# BRUCE MONTGOMERY/EDMUND CRISPIN:
## A LIFE IN MUSIC AND BOOKS

*To my parents, for their constant encouragement*

# Bruce Montgomery/Edmund Crispin: A Life in Music and Books

DAVID WHITTLE
*Leicester Grammar School, UK*

**ASHGATE**

Published by
Ashgate Publishing Limited
Gower House
Croft Road
Aldershot
Hampshire GU11 3HR
England

Ashgate Publishing Company
Suite 420
101 Cherry Street
Burlington, VT 05401-4405
USA

Ashgate website: http://www.ashgate.com

**British Library Cataloguing in Publication Data**
Whittle, David
  The life and music of Bruce Montgomery/Edmund Crispin
  1. Montgomery, Bruce, 1921–1978 2. Crispin, Edmund, 1921–1978
  3. Composers – Great Britain – Biography 4. Novelists,
  English – 20th century – Biography
  I. Title
  780.9'2

**Library of Congress Cataloging-in-Publication Data**
Whittle, David, 1958-
  Bruce Montgomery/Edmund Crispin : a life in music and books / by David Whittle.
       p. cm.
  Includes bibliographical references and index.
  ISBN-13: 978-0-7546-3443-0 (alk. paper)
  ISBN-10: 0-7546-3443-4 (alk. paper)
  1.   Montgomery, Bruce, 1921–1978 2.   Authors, English—20th century—Biography.
3. Composers—England—Biography. I. Title.

  PR6025.O46Z95 2007
  780.92—dc22
  [B]
                                                              2006021119

ISBN 978-0-7546-3443-0

Printed and bound in Great Britain by TJ International Ltd, Padstow, Cornwall.

# Contents

# List of Plates

Uncredited illustrations are from the collection of Sheila Rossiter.

# List of Music Examples

# Acknowledgements

I have been very fortunate to meet nothing but generosity in the writing of this book. Montgomery's friends and acquaintances have been unfailingly helpful and willing to speak to me, as have custodians of archives and other material. In particular, I must mention Dr Judith Priestman, Dr Peter Ward Jones and the staff at the Bodleian Library for permitting me to sift through Montgomery's papers before they were catalogued, and for their help in fielding questions. I am also grateful to Merton College and St John's College, Oxford, for providing me with accommodation and other facilities.

Many individuals have helped me enormously, and their interest in the project, and in many cases their hospitality, has made the toil of research a pleasure. It is a strange feeling (almost one of impertinence) to quiz people who knew Montgomery and from their recollections paint a portrait of a person I will never meet. Their eagerness to talk about Montgomery demonstrates, I think, the esteem and affection in which he was, and is, held. I owe some of them a particular debt. By the end of my conversations with Brian Aldiss I felt very well informed about the development of science fiction, having known more or less nothing about it previously. He has been a great supporter of the biography. The late Geoffrey Bush was also an enormous enthusiast for the project and kept me up to the mark with notes and jottings. The detailed reminiscences of Colin and Mary Strang and Audrey Stock were all the more pleasurable for having taken place whilst enjoying their lively and convivial company. In the early stages of my research I greatly appreciated Robert Pascall's wise advice whilst trying to fashion a thesis out of the material. I must also thank my friend and colleague Charles Paterson who inadvertently set me on the Montgomery trail; his eager discussions of twentieth-century English music and detective fiction are always illuminating. I am most grateful to Phil Clymer and Chorion for readily allowing me to quote so extensively from Montgomery's novels.

I am very happy to acknowledge the following people and organisations: the late Sir Kingsley Amis, the late Sir Thomas Armstrong, Sir Malcolm Arnold, Joan Bagley, Julie Baldwin (Collins Publishers), J.G. Ballard, Betty Baly, the late Jacques Barzun, Jean Bell, the late Revd J.G. Bishop, the late Bill Blezzard, Christopher Bornet (Royal College of Music), Richard Braine, BBC Natural History Unit, Geoffrey Brown (Merchant Taylors' School), James Brown, the late Geoffrey Bush, Rev. C.A. Cardale, the late Humphrey Carpenter, Michael Charlesworth (Shrewsbury School), Charles Cleall, Robert Conquest, John Noble Cooper, Cecil Cope, Caroline Cornish (BBC Written Archives Centre), Rosi Crane (BBC South & West), the late Julian Critchley, Constance Cruickshank (Faber and Faber), the late Mary Peel Davies, Oliver Davies (Royal College of Music), Kieran Doyle, the late Ruth Dyson, *Evening Standard*, Percy Everett, Elizabeth Ferrars, The Film Institute of Ireland, Dick Francis, Anthea Fraser (Crime Writers' Association), Dr M.R. Freedland (St John's College Society), Spencer Freeman (Novello), Brian and Nancy Galpin,

Douglas Gamley, Michael Gilbert, Alexander Gleason, Livia Gollancz (Victor Gollancz Ltd), Ron Goodwin, Hilary Goodworth, Richard Gordon, Douglas Greene, Richard Hardcastle, George Hardinge, Harry Ransom Humanities Research Center (University of Texas), Desmond Hawkins, Capt. M.J. Henderson (Band of the Irish Guards), the late Patricia Highsmith, Sheila Hodges, Erica Hutchinson (Performing Right Society), the late Michael Innes (J.I.M. Stewart), the late Arthur Jacobs, Barbara James, John Jenkins, Sir Anthony Jephcott, Micky Jones, H.R.F. Keating, Michael Kennedy, Brian Ladd, Philip Lane, J.C. Larkin, Zachary Leader, N.A. Lee (University of Bristol), Leicester Probate Sub-Registry, Helen Leiper (Oxford University Press), Anthony Lejeune, Christopher Longuet-Higgins, Macmillan Publishers Ltd, Eileen Mann, Robert McNeil, Graham Melville (British Film Institute), Jamie Milford, Eleanor Millard, Janet Moat (British Film Institute), the late Charles Monteith, David Morgan, Andrew Motion and the Executors of the Estate of Philip Larkin, Music Publishers' Association, Northwood Preparatory School, Office of Population Censuses and Surveys, Pauline Oldham, Imogen Painter, the late Theodore Pantcheff, Ann Parker, Christopher Parsons, Muriel Pavlow, Leslie Phillips, Kate Pool (Society of Authors), Michael Powell, Josephine Pullein-Thompson (PEN), Peter Rogers, the late Bernard Rose, the late Alan Ross, Royal College of Organists, Sheila Rossiter, Edwina Sampson, Jennifer Savery, David Shapland, Bryan Shaw, John Shirley, Nigel Shortman, Nigel Simeone, Joyce Sims, Elspeth Slaughter, Wyn Smith, Tony Soper, *The Spectator*, Veronica Stallwood, J.S. Sudbury, Gavin Sutherland, the late Donald Swann, Eric Sykes, the late Julian Symons, Mary Thairlwall, the late Gerald Thomas, Stephen Tothill, Ursula Townsend, Jeni Turnbull, F.P. Turner (Rank Film Distributors), the late Michael Underwood, the late John Wain, Anna Walne, Elizabeth Wells (National Sound Archive), West Country Writers' Association, the late David Whiffen, the late David Williams, Alan Willmott, A.J. Wright.

I am grateful to the following copyright holders for permission to reproduce material:

Quotations from Montgomery's novels are reproduced with the kind permission of Rights Limited. Copyright © Rights Limited, a Chorion company. All rights reserved.

Letters to Montgomery from Oxford University Press are reprinted by permission of the Secretary to the Delegates of Oxford University Press.

Extracts from *The Letters of Kingsley Amis* (edited by Zachary Leader) are reprinted by permission of HarperCollins Publishers Ltd.

Extracts from *Memoirs* by Kingsley Amis are used by kind permission of The Random House Group Limited and Jonathan Clowes Ltd, London, on behalf of the Literary Estate of Sir Kingsley Amis. Copyright © 1991 Sir Kingsley Amis.

The extract from a letter to the author from J.I.M. Stewart is used by permission of A.P. Watt Ltd on behalf of Michael Stewart.

Extracts from letters to Montgomery and the author from Julian Symons are reproduced with permission of Curtis Brown Group Ltd, London, on behalf of the Estate of Julian Symons. Copyright © Julian Symons.

The extracts from *Mary Ambree* by Montgomery are reproduced by permission of Oxford University Press.

The plate from *Raising the Wind* is reproduced by permission of Canal+ Image UK Ltd.

I am happy to acknowledge quotations from Montgomery's forewords to *Best SF* and *Best Detective Stories*.

All musical extracts are © Novello unless otherwise stated.

The letters from Philip Larkin are © Faber and Faber.

I must express my gratitude to those who have corresponded with me and who have granted permission for extracts from their letters to be quoted. Every effort has been made to contact copyright holders of the remaining material.

I am indebted to Rachel Lynch, Heidi May and Sarah Charters and the editorial team at Ashgate for putting up with my increasingly manic demands as the pressure has grown. My thanks go to Andrew Baker-Munton, Charles Paterson, Pat Walne and my parents for reading and commenting on the typescript. I need hardly add that any remaining infelicities are entirely my own responsibility.

And finally, I must mention my late cat Montgomery, whose name and frequent looks of reproof did much to stir my feelings of guilt during the many moments of literary lethargy.

Oakham
2006

# Introduction

On Thursday 24 August 1961 at the Plaza Theatre, Lower Regent Street SW1, a film, *Raising the Wind*, was given its premiere. A comedy set in a music college, it was immediately compared to *Doctor in the House*, a 1954 release which followed the antics of medical students. The cast included many stalwarts of British comedy of the period, some of whom appeared in both films: Kenneth Williams, Leslie Phillips, Liz Fraser, James Robertson Justice and Sid James were notable amongst them. Producer Peter Rogers and director Gerald Thomas were a well-established pairing, responsible for the increasing number of films in the *Carry On* series.

The members of the production team and cast, gathered in their evening dress at the Plaza, were cheered by news of pre-release bookings at coastal resorts. At the Forum Cinema on Jersey, for instance, *Raising the Wind* had taken more at the box office than any film so far in 1961. Reporting the premiere with a double page spread of photographs, *Daily Cinema* announced that pre-release bookings had 'scored a shattering success [...] exceptional bookings [at coastal resorts] giving every indication that *Raising the Wind* is destined to be one of Anglo's all time box-office giants'.[1]

For one man the premiere represented a particular success. Bruce Montgomery, not yet 40 years of age, was responsible for the storyline, screenplay and musical score of the film. He had also conducted the music and acted as technical advisor. Such a wide-ranging creative contribution remains highly unusual, if not unique. That Montgomery had written the music was not unexpected: *Raising the Wind* was his fortieth film score. This number included the four *Doctor* and five *Carry On* films so far released. What was less expected, perhaps, was that he should have written the screenplay of a film which the *Observer* reviewed as 'a jolly British romp'.[2] Yet, under his pen-name of Edmund Crispin, Montgomery was the author of eight highly acclaimed detective novels and many short crime stories in whose pages the farcical often makes an appearance.

The production had been a very happy one, with Montgomery in his element as technical advisor. The members of the orchestra enjoyed having a more important role than in most films, and particularly relished having to play the *William Tell Overture* so fast that it ended in total disarray. Montgomery had coached Leslie Phillips to conduct so well that the orchestra applauded the actor. With Peter Rogers and Gerald Thomas backing him, Montgomery was already at work on a sequel.

In reply to a letter of congratulation on *Raising the Wind* from Josephine Bell, a fellow writer of detective novels, Montgomery wrote: 'It isn't a picture calculated to raise the cultural tone of the nation.'[3] Despite this realistic, if rather gloomy,

---

1    *Daily Cinema*, 28 August 1961
2    *Observer*, 27 August 1961
3    RBM to Josephine Bell, 5 October 1961

appraisal of his work, the film marks the culmination of the most successful years of Montgomery's career. He was regarded with esteem by devotees of the detective story for his eight novels, even though the last had appeared eight years previously, and was frequently called upon as an authoritative commentator on the genre by journals and the broadcasting companies. He had also established himself as a distinctive writer on science fiction. The series of *Best SF* anthologies he edited for Faber from 1955 have since been described as 'crucial in establishing valid critical standards'.[4] He had written the scores for some of the most prominent British films of the 1950s; he had a large body of serious concert music in the catalogues of Novello and Oxford University Press; he had earned a lot of money from film work and royalties; a house was about to be built to his own specification in Devon. Yet despite these other activities, Montgomery regarded himself first and foremost as a composer of concert music. He had been working for this time when he would have sufficient money to be able to concentrate on composing such music.

*Raising the Wind* was almost Montgomery's last film score. He had often found it difficult to complete music on time, and in 1962 he reduced the recording schedule for *Carry On Cruising* to chaos when he failed to produce most of the score. It was the last straw for Peter Rogers and Gerald Thomas. They never employed him again. Montgomery had been a heavy social drinker for some time, and this rejection (with the subsequent loss of its ample remuneration) pushed him into alcoholism. The effect on his constitution, which had never been robust, was catastrophic.

In the remaining seventeen years of his life, Bruce Montgomery's musical output was negligible. He completed only one more novel. He had made a musical and literary name for himself by the age of 30, well before his Oxford friends and contemporaries Kingsley Amis and Philip Larkin made their names as men of letters. Yet he seems to have seen what was coming. In June 1956, not long after *Lucky Jim* had propelled Amis to fame and *The Less Deceived* had established Larkin, Montgomery wrote to the latter:

> What with Kingsley becoming a prominent literary figure, and now you, I feel like an ageing hare overtaken by squads of implacable tortoises. There's still time, I suppose, for me to switch to some pursuit more highly esteemed than either film music or detective fiction – but should I be any good at it if I did? And what would become of the big cheques I so much enjoy receiving?[5]

The doubts that Montgomery habitually harboured about his work are evident. The story of his life is that of a gifted man to whom success came early and easily in different fields. The question his life poses is why the 'ageing hare' aged quite so abruptly.

---

4     *Trillion Year Spree*, Aldiss, p. 628

5     RBM to Larkin, 19 June 1956

# Chapter 1

# 'Daydreaming child with nice manners': 1921–1928

There is little in Bruce Montgomery's family history to suggest such diverse musical and literary talents. On the back of the distinctive green Penguin paperbacks in which his detective stories were published, Montgomery is described as of 'Scots-Irish parentage'. His father, Robert Ernest, the second son of William Jamison and Eleanor Harper Montgomery, was born in Belfast on 9 July 1878. Robert's father was a merchant originally from Bangor, County Down. By the time Robert entered King's College London, the family had moved to a house in Balfour Avenue, Hanwell, in west London, and Robert's brother had already emigrated to Australia where he started an eiderdown factory. The second of Bruce Montgomery's three sisters, Sheila, recalls hearing of her paternal grandfather's death whilst skating with her father on a pond near the family home at Chesham. Thereafter, the girls would stay occasionally with their grandmother in Hanwell. Eleanor Montgomery was a strict member of the Plymouth Brethren, and the girls were expected to worship with her.

Robert Montgomery joined the civil service in 1898 as a Second Class Clerk in the India Office and spent his whole working life serving the interests of a country he never actually visited. By the time Bruce was born in 1921 Robert was Principal Clerk. He was an intelligent, thorough, honest and placid man, never known to use strong language about anything or anyone. Once in a while, every three years perhaps, he might lose his temper over some trivial matter, but it was soon forgotten and no grudges were borne. The meticulousness that Bruce showed in certain aspects of his life came from his father's side of the family. Robert's qualities were doubtless a consequence of his firm religious faith, and it was through the church that he met his wife.

Bruce Montgomery's mother, Marion Blackwood Jarvie, was ten years her husband's junior. Her side of the family was far less stable. Born in Cramond, a village on the banks of the Forth outside Edinburgh, on 18 September 1888, she was brought up by her grandparents. She told her own children that her parents had drunk themselves into paupers' graves. On another occasion, it was made clear that her father had drunk away a fortune. Bruce's own reliance on alcohol in later life may have owed something to the influence of his mother's family. Whereas on his father's side Montgomery claimed in later life to be descended from 'various Earls of Arundel, Shrewsbury and Eglinton',[1] his mother's family boasted a more colourful history. Marion's father thought he was an illegitimate descendant of

---

1    *World Authors*, Wakeman, p. 344

Bonnie Prince Charlie and his grandchildren wore the Royal Stewart tartan in their childhood. Bailey Nichol Jarvie, otherwise known as Rob Roy, was also claimed as an ancestor. A less glamorous relative was the Laird of Blackwood, a small village south of Glasgow.

It was while Marion Jarvie and her two sisters were living with relatives in London that she joined the choir of St Andrew's Presbyterian Church in Mount Park Road, Ealing. Also in the choir was Robert Montgomery. He proposed to Marion several times before she accepted him in a telegram he received whilst playing cricket at Horsham. They were married at St Andrews by the Reverend Herbert Wylie on 22 August 1910. The Montgomerys were sufficiently sentimental to return there for the christening of their youngest daughter, Elspeth.

The couple made their home at Chesham Bois in Buckinghamshire. The house was named Blackwood after Marion's ancestral laird and stood on Bois Lane, at the corner of Stubbs Wood. All four children were born at Blackwood. The first three were all girls: Eleanora (known as Nora) was born on 4 May 1911; Sheila on 13 March 1913; Elizabeth, always called Elspeth, on 9 January 1916.

The fourth child, Robert Bruce, was born on 2 October 1921, well over five years after the arrival of Elspeth. The boy was always known as Bruce and was called quite openly his parents' 'afterthought'. He was given a spider on every birthday to celebrate his names.[2] After three girls the proud parents were delighted to have a boy, but their joy was slightly tempered by the infant's congenital deformity of the feet. Before the birth Marion Montgomery had been visited with a premonition that there would be something wrong. She was right: both of Bruce's feet were turned in. This meant frequent operations until the age of 14; it also meant that he had to wear callipers well up to his shins.

When Bruce was two years old, the family moved to a new home, Domus in Stubbs Wood Lane, just around the corner from Blackwood. This big house in a rural setting was built for them, much of it to Robert Montgomery's design. There were six bedrooms, a dining room, a lounge and a large drawing room which was used for dances, musical evenings and Marion Montgomery's many bridge parties. On warm summer nights the children were sometimes allowed to sleep downstairs in the L-shaped verandah. The acre of garden gave evidence of Robert Montgomery's sporting enthusiasms. There was a nine-hole putting lawn, and on the tennis court Mr Montgomery, true to his character, would play his game as a steady doubles partner and leave the flashy shots to others. The children's interests were served by a swing and a see-saw. They could also play in the wild section and amongst the cherry trees. Robert Montgomery was particularly fond of roses, and the garden was full of standard and bush varieties. At Christmas, when Eleanor Montgomery and Aunt Lucy, one of Robert's sisters who lived with his mother at Hanwell, came to stay, there was always a vase of roses on the dinner table. A gardener was employed for most days of the week.

It was a happy family life for the four children. Robert Montgomery's quiet character was rarely ruffled by his wife's more variable temper. Arguments between

---

2    To commemorate the Scottish king Robert the Bruce (1274–1329) who, whilst hiding in a cave, took heart from the persistence of a spider weaving its web.

the two were so rare that it was quite an event when Sheila once reported that she had overheard one. Neither Marion nor Robert retained a brogue from their upbringing, but Marion occasionally used some strange Scottish words with a bit of an accent.

The church was a very important part of Robert Montgomery's life. He was a prominent member of the Free Church in Amersham where he formed the choir, became Choir Secretary and then served as Treasurer of the Church for many years. Marion Montgomery was a devoted bridge player. The family's interest in the game was such that the children even played a hand or two sometimes before leaving for school in the morning. Their father's strict religious beliefs meant that no money could be played for. Marion seemed rarely to be in when the children came from school, and they were looked after by their live-in maid. Olive was first engaged at the age of 14 when Nora was born. She remained with the family until Bruce left school. Olive always called Marion 'mummy', and Bruce was known as 'my Brucie boy'. When she left the Montgomerys, Olive went to Canada, married an old widower friend and gave birth to a boy whom she christened Bruce.

As one of the family, Olive accompanied the Montgomerys on their annual summer holiday. Robert took the whole of August off, Domus was let to help pay for the rent of the holiday home, and the whole family transferred to the south coast. Broadstairs, the Isle of Wight and Hayling Island were favourite haunts. By the time Bruce was a teenager, Fowey in Cornwall had become established as the regular summer retreat.

Bruce Montgomery wrote later of his childhood:

My mother was Scottish and my father an Ulsterman; I myself was born in England. My upbringing was in the twenties and thirties, conventionally middle-class, and I look back on it with pleasure and gratitude. The middle-class standards demonstrated to me then still seem to me worth serious consideration. They were kindness, politeness, strictness in money matters, conscientiousness in work, marital fidelity and a regular (in all senses) life. Religion was there too, but was an option – i.e., up to the age of fourteen or so some small acquaintance with it was obligatory, but after that one was left to choose for oneself. Since children are at their happiest when bombinating inside a framework of unoppressive but definite rules and conventions, I was happy, and although I have often failed to live up to those *bourgeois* standards, I've always regretted my failures. For all its limitations, decent *bourgeoisisme* seems to me not at all a bad or unreasonable code to live by – or to write by, either.[3]

Bruce, as the only boy, was spoiled by his mother: she went as far in his adulthood as to wash his first car. He had inherited the Titian hair which had made Marion quite a belle in her youth. The sisters were pleased to have a little brother whom they could take out in his pram, even if Sheila did once tip him out of it. Elspeth used to lead him to his first school, Chesham Bois High School, a dame school run by three elderly sisters. Elspeth would ride her bicycle whilst Bruce followed on his fairy-cycle. It was two miles each way, and he could recite the names of all the houses they passed. With no school lunches they had to go each way twice every day. As Bruce always had his feet encased in plaster or callipers from surgery, this was no

---

3    *World Authors*, Wakeman, p. 344

easy journey. Sheila taught him to ride a proper bicycle later. But Bruce did not see much of his sisters after they were sent away to Crediton High School in Devon, their father having decided that if the girls were going to board, they might as well be a good distance away.

Towards the end of his life, Bruce Montgomery described himself as a 'timid, lazy, daydreaming child with nice manners'.[4] These nice manners did not prevent him from saying exactly what he thought, however. At the age of seven he was obliged to attend a children's party. As he left he said to his hostess: 'Thank you very much. I have not enjoyed myself, but it was not your fault.'[5] Bruce's 'obligatory' acquaintance with religion was confined to attendance with his sisters at services on Sundays, usually having to endure sermons which lasted at least half an hour. The daydreaming was a result of his having to amuse himself, partly because of his regular confinements for surgery and partly because his sisters were away at school. He slept with a toy pistol, caps primed, under his pillow.

When he was four years old, Bruce was taken on an outing to a nearby farm. Elspeth and he were stroking a horse when the animal suddenly kicked out and split open the boy's head. There was a lot of blood and the family was very alarmed. The curtains in the house were drawn. The girls, who at one stage wondered if he would live, were relieved to hear that there was no lasting damage except for a horseshoe-shaped scar on the top of his head which could be seen only when the wind ruffled his hair. Opinion in the family was that this kick gave impetus to Bruce's brain and was responsible for his subsequent academic career.

In 1925, some time later than their friends, the Montgomerys bought their first car, a second-hand open Peugeot. Robert Montgomery was never the best of drivers. His wife said that on hills he always went backwards to go forward. Even so, the car was very useful particularly for getting Robert to his work in London during the General Strike. It was also useful for getting Bruce to Amersham station for his daily train ride to his new school.

---

4       Ibid.
5       'Fen's Creator', Critchley

# Chapter 2

# 'An intellectual snob': 1928–1940

In 1928, when he was seven, Montgomery started at Northwood Preparatory School. This school had been founded in 1910 by Francis Terry, the third son of a Nottinghamshire clergyman. There were about 80 pupils, all but a handful of whom were day boys. The boarders lodged with Mr Terry and his wife, and those whose parents lived abroad often remained with the couple during the holidays. The boys came mostly from middle-class professional families, some of whom ran their own businesses. There were a few sons of traders. Because of the headmaster, the school was known locally as Terry's.

Frank Terry was primarily a disciplinarian, and he kept a cane on his desk during lessons. The boys regarded him with a mixture of 'awe and healthy respect',[1] but found him firm and fair. The atmosphere of the school was contented, probably because Terry kept everything firmly under control. He had read History at Oxford, but at Northwood he taught in most areas of school life, including Latin and games. At the end of lessons Terry would line up his pupils and move them up or down the order depending on the answers to his questions. Five minutes before the end of a games session he would blow his whistle and exhort each boy to use up all his energy in the time that remained. At the opening of new buildings in March 1912, Terry spoke of his view that the job of a preparatory school education was to 'form habits in its pupils, to awaken and maintain interest and to stimulate effort'.[2] He thought that his school should not fill boys with stock ways of impressing examiners but should lead them to think on their own. The way to do this was to organise their instruction very carefully. Terry expected his staff to spend a good deal of their holidays planning the work of the next term. He wrote very full reports on each boy at the end of every term and staff were instructed to do the same. Loyalty to the school was everything and Mr Terry led by example. Many boys recall him marching up and down the touch line during matches shouting 'Buck up, Northwood!' This phrase was the last line of the school song:

So let's cheer, Boys, cheer the Old School
As along through life we go.
Keep it firm in our affection
Because we love it so.
And in far off years may the same loud cheers
Ring out where we have stood

1    *History of Terry's*, p. 6
2    Ibid., p. 3

As we pass the torch-light onward
Singing 'Buck up, Northwood'.[3]

The headmaster was active in all aspects of the school and could often be found stoking the boiler, mowing the lawns and clipping the hedges.

The facilities of the school seem rather spartan by modern standards. There was a long hall, fitted with wall bars and climbing ropes, which was used for assembly. Immediately afterwards this hall would be converted into six classrooms by shutters. The rattle of these shutters being pulled down became a characteristic sound of the school day. They also served another purpose. One day Terry became particularly enraged by a stupid answer in class. He hurled his pen at the offender and missed him, but the pen lodged, quivering, in the wooden shutter behind.

The subjects of the academic curriculum were Scripture, English, French, Latin, Mathematics, Geography and History. Terry was particularly keen on neat handwriting, correct spelling and clear expression. He believed that this last quality was helped by a thorough understanding of Latin. Scripture was considered particularly important. The day started at 9 a.m. with prayers and Scripture teaching. Four lessons followed in the morning with a break of half an hour between 10.45 and 11.15 a.m. Half of this break consisted of some sort of drill in the playground. This drill prepared the boys for marches and parades, particularly on Empire Day. On Monday, Wednesday and Friday afternoons there were lessons; on Tuesday and Thursday all boys were coached in games by Mr Terry. Fencing and boxing were encouraged. There was an active contingent of scouts.

Montgomery had few friends at Terry's. The academic side of the school suited him, but he found himself at a disadvantage when it came to physical activities. He could not take part in games because of his disability, and he was often absent having surgery on his feet. These operations took place at the Royal National Orthopaedic Hospital in Great Portland Street. Lying in bed during a visit in November 1936 he saw the flames in the sky as the Crystal Palace burnt down. The treatment consisted of having his feet turned outwards and kept there with plaster. Montgomery never used crutches, but after each operation he was left with a walking plaster and a wooden sole. His mother used to massage his feet, more from a desire to help than with any hope of moderating the problem.

Although he changed his views on exercise in later years, Montgomery's reaction to his lameness at Terry's was typical of a young boy. He resented that he could not join in the activities at school. Swimming was one form of exercise he could take, although the Saturday morning sessions in spring at the Rickmansworth baths were marred by a tendency for the water from the river Colne to be full of tadpoles. To fill the time that would otherwise have been taken up by sport, the boy began to read widely and take piano lessons. Sensing Montgomery's needs, his parents encouraged him. There were plenty of books in the house, including the latest encyclopaedias. His parents also passed on their love of music. They held musical evenings in the drawing room with their friends, particularly Nora and Ted Bray. Ted Bray had a

---

3     John Noble Cooper

very good tenor voice and was in the choir with Robert Montgomery at Amersham. His wife was a piano teacher in Chesham Bois.

One teacher who certainly made an impression on Montgomery at Northwood was Mlle Natalie Laurent. She taught French and the school laid great emphasis on this. French plays were produced regularly, with Mr Terry giving a synopsis in English before they were performed for parents, often on Speech Day. Most of the work was oral, and pupils of hers spoke with a proper French accent, to the extent that at their public schools many had this accent drummed out of them as being not sufficiently 'English'.[4] The music teaching at the school was limited to piano lessons. A few years before Montgomery went to Terry's, someone with whom he was to come into contact at Oxford came to present the prizes on Speech Day. Sir Hugh Allen held two important positions: Director of the Royal College of Music and Professor of Music at Oxford University. On this occasion Mrs Terry conducted the boys in a rendering of *Barbara Allan*, deemed appropriate as Sir Hugh had a daughter called Barbara. Mrs Terry did not know that Sir Hugh had become rather irritated by the frequency with which this song was performed for him on ceremonial occasions.

Despite his growing interest in music, books and languages, Montgomery favoured no particular subject at this stage of his schooling. In the light of the difficulties he experienced developing a career in a single discipline, two comments he made when he was about seven or eight years old show that consistency was a problem not only in later life. During the evening meal one Sunday after church, Montgomery was discussing what he would be when he grew up. Having pondered and dismissed the usual things (engine driver, fireman) he suddenly ended by announcing: 'I don't really know. I expect I shall marry Jane [the small girl who lived next door] and be the father of some small child.'[5] On another occasion he decided that he would never marry but have lots of cats.

To follow his education at Terry's, Montgomery had been entered (shortly after birth) for Merchant Taylors' School, at that time situated in Charterhouse Square in the City of London. It was intended that Montgomery should board there, but in 1933, the year before he was due to go, the school moved conveniently to Northwood. Indeed, in 1930, the Headmaster of Merchant Taylors' was the guest of honour at Terry's prize giving. The links with Merchant Taylors' had always been quite strong, but with the school's immediate proximity these links became even stronger. Montgomery gained a scholarship. On coming home from Terry's each evening it was Montgomery's habit to sit and tinker at the Broadwood baby grand piano in the drawing room, still with his cap on his head and his satchel round his shoulders. Some time after he had taken the scholarship exam, his mother asked him how he had got on. 'Oh, I've got it,' he replied, without ceasing to play.[6] He had known for some time but had not bothered to tell anyone. He entered Merchant Taylors' in September 1934 at the age of almost 13.

---

4    *History of Terry's*, p. 9
5    Sheila Rossiter
6    Ibid.

Merchant Taylors' School had been at its new purpose-built site for only one year, and the facilities were rather different from those Montgomery had been used to at Terry's. Set in large grounds, with plenty of space for a fine gymnasium, games' pitches, squash and fives courts and even a lake for sailing, everything was new. There was a good atmosphere amongst the 500 pupils. Bullying was virtually unknown, perhaps because, like Mr Terry, the Monitors were permitted to use the cane. The teaching was exemplary and the staff admired by the pupils. Those pupils who advanced beyond Matriculation were particularly stretched. Like Terry's, there was little social mix amongst the pupils. Many left the school after Higher Certificate, or before if they were to enter the professions or their family's business. Unlike Terry's, though, the religious observances of the school were not rigorous. There was little else apart from prayers at morning assembly.

Montgomery continued his practice of taking the train to Northwood every day. Even if his parents had wanted him to board as originally intended, the proximity of the school and his foot condition precluded it. Montgomery must have been very pleased with the heavy emphasis on the arts in the school. There were plenty of music practice rooms with pianos, and the School Hall housed a pipe organ. Societies flourished. The well-stocked library was another place in which he spent a lot of time.

Montgomery entered Merchant Taylors' in Spenser House, named after the Elizabethan poet Edmund Spenser (*c*.1552–1599) who was a scholar of the school, and was first put into Upper IVC until it was realised that he had been under graded on the entrance exam. He was moved to Upper IVA for the remainder of the first term and finally upgraded again in January 1935 to spend the rest of the academic year in Modern Division A. This meant that he had to specialise. The school had three 'sides': Classical, Modern and Science. The influence of Mlle Laurent showed, and Montgomery chose Modern Languages, starting to learn German in addition to French. He sat his School Certificate exams in December 1935, adding some extra credits in the summer of the following year.

With his sisters being away at school, Montgomery must have felt at times as if he were an only child. Since this was combined with a physical disability and his continuing inability to participate in active pursuits which were the mainstream of school life outside the classroom (the Officers' Training Corps and the Scouts, for instance), he made his own interests. The worst of the deformity of his feet was now past, though. At the age of 14 Montgomery had his final operation, which reduced his lameness to a slight limp. With four children, his father's financial obligations meant that he had to borrow money for this operation from his wife's sister, maiden Aunt Mary. This detail was only known to Robert Montgomery and his sister-in-law until Aunt Mary divulged the secret to the family. By now, however, Montgomery was not worried that he could not become involved in sport. His lameness gave him an excuse for avoiding something for which, a friend and contemporary later said, he was not temperamentally suited. He was much more interested in playing the piano, listening to music and, later, going to the pub.[7]

---

7    Colin Strang

He did do remedial gymnastic classes on his own once or twice a week, but apart from that he channelled his abilities and enthusiasms into the academic pursuits that were open to him. This was helped by his friendly academic rivalry with a boarder who rejoiced in the name of Theodore Xenophon Henry Pantcheff, and who later became a distinguished servant of the British Crown. Pantcheff worked for British Intelligence in Germany during the years immediately after the Second World War, and following work in the diplomatic service in Africa he became an acknowledged senior advisor on that continent. Montgomery and Pantcheff entered Merchant Taylors' on the same day and were in the same forms all the way up the school, a distinction no one else shared with them. This rivalry had the benefit of prompting the boys to efforts they might otherwise have never made. His sister Sheila once received a phone call from Montgomery at Merchant Taylors' asking if she could come and pick him up in the car because he had so many prizes to carry.

Despite the great friendship between the two boys at school, they met only once afterwards. In 1942 Pantcheff was dining with a friend in an Oxford restaurant when Montgomery walked up to their table and said in his most pompous voice: 'By the powers that be, it's Pantcheff!' This expression became a byword in the Pantcheff family.[8]

There were two piano teachers at Merchant Taylors': Kendall Taylor, a well-known concert pianist, took the better pupils whilst Mr Barnes, who had lost three fingers in the First World War but still managed to play Beethoven Sonatas, was responsible for the lesser lights. Montgomery was taught by Taylor. He also took organ lessons with Mr Waller, the Geography master, a 'rather ferocious chap who played the organ not particularly well'.[9] Apart from this, most of Montgomery's serious musical education seems to have happened away from school. At the time he started at Merchant Taylors', Montgomery and his family met Godfrey Sampson on holiday at Fowey. Sampson, born in 1902 and thus almost twenty years Montgomery's senior, hailed from Gloucester and had attended Westminster School and the Royal Academy of Music where he had been Mendelssohn Scholar in 1927. By 1934 Sampson had made a name for himself as a composer and was a professor of composition at the Academy. He lived in Claygate in Surrey, was organist at the parish church and taught at Milbourne Lodge School when his duties at the Academy permitted. The son of a clergyman, Sampson was a tall, slender man with a terrific sense of humour and strong religious convictions. He tended to dress smartly and soberly, and was not keen on being seen as an artistic type.[10] Sampson and Montgomery agreed with each other on sufficient things (an obsession with music and a loathing for sport, for example) to make this a very good friendship. Sampson soon realised that the boy had a great deal of musical potential, and his influence on Montgomery's development and career was enormous.

Sampson's encouragement consisted of introducing Montgomery to a wide variety of music, advising him on composition and improving his organ playing. Montgomery's interest in the organ had started early. On being told that the boy

---

8      Theodore Pantcheff to author, 2 October 1989

9      Brian Galpin

10    Edwina Sampson

played the piano, his orthopaedic surgeon had suggested he learn to play the organ as the pedal work might help the problems with his feet. He took every opportunity to further his knowledge of organs. On one of the earliest holidays in Fowey when Sampson joined the family, he and Montgomery took a boat up the river Fowey, hauled it onto the bank and then played on the organ in a village church without asking permission. Sheila was horrified by their forwardness. By the age of 15, although he was almost entirely self-taught, Montgomery was playing the organ at his father's church with Sheila sometimes operating the hand pump. (Sheila said that she would pump for anyone if it meant that she could be in the choir.) In June 1936 Montgomery gave an organ recital at the Free Church in Amersham; the programme included *Toccata and Fugue* in D minor by Bach, Murrill's arrangement of *Crown Imperial* by Walton, as well as works by Coleridge-Taylor, d'Evry, Halsey and Harvey Grace. Godfrey Sampson gave the young performer vital advice: 'Have a collection to cover expenses – there won't be any, so you can pocket the lot.'[11]

In May 1937, when Montgomery was 16, his sister Elspeth was married at St Mary, Moorgate, after receiving her Catholic instruction there, something the strict Orangeman Robert Montgomery had wanted nothing to do with. Montgomery played for the ceremony on another organ which had to be pumped by hand. After the service he was furious, claiming that the instrument had made a noise 'like a seagull'.[12]

Sampson invited Montgomery to concerts and lent him books on orchestration. During Montgomery's convalescence in 1936 from one of his operations, Sampson told him to spend the time studying Stewart Macpherson's book on counterpoint in two and three parts. When Montgomery was 14 Sampson spoke to Douglas Hopkins, the organist of St Paul's Cathedral, and arranged for the boy to sit in the organ loft during a service. Montgomery's love of Wagner can be traced to the enthusiasm Sampson entertained for the composer. Postcards from Sampson were addressed in such terms as 'Herrn Komponist R.B. Montgomery' or referred to Montgomery as 'Beckmesser', a character in Wagner's *Die Meistersinger*.

The surviving letters from Sampson to Montgomery show that the friendship also had a firm teacher/pupil aspect. Sampson had a strong will and liked to get his own way. Towards the end of 1936 Montgomery was learning two preludes and fugues by Bach for Sampson who refused to let the boy play the organ at Claygate until he had learned them properly. Sampson insisted that Montgomery must master them thoroughly and wrote 'on this point you are, at present, <u>flagrantly</u> weak'.[13] In one letter Sampson gave Montgomery a lengthy discourse on how to develop a theme (something he was never, even in his maturity, much concerned with). After an examination of Montgomery's latest piece in 1937, Sampson noted an aspect of Montgomery's style which was to remain constant: 'The sudden changes of key in places [are] piquant and really musicianly.'[14] In the same letter Sampson advised Montgomery against his habit of using themes from previous works. Unknown to

11    Godfrey Sampson to RBM, 15 January 1936
12    Elspeth Slaughter
13    Godfrey Sampson to RBM, 24 November 1936
14    Ibid., 4 October 1937

both of them at the time, this tendency was to be of great use when Montgomery came under the pressures of composing music for films.

Of this period in his life Montgomery later wrote:

> The start of my writing and composing was, I think, a matter of compensating for the lameness which at school (Merchant Taylors') prevented me from taking part in games and athletics. Overdoing it, I became a prig and an intellectual snob.[15]

Although he never joined the choir, Montgomery took some part in school music-making. His performances in school concerts are documented in the school magazine, *Taylorian*. In June 1936 he sang in Horn's duet setting of *I Know a Bank* ('in which the voices were very well matched')[16] and also appeared as one of three accompanists for the National Anthem. On other occasions he performed, with B.H. Balkwill, the piano duet version of Arthur Benjamin's *Jamaican Rumba*, played the piano part in Hummel's *Trio for Wind Instruments* ('which carried well deserved applause')[17] and accompanied in 'a very capable performance'[18] of the first movement of the *Violin Sonata in G* by Beethoven. He also played the organ part in an unusual arrangement, for two pianos (eight hands) and organ, of the *Minuet* from Beethoven's *Symphony No. 1.*, the acerbic reviewer (who enjoyed himself immensely elsewhere in the notice) commenting that 'the result would have been better still if the tone of the grand piano had not been too much for the upright'.[19]

The combination of Sampson's counsel and his own listening meant that for his age Montgomery knew a prodigious amount of music. Whilst still at school he was already very knowledgeable about the latest developments. He was an admirer of Walton's *Belshazzar's Feast* (first performed in 1931) and he followed avidly the contemporary career of Richard Strauss. His taste was eclectic. In November 1939, with the same Balkwill with whom he had performed the *Jamaican Rumba*, Montgomery lectured the Three Sixths Class at Merchant Taylors' on ballet, an interest he was to develop at Oxford. The event was considered 'a great success, though hampered by a faulty gramophone, which, after the most terrible struggle, could only be heard by three or four rows'.[20]

> Montgomery began by defining ballet, and went on to say that ballet was by no means an effeminate occupation; it demanded the greatest possible staying power and the physique of an athlete. Moreover, the dancer had to have perfect control over every muscle, for not only did he have to exert himself continually, but he had to look graceful into the bargain. After mentioning a few of the different types of ballerina, Montgomery told us something about the task of the choreographer. In ballet the creative power was represented by the music, and the art by the interpretation of the various dances; and in the latter there was scope for the individuality of the choreographer. He was largely responsible for the success of the production, and had to be an expert in costumes, music, dancing, and painting – for

15    *World Authors*, Wakeman, p. 344
16    *Taylorian*, Vol. 57, July 1936, pp. 164–165
17    Ibid., Vol. 57, July 1937, pp. 364–365
18    Ibid., Vol. 59, December 1939, p. 33
19    Ibid., Vol. 58, March 1939, p. 288
20    Ibid., Vol. 59, December 1939, p. 30

scenery plays a very considerable part in ballet. Ballet music consisted either of separate tunes strung together or of a whole piece specially composed for ballet – as, for instance, well-known compositions of Tchaikovsky and Stravinsky. The theme might be merely an attempt to convey a certain atmosphere, or it might be a complete story. Montgomery concluded with some general remarks about national ballets – Spanish, French, Russian, and finally English; he expressed his great appreciation of the Vic-Wells ballet.[21]

Montgomery also read a great deal. Being a 'prig and an intellectual snob' had unfortunately affected his popularity amongst his fellow pupils. The combination of a strong intellect, lameness and the absence away at school of his sisters had left him as something of a loner, a situation that was altered only when he met similar minds at Oxford.

The first surviving composition of Bruce Montgomery is a hymn tune. In 1934, at the age of 13, he wrote the tune which he called *Chesham Bois*. It was printed privately. It was used during a service at Amersham Free Church, and his mother swelled with pride as the congregation sang her son's music. It is an attractive melody in typical nineteenth-century fashion, reminiscent of Stainer, competently if rather repetitively harmonised. Mary Brownrigg observed at Oxford, perhaps somewhat illogically, that Montgomery had such a feeling for harmony it was likely he never had any formal instruction in it. It is hard to imagine, however, that no help was given to him. The grasp of harmony shown by this 13-year-old is more advanced than one would expect. Even so, Montgomery must have been very proud to have had a composition printed. The person most likely to have helped with the harmonisation, Godfrey Sampson, longed to hear about the tune's first outing and was, as always, full of good advice: 'If you're given proofs to correct be very careful – it's so easy to pass over a musical misprint, & once passed every organist & choir the world over will happily sing it, all unsuspecting.'[22]

Towards the end of his life, Montgomery wrote: 'I learned piano and organ and started to compose at the age of 14 – dreadful rubbish, as you'd expect.'[23] Apart from his hymn tune, nine other works which he wrote before going up to Oxford survive in manuscript. Another piece, *The Sands of Dee* for chorus and orchestra, written in 1935/6 is referred to as being 'fortunately lost' in a catalogue of his music which Montgomery compiled some time in 1951. With the optimism of youth, and the connivance of Sampson, he sent various works to publishers. 'I am so sorry, & hope you won't be too disappointed, but the enclosed letter tells its own tale', Sampson reported after one rejection, 'not, however that it's discouraging – on the contrary, and considering your tender years, it's just the opposite.' He was keen to make sure that Montgomery became wise to the ways of the world: 'If you care to try other publishers I should, but they're all devils remember.'[24]

*Pilgrimage*, a work Montgomery completed in the month of his 17th birthday, might be listed as 'juvenilia' by its composer in his own catalogue, but it shows that he was developing the musical style and tendencies which mark out his later

---

21     Ibid.

22     Godfrey Sampson to RBM, 4 December 1934

23     'Edmund Crispin', Montgomery

24     Godfrey Sampson to RBM, 24 November 1936

works. The great majority of Montgomery's published music is vocal, with the words generally taken from verse of the sixteenth and seventeenth centuries. These observations are true of this work; it is for SATB with piano or organ, and the text is by Sir Walter Raleigh (?1554–1618). Musically, the language is not yet as heavily chromatic as his mature style, and it is devoid so far of what was to become his harmonic fingerprint, a rapid swerve away from and back to the key of the moment, although the central section of a work which begins and ends in B flat major moves fairly quickly through D major and F sharp major and thence via a chromatically descending bass back to the tonic. Even so, certain progressions which soon became characteristic of his work make an early appearance.

The overall impression is that influences of Vaughan Williams, Parry and Stanford are not far away. The rise and fall of the opening instrumental passage (which recurs during and at the end of the work, giving it a pleasing sense of shape) and the broad initial choral phrase (with its chromatic descending inner line) are typical. Twice in the work Montgomery uses a favourite progression (II–V–I) which he embellishes in different ways. In the first instance ('My bottle of salvation') a dominant 9th (on G) with an appoggiatura rising from the sharpened 11th is immediately followed by a dominant 13th (on C) which itself leads to a dominant 7th (on F). On the second occasion ('on ev'ry milken hill') a minor 7th is added to II, followed by a dominant 13th leading to the tonic with an unprepared suspension on the 2nd [Example 2.1].

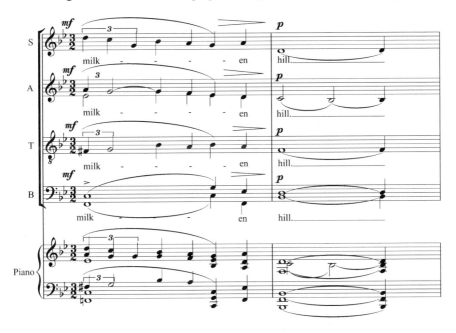

**Example 2.1** *Pilgrimage*

Three other chords used in this work became favourites: a dominant 7th with an augmented 5th at the top and a raised 8th ('the bowl <u>of</u> Bliss'), chord VII with raised

3rd and 5th set against a tonic pedal ('And drink mine everlasting <u>fill</u>'), and towards the end of the work ('it will <u>thirst</u> no more') Montgomery uses a dominant 9th on E flat which resolves not to an A flat, but to a chord of B flat with added 2nds and 6ths [Example 2.2].

This last chord adds spice to the setting of the word 'thirst', but at this stage in his career Montgomery had a more developed sense of harmony than he did of word setting (*Pilgrimage* shows some immaturity in this latter area: at one point, for instance, he attempts to set 'quiet' to a single semibreve, at another he stresses the final syllable of 'pilgrimage' on the first beat of a bar). Even at his peak Montgomery was, in his own words, 'an incurably elaborately harmonic composer'[25] in the sense that the chords he employs are often of more interest than, say, his use of rhythm or word painting. In *Pilgrimage* his use of rhythm is undemanding. In other circumstances this might be a criticism, but here it creates a reflective atmosphere which suits the mood of the poetry.

**Example 2.2 *Pilgrimage***

Sampson was constantly on the lookout for ways in which to encourage and chivvy his young friend in his work, and Montgomery sent completed compositions straight to him for comment. 'At first glance', Sampson wrote after receiving the manuscript of another choral piece (*Jesu, that dost in Mary dwell*), 'it looks a little too unconventional in places to be suitable for a normal church anthem. Publishers always fight shy of such things remember.'[26] Sampson's comments after a more thorough examination of the score show how well he mixed rigorous criticism with encouragement. Following a series of specific, mostly moderately negative, observations, he concludes in a more general and positive vein:

> All this is very frank – but I don't think you would wish me to be otherwise. Also, it is only my opinion, & many better judges may think differently. If I may offer a word of advice, when you embark on a work, decide what it is going to be & stick to it. It is fatally

25    RBM to Geoffrey Bush, 9 February 1965
26    Godfrey Sampson to RBM, 30 August 1940

easy to be carried & in the heat of writing include something quite out of the picture – but experience, & experience only is, I think, the cure for that. Don't think I am talking like an old man, but I have been at the game for twenty years. At any rate your anthem is better than I could have done at your age – if that's any comfort. Go on writing. It's the only thing to do.[27]

Montgomery was fortunate to have such a capable teacher. Sampson may have been indulgent with his time, but he was a stern taskmaster who took every opportunity to make sure that his pupil thought deeply about the work he was producing. As a result, by the time Montgomery left school he was the possessor of a more secure composition technique than most people of his age.

In the spring of 1937 Montgomery made his first trip abroad on his own to stay with a family in Dresden. It was a tense time to be visiting Germany. When the 15-year-old arrived at Southampton on 4 April to set sail for Cuxhaven on the SS *Hansa*, he fell in with a Dr Nutzel, a lawyer and enthusiastic Nazi, with whom he had conversations about politics, Nazism, art and religion, made comic by the limits of the one's English and the other's German. Montgomery's letters home frequently reassure his mother about his safety. On the 4th he wrote: 'I'm very happy, mother, so don't worry or anything like that',[28] and on the 6th he wrote again: 'I forgot to say that when we reached the ship the whole orchestra struck up *Deutschland über Alles* and everyone did the Hitler salute and it was all most impressive.'[29] The start of the voyage was bedevilled by mists. Montgomery had the cabin to himself, and he was woken and called to meals 'by a sort of German folk tune played on the cornet'.[30]

The ship arrived in Cuxhaven early in the evening of the 7th, whereupon the band burst forth into *Deutschland über Alles* again 'and everyone on the quay froze stiff. It was the most amazing sight.'[31] He took the train to Hamburg, arriving close to midnight. He was supposed to have been met by friends of Nora, but no one appeared. With his limited German he managed to communicate with a railway official, and he telephoned the family. As he did not know their address, it was fortunate for Montgomery that the family he was due to stay with (the Grauerts) were the only ones with that name listed in the telephone directory. He stayed for one night, and then travelled by train to Dresden via Leipzig.

He stayed with the Fickler family in their flat on Regensburger Strasse. Godfrey Sampson had instructed Montgomery what to see and do in Dresden, and he lost no time in booking seats for three operas: *Tristan and Isolde*, *Die Walküre* and *Elektra*. He kept up a stream of letters home which his mother was instructed to number and retain so that they formed a diary of his trip. They are remarkably enthusiastic and mature in style, with occasional lapses into schoolboy expressions such as 'I shall have piles to tell you when I get home.'[32] He gives details of what he notices, such

27    Ibid., 9 September 1940
28    RBM to parents, 4 April 1937
29    Ibid., 6 April 1937
30    Ibid.
31    Ibid., 7 April 1937
32    Ibid., 10 April 1937

as the fact that Germans don't cross their legs, and 'the extraordinary prevalence of plus-fours, or K-nickerbockers, as they are called here'.[33]

He saw *Tristan and Isolde* on the 11th, and wrote home shortly before it saying that he was to sit in the fifth row of the stalls. 'I am terribly excited,'[34] he proclaimed, at the same time admitting to slight feelings of homesickness. The next day he reported that Martha Fuchs as Isolde was magnificent and there were 'over twenty curtains! I counted. [...] They have changed Walküre to Oberon – most aggravating.'[35] He clearly loved this immersion in music. He heard Beethoven's *Ninth Symphony* and followed it in the score he had bought (the expense of which worried him), noticing that the clarinets 'were a bit shaky and got behind at one point, causing confusion'.[36]

He went to *Rigoletto*, but thought it 'trivial'.[37] His later interest in art was not yet developed. He visited some galleries, but reported to his mother that 'I don't appreciate pictures as I should.'[38]

He discovered that his ship, the New York, was returning to England on 22 April, two days earlier than he had expected, so he had to change his arrangements. 'It is tremendous fun, doing all this myself. I feel so responsible and experienced.'[39] He also had to husband his finances. He was paying for his board and lodging and his money was running low, but he was determined to go to the opera in Berlin on the way home 'as by a lucky chance, *Die Meistersinger* is on the night I am there!! That I could not miss. I shall also be there for Hitler's birthday.'[40] He stayed at the Hotel Nordland on the 19th and was home by the 24th.

In April 1938 Montgomery composed his *Rondo Rhapsody*, scored for cor anglais, horn, harp and string quartet. The work was completed in Paris on another of his trips abroad. On this occasion he was lodging in a pension. During the chilly weather, the chambermaid was in the habit of warming the lavatory seat for him by sitting on it. The job done, she would knock on his door and say, 'C'est chauffé, Monsieur Robert.'[41] This was the only place he was known as Robert, because the French found the name 'Bruce' unfamiliar.

When his detective novels were published by Penguin, Montgomery's biographical note stated: 'He travelled a certain amount before the war, particularly in Germany, where he totally failed to prognosticate the subsequent course of events.' What his views were as war edged nearer are not known. As his lameness meant that active service was out of the question, the dangers of war were undoubtedly further from his mind than from those of his contemporaries who might expect to be called up. Still at school, he had important things on his mind. In the summer of 1939 he passed his Higher School Certificate in French and German, with subsidiary Latin, English

---

33     Ibid.
34     Ibid., 11 April 1937
35     Ibid., no date
36     Ibid., 14 April 1937
37     Ibid.
38     Ibid., 10 April 1937
39     Ibid., 11 April 1937
40     Ibid., 14 April 1937
41     Colin Strang

Literature and Geography. A few months later in the autumn, just after war had broken out, he sat the scholarship exam for Oxford in French and German. He passed and was awarded the Sir Thomas White Scholarship for Modern Studies, a closed award for pupils from Merchant Taylors', at St John's College. Things might have turned out rather differently, though. Towards the end of 1938 Godfrey Sampson had contacted his friend Boris Ord, organist of King's College, Cambridge, with the intention of encouraging him to take Montgomery. Early in the summer of 1939 Sampson wrote to Montgomery that he still had not heard anything definite from Ord, but that it was 'his [Ord's] suggestion that I should take you up [to Cambridge] between July 8th and August 8th. However, I shall be there in September and if he is also, so must you be.'[42] Nothing further happened.

Montgomery's school report for the Christmas Term 1939 shows many of the characteristics his later work would display. 'He pursues his reading with a very lively interest and well-founded discrimination,' states his English master. 'He becomes less exclusively intellectual and develops breadth of sympathy. His writing shows real promise.' In French Literature he was 'still inclined to be "showy"'. In a remark that was to be true of his work as a critic, he was judged to be 'pleasantly unwilling to let others get away with vague or unwarranted obscurities'[43] by the master who led a general studies programme. His interest in verbal jousting is shown by reports in the school magazine. In February, he contributed to a debate on the motion 'This House would rather live in a house than a flat':

> Nothing deterred, Mr. Montgomery informed the House that he would rather live in a flat among fields than in one of a swarm of hideous villas disfiguring the countryside.[44]

In the report of another debate, this time on the motion 'This House considers the physical education in this School to be inadequate', there is merely the somewhat bald and enigmatic statement: 'Mr. Montgomery expounded Plato.'[45] His status within the school was such for him to become a Prompter (the junior of the two ranks of school prefect) in 1938, and a Monitor (senior prefect) in 1939.

His scholarship to Oxford safely secured, Montgomery had some time on his hands. In the Spring of 1939, towards the end of his time at Merchant Taylors', Montgomery went to help at the Rickmansworth Food Office. Volunteers were needed to write names and addresses on ration books, and to help with clerical duties. Montgomery went there for a couple of hours after school each day and met his first girlfriend. Muriel Pavlow, later to become an established film actress in, coincidentally, some of the films for which Montgomery composed the music, was at that time a young actress who lived in Rickmansworth with her parents. She had returned home because the war had temporarily reduced the entertainment industry. Now nearing her 18th birthday, Muriel had been on the stage since she was 14.

Muriel and Montgomery soon became friendly. At that time Montgomery came across as a quietly spoken person with a marvellous sense of humour. He was

---

42 Godfrey Sampson to RBM, no date
43 School report, Christmas Term 1939
44 *Taylorian*, Vol. 58, March 1939, p. 278
45 Ibid., Vol. 59, March 1940, p. 95

not at all shy, and seemed happy enough with his schooling. His straightforward, easy-going nature bordered on laziness (in 1938 Godfrey Sampson had written to Montgomery: 'You have an indolent nature but an active mind'),[46] a trait that was to dog him in later life. He talked a lot about music and seemed to be heading for a career in that direction, despite being on the verge of reading Modern Languages at Oxford and being expected, by his father at least, to join the Civil Service thereafter. Muriel was aware how superior Montgomery was to her intellectually.

They had evenings out at the Odeon in Rickmansworth (seeing *The Wizard of Oz*, a favourite of Montgomery's, at least four times) and at The Millstream, a restaurant in Amersham. They thought it was very daring to have a drink before dinner and half a bottle of wine with it. Montgomery was always very good about seeing Muriel home, walking the 20 minutes from her house to Rickmansworth Station before taking the last train back to Amersham. On one occasion, on the eve of Muriel's 18th birthday in June 1939, they had talked and were very late arriving home. The pair met Muriel's mother at the end of the road; she was in a state of panic and about to ring the police.[47] The friendship survived Montgomery's move to Brixham with his parents, and continued into his time at Oxford.

Although they met by chance, Montgomery's friendship with Muriel was timely in that he had for some years taken an interest in amateur dramatics. One of his last school reports noted that 'He has found time to read a good deal and to make a very helpful contribution to our study of plays and poetry.'[48] His friendship with Muriel meant that he could indulge this interest. At the Playhouse in Amersham there was a repertory company led by Sally Latimer. The theatre was a converted cinema and the company had only recently been started. Good productions were common. Montgomery was interested in what went on, and used to help out by playing the piano for them. His experiences here were to grow into a much deeper interest in the theatre by the time he reached Oxford.

Montgomery's father had been due to retire in 1938, but the approach of war meant that he kept at work for another year. As recognition of his work at the India Office, it was proposed that Robert Montgomery should be created a Knight Commander of the Indian Empire. His wife, however, would have none of it, claiming that she wanted to remain an ordinary housewife. Marion Montgomery won. In the end Robert was appointed a Commander of the Indian Empire.

With their son about to leave home for university, the Montgomerys decided to move in readiness for their retirement. This meant severing their connection with Amersham Free Church. Robert Montgomery was presented with an elaborate and beautifully drawn inscription which thanked him for his twenty-seven years of faithful service as a chorister and wished him a happy and healthy retirement. When the girls had left home, the family had moved from Domus to a smaller house in Amersham-on-the-Hill. Now they decided to move further afield. Robert Montgomery had always wanted to live in Fowey in Cornwall and have a boat in which he could go fishing. But they did not move quite that far. Several months

46    Godfrey Sampson to RBM, 6 September 1938
47    Muriel Pavlow
48    School report, Easter Term 1939

before Bruce Montgomery went up to Oxford in October 1940, his parents moved to Rock Hill House, overlooking the harbour in Brixham, Devon.

# Chapter 3

# 'A seminal moment': 1940–1943

After schooldays during which, as we have seen, Montgomery himself considered that he had become 'a prig and an intellectual snob'[1] and as a result made few friends, his arrival at Oxford created an opportunity for change. Initially, however, little seemed to alter. The impression he made on his contemporaries was formidable. 'There was no doubt, though, who, of us all, appeared the most sophisticated, best-read, widely connected and gifted. Bruce Montgomery [...] may have been slightly older than us, but he was light years ahead in experience,' wrote Alan Ross,[2] with whom Montgomery shared tutorials in his first year. He made a great impression, too, on Kingsley Amis, who went up two terms after Montgomery:

> I must have seen Bruce Montgomery on my first morning in St John's in 1941 coming out of his staircase in the front quad to go to the bath-house. [...] I felt rather like a recruit getting his first sight of a full colonel in red tabs, spurs, etc.: here was an *undergraduate*, the real thing. This man, along with an indefinable and daunting air of maturity, had a sweep of wavy auburn hair, a silk dressing gown in some non-primary shade and a walk that looked eccentric and mincing, though I found out later that it was the result of a severe congenital deformity in both feet. [...] When more fully attired, he inclined to a fancy-waistcoated, suede-shoed style with cigarette-holders and rings.[3]

Although Montgomery's showy dress sense made Amis 'uneasy',[4] he was still an impressive figure; that he drank spirits in the bar of the Randolph Hotel, particularly at lunchtime, whilst most undergraduates took beer in public houses added to his reputation. Because of this 'formidable exterior',[5] Philip Larkin did not get to know Montgomery as a friend until his last year at St John's, despite it being normal for the few undergraduates reading humanities to meet together:

> Bruce's modern languages–Playhouse–classical music–Randolph Hotel ambience conflicted sharply with my own. Of course, I had seen him about, but it hardly occurred to me that he was an undergraduate, not in the same sense that I was. Wearing an air raid warden's badge and carrying a walking stick, he stalked aloofly to and fro in a severe triangle formed by the College lodge (for letters), the Randolph bar and his lodgings in Wellington Square.[6]

---

1    *World Authors*, Wakeman, p. 344
2    *Blindfold Games*, Ross, p. 144
3    *Memoirs*, Amis, p. 71
4    Ibid.
5    Introduction to *Jill*, Larkin
6    Ibid.

It was not only this physical exterior that intimidated his contemporaries. They were also aware that he was a good pianist, organist and composer. He had painted a picture of his school which was displayed in his rooms; it was a watercolour and consisted of a number of extraordinary lines, mostly vertical, in very delectable pale colours. There were other paintings, but this was the only framed one. He had also written a book called *Romanticism and the World Crisis* as well as essays on various authors. Montgomery was himself aware to a certain extent of the image he projected, but in his turn he realised the qualities of his friends. He felt that his 'dislikeable characteristics were to some extent modified when I met various fellow undergraduates whose minds seemed to me much better than my own. [...] In that sceptical generation, with its distaste for pretentiousness and humbug, I found many of my best friends, losing at least some of my own pretentiousness and humbug in the process.'[7]

The impression Montgomery gave soon faded when people got to know him. 'Beneath this formidable exterior [...] Bruce had unsuspected depths of frivolity, and we were soon spending most of our time together swaying about with laughter on bar-stools.'[8] Elsewhere, Larkin refers to Montgomery's 'genial sense of the absurd'.[9] Amis agreed: 'Like me, Philip [Larkin] had found Bruce a little intimidating at the start, though he was the gentlest of souls (I only saw him angry once, when I had stigmatised Malcolm Arnold's overture *Beckus the Dandipratt* as marred by fake jollity).'[10] Ross felt the same: 'His familiarity with writers, painters and musicians I had never heard of, made me reluctant to expose my own ignorance in his presence, but he was always wryly polite, sympathetic and generous in the communication of his own enthusiasms.'[11]

Montgomery's enthusiasms were indeed wide. Ross noted that 'his knowledge appeared encyclopaedic'.[12] He was remarkably well-informed about the very latest developments in music and literature, particularly in Europe. He shared rooms in his first year with Colin Strang. Strang was also a former pupil of Merchant Taylors', but he and Montgomery had not become friends until working at the Rickmansworth Food Office shortly before going up to Oxford. Strang was the owner of a gramophone, and he bought the records which Montgomery suggested. He favoured the Romantics: the third piano concertos of Prokofiev and Rachmaninov were often played, and the late-Romantic music of Wagner and Richard Strauss retained its appeal. As time went on Montgomery became particularly keen on Brahms and grew to detest Berlioz.[13] In general he ignored Mozart and Beethoven, castigating the latter for writing one climax after another with nothing in between.[14] He was devoted to Bach and had a thorough knowledge of the cantatas; any choir he took would sing at least one

---

7     *World Authors*, Wakeman, p. 344
8     Introduction to *Jill*, Larkin
9     Foreword to *Fen Country*, Larkin
10    *Memoirs*, Amis, p. 72
11    *Blindfold Games*, Ross, p. 145
12    Ibid.
13    Jacques Barzun to author, 14 February 1990
14    Colin Strang

of them. He rarely took an interest in earlier music. Montgomery was particularly drawn to recent work by leading English composers. *Music for Strings* by Arthur Bliss (1935) joined *Belshazzar's Feast* in impressing him deeply. He kept a close eye on the career of Constant Lambert. He had reservations about Vaughan Williams, because he thought the composer had 'tarred everybody of that generation'.[15]

*At Swim-Two-Birds* by Flann O'Brien, first published in 1939, delighted Montgomery by its use of word play. For the same reason he enthused about the poetry of Edward Lear. Strang recalls that he took a dim view if people supposed he was referring to Shakespeare when he asked if they liked Lear. He would demolish anyone who thought that Lear's habit of repeating the first line at the end made him a bad poet. He held that this was one of the strengths as this last line would often accommodate the key word of the limerick. He particularly loved the limerick which begins: 'There was an old man who supposed the street door was partially closed', and frequently discussed what an odd thing this was to suppose. He was always ready to propound his love of Wyndham Lewis. Lewis was a great supporter of Classicism against Romanticism, and Montgomery had the notion that Romanticism was at the bottom of the trouble that led to the war. This led to an odd mixture of views. He admired Romanticism in music but did not care for the same trend in literature: he was keen on contemporary music but 'had little use for contemporary poetry, the result probably of an excess of Wyndham Lewis'.[16] Montgomery believed that Hitler was somehow a product of Romanticism. This theory was responsible for the unpublished 160-page extended essay *Romanticism and the World Crisis* which he completed in 1942. The authors acknowledged in the foreword show something of the breadth of his reading: Henri de Montherlant, Charles Maurras, Julien Benda, Hermann Keyserling and Lewis are all cited. The work is subtitled an 'Essay on the Culture and Politics of the XXth Century'. With titles to chapters such as 'The Apotheosis of emotion and the intellectual alternative', it is hardly surprising that the existence of the work struck terror into his contemporaries.

Montgomery's literary endeavours were encouraged by his friendship with Charles Williams, who worked for Oxford University Press. Williams (1886–1945) wrote poetry, books on theology, and supernatural thrillers; he was also a member of the 'Inklings', a literary group which included Tolkien and C.S. Lewis. Sometimes these writers would read passages from their work in progress to Montgomery and his contemporaries, and Montgomery heard snatches from *The Lord of the Rings* in this way.[17] It is probable that Montgomery first met Williams when he tried to interest Oxford University Press in publishing *Romanticism and the World Crisis*. They met regularly to talk about books in conversations that were regarded by Montgomery's friends as highly intellectual. Montgomery was entertained by the habit Williams had of continuing at the next meeting with the half sentence he had broken off with as he caught his bus at the end of their previous encounter ('As I was saying, my dear

---

15    Mary Strang
16    Ibid.
17    Joan Bagley to author, 20 June 1990

fellah…').[18] The influence was not all one way; Montgomery took Williams out for meals and lent him novels by John Dickson Carr.

With this sort of stimulation, it is not surprising to find Montgomery writing an informed letter to the editor of the *Times Literary Supplement*. He was outraged by a letter from a Dr Oscar Levy which dealt with the quarrel between Nietzsche and Wagner. Levy attacked Wagner, claiming that he would have keenly embraced the Nazi ethos whereas Nietzsche would not. Montgomery wrote back in forthright terms. He accepted that Wagner would probably have been a Nazi, but he warned that 'Dr Levy's interpretation […] must not be taken as implying that Nietzsche would have been innocent in this respect.'

> Nietzsche's thought was often so confused and inconsistent, its cadre so pretentious and obscure, that almost anything can be proved by rummaging through his works. Wagner's, which is as mediocre as Dr Levy suggests, has the very vulnerable merit of being comparatively plain. Whitewashing Nietzsche may be all very well; but if it is to entail as a corollary the vast and hazily damning generalizations on Wagner of which Dr Levy is guilty, then it is time that the political dangers of Nietzsche's philosophy were finally and definitively pointed out.[19]

He makes his point by quoting from Nietzsche: 'Zarathustra says: "I divine that ye would call my Superman – 'the Devil!'"' And indeed we do.' The tone of the letter suggests that Montgomery enjoyed writing it. As a combination of his musical, literary and linguistic studies, this was an ideal subject.

So he comes across as a sophisticated and wealthy young man. He cultivated the right people, but his learning was clearly self-imposed. He still avoided physical activities and, as he noted, took refuge in music and books. There was no reason whatever why he should appear wealthy, but he certainly had the money to drink in the Randolph and smoke ferociously (his fingers were usually stained by nicotine). He loved conviviality. Hours were spent in propping up bars, chatting all the time, telling funny stories and anecdotes or making puns on people's names. One of the puns that he often made concerned Sir Edward Maufe, the architect of the Oxford Playhouse and of the extensions at St John's College. Maufe was late arriving at a dinner over which Sir Edwin Lutyens was presiding:

> 'Excuse me, Sir Edwin, I'm Maufe,' he explained.
> 'My dear fellow,' replied Lutyens, 'you can't go now, you've only just arrived.'[20]

Thus, upon closer acquaintance Montgomery was not at all intimidating. He accepted anyone who was happy to listen to him. Strang recalls that 'he was part of everyone's gang'.[21] Larkin painted a vivid picture of his love of sitting on licensed premises talking about art:

---

18    Colin Strang
19    *Times Literary Supplement*, 28 February 1942, p. 103
20    Colin Strang
21    Ibid.

Under his immediate influence I suddenly revolted against all the things I'd previously worshipped – poetry, law, psychoanalysis, seriousness.....and so forth. It was like being back in the fourth form again. Bruce's irresponsibility and self-confidence were exactly what I needed at the time and our friendship flared up like a flame in oxygen [...] We spent a great many evenings drinking together in the Gloucester Arms, or more often the Lord Napier in Observatory Street.[22]

Larkin repaid the compliment by attempting to broaden Montgomery's horizons:

In return I played him Billie Holiday records and persuaded him to widen his circle of drinking-places. One night the Proctor entered one of these and I was caught by the bullers at a side door: Bruce, on the other hand, simply stepped into a kind of kitchen, apologized to someone he found ironing there, and waited until the coast was clear. 'When will you learn,' he reproved me afterwards, 'not to act on your own initiative?'[23]

Larkin introduced Montgomery to more jazz than just Billie Holiday:

I talk to Bruce Montgomery about jazz a good deal. He is the last person I should have thought would have liked it, but in our last term at Oxford he took a liking to some of our records, particularly the Chicago Rhythm Kings' 'I've Found a New Baby'. His classical training and taste make it impossible for him to like jazz for simple rhythm or power (he does not like Bessie Smith) but he tells me that small-group improvised counterpoint is parallel to the counterpoint of Bach, and that both types of music head their genres and are somewhat connected. This sounds sensible enough to me. His eclectic taste makes me aware of how much mediocre stuff we have, though not as much as he would say.[24]

It is typical of Montgomery's approach to such things that he would look further into the genre, but given that particularly in later life his artistic tastes were nostalgic, it is not surprising that he enjoyed the same types of traditional jazz as Larkin. He never did like Bessie Smith, though, referring to her as a 'phlegmy bawler'[25] in a letter to Larkin over thirty years later.

Despite this self-confidence, Montgomery was something of a hypochondriac, a trait he was never to lose. Because of his disability and his consequent lack of exercise he had a rather pale complexion, and he worried about his heart, with good cause considering how much he drank and smoked.

The Oxford Montgomery arrived in was one altered greatly by the war. There were far fewer undergraduates, and he found it easier to make his mark in music than he might if he had come up under more normal circumstances. Because the appointed organ scholar had joined the forces, Montgomery found an opportunity to take charge of music in the chapel at St John's. He was paid £15 a year for his work as organist. In July 1941 Godfrey Sampson wrote to congratulate him on various successes, 'especially as University organist and organist of Great St Mary's [presumably Sampson intended St Mary the Virgin, the University Church]. Who

---

22    *Philip Larkin*, Motion, p. 88
23    Introduction to *Jill*, Larkin
24    Larkin to J.B. Sutton, 17 October 1944
25    RBM to Larkin, 12 February 1977

carries on there in the Vac? I feel rather proud too, as I did slightly help to fertilize the musical seed within you.'[26] During his three years he became involved in a great many musical events, some of which managed to include his love of theatre and ballet.

He was active as a conductor, particularly with choirs. He had a very good technique, and rehearsals with him were popular because he was amusing and knew what he was doing. He always used a baton, even with choirs, making small precise movements. His other hand often remained in his waistcoat pocket, something he learned from Richard Strauss. Montgomery once told Colin Strang, with approval, two of Strauss's rules for conductors: 'The left thumb should never leave the waistcoat pocket. Never look encouragingly at the brass.'[27]

Montgomery often played the piano for the University Ballet Club, sometimes as a duet with Donald Swann. Twice he accompanied performances by two members of Madame Rambert's company. After one of these concerts he attended a party at which Madame Rambert made an appearance. He was very excited by this and talked about it for weeks, quoting a clerihew that Madame Rambert had delivered: 'Alcibiades met ze pleiades, and took ze bodices off those most delightful goddesses.'[28] The music he played for these concerts consisted mostly of contemporary works by the likes of Poulenc, Walton, Ravel, Lord Berners and Lambert. The last composer was the subject of an article by Montgomery which appeared in the Trinity Term 1943 edition of *Arabesque*, the magazine of the Ballet Club. As in a previous article on the subject of music in ballet in general, Montgomery showed that he was very well versed in the work of contemporary composers for the genre. He loved Lambert's *Rio Grande*, and in one performance of the work by the University Musicians' Club he 'dazzled' Arthur Jacobs 'by not only conducting but stepping down to play the piano cadenza'.[29]

Montgomery continued the interest in theatre that had been kindled by Amersham and Muriel Pavlow. He haunted the bar and back regions of the Oxford Playhouse. In July 1942 he directed the music there for performances of *The Ascent of F6* by W.H. Auden, Christopher Isherwood and Benjamin Britten, having the previous year played the piano for performances of the same play given by the Christ Church Dramatic Society in which Michael Flanders played Ian Shawcross. His friendship with Muriel Pavlow had continued, by letter at least, after his move with his parents to Brixham and thence to Oxford. It seems that Montgomery was more keen on her than she was on him. Initially Muriel was also very ardent, but this soon changed: she did not always seem to know her own mind, one moment claiming that she loved Montgomery (Robbie, as she called him) more than anything, the next wondering what she saw in him. By November 1940 Muriel's mother was convinced that her daughter would marry Montgomery, but Muriel made it very clear that this was not going to happen. When she tried to break with him Montgomery put it down to their separation, but Muriel was sure that this was not the reason. The friendship

---

26    Godfrey Sampson to RBM, 24 July 1941
27    Colin Strang
28    Ibid.
29    Arthur Jacobs to author, 21 January 1992

had its stormy moments and by the middle of 1941 the split had been made, with Muriel telling Montgomery that he had begun to bore her – yet she was very keen to keep in touch and on good terms with him. The relationship had never really been more than that, with a lot of fun and a kiss on the cheek being as far as it went. Muriel was determined to follow her career whilst keeping her options open.[30] Matters became complicated by June 1941 as Muriel was in rep at Oxford, but as far as she was concerned marriage was still out of the question. Kingsley Amis believed that Montgomery wanted to marry Muriel, and that not doing so was a great disappointment to him.[31] The fact that he dedicated his first published book to her in 1943 was an indication of his feelings. She appeared at the Playhouse fairly regularly during Montgomery's Oxford years. One of her major roles there was in *Mary Rose* by J.M. Barrie. Montgomery attended the first night and told Muriel that the moment she came back on stage, with her cloak seemingly still moving after she had stopped, was one of the most thrilling things he had ever seen.[32] A friendship of some sort was maintained. Whatever the state of the relationship, it did no harm to Montgomery's reputation to be seen with an up-and-coming young actress.

Montgomery was writing music and plays, and sometimes combining the two. In November 1942 he composed eight pieces of incidental music for a performance of *Everyman* by the Student Christian Movement. Compared with the flood of music he produced in the years immediately after Oxford, his time as an undergraduate produced only a small amount. At some stage he went to Thomas Armstrong, then organist at Christ Church, for composition lessons.

I remember Bruce Montgomery as an undergraduate very well, a clever, attractive and friendly young man – very quick to understand the full implications of basic principles of harmony and counterpoint, and not so rebellious about academic music studies as some of his contemporaries. In music, at that time, he seemed pretty conservative and perhaps too anxious to produce something well-written, approachable and performable to be very experimental.[33]

In a further comment Armstrong added: 'Highly gifted as he was, he might have been a more prolific and perhaps [...] more individual composer if he hadn't had so many other talents and interests.'[34] Armstrong also gave Montgomery conducting lessons. After they had graduated, Montgomery played the organ at the wedding of his friend Brian Galpin who had been at Hertford College. He also composed the march to which the bride entered. As the newly-wed pair left the church he was tackling the usual *Wedding March* by Mendelssohn and was about to avoid the tricky middle passage when there was a tap on his shoulder and a voice saying: 'Don't funk it!' It was Thomas Armstrong.

Two important pieces Montgomery composed during his Oxford years were his first published works which, although not appearing in the Oxford University Press

30   Muriel Pavlow
31   Sir Kingsley Amis
32   Muriel Pavlow
33   Sir Thomas Armstrong to author, 10 January 1990
34   Ibid., 28 January 1990

catalogue until 1944, were both written in 1941. Dedicated to his parents, although the original manuscript awards this honour to Godfrey Sampson and his church choir, *My joy, my life, my crown!*, an anthem for SATB with organ accompaniment to words by George Herbert (1593–1633), is a straightforward and charming piece whose broadly-sweeping and memorable melody is used for each of the three verses. This strophic structure is varied in common fashion: the first verse is for trebles only, the second for SATB in harmony with only occasional short organ phrases, and the third is for the whole choir in unison with harmony at the very end. The work contains (particularly in the organ passages which precede and link the verses) the first signs of what was to become a characteristic Montgomery harmonic fingerprint, the sudden, short chromatic swerve in which the original key is returned to almost before the ear realises quite the extent to which the music has left it. Indeed, acceptance of the piece for publication was conditional, amongst other revisions, on Montgomery toning down this tendency: 'The slight touch of F major in the opening symphony [this in a piece in D major] seems forced', wrote his editor, 'because it is repeated later and never goes very far along the new track.'[35] Before the final verse the organ has a quick swerve into B flat major. Generally, though, the key relations are carefully placed and secure; the combination of this, a contrapuntally supportive bass line and the harmony and texture is clearly designed in its simplicity to throw emphasis on the melody. Near the close there is a telling use of the flat-seventh, a device which recalls English Renaissance choral style and which Montgomery favoured in later works. The strophic setting precludes a detailed response to word setting, but there are clear signs that Montgomery is developing this aspect of his craft. By judiciously alternating bars of differing time signatures (particularly 4/4 and 3/2), he succeeds in giving a flow to his melody which at the same time manages to avoid any hint of rhythmic predictability. By drawing out the conclusion of the last verse and adding harmony, Montgomery brings out the importance of the final words: 'God writeth "Lov'd"'. This anthem is an accomplished and engaging work which deserves to be heard more often, its relatively modest choral demands making it ideal for church choirs.

It is instructive to make a brief comparison with an anthem for the same forces composed by his mentor Godfrey Sampson a few years earlier. Published by Novello in 1938 and mentioned in *Holy Disorders* (Montgomery's second novel), *Come, my Way, my Truth, my Life!* is also a setting of a text by George Herbert. Its three four-line verses are set in a more varied way: the first begins with tenors and basses in unison before branching into four-part harmony; the second starts with just sopranos before breaking into harmony; the last is in unison until the closing chords in similar fashion to Montgomery. Both settings also make use of augmentation at their close. There are superficial differences: the new music for the second half of the second verse means that Sampson's anthem is not entirely a strophic setting, unlike *My joy, my life, my crown!* Sampson never leaves his choir unaccompanied by the organ whereas Montgomery does. There are notable similarities: the use of a broad, flowing melody, the occasional switches between time signatures of 4/4 and 3/2 to maintain the rhythm of the words, and the use of the flattened seventh at cadence

---

35    Norman Peterkin (OUP) to RBM, 27 January 1944

points. More important, perhaps, is the harmonic language. Both write generally in a conservative tonal style with well-considered modulations. Mention has been made above of Montgomery's developing trademark 'swerve' in the organ interludes, and in *Come, my Way, my Truth, my Life!* there are moments when Sampson does much the same, although not to the same extent. In his link passage between the first two verses Sampson, from his tonic of F major, flirts with A flat major, and between the second and third he shifts to D flat major. The cumulative effect of these similarities certainly suggests that for his first published work Montgomery had absorbed the advice he had been given over the years by Sampson, yet there are signs that he was preparing to branch out in his own direction.

*Two Sketches for Pianoforte* was published almost simultaneously with *My joy, my life, my crown!* One of the three purely instrumental works in Montgomery's published catalogue, these are short impressionistic pieces. His publisher was surprised that they had been submitted, as Montgomery had previously indicated that he was not interested in writing for the piano. Originally called *Nocturnes*, it was suggested that this title was 'so associated with a certain type of piece' that it would be better to rename them 'Preludes or Sketches or Etchings'.[36] Dedicated to Diana Gollancz, the pieces show more clearly than *My joy, my life, my crown!* the direction in which Montgomery's music was going, and in many ways they are typical of his later work. They make use of quite advanced chromaticism, particularly in sequential passages indebted to the cycle of fifths, and the music ranges through an array of keys whilst always being able to return to the tonic without any sense of artifice. There are frequently great fistfuls of notes in each chord, something that one reviewer (Robin Hull in *The Chesterian*) thought could have been 'more vigorously pruned',[37] and a tendency the composer himself was well aware of, observing later in life that 'I have the greatest difficulty in writing any chord in less than seven real parts and still feeling that it was worth writing.'[38] Despite the tonal peregrinations, there is an assured grasp of structure and the *Two Sketches* show how comfortable Montgomery was with small-scale works. Although always melodic, in general Montgomery's works often gain their distinction from his harmonic invention and the ways in which this invention underpins the melody (*My joy, my life, my crown!* is relatively unusual in that the single melody dominates the work). In the *Two Sketches* added 6ths, 7ths and 9ths abound, and there is great use of appoggiaturas, often as a raised 11th over a dominant 7th. The impressionistic nature of the pieces is increased by this dense harmony, and the raised 11ths often suggest the whole tone scale idiom associated with Debussy and his school. Of the two pieces, the first has a broader melody than the more episodic second, and it is worth noting that although in F major (originally F# major but transposed for publication), the lack of the leading note at cadence points in this melody leaves traces of modality which are characteristic. Montgomery's performance instructions make clear the nature of the pieces: 'The playing of these Sketches should be rubato throughout, and the indications of tempo, etc., are to be regarded less as specific directions than as a

---

36 Ibid.

37 *The Chesterian*, uncertain date

38 RBM to Geoffrey Bush, 9 February 1965

rough general guide to the form which the rubato should take.'[39] Asked for people who might like to receive copies of the sketches, Montgomery suggested Sir Hugh Allen, Thomas Armstrong and Ernest Walker: 'All of them have been kind enough to take an interest in my work, and Sir Hugh heard these two pieces when they were first written. He swore they were inconsistent in idiom! – an objection I've never been able to understand.'[40]

At the same time, Montgomery was trying his hand at popular songs and blues which he called 'my jazzies'.[41] One of his party pieces at the time was to play and sing *Moonlight Becomes You* and other Bing Crosby songs. When he vamped at the piano, Larkin sometimes contributed the occasional note in the treble whilst Montgomery played the bass. When Montgomery discovered that Mary Miles, a fellow undergraduate, had an uncle in the publishing trade, he was immediately interested. Montgomery rarely missed an opportunity to meet people who might help him in his work. Miles took him to London to see her uncle. Nothing came of this introduction, but Montgomery gained something from the trip when the pair went to watch Constant Lambert conduct in the afternoon.

Montgomery was also busy writing plays. Before going up to Oxford he had become friendly with Ronald Lloyd Jones, to whom he dedicated *Romanticism and the World Crisis*. Lloyd Jones was a colleague of Sally Latimer's at the theatre in Amersham. Montgomery sent Lloyd Jones drafts of a play he was writing called *The Lion and the Fox*. They had planned to try and persuade Latimer to stage it at Amersham, but the chances of this happening disappeared when a play Lloyd Jones was directing there was abandoned as a disaster. This misfortune ended Montgomery's dramatic work for some time and Lloyd Jones, having joined the RAF, went missing in action over NW Germany in 1943.

Montgomery's contribution to the war effort during his time at Oxford took the form of work as an air raid warden. He volunteered for this, was trained and passed a quite demanding examination. In the collection of his papers in the Bodleian there is a delightfully wry account of a weekend's full-scale civil defence exercise in which he was put in charge of a Fire-Control Centre in a cellar of All Soul's. Having complained to the Authorities that he could not manage single-handed, they sent him two keen volunteer assistants. These turned out to be Lord David Cecil[42] and Dr A. L. Rowse.[43]

Cecil and Rowse dealt with the paperwork detailing which incidents had been answered by which trailer-pump whilst Montgomery took the telephone messages. The calls became more and more frantic:

> Towards tea-time an exceptionally clotted mass of directives came in from Balliol all at once. 'Where,' I said to Rowse in some despair, 'is trailer-pump number five?' 'It's there,' he said, pointing to a hook on the board. I said irritably 'I'm sorry, but I don't think it

---

39     Note on *Two Sketches*

40     RBM to Norman Peterkin, 20 September 1944

41     Colin Strang

42     Lord David Cecil (1902–1986), scholar and biographer of, amongst others, Thomas Hardy and Jane Austen

43     A.L. Rowse (1903–1997), historian

can be. Didn't we send it off half an hour ago to put out the King's Arms?' 'Cecil,' said Rowse sternly, 'where is number five?' Cecil looked up from the Incidents Book. 'Wowse, Wowse,' he said, infected by the general panic, 'I cannot wead my <u>witing</u>!' But before any of us had a chance to sort this out, Balliol was on the telephone again. 'All Souls,' it said dramatically, 'is on fire!'

'All of it?' I said, testily.

'Yes, all of it.'

'In that case Rowse and Cecil and I are being roasted to death.'

There was a pause, and then Balliol said 'Wait a minute, will you?' Then there was an even longer pause. In the background I could hear telephones ringing, chatter, people stamping to and fro. In the middleground a muttered consultation was going on. Presently a voice came back and said 'No, just part of it.'

'Which part?'

'Wait a minute,' the voice said again, and there was another long pause. Eventually, 'The Warden's Lodgings.' I heard.

'Whereabouts are they?'

'<u>I</u> don't know, I don't know. You've got Rowse there. haven't you? Well, he <u>lives</u> there. Ask him.'[44]

Events quieten down. On the Sunday Montgomery finds himself in more congenial surroundings, on the top of the Playhouse, instructing the company what to do in the event of an attack.

Whilst his friendship with Muriel Pavlow was petering out, Montgomery was presenting his best side to other women. He had a great effect on many female undergraduates in his sphere because on the whole they had been brought up quite strictly in sheltered and cloistered single-sex schools. Few of them had met anyone with such a breadth of reading and experience or who was socially so entertaining. Amis drew the conclusion from Montgomery's treatment of women in his books that he had terrible trouble with girls, of what sort he was not sure. Some people thought he might be homosexual, perhaps because of the way he dressed, but Amis did not think so and never saw any evidence. Montgomery apparently thought that Amis might be homosexually inclined. After Amis had joined the St John's choir, and left it almost immediately, Montgomery confided to Larkin that he thought Amis had been drawn to him 'in a very personal way'.[45] There is no evidence at any time in his life that Montgomery was homosexual, but there are grounds for thinking that he made a lot more of his love life than existed. He cut quite a dash when he paraded Muriel, who was already quite well known as an actress, on her visits to Oxford, even though as we know the relationship, on whatever level it actually existed, was more or less over. He added to this impression by indicating 'unlikely' girls from St Hugh's in a choir he conducted and asking a friend 'Who's that in the fourth row back?'[46] The evidence suggests that he was 'strongly heterosexual, but in a contemplative way'.[47] Later in his life the problems Montgomery had with women became much clearer.

44    Untitled essay, GB-Ob. MS. Eng. C. 3929

45    *Memoirs*, Amis, p. 71

46    Mary Strang

47    Geoffrey Bush

One girl friend who was to have some effect on his early career was Diana Gollancz. Daughter of Victor Gollancz, the publisher, she was an art student at the Slade, which had been evacuated from London to the Ashmolean Museum in Oxford. To what extent their relationship prospered is also difficult to tell (she was friends with everyone), but Diana was certainly captivated by Montgomery's urbanity. She was a pretty, dark, Middle-eastern looking girl, and was a regular visitor to tea at Montgomery's rooms in Wellington Square. Diana, Larkin reported, 'seemed boundlessly good-natured and endearingly silly',[48] and her frivolous high spirits mixed well with Montgomery's often frivolous intellect. Muriel Pavlow recalls that Montgomery was very enamoured of Diana and talked about her a good deal. Muriel was rather pleased that he had found someone else, and this helped complete the separation of their ways. If, on the other hand, Montgomery was using his friendship with Diana to try and make Muriel jealous, it did not work.

It was to Diana's father's firm that Montgomery submitted his first novel. The genre of work he produced was rather unexpected, as he recalled later:

> I was with one of those rare creatures, a genuinely bookish actor, in a pub in Oxford. We normally talked books. And we did so on this occasion. How the conversation got round to John Dickson Carr I can't quite remember, but I do remember the tone of mingled reproof, reproach and amusement with which my friend said, 'Oh, haven't you read John Dickson Carr?' I was a bit of an intellectual snob in those days, and thought the detective story rather beneath my notice. However, you didn't ignore advice about books from John Maxwell (my friend) [Maxwell had been stage manager for the production of *The Ascent of F6* at the Playhouse for which Montgomery had directed the music], and on our way back to my lodgings he called in at his, and he lent me a copy of *The Crooked Hinge*.
>
> I went to bed with it not expecting very much. But at two o'clock in the morning I was still sitting up with my eyes popping out of their sockets at the end of one of the sections – I think the third – with the doctor looking after the nerve-wracked maid saying, 'You devil up there, what have you done?'
>
> And of course I finished the book that night. It was to be a seminal moment in my career and to alter it entirely, for although subsequently I read and enjoyed other detective-story writers, in particular Michael Innes and Gladys Mitchell, it was Carr who induced me to try my hand at one myself, thus creating Edmund Crispin.[49]

Montgomery wrote his first story at breathtaking speed during ten days of the Easter Vacation of 1943, using (according to Larkin) 'his J nib and silver pen-holder'.[50] Clearly he did not let his approaching Finals get in the way. On 21 April he wrote to Victor Gollancz:

> My dear Mr Gollancz,
> I have just finished a detective novel (now in process of typing) and am wondering if it would be of any interest to you. I have tried your patience with so many of my MSS in the past, that I hesitate to foist another on you without warning. But Diana tells me your

---

48    *Philip Larkin*, Motion, p. 87
49    'Edmund Crispin', Montgomery
50    Introduction to *Jill*, Larkin

firm is always ready to consider detective fiction, and I think you may find this a passable example of the genre.[51]

It is likely that Montgomery had tried Gollancz with *Romanticism and the World Crisis* (Charles Williams told him that he had 'written one of the more intelligent manuscripts that I have seen for years' and had tried to help Montgomery with finding an agent),[52] but what other manuscripts he submitted remain unknown. Anthony Jephcott, who had rooms in the same house as Montgomery in Wellington Square, recalls seeing a typescript of a novel, never published and set in the future, which started with the sinking of a passenger liner which struck an undetected mine left over from the war.[53] Gollancz agreed to see this latest novel, and Montgomery submitted *The Case of the Gilded Fly* on 7 May, noting in his covering letter: 'It is a trifle shorter than the average, but in these days of paper shortage I dare say that will not be a disadvantage!'[54]

Gollancz wasted no time in making his decision, writing on 24 May. He had read the novel himself, commenting that 'the plot is adequate, though not particularly brilliant. Its somewhat pedestrian character is, I think, offset by the general "cleverness" of the thing as a whole.'[55] He also thought that the title could be improved. Montgomery was entertaining Donald Swann in his rooms when he discovered that his novel had been accepted for publication. Another friend, Brian Galpin, was the witness when Montgomery signed his first contract with Gollancz. It was the start of his literary career.

---

51    RBM to Victor Gollancz, 21 April 1943 (Gollancz Archive)
52    Charles Williams to RBM, 7 December 1942
53    Sir Anthony Jephcott to author, 25 June 1990
54    RBM to Victor Gollancz, 7 May 1943 (Gollancz Archive)
55    Report, Gollancz Archive

# Chapter 4

# 'What a bloody business': 1943–1945

The image of sophistication which Montgomery had projected to his Oxford friends was increased by the knowledge that a book of his was to be published. The novel, however, would not appear for nine months and, with final exams to sit, Montgomery had more pressing matters on his mind. It seems that his preoccupation with other things, not least writing a full length detective novel in the vacation immediately before his exams, had its effect. 'Incidentally, my interest in the theatre, in music and in books caused me to neglect my studies and get in modern languages an ignominious Second, when if I'd worked reasonably hard I'd probably have managed a First. However, it was not a substitution I regret at all.'[1] His contemporaries agree with this: 'I do have memories of […] his appearance, almost certainly cultivated but misleading, in doing no work at all.'[2] Larkin enlarged on this:

> Bruce was lazy but with a far more brilliant brain than I; I was lazyish, but vaguely industrious, doing a great deal of undirected work. He was expected to get a first by nearly everyone, and the responsibility weighed on him, driving him to the bar of the Randolph but rarely to his desk and books.[3]

Amis recalls that a report written by Montgomery's tutor read to the effect that 'Mr Montgomery is very charming, extremely courteous, but seems to have done no work at all.'[4] Colin Strang suspects that he never went to lectures, believing them to be a waste of time, but had a great facility for writing essays for his tutorials, the only teaching he was required to attend. Montgomery knew the languages very well and quite enjoyed writing essays, so he lived on his wits and cruised through university. As at school, he enjoyed theorising and reading. He could read the necessary books and write any essay very quickly.

Montgomery's fledgling flirtation with literary success led to Larkin also taking time away from his studies:

> I sometimes wonder if Bruce did not constitute for me a curious creative stimulus. […] Even in that last term, with Finals a matter of weeks away, I began an unclassifiable story called *Trouble at Willow Gables*, which Bruce and Diana Gollancz would come back to read after an evening at The Lord Napier. Possibly his brisk intellectual Epicureanism was just the catalyst I needed.[5]

---

1    'Edmund Crispin', Montgomery
2    David Whiffen to author, 14 May 1990
3    *Philip Larkin*, Motion, p. 88
4    Sir Kingsley Amis
5    Introduction to *Jill*, Larkin

This 'unclassifiable' story was set in a girls' school and was full of voyeurism and sado-masochism. It was written as a private entertainment but showed aspects of Larkin's character which remained with him, in a contemplative rather than active way, for the rest of his life. In a second story, *Michaelmas Term at St Bride's*, several of the characters have moved on to university. Both Montgomery and Diana Gollancz feature, the former when his first novel is presented at a party to someone who thinks it is by Lord David Cecil or Lord Berners, and he is later pointed out drinking in a bar. This story was never completed, but Montgomery was presented by Larkin with one of only two copies of the poems of Brunette Coleman, the pseudonym under which Larkin hid for these youthful titillations. This does indeed seem a 'curious creative stimulus', but before long Montgomery was given the opportunity to offer more conventional and far-reaching literary advice.

It had always been assumed in his family that Montgomery would enter the Civil Service. He had other ideas. The acceptance of *The Case of the Gilded Fly* made him think of the possibilities of a career in writing, and he looked for a post which would tide him through the war. Schoolmasters were in great demand, and he soon found a teaching post at Shrewsbury School, a private boarding establishment for approximately 500 boys. It was a fortunate move for him. A few months after he started at Shrewsbury in September 1943, Philip Larkin, believing Montgomery's proximity to be a 'good omen',[6] was appointed to a librarian's position in the public library at Wellington, only ten miles and a short train journey away.

Montgomery was a useful recruit, being able to teach English and Music as well as Modern Languages. Indeed, he spent more of his time taking English classes than anything else. Compared with the realities of war, teaching was a comparatively idyllic occupation, and it was not difficult to forge civilised relations between staff and pupils. Montgomery was highly respected by both boys and staff for his intellect, and his reputation as an up and coming author did him no harm. All the 50 or so staff were either too old for military service or, like Montgomery, handicapped in some way. His individuality and enthusiasms made 'a refreshing change from the run of Shrewsbury schoolmasters':[7]

> Public-school masters, I found, ran to type. Leather-patched and grubby with tobacco, they taught whatever they had to teach with vigour and a numbing conventionality. Those with character tended towards dottiness [...] But Bruce Montgomery was neither dull nor dotty. Young, red-haired, lame and flamboyant, he blew down the musty corridors of the Schools Building doing us all a power of good. His favourite English lesson was to read aloud the ghost stories of Montague James.[8]

Montgomery's gift of wit made him immensely entertaining. He played the organ in chapel and took congregational practices early on a Friday morning. On one occasion he started all 500 boys and the staff on a hymn. Within seconds, enraged by the feeble result, he thumped the lectern and shouted: 'Stop! Stop!' Everyone froze. 'Getting you lot to sing,' he thundered, 'is like prodding an elephant with a

---

6    *Required Writing*, Larkin, p. 31
7    Julian Critchley to author, 2 May 1990
8    'Fen's Creator', Critchley

toothpick!' The place collapsed in laughter. When the hymn was restarted, the boys took the roof off.[9]

In many ways, the post suited Montgomery. His handicap limited his participation in school life (he was not expected to take games, for instance) and as a consequence he had more free time than other staff. He was able to indulge his interests of writing music and novels, and he was known to read up to three detective novels in one day. A colleague, Stephen Tothill, frequently found Montgomery staggering under the weight of books from the school library.[10] He was particularly keen on forensic science and consulted various sources to make sure that its use in his novels was accurate (*Swan Song* includes a particular instance of this). As at Oxford, he was eager to introduce others to new music. One colleague who had a gramophone soon found himself introduced to *Belshazzar's Feast*.[11]

Montgomery made one notable foray into helping with activities outside the classroom. During Easter and Summer holidays the pupils were put at the disposal of short-staffed farmers. Classed as agricultural workers, the boys were paid and given double rations, and their parents were delighted by the marvellous condition in which they returned home. Montgomery joined Stephen Tothill in running a summer harvest camp at Tetbury in Gloucestershire. The boys lived in tents whilst the two staff and the cooks were billeted in the house. There were various incidents. It was a very hot summer and the local well ran dry. The boys were on the point of being sent home when, in desperation, the WAEC (War Agricultural Executive Committee) managed to persuade a local farmer to lend his water wagon. This was duly brought over pulled by a horse and filled from a stream, permission for which had to be given by a neighbouring parish council. The water came out of the wagon brown with rust. The two staff again decided that the boys would have to be sent home. However, a local doctor who had worked abroad told them that if they filtered the water through two handkerchiefs and then boiled every drop, it would be drinkable. Tothill and Montgomery took the dramatic decision to keep the vital work force, and to their relief the water purification scheme worked. No one was ill.

On the fourth day an enormous barrel of cider arrived for them, an unprecedented gift arranged by the local committee. Montgomery pounced on it and climbed on top, but in his enthusiasm knocked the tap into its hole, breaking the seal and releasing the pressure. The tap was promptly blown out and a mass of cider was lost. Both Montgomery and Tothill were soaked in their efforts to stem the flood, with Montgomery shouting: 'Get that tap in, Stephen!' whilst holding pans and other receptacles to try and rescue some of it. The flow was finally tamed, but within ten minutes both soused men became the target of all the local wasps and had to take off every stitch of clothing to fight them away.

Montgomery had his car, a Hillman Minx, at the camp. When he discovered that Tothill did not drive, he encouraged him to have a try. Tothill had no experience at all of driving, which showed when he was proceeding down a country lane and misjudged the speed for a corner. With Montgomery yelling 'Brake! Brake! Brake!',

9      Stephen Tothill

10     Ibid.

11     Michael Powell to author, 28 September 1989

Tothill took the right-angle rather quicker than he should, went on to the wrong side of the road, hit the hedge with his right wing and came, not very gracefully, to a halt. Whilst Tothill hoped a large hole would swallow him up, Montgomery inspected the damage (a recognisable dent in the wing), swore and said: ' That makes three, Stephen', referring to the number of dents on his car.[12]

It seems that despite these excitements Montgomery did not find teaching terribly attractive. One letter to Larkin finishes: 'I must go and teach, God help me. What a bloody business.'[13] Most of the letters to Larkin seem to have been written whilst he was taking a class. In one of them he gives an indication of his methods:

> Well, here I sit – taking a class for a colleague who took a class for me when I failed to return here from Oxford – sitting on a high dais in a gown and looking very grim at a lot of boys engaged in sleeping, doodling, and in some cases actually working [...] my method of taking a class being to say 'go on reading from where you left off.' [...] Forgive me while I tick two boys off for talking.
>
> (There, I've done it! 'Barton and Treves, if you don't stop that persistent gabbling, I shall kick you out of the room.' Unsubtle, perhaps, but effective.)[14]

In the same letter he gives another snapshot of himself in action during a French class:

> A boy has just asked the meaning of 'galopante'.
> 'Well, think. What part of speech is it?
> 'Imperfect, sir.'
> 'No, it isn't, it's the present participle. What verb does it come from?'
> 'Galopifrei, sir.'
> 'No, of course not, it comes from 'galloper'. What does that sound like?'
> 'Gallop, sir.'
> 'Yes, well, exactly.'
> 'It doesn't make sense, sir.'
> 'Oh Lord. Bring the book up here. Now, let's see, where is it? Ah, yes. Well, 'palpitation galopante', it's – it's – no, it doesn't seem to make sense, does it?
> 'Perhaps there's a misprint, sir.'
> 'No, look here, wait a minute, what are you talking about, of course it makes sense. It means his heart was beating very fast.'
> 'Oh, does it, sir?'
> 'Yes. I'm surprised you didn't see that at once.'
> 'Yes, sir.'
> 'Well, go and sit down, boy, don't hover about.'
> 'Yes, sir.' (THE BOY sits down. THE MASTER resumes his writing).[15]

One of his reluctant piano pupils recalls that Montgomery seemed equally uninterested in attempting to teach him, and was easily persuaded to spend most of

---

12    Stephen Tothill.
13    RBM to Larkin, 20 October 1944
14    Ibid., 22 November 1943
15    Ibid.

the lesson playing to the boy.[16] Ten years later, Montgomery ruminated on his career as a schoolmaster:

> Like all the more uncomfortable periods of one's life, Shrewsbury seems very lively and interesting in retrospect – but all the same, wild horses would be needed to drag me back there these days.[17]

It was clear then that music was his first love and, as he said to Tothill, 'The reason I churn out the detective novels, Stephen, is that it allows me to play music.' Tothill recalls that there was always an undercurrent of money with Montgomery, something that was hard to relate to his background and which frequently recurred in his later life (in 1953 Amis commented that 'Perhaps I haven't got to have it [money] like Bruce has').[18] There was an incident with the Headmaster (John Wolfenden, later to become Vice-Chancellor of Reading University and Director of the British Museum and, more famously, chairman of the committee which in 1957 recommended decriminalising consensual homosexual behaviour in private) which had its origins in money. Montgomery lodged in the house of a very elderly Old Boy of the school, just behind the school-owned quarters which accommodated other bachelor staff. During 1945 he decided that he resented paying the amount of rent demanded from him, and went to see the Headmaster to negotiate cheaper lodgings. Wolfenden dug his heels in, goading Montgomery to say to him: 'Headmaster: this is a case of Dives and Lazarus, isn't it?' Tothill regarded this as an almost suicidal statement for a junior temporary member of staff to make to such a powerful man. Montgomery stayed where he was.

Montgomery and Larkin met at least weekly, usually on licensed premises. Tuesday was a favourite: not only was it Larkin's day off but, as it was also Shrewsbury's market day, the pubs stayed open throughout the afternoon. Larkin would often go to Shrewsbury on a Saturday evening and they would chat in The Red Lion. Montgomery sometimes travelled over to Wellington for a session in The Raven. The main purpose seemed to be to consume considerable amounts of alcohol. Whilst asking whether he ought to come to Wellington to help Larkin settle in, Montgomery showed the way his mind was working:

> I am shifting my piano teaching out of Tuesday evening – but can't, unfortunately, shift afternoon school (without becoming Headmaster), which doesn't end till 6.20. Fortunately, though, this is just ten minutes before they open,[19] so no time is lost.'[20]

'Well,' a later letter to Larkin begins, 'I must say I was rather drunk last night; and felt it this morning. Still, it was quite an amusing party [...] You somewhat alarmed me by suddenly falling over a wall like that, and I sincerely hope you're all

---

16    Ann Parker to author, about Richard Parker, 25 September 2001
17    RBM to Stephen Tothill, 4 June 1954
18    Amis to Larkin, 26 November 1953, *The Letters of Kingsley Amis*, Leader (ed.) [hereafter LKA]
19    Montgomery had clearly forgotten about market day opening hours
20    RBM to Larkin, 27 November 1943

right. You recovered your equanimity with remarkable speed, but write and reassure me. There's nothing like a good evening's drinking, is there? Oh…oh…my head.'[21] Later, Amis recalled another consequence of their recreation:

> In those days, before he started making real money, Bruce had been a beer-drinker, a fanatical one by Philip's account, setting a cruel pace and insisting on being closely followed. After a prolonged session, the pair had the hardihood to attend a meeting of the school literary society. Philip found himself in the chair furthest from the door with hundreds of boys, many sitting on the floor, between him and any exit. Quite soon after everybody was settled a tremendous desire to urinate came upon him. Finding he could not face causing the upheaval that must have attended his leaving the room, and reasoning, if that is the word, that he was wearing a lot of clothes, including, in those days of fuel rationing, a heavy overcoat, he decided to rely on their absorbent qualities and intentionally pissed himself. It turned out that he had miscalculated, and under his chair there rapidly formed a pool of…[22]

There was the question of what to talk about whilst in the pub:

> When we were drinking last Bruce and I ran so far out of conversation that we were reduced to compiling a list of sexual perversions on the back of an envelope, and planning to write a little library of short novels, one around each. It was the pleasantest kind of castle-building, as we each knew we had no such intention. I scored heavily with the inclusion of mastigophily, of which he had not heard. We divided them up equally between ourselves. Dropping ONANISM as too trite, he put in a claim for SADISM and SODOMY (male) while I bagged LESBIANISM and ANAL EROTISM. He brought up MIXOSCOPY, and we discussed for some time PAEDERASTY and what I call WILLOWGABLISMUS. It was interesting to see what was left out at the end. Neither of us had much feeling for BESTIALITY or MASOCHISM, though we good-naturedly undertook them, one each. But I forget which. [23]

Fortunately this was not the summit of their literary conversations. They eagerly discussed each others current projects; Montgomery was awaiting the publication of *The Case of the Gilded Fly* (called 'The Gelded Fly' by Larkin) and was well on with his next mystery *Holy Disorders*, despite claiming that 'one doesn't get long enough consecutively to work at it, and beer holds one up rather, too.'[24] He told Alan Ross that 'Like Trollope I've taken to getting up early and writing for two hours before breakfast. But I always feel so ill that the light-hearted spirit of comedy comes slowly….'[25] Larkin was writing poetry and was now also completing his novel, *Jill*.

In later life, when his literary and musical creative gifts deserted him, Montgomery compensated to a certain extent by becoming a respected critic. His wide knowledge of books and his clear and honest thinking made him an ideal reviewer, and many aspiring authors, some of whom became respected writers themselves, wrote

---

21     Ibid., 19 November 1944

22     *Memoirs*, Amis, p. 59

23     Larkin to Amis, 9 July 1945, *Selected Letters of Philip Larkin*, Thwaite (ed.), hereafter [SLPL]

24     RBM to Philip Larkin, 27 November 1943

25     *Blindfold Games*, Ross, p. 147

appreciatively to Montgomery of the helpful words of support and advice that he had given. In many ways this work started in Shropshire with Larkin during a period when they were thrown on each other's company. More importantly, it was during a formative period for both of them. Montgomery lectured Larkin on not being sufficiently determined to succeed – and not just with his writing:

> Is this Orwellian gabble about sharing a bed <u>literally true</u>? If it is, I must say you rather alarm me. Surely you can get a <u>bedroom</u> to yourself. I don't think you push and agitate enough. You set out with the idea that the whole thing's going to be beastly, become resigned, and not unnaturally discover that it <u>is</u> beastly. It's the same with your literary work. You set out with the conviction that anything you write will be a minute thing, nugatory and immature, and the human mind being on the whole an obedient instrument, of course it turns out like that. More will-power, Philip! More determination, you scagot![26]

Montgomery inspected Larkin's poetry and made valuable suggestions, particularly for the collection published in 1945 as *The North Ship*. He countered Larkin's infatuation with Yeats: 'He's all right you know, but his ideas are unusually daft, even for a poet. [...] And I should have liked to have given him a biff on the kisser and then asked him if he still thought good strong blows were delights to the mind. He lacks vividness, too, the memorable line.'[27] On another occasion Larkin recalled 'Bruce Montgomery snapping, as I droned for the third or fourth time that evening *When such as I cast off remorse, So great a sweetness flows into the breast...*, "It's not his job to cast off remorse, but to earn forgiveness." But then Bruce had known Charles Williams.'[28] Montgomery let Larkin know that he thought the aim of some of the poems that would make up *The North Ship* was not clear. 'Now and then I do a poem,' Larkin wrote, 'which Bruce reads dolefully and says, "It won't do, you know, it's not as good as the others." This tends to annoy me but he is probably right.'[29] Later, Larkin's inscriptions in the copies of his poetry and novels that he presented to Montgomery show his appreciation of his friend's advice; in *A Girl in Winter* he wrote 'To Bruce, whose consistent critical enthusiasms and encouragement resulted in this book'.[30] More public demonstrations were the dedications to Montgomery of the first poem in *The North Ship* (1945) and of his second novel *A Girl in Winter* (1947). In return, Montgomery made it clear that he was grateful for help with aspects of two of his novels, *Holy Disorders* and *The Moving Toyshop*, the latter being dedicated to Larkin. Montgomery even sent Larkin occasional pieces of his own poetry for comment. Kingsley Amis, despite his frequent criticisms of Montgomery's ability as an author ('I hope Bruce composes better than he writes words' he remarked in 1947)[31] also despatched work occasionally for scrutiny. 'Bruce sent the Legacy back with a number of comments,' Amis reported of a novel which remained unpublished.

---

26    RBM to Larkin, 27 November 1943
27    Ibid., 3 November 1944
28    *Required Writing*, Larkin, p. 29
29    *Philip Larkin*, Motion, p. 115
30    Ibid., p. 116
31    Amis to Larkin, 27 December 1947 [LKA]

'[H]e said "the women are all frightful", [...] it surprised me that he said it abt. Steph [...] but I think he's pretty right, alack, abt. Jane.'[32]

*The Case of the Gilded Fly* was published in February 1944. It sold well and received respectable reviews, most of which regarded it as a promising debut and looked forward to his next book. Typical was the unsigned notice in the *Times Literary Supplement:*

> Anyone who wishes to know what 'bloodcurdling' means has but to read 'The Case of the Gilded Fly' late at night in a lonely house. There is in it a ghost story which creates the afraid-to-look-over-your-shoulder feeling exquisitely. [...] His book, a merger between detective story and Oxford novel, is constantly amusing either because of his wit or else because of his excessive worldliness. [...] The story, readable in itself, excites keen interest in what Mr. Crispin will write next.[33]

The influence of John Dickson Carr is obvious; their detectives, Gervase Fen and Gideon Fell, even have the same initials. The murder itself is of the locked room variety much favoured by Carr. A body is discovered, not in a locked room as such, but in a room into or out of which no one could possibly have come at the apparent time of the murder. The fact that the shot that is heard is not the one that kills the victim becomes, in the sense that things are not always what they seem, a favourite device of Montgomery's, particularly in his short stories. *The Crooked Hinge*, Montgomery's stimulus, has more than a touch of the supernatural about it. Montgomery's plot has little of that, but he introduces a ghost story into the book which, whilst having no direct bearing on the story, certainly adds flavour. His reading of ghost stories to the boys at Shrewsbury was perhaps research for his own writing.

In the first few pages Montgomery mentions or quotes from authors such as Beerbohm, Dunbar, Eugene O'Neill, Shakespeare and Voltaire, leading reviewers to suspect that 'Edmund Crispin', the pseudonym Montgomery adopted, was an Oxford don or indeed a further alias of J.I.M. Stewart (already known as Michael Innes), himself later an Oxford don and already an established writer of detective fiction. Montgomery explained that he assumed a pen-name with the intention of retaining his real name for composing music. How he arrived at his alias and his detective was known to Larkin:

> temperamentally he inclined more to the academic comedies of Michael Innes; 'Gervase Crispin' in *Hamlet, Revenge!* gave Bruce half his pseudonym (originally 'Rufus Crispin', from his own wavy red hair) and half the name of his detective, Gervase Fen, whose other name evoked his Oxford tutor, W.G. Moore, by way of 'Lead, Kindly Light' ('O'er moor and fen'). Fen reproduced much of Moore's appearance, and some of his mannerisms, but the caricature was an affectionate one.[34]

Amis thought that Fen, styled as Professor of English Language and Literature in the University of Oxford, was like Moore in physical appearance but not in

---

32    Ibid., 16 January 1949 [LKA]
33    *Times Literary Supplement*, 11 March 1944, p. 129
34    Foreword to *Fen Country*, Larkin

character. Whereas Fen is eccentric and usually rather manic, Moore was a much more orthodox sort of don.[35] Moore made it clear that he suspected he was Fen and laughed about it, although Montgomery thought differently: 'He [Moore] doesn't quite realise he's Fen.'[36] Years later Montgomery admitted that Fen was based in part on Moore, 'but as with most detectives, I think there is a good deal of his creator in him'.[37] He said that there had been modifications as the years went by: 'Still, even now I myself think of Fen as <u>looking</u> like Moore, and even in some ways talking like him.'[38] Moore said that he could forgive Montgomery everything except the reference to Fen's wife which he took to be a portrait of his wife, Joy. In reality she was a well-built woman of great character and charm whose large glasses did nothing for her appearance.[39] In the book she appears as 'a plain, spectacled, sensible little woman incongruously called Dolly'.[40] Within Moore's family it was understood that he had sent Montgomery down for not working (this was not the case) and the creation of Fen was his revenge.

Fen is introduced early in the novel, as he returns to Oxford by train:

Gervase Fen, Professor of English Language and Literature in the University of Oxford, frankly fidgeted. At no time a patient man, the delays drove him to distraction. He coughed and groaned and yawned and shuffled his feet and agitated his long, lanky body about in the corner where he sat. His cheerful, ruddy, clean-shaven face grew even ruddier than usual; his dark hair, sedulously plastered down with water, broke out into disaffected fragments towards the crown. In the circumstances his normal overplus of energy, which led him to undertake all manner of commitments and then gloomily to complain that he was overburdened with work and that nobody seemed to care, was simply a nuisance. And as his only distraction was one of his own books, on the minor satirists of the eighteenth century, which he was conscientiously re-reading in order to recall what were his opinions of these persons, he became in the later stages of the journey quite profoundly unhappy. He was returning to Oxford from one of those innumerable educational conferences which spring up like mushrooms to decide the future of this institution or that, and whose decisions, if any, are forgotten two days after they are over, and as the train proceeded on its snail-like way he contemplated with mournful resignation the series of lectures he was to deliver on William Dunbar and smoked a great many cigarettes and wondered if he would be allowed to investigate another murder, supposing one occurred.[41]

Later in the novel, another character gives his views on Fen:

Nigel reflected [...] that there was something extraordinarily school-boyish about Gervase Fen. Cherubic, naïve, volatile, and entirely delightful, he wandered the earth taking a genuine interest in things and people unfamiliar, while maintaining a proper sense of authority in connection with his own subject. On literature his comments were acute, penetrating and extremely sophisticated; on any other topic he invariably pretended

---

35    Sir Kingsley Amis

36    Brian Aldiss

37    RBM to Jan Broberg, 26 October 1959

38    RBM to Miss Balmer, 19 August 1968

39    Wyn Smith

40    *The Case of the Gilded Fly*, Chapter 5

41    Ibid., Chapter 1

complete ignorance and an anxious willingness to be instructed, though it generally came out eventually that he knew more about it than his interlocutor, for his reading, in the forty-two years since his first appearance on this planet, had been systematic and enormous. If this ingenuousness had been affectation, or merely arrested development, it would have been simply irritating; but it was perfectly sincere, and derived from the genuine intellectual humility of a man who has read much and in doing so has been able to contemplate the enormous spaces of knowledge which must inevitably always lie beyond his reach. In temperament he was incurably romantic, though he ordered his life in a rigidly reasonable way. To men and affairs, his attitude was neither cynical nor optimistic, but one of never-failing fascination. This resulted in a sort of unconscious amoralism, since he was always so interested in what people were doing, and why they were doing it, that it never occurred to him to assess the morality of their actions.[42]

Fen's capricious demeanour can alter very suddenly:

The change in Fen, he [Blake] told himself, was astonishing. His usual slightly fantastic naivety had completely disappeared, and its place was taken by a rather formidable, ice-cold concentration. [...] At the opening of an investigation, the mood was invariable, as always when Fen was concentrating particularly hard; when he was not interested in what was going on, he relapsed into an excessively irritating form of boisterous gaiety; when he had discovered anything of importance, he 'quickly became melancholy', after the manner of the young lady whose folly induced her to sit on a holly; and when an investigation was finally concluded, he became sunk in such a state of profound gloom that it was days before he could be aroused from it. Moreover, these perverse and chameleon-like habits tended not unnaturally to get on people's nerves.[43]

As Fen is never again painted so fully in later novels, these passages have been quoted at length to show the point from where Montgomery started with him. Fen's inclination to boredom comes out in his acerbity and rudeness towards other characters:

On his arrival Fen had been extremely rude to him – but then he was habitually rude to everyone; it was a natural consequence, Nigel decided, of his monstrous and excessive vitality.[44]

His most abusive attack is launched against a suspect, Donald Fellowes, who is reluctant to co-operate:

Fen got to his feet; he towered over Donald as a liner towers over a tug. 'You are,' he said, 'without exception the most imbecile ignominious cretinous poltroon it has ever been my evil fortune to meet. What is worse, you become more imbecile, ignominious, cretinous and poltroonish with every hour that passes.[45]

Fen is clearly a lover of Lewis Carroll's *Alice's Adventures in Wonderland*. Early on he is seen rushing away from Blackwell's bookshop saying 'Oh dear, oh dear, I

42    Ibid., Chapter 13
43    Ibid., Chapter 6
44    Ibid., Chapter 5
45    Ibid., Chapter 10

shall be too late!' like the White Rabbit,[46] and later is described as waking up 'like the Dormouse, with a little shriek'.[47] During moments of high excitement he often comes out with expressions such as 'Oh my fur and whiskers!',[48] and these continue in the later novels. At one point Fen manages to combine these with his acerbity when speaking to his wife:

> 'You can't come and see it,' Fen answered rudely, 'there's no room.' The phraseology of the more abominably offensive of creatures in Alice tended to insinuate itself into his conversation.[49]

Although, to satisfy the Gollancz libel lawyer, Montgomery issued a disclaimer at the front of the book that the characters and setting with the exception of Oxford itself were imaginary, he clearly was writing about places and people he knew. As we have seen, Fen was based to some extent on his tutor. His linguistic studies were responsible for the name of the murdered woman, Yseut, whose father was an expert on medieval French literature. The story is set in a drama company in Oxford which bears a striking resemblance to the Playhouse which Montgomery knew well. The unpleasant atmosphere of back-stabbings and bitchiness may well have been based on Montgomery's experiences in Amersham and Oxford. Some of the other characters take after Montgomery himself, to the extent that one wonders how autobiographical the novel is. For instance, Donald Fellowes ('addicted to bow ties and gin') is organist at Fen's college: 'As an undergraduate he had been so much occupied with music that his tutors (he was reading history) had despaired, and as it turned out with reason, of ever getting him through anything.'[50] As for Nicholas Barclay, 'a brilliant academic career had been prophesied for him', but he began to question the worth of the academic life 'and had taken to drinking, quite amiably, but persistently'.[51] Yseut is 'sexually knowledgeable without being sexually experienced',[52] an interesting observation given his contemporaries' suspicions about Montgomery's own love life. Robert Warner, the director of the company, has a Jewish mistress (Diana Gollancz was Jewish). There are a number of the in-jokes which appear in all his books. Diana is the name of someone in the cast. Bruce is the name of the gloomy rehearsal pianist. In a clear reference to Godfrey Sampson, Montgomery has Donald Fellowes announce: 'As soon as this term's over, I'm going to volunteer for the R.A.F. It seems to contain most of the organists in the country anyway.'[53]

The plot allows Montgomery to show off his musical knowledge at vital points. Wagner's overture to *Die Meistersinger* blasts so loudly that a fatal shot is barely

---

46    Ibid., Chapter 2
47    Ibid., Chapter 7
48    Ibid., Chapter 10
49    Ibid., Chapter 12
50    Ibid., Chapter 1
51    Ibid.
52    Ibid.
53    Ibid., Chapter 12

heard:[54] 'if he chose his moment well – say the fortissimo re-entry of the main theme just before the contrapuntal section where all three themes are played together – there was little chance of its being heard'.[55] Confirmation of the murderer's identity is given by the combination of stops that are left drawn on an organ. There are other opportunities for Montgomery, via Fen, to give his views on music, as he does when told that the setting for evensong is Dyson in D ('Nice,' commented Fen, 'theatrical, but nice. […] Musically, it's a battle of religion and romance, of Eros and Agape')[56] or when discussing the 'rich Teutonic concoction'[57] of Richard Strauss's *Ein Heldenleben*. He makes the most of his studies to have Warner give a short lecture on eighteenth-century French drama, and Fen pontificates on Pascal's view of human justice.

The flippant side of Montgomery's writing is clearly in evidence. Fen comes out with what would, in the later eight novels, become typically pert expressions such as 'In fact, I'm the only literary critic turned detective in the whole of fiction',[58] or 'Heaven grant Gideon Fell [Carr's detective] never becomes privy to my lunacy.'[59] Mid-way through the novel, a discussion about the murder between Fen and the Chief Constable, Sir Richard Freeman (by a nice irony himself an amateur literary critic), changes into a comparison between their methods and those of a detective story writer:

> Sir Richard roused himself acerbly. 'Really, Gervase: if there's anything I profoundly dislike, it's the sort of detective story in which one of the characters propounds views on how detective stories should be written.'

A few paragraphs later, after Fen claims to know who the murderer is but will not yet tell, the subject occurs again:

> Sir Richard lifted both hands, palms outward, in the conventional mime for despair. 'Oh, Lord!' he said. 'Mystification again. I know: it can't come out till the last chapter.'[60]

It should be noted here that Montgomery was not the only author to exaggerate the artifice of the detective story. For instance, in *The Hollow Man* (published in 1935), Montgomery's muse John Dickson Carr has this exchange between his detective, Gideon Fell, and another character:

> 'I will now lecture,' said Dr Fell, inexorably, 'on the general mechanics and development of the situation which is known in detective fiction as the 'hermetically sealed chamber'. Harrumph. All those opposing can skip this chapter. Harrumph. To begin with, gentlemen!

---

54    Montgomery may have been influenced in this by the Albert Hall scene in Hitchcock's 1934 film *The Man Who Knew Too Much* where an assassin waits for a cymbal clash to cover the sound of his gunshot before he shoots a visiting foreign official.

55    *The Case of the Gilded Fly*, Chapter 15

56    Ibid., Chapter 8

57    Ibid., Chapter 10

58    Ibid., Chapter 5

59    Ibid., Chapter 10

60    Ibid., Chapter 8

Having been improving my mind with sensational fiction for the last forty years, I can say – '

'But, if you're going to analyse impossible situations,' interrupted Pettis, 'why discuss detective fiction?'

'Because,' said the doctor, frankly, 'we're in a detective story, and we don't fool the reader by pretending we're not. Let's not invent elaborate excuses to drag in a discussion of detective stories. Let's candidly glory in the noblest pursuits possible to characters in a book.'[61]

Even Dorothy L. Sayers, in *Five Red Herrings* (1931) follows a similar path:

'See here, Wimsey, you're not going to turn round now and say that the crime was committed by Mrs Green or the milkman, or somebody we've never heard of? That would be in the very worst tradition of the lowest style of detective fiction.'[62]

Later in the same chapter a character says: 'No. He hadn't an accomplice. But he was a student of detective literature.'[63] It is this style which Amis has found hard to stomach. In the remarkably (and unnecessarily) peevish chapter on Montgomery in his memoirs, Amis admits that 'There are good things in all of them', but now claims to find Montgomery's books 'unreadable'. He refers to their 'constant flippancy and facetiousness of style, an excessive striving after high spirits or their effect'. He also puts forward the view that, in *The Case of the Gilded Fly*, at 'two vital points, those involving the crime itself and the denouement, the author introduces grotesque improbabilities'.[64] Something needs to be said about these accusations. The first is that *The Case of the Gilded Fly* is Montgomery's first novel and his first attempt at a detective story. He never made any secret of his view that the genre should be seen as a diversion and not as high art, although it should be pointed out that there are few of the comic set-pieces and none of the ludicrous characters which appear in most of his later novels. He was aware of the type of book he was writing. 'Here's the piece of nonsense,' he wrote when he sent a copy of the novel to Alan Ross. 'I won't go into lengthy apologies for all the bad bits (there are many).'[65] Whilst he was writing his next story he was more frank to Larkin: ' "Holy Disorders" is already about four months gone, and is turning out well. Still, I admit – it's not a work of literature in the sense that "Jill" is. I'm just an old hack, that's all – scribble, scribble, scribble.'[66]

The other point which needs to be made is that whereas Amis attacks Montgomery for improbabilities in his plot, he has praised John Dickson Carr's *The Crooked Hinge* for what appears to be the same tendency: 'The explanation is simple and entirely plausible, but you would just not happen to think of it.'[67] It seems to this author that the sudden revelation at the denouement that Carr's murderer has artificial legs is just as improbable as anything Montgomery dreams up – and is none the worse for

---

61   *The Hollow Man*, John Dickson Carr, Chapter 17
62   *Five Red Herrings*, Dorothy L. Sayers, chapter entitled *The Murderer*
63   Ibid.
64   *Memoirs*, Amis, p. 73
65   *Blindfold Games*, Ross, pp. 146–147
66   RBM to Larkin, 22 November 1943
67   Quoted on cover of *The Crooked Hinge*, John Dickson Carr, Xanadu Publications

it. There are many detective stories which could have the same accusation thrown at them.

The fact remains that it is these qualities of 'high spirits' and 'flippancy' that are largely responsible for the popularity of Montgomery's novels. *The Case of the Gilded Fly* contains various other devices that were to become characteristic of Montgomery's work. There is the first in a long line of singular animals whose eccentricities of behaviour are matched only by their eccentricities of appearance:

> The only salient feature of the small, rather shabby public bar was an enormous nude parrot, which had early contracted the habit of pecking out all its feathers, and which now, with the exception of the ruff and head, which it could not reach, presented a dismal and ludicrous grey, scraggy body to the gaze. It had been given to the proprietor of the 'Aston Arms' in a fit of lachrymose gratitude by a visiting German professor, and was in the habit of reciting a lyric of Heine, which feat, however, it could only be induced to perform by the careful repetition of two lines from the beginning of Mallarmé's *L'Apres-midi d'un Faune*, this appearing to start some appropriate train of suggestion in its mind. This aptitude aroused the deepest suspicions in such soldiery as frequented the 'Aston Arms', equalled only by their suspicion of those of their countrymen who were capable of similar or greater achievements in the same direction; it was employed by the proprietor to warn customers of the imminence of closing-time, and the raucous tones of *Ich weiss nicht, was soll es bedeuten, das ich so traurig bin* were the normal prelude to more forcible means of ejection.[68]

Characters in Montgomery's novels often fall in love as soon as they meet (or even before, as Nigel Blake does here with Helen Haskell) and are engaged just as quickly (as also happens here). There is invariably a brief appearance by an artisan, usually male, who speaks with either a brogue or in somewhat basic language with an abundance of dropped aitches. Here this rôle is take by Joe Williams, a stonemason who is in the vicinity at the time of the murder. Fen usually manages to co-opt an assistant for each of his cases. In this novel it is one of his former students, Nigel Blake, who, like Richard Cadogan in *The Moving Toyshop*, imagines himself to be visiting Oxford as part of his holiday.

There is one further aspect of *The Case of the Gilded Fly* that needs to be considered. In his book *The Movement*, Blake Morrison refers briefly to Montgomery's important early influence on this literary development. Something more needs to be said about this here. The Movement was defined and given its name in an unsigned article in the *Spectator* on 1 October 1954. Now known to have been written by the literary editor of the journal, J.D Scott, the article stated that the Movement

> is bored by the despair of the Forties, not much interested in suffering, and extremely impatient of poetic sensibility, especially poetic sensibility about the 'writer and society'. So it's goodbye to all those rather sad little discussions about 'how the writer ought to live', and it's goodbye to the Little Magazine and 'experimental writing'. The Movement, as well as being anti-phoney, is anti-wet; sceptical, robust, ironic, prepared to be as comfortable as possible.[69]

---

68   *The Case of the Gilded Fly*, Chapter 10
69   *Spectator*, 1 October 1954

Of the authors named in the article, Kingsley Amis and John Wain were contemporaries of Montgomery's at Oxford, and other friends of his who were later considered part of the group included Philip Larkin and Robert Conquest. This is not the place to rehearse the arguments about the validity of grouping these and other writers together (some of the named authors subsequently claimed to be unaware of belonging to any such trend), but there are clear signs of the points made by J.D. Scott in Montgomery's early novels. Although Fen and his creator scatter literary and other intellectual allusions with abandon as if to make sure that no one will doubt their credentials, there are frequent incidents in which both of them demonstrate a pragmatic, at times subversive, approach towards so-called artistic sensibilities. In *The Case of the Gilded Fly*, Fen states his views:

> I'm inclined, you know, to take the philistine view that there's a good deal of hooey about the artistic temperament. So many of the greatest artists have been without it, or rather they've had sufficient low cunning to satisfy their beyond-good-and-evil tendencies *sub rosa*, without arousing the wrath of society. The artistic temperament is too often only an alibi for lack of responsibility.[70]

To make sure this message hits home, Montgomery has a playwright as the murderer. Robert Warner, who shares his surname with a character in Larkin's first novel *Jill*, does not view himself or his art through rose-tinted spectacles, but he makes sure that people realise he is an intellectual:

> It's all vanity really. Costals, in Montherlant's novel, is the quintessential type of the artist – the self-sufficient, childish, ruthless egotist. Pulled to pieces, that's certainly all I amount to.[71]

Warner expands on this later in the novel when asked why he writes:

> 'For money – and for the sake of showing off; I think that's why most men, even the very greatest, have written. The Creation of Art' – he succeeded in making the capitals articulate – 'is an object which seldom enters into their calculations. Necessarily. Most original artists don't know what art is, or beauty. They're almost invariably hopeless critics; writers never know the first thing about music, or musicians about writing, or painters about either, so it can't be beauty they're all intent on. That presumably is a sort of incidental occurrence, like the pearl in an oyster.'[72]

In *Holy Disorders*, a villain kicks out one of Fen's teeth after he has been subjected to a short character assassination:

> I know your type of undergraduate so well. It's always existed in Oxford – over-clever, incapable of concentration or real thought, affected, arty, with no soul, no morals, and a profound sense of inferiority.[73]

---

70     *The Case of the Gilded Fly,* Chapter 11
71     Ibid., Chapter 12
72     Ibid., Chapter 10
73     *Holy Disorders*, Chapter 13

In *The Moving Toyshop*, there is a rather rough-and-ready lorry driver who is an avid reader of D.H. Lawrence ('that's all I am – nothin' but a soul-less machine').[74] Fen debunks literary sensibilities by introducing various games such as 'Detestable Characters in Fiction' (Lady Chatterley and her gamekeeper and almost everyone in Dostoevsky are amongst those who come under fire), 'Unreadable Books' (*Ulysses* is the first of the suggestions) and 'Awful Lines from Shakespeare' (Fen is interrupted before he can make a start), rather along the lines of Montgomery and Larkin's game of Sexual Perversions. More important, perhaps, is the character of Fen's assistant in his detection, a poet by the name of Richard Cadogan. In the course of a lengthy discourse on the disparate nature of poets ('Wordsworth resembled a horse with powerful convictions [...] Whitman was as strong and hairy as a goldrush prospector [...] Shelley believed every lunatic idea under the sun'), Cadogan announces: 'No, there isn't such a thing as a poet-type.'[75]

In *The Case of the Gilded Fly* Fen shows an apparent disdain for the tools of his trade when he is found by Robert Warner, the playwright, in Blackwell's reading a book from the shelves and cutting the pages with a penknife. When Fen is told off by one of the assistants, Warner reports this exchange:

> 'Young man, this bookshop was dunning me for enormous bills long before you were born. Go away at once, or I'll cut out all the pages and scatter them on the floor.' The assistant went, in some dismay, and he turned to me and said, 'Do you know, I was afraid I was going to have to.'[76]

Fen also demonstrates a subversive view of authority, particularly in his reminiscences of being a proctor, a university official whose job was to ensure that students obeyed the rules:

> 'When I was a proctor,' he said, 'I used to have great difficulties – about pubs, I mean. The people I found in pubs were invariably my most brilliant pupils, and I wanted nothing better than to stop and drink and talk books with them. So I used only to come when I simply had to, and then march through, with a stern expression, taking no notice of anyone. When the junior proctor was going out, I discovered his itinerary and rang up my best friends and warned them. All very illegal, I fear.' He sighed.[77]

Fen continues his war against proctors in *The Moving Toyshop*.

Montgomery's influence on and contribution to the Movement cannot be overstated for the simple reason that his first published work which displays these characteristics preceded that of any of the more prominent members of the group, in most cases by the best part of ten years. Largely a nostalgic figure in his creative work, here for once Montgomery led the way. His ability to mix intellect with robust anti-pretension had a great influence on two of the leading lights, Larkin (who called him 'one of the few low-brows I know')[78] and Amis, at a time when

---

74      *The Moving Toyshop*, Chapter 6
75      Ibid., Chapter 12
76      *The Case of the Gilded Fly*, Chapter 2
77      Ibid., Chapter 10
78      Larkin to Norman Iles, 2 September 1943 [SLPL]

his star was ascending more quickly than theirs. This influence was undoubtedly disseminated further by them as they climbed higher into the literary world. It was not Montgomery's fault that he was working this combination into detective fiction, a genre often mistakenly considered far from the equal of the poetry and literary novels that Larkin and Amis would eventually produce.

Montgomery's success produced a mixture of envy and criticism in his friends. 'When I see Bruce raking in money off two continents for a bit of stuff he turned out in three weeks, there is something savage in me and I want to strike things with my fist and my eyes go dark and there is a beating in my throat,' Larkin wrote to Amis.[79] He confided to another friend: 'I have seen reviews and handled copies like the Israelites picking up the manna & wondering what in fuck it was.' The fact that 'most of the reviews have been favourable, and that surprises me, because the book is not terribly good, even when one makes allowances for the kind of book it is'[80] at least gave Larkin more confidence to continue looking for a publisher for *Jill*. Montgomery was doing his best to encourage Larkin; he thoroughly enjoyed *Jill* but suggested some alterations for the last chapter and said that he would give it to his friend Charles Williams at Oxford University Press who was in turn likely to send it to T.S. Eliot at Faber. 'This is such a tenuous and dizzy chain of impossibilities that I don't place much faith in it,' Larkin wrote.[81] Montgomery's agent, Peter Watt of A.P. Watt, was easily persuaded to take on Larkin's second novel, *A Girl in Winter*. Having criticised Montgomery's next novel, *Holy Disorders* ('I don't like all those silly literary allusions [...] there is a lot of pointless facetiousness'), at least Amis admitted that 'what I say is largely inspired by envy and I can't write *at all*, but I felt I had to tell somebody about it. Bruce says he doesn't like it much either. But what an intelligent and charming person he is.'[82] Later, writing to Larkin, Amis came up with a scheme for their joint success: 'It seems to me that if we three could pool our resources – i.e if Bruce gave you some of his facility, and me some of his success, and if both of us gave him some of your talent – the world would be solidly the gainer, yas [*sic*], and so would we.'[83]

In a letter, Montgomery informed Alan Ross 'There has been a succession of girls, none of them interesting. Women have never inspired my work, so all this amatory activity has done nothing but hold it up.'[84] Women certainly found Montgomery attractive, and it was his particular gift to appeal to them as a comforter after unhappy relationships. During his time at Shrewsbury, he was actively pursued by two, was more than friendly with another and had not given up on Muriel Pavlow (she spent the weekend at Shrewsbury in November 1944).

None of Montgomery's letters from these relationships are known to survive, but from those written to him by both Nan Feeny and Peggy Bailey it seems that they did not receive a great deal of encouragement, at least as far as any sort of commitment

---

79    Larkin to Amis, 9 July 1945 [SLPL]

80    Larkin to J.B. Sutton, 8 February 1944 [SLPL]

81    Ibid., 26 February 1944 [in *Philip Larkin*, Motion, p. 124]

82    Amis to Larkin, 10 February 1946 [LKA]

83    Ibid., 30 July 1950

84    *Blindfold Games*, Ross, p. 147

was concerned. They both lived some distance from Shrewsbury (Feeny in Ruislip, Middlesex, and Bailey in Stoke-on-Trent) and much of their correspondence is spent in trying, usually with little success, to arrange meetings with Montgomery.

Nan Feeny, who worked in the Intelligence Department of *The Times* and to whom Montgomery had been introduced through his friendship with Ronald Lloyd Jones, now missing at war, wrote many letters in which she protests her affection for Montgomery. Nan was in an unsatisfactory marriage; her husband had imposed a regime of celibacy six months into their six year marriage and was now away at the war, and she was impressed by Montgomery's urbanity and charm. She was determined to spend as much time as she could with him, even if that meant letting matters go no further than a very good and platonic friendship.

Initially she made sure that Montgomery knew what he was up against when he was due to stay with her: 'At this point I ought to mention that, in case I have made you think otherwise, I do NOT dispense with my pillow. So if you come, bring your hot-water bottle! There is no particular reason why I'm saying this, so don't take it amiss – it's just that I like to get things straight from the start. [...] However, I do share whole-heartedly your lust for liquor.'[85] With the exception of Muriel Pavlow, on whom he appeared genuinely keen, Montgomery usually ended up fending off women when they became too serious about him. There are the unmistakable signs of this happening with Nan. He tells her on one occasion that he is 'selfish, inconsiderate, vague and nervous',[86] on another that he is afraid of women.[87] Nan had had some sort of (probably platonic) fling with Ronald Lloyd Jones, because Montgomery indicated that he was nervous about 'stepping into dead men's shoes'.[88] Nan told him not to worry about that, because Lloyd Jones had not succeeded in getting her 'to unbend an inch'.[89] Although very keen to get to know Montgomery better, she was certainly not pushing him; because their time together was always so short, 'I don't get a chance to know what you are really like. Bed, I suppose, is one place to find out, but I really prefer to approach things the other way, and that's one reason why I am far from an eager or willing lover.'[90] Her mask slipped once: 'I have a somewhat disturbing recollection of having attempted to traduce my customary continence, and if I upset you, I can only beg you to blame the delightfully large amount of drink you gave me [...] And darling you mustn't get tight every night so that you spend your time falling down.'[91]

Montgomery always seemed to foot the bill when he took women out, and this increased their regard for his worldliness. Nan certainly thought he had plenty of money. We have already seen the impact Montgomery's apparent sophistication had on women, and Nan was no different: 'There are times with you when I become overwhelmed by a feeling of futility [...] You have so much and do so much that by

---

85    Nan Feeny to RBM, 13 October 1943
86    Ibid., 1 February 1944
87    Ibid., 9 June 1944
88    Ibid., 8 May 1944
89    Ibid.
90    Ibid.
91    Ibid., 30 November 1944

contrast I feel miserably insignificant.'[92] Despite all this, she still wanted to continue seeing him: 'I want to know you for ever and ever. I'm not interested in love and sex and everything that goes with it, I just want to go on knowing you.'[93] Whilst trying to understand his behaviour, Nan makes an astute observation on Montgomery's relations with women: 'as you say so little of a personal nature to me, lack of physical happiness may be another cause'.[94] She had previously declared that 'ours is the most extraordinary friendship, or whatever the word is, that I have ever taken part in'.[95] Nan constantly attempted to arrange meetings with Montgomery, but he succeeded in side-stepping most of them. 'I could potter about or sleep till you were free to make your delightfully dishonourable advances,' she wrote on one of these occasions. 'Will you take me out and make a fuss of me and give me evenings such as our first which I always remember?'[96] Later she suggested that his indifference was beginning to succeed: 'I never forget you, but you have become something of a dream I keep remembering vividly. You obviously have no idea how much I want to be with you again.'[97] Fortunately for Montgomery, Nan fell in love with a Canadian journalist towards the end of the war but was still keen to keep in touch with him.

Montgomery's simultaneous friendship with Peggy Bailey followed a similar path, but with Peggy being a single woman at least one complication was removed. She also became more ardent in her pursuit of him than Nan. He was introduced to her by a colleague at Shrewsbury and they went out for dinner on a number of occasions towards the end of 1944. After one of these meetings she told Montgomery: 'I can't imagine you teaching divinity, but then I can't imagine you teaching anything [...] to me you seem the last person on earth to be a schoolmaster.'[98] At another she could not pluck up the courage to ask Montgomery why he was not fighting, so she did it by letter instead. This made him resentful and angry: 'Why do you want to impress upon me the fact that you didn't volunteer from patriotic and idealistic motives?' she asked. 'Personally I think these motives are pretty good myself.'[99] Although Montgomery's disability ruled him out of active service, a letter from Godfrey Sampson makes it clear that he had other irons in the fire before accepting the job at Shrewsbury ('I am much intrigued to hear about your offer of a commission in this racket [Sampson was an Intelligence Officer], and though for my own sake I wish you were coming, you are wise to keep out of it').[100] Montgomery seems to have had an ambivalent attitude towards the forces; on the way back from seeing Peggy in Stoke he was upset by the antics of three RAF officers, and she reported that he had a lack of sympathy with the RAF.[101]

---

92    Ibid.
93    Ibid., 14 January 1946
94    Ibid., undated
95    Ibid., 8 October 1944
96    Ibid., 9 June 1944
97    Ibid., 1 November 1944
98    Peggy Bailey to RBM, 5 October 1944
99    Ibid., 19 October 1944
100   Godfrey Sampson to RBM, 22 April 1943
101   Peggy Bailey to RBM, 25 October 1944

Montgomery began to sense that things were getting too serious for him, and his campaign of withdrawal started when he told Peggy that he knew next to nothing about women. This did not put her off. In March 1945 she told Montgomery that she had fallen in love with him. 'I love everything about you,' she wrote, and included in this the wave in his hair, his walk, voice, smile, even his yellow waistcoat. Then came the usual response to his urbanity: 'Soon after I first met you, you told me that you thought you were falling in love with me [...] I was a little scared of you too (I still am) [...] To me you seemed so much a man of the world [...] so adult and sophisticated [...] in fact everything I am not.'[102] She was unsure about Montgomery's feelings towards her and wanted to know where she stood. She had not been very impressed when he had produced a glamorous photograph of Muriel Pavlow and proceeded to tell her that he had Muriel in mind for the lead of a play he was intending to write. Why did he carry a picture of her if they had split up? When Montgomery told Peggy that he was not in love with her, she went off to the coast to try and forget about him – but failed. Her next ploy was to try and remain friends with him, in the hope that Montgomery might grow to love her. He was worried about keeping up a 'patchwork friendship' and told Peggy that his feelings for her were 'physical – nothing more'.[103] Montgomery also doubted that Peggy was in love with him physically; she put this down to her being undemonstrative as a result of shyness and inexperience. In the end the relationship petered out, and 18 months later Bailey was writing from Cambridge to say that 'after much trial and tribulation' she had recovered from her 'unfortunate affair of the heart. What a stupid little idiot I was and how intensely irritating and tedious you must have found me.'[104] These friendships are the first signs that Montgomery did indeed have 'terrible difficulties'[105] in his relationships with women, problems which became more obvious in later years.

Montgomery kept up his friendship from Oxford days with Mary Miles (now Brownrigg). They attempted to meet from time to time in either Darlington or Leeds as Brownrigg was by now County Music Organizer to Yorkshire Rural County Council. In December 1944 she asked Montgomery to 'lend tone'[106] and conduct at a summer school at Newburgh Priory near York the following August. In 1946 Brownrigg made an attempt to enlist Montgomery for a motoring tour of Switzerland. After some initial interest, the scheme foundered. Montgomery was always keen on his creature comforts and he was unlikely to have been impressed by the possibility of being accommodated in a tent: 'I expect you might want something a bit more comfortable,' Brownrigg realised. 'Have you ever slept in straw?'[107]

The invitation to 'lend tone' at Newburgh Priory came about because of Montgomery's increasing success as a composer. During 1944 he had been very busy writing and submitting works to publishers. As we have seen, in January

---

102    Ibid., 18 March 1945

103    Ibid., 28 April 1945

104    Ibid., 11 November 1946

105    Sir Kingsley Amis

106    Mary Brownrigg to RBM, 20 December 1944

107    Ibid., 20 January 1946

Oxford University Press accepted the *Two Sketches for Pianoforte*, and the anthem *My joy, my life, my crown!*, both composed during Oxford days. The latter had been previously submitted and rejected, but on re-submission it was accepted after certain minor revisions. The publishers also accepted a two-part song with piano accompaniment *Spring, the sweet Spring*, a setting of words by Thomas Nashe (1567–1601). Reviews in *The Musical Times* were encouraging. The 'nice diatonic discords' of the *Two Sketches* 'recall, with a necessary tincture of time-spice, the sort of thing that writers such as young Dale were producing when this bitter century was as yet an innocent babe. Happily, some young writers still cannot help going romantic.' The reviewer was reminded, 'if only in a chord or two' of Delius and Ireland.[108] The anthem 'followed the English tradition […] and [Montgomery] has succeeded in his attempt to catch the mysticism of the poem. A strong simplicity of harmonic structure allied to real devotion is characteristic in this useful and quite simple little work.'[109]

*Spring, the sweet Spring* was published later in 1945, as was *Sally in our Alley*, a part song rejected by Oxford University Press in May 1945 on the grounds that it was not a sufficiently striking setting of familiar words and because paper shortages were limiting new ventures. It was subsequently accepted by Novello, the company that was to publish the great majority of Montgomery's work. When it was rejected by Oxford University Press, Norman Peterkin (whom Montgomery normally dealt with) was away on sick leave. After its acceptance by Novello, Montgomery was anxious not to queer his pitch in Oxford. 'I suppose Mr May told you (or he may not have done) that he returned my setting of "Sally in Our Alley" recently,' he wrote to Peterkin. 'I only mention this because Novellos have accepted it, and I should not like you to think that I have treacherously deserted you after all your kindness!'[110] Peterkin replied that, given the reader's report, his deputy had been right to return the work, but he reassured Montgomery: 'I am glad for your sake that Novellos have taken it on, and I know you will not let this interfere with our arrangement that you let me see all that you write.'[111]

*Spring, the sweet Spring* is a typical work, lively and full of harmonic sequences and switches between C and A flat majors. (Two partsongs rejected by Oxford University Press in 1944, one which remained unpublished, *Blow, Blow thou Winter Wind*, and another published by Novello in 1948, *Gather Ye Rosebuds*, failed because the 'sudden key switches are difficult'.)[112] *The Musical Times* referred to Montgomery's 'newer harmonic outlook', and its one criticism was that the texture of the piano accompaniment needed a lighter touch.[113] The chromatically sliding accompaniment brings the music of Peter Warlock to mind at times. At the end, a passage firmly in C major brings tension to the climax by suddenly shifting solely for the penultimate chord to A flat major before returning to the tonic. This type of

---

108   *The Musical Times*, November 1944, p. 339
109   Ibid., February 1945, p. 52
110   RBM Norman Peterkin, 4 August 1945
111   Norman Peterkin to RBM, 8 August 1945
112   OUP to RBM, 27 January 1944 (OUP Archive)
113   *The Musical Times*, September 1945, p. 279

harmonic swerve at the end of pieces became a favourite device of Montgomery in his later works. Godfrey Sampson liked the song: 'Should I insult it by saying it was quite Sampsonian in places? And could I compliment it more? I particularly enjoyed the bit where the erudite birds tu-whit etc. in augmented phrases. Those must have been the parent birds as distinct from the fledglings.'[114]

*Sally in our Alley* is rather different. To words by Henry Carey (?1687–1743) in places it is reminiscent of Sullivan and gives the impression of being Montgomery's attempt at a contemporary madrigal. Although the inevitable harmonic swerves are present, there are passages of a more sustained diatonic nature than are usually found in his compositions. Although this commentator cannot agree with Godfrey Sampson's view that it was his student's best published composition so far,[115] it undeniably has its moments. There is a strong melodic invention and an even stronger sense of drama, with strategic rallentandos and pauses. When the tenors and basses trumpet out 'But let him bang his bellyful' we really are called to pay attention. There is an engaging skittishness about the partsong which is reinforced by the jolly refrain at the end of each verse. *The Musical Times* limited its review to commenting on the sense of fun the composer had produced, which is certainly true.[116]

114   Godfrey Sampson to RBM, 2 April 1945
115   Ibid., 17 February 1946
116   *The Musical Times*, April 1946, p. 116

# Chapter 5

# 'You mustn't mind if I pay for it': Music and Novels 1945–1952

By the close of 1945 the success of his writing and the end of the war had allowed Montgomery to finish teaching at Shrewsbury. *Holy Disorders* was about to be published in Britain, *The Case of the Gilded Fly* had been brought out in America (renamed *Obsequies at Oxford*) and progress on his third novel, *The Moving Toyshop*, was well advanced. He moved to his parents' house in Brixham.

The action of *Holy Disorders* takes place in a cathedral city called Tolnbridge and involves a ring of Nazi spies. The book has many of the qualities of *The Case of the Gilded Fly*. The supernatural, black magic and the burning of witches is an important part of the plot (the influence of John Dickson Carr is still evident) and detection takes second place to a cast of characters; a friend agreed with Montgomery that it was a poor detective story, but an amusing one.[1] Although not exactly a locked-room mystery, the main murders take place in the locked cathedral. There is the usual scattering of literary allusions: Shakespeare, Kant, Donne, Dunbar (whose poetry Montgomery was currently setting in his musical work), Rochefoucauld, Mallarmé and Graham Greene are just some who make an appearance; Fen enlists, inadvertently, a minor aristocrat by the name of Henry Fielding to help him with the investigation, and this leads to a running joke about the authorship of *Tom Jones*. Montgomery's high spirits and in-jokes are again in evidence: when he hears that Scotland Yard is to send down one of its best men, someone called Appleby (the name of Michael Innes' fictional detective), Fen objects:

> 'Appleby! Appleby!' howled Fen indignantly. 'What do they want with Appleby when I'm here?' He calmed down slightly. 'I admit,' he said, 'that he's very good – *very* good,' he ended gloomily.[2]

Elsewhere the local inspector makes a literary allusion. 'It is always my fate', he [Fen] said, 'to be involved with literary policemen,'[3] a reference to his friendship with Sir Richard Freeman, the Chief Constable of Oxford. When describing a knot that can be untangled from a distance, Fen names it the Hook, Line and Sinker because 'the reader has to swallow it'.[4] There are plenty of other examples. The outstanding comic set-piece comes when Canon Garbin remains blissfully unaware of the extent to which his study reproduces the setting of Edgar Allan Poe's *The*

---

1     Peter Oldham to RBM, 22 June 1946
2     *Holy Disorders*, Chapter 5
3     Ibid., Chapter 5
4     Ibid.

*Raven*. Garbin's gloomy room is inhabited by a bird which was sold to the cleric by a 'foreign sailor with a tragic history'.[5] It is reputed to speak, but has never done so. Fen's interview with Garbin, to which he has been accompanied by Geoffrey Vintner, gradually becomes more chaotic as Fen fails to resist opportunities to quote from the poem, with the scraping of branches on the window lattice presenting a particularly inviting opportunity. Eventually the interview breaks down completely:

'And now, [said Garbin] is there anything else?'

'Is there,' said Geoffrey, 'is there balm in Gilead?'

Fen hastily retired to make a close examination of one of the bookcases. 'I see you have here' – he hesitated, and went on in a weak, quavering voice – 'many a quaint and curious volume of forgotten lore.'

It was at this point that the interview really got out of hand. Geoffrey was hardly able to contain himself, and Fen was scarcely better. The gravity and incomprehension of Garbin made matters worse. What he thought was going on it is impossible to say; perhaps he fancied Fen and Geoffrey to be engaged in some recondite form of retaliation for his earlier outspokenness. At all events he said nothing. Hasty farewells were made. At the door Fen turned to look at the raven again.

'Take thy beak,' he said, 'from out my heart, thy form from off my door.'

'His eyes,' said Geoffrey, 'have all the seeming of a demon's that is dreaming.' Then they went out, in some haste. At the front door, Fen recovered himself sufficiently to ask Garbin one more question.

'Do you know the poetry of Edgar Allan Poe?'

'I'm afraid not. I have no great use for verses.'

'Not his poem, *The Raven*?'

'Ah. There's a poem about a raven, is there? Is it good? I know nothing about these things.'

'Very good,' said Fen with the utmost gravity. 'You would find much in it to interest you. Good morning.'[6]

The first murder in the book is that of the cathedral organist. As in *The Case of the Gilded Fly*, events in the organ loft are again vital to the plot, as indeed is an effect that is possible on a large instrument in a large building. Geoffrey Vintner, composer, organist and friend of Fen's, is a leading character, and it is clear that he is based to a certain extent on Godfrey Sampson. Vintner is, like Sampson at the time Montgomery wrote the book, a confirmed bachelor disinclined to leave his cottage in Surrey. Vintner was bred in a country rectory: Sampson's father was a clergyman. At Tolnbridge Vintner decides that the choir will sing Sampson's *Come, My Way*.[7] Sampson had actually helped Montgomery with background information, particularly over the functions of both chapter and clergy houses.[8] It seems that originally the book was to be dedicated to him: 'don't forget you have promised to dedicate the Cornish one [it is actually set in Devon] to me in memory of many

5    Ibid., Chapter 8
6    Ibid.
7    Ibid., Chapter 8
8    Godfrey Sampson to RBM, 26 and 29 January 1944

adventures together therein'.[9] It seems more than coincidence that the novel is set in the area of South Devon where Montgomery's parents lived.

Fen has developed into an even more abrasive, splenetic, testy, irritating and occasionally sulky character than he was in *The Case of the Gilded Fly*. It is not only his friends who are subjected to verbal assaults; even the inspector leading the investigation is told at one stage that he is too stupid to understand a point Fen has just made. He continues to plough his own furrow: 'Considerateness and sensitivity to conventional atmospheres were not […] Fen's strongest points.'[10] The ever restless Fen is a person who takes up, and just as quickly drops, new enthusiasms, as Vinter explains:

> 'My better self persuades me that he's a normal, sensible, extremely healthy-minded person, but there are times when I wonder if he isn't a bit cracked. Of course, everyone has these obsessions about some transient hobby or other, but Fen's personality is so' – he hesitated over words – '*large* and overwhelming, that when he gets bitten it seems like a cosmic upheaval. Everything's affected for miles around.'[11]

In *Holy Disorders* he is fascinated by insects and is likely to be found studying moths when becoming bored by the investigation. This new craze pays dividends for him, as his collection of bees, wasps and hornets plays a major part in his escape from a pistol-wielding villain. He spends even more time in public houses and claims that discovering the murderer would be made easier if others followed his example:

> 'And I – what was I doing?' Fen frowned with concentration. 'Yes, I have it: I was just going into a pub. I knew there was something familiar about six o'clock. If everybody had had the sense to go into pubs as soon as they opened their doors, this thing wouldn't have happened.'[12]

The other characteristics of Montgomery's novels are mostly in evidence. An unappealing left-wing worker menaces passengers on a train, dropping his aitches with abandon; continuing his habit of commandeering a different sidekick, or sidekicks, for each adventure, Fen here enlists Vintner and Fielding; Montgomery makes the most of his musical knowledge, particularly when Fen grills the landlord of the Whale and Coffin, a lover of church music; Geoffrey Vintner falls in love with the daughter of the Precentor as soon as he looks at her and proposes marriage almost immediately. Montgomery's unattached young women are usually described in idealistic and stylised terms, and his young men never have to go through the thrill of the chase. As we have seen, it seems that this was Montgomery's own preferred approach to girlfriends – in general he did not appear keen to make too much effort. Vintner has his suspicions about women, ones that we shall see were shared by Montgomery in his advancing years:

---

9    Ibid., 17 March 1944
10   *Holy Disorders*, Chapter 9
11   Ibid., Chapter 3
12   Ibid., Chapter 9

He also laboured, as a result of reading books, under the delusion that every unmarried woman he met was hunting, with all the tricks and subterfuges of her deadly and mysterious sex, for a husband, and congratulated himself inwardly upon hair-raising escapes from several women who in point of fact had never even considered marrying him, and who had merely used him as a temporary paramour and offered him the honourable courtesy of the sex, a good-night kiss at the end of an evening enjoyed at his expense.[13]

Later, Vintner expands on his feelings in a way that was again to be true of Montgomery in the coming years:

Bachelorhood, complacent in a hitherto indefeasible citadel, was startled into attention and began to peer anxiously from behind its fortifications. Discomfort, it whispered persuasively: inconvenience. All your small luxuries, your careful arrangements for peace of mind, would go by the board if you got married. Women are contemptuous of such things, or if she should turn out not to be, why marry her at all? Why have a mirror to reflect your own fads, to flatter your face? Pointless and silly. You'd much better remain as you are. Your work, too – a wife would insist on being taken out just when you were struggling with a particularly good idea. And what would become of your Violin Concerto with a baby howling about the house? You're an artist. Artists shouldn't get married. A little mild flirtation, perhaps, but nothing more.[14]

In *Holy Disorders* Montgomery pays homage to Evelyn Waugh, something that also occurs in later novels. Justinian Peace, brother-in-law to the Precentor at Tolnbridge Cathedral, has his doubts:

'Good heavens,' said Geoffrey, 'Not like Mr Prendergast?'
'I beg your pardon?'
'In *Decline and Fall*.'
'I'm afraid I've never read Gibbon,' said the other [Peace] [15]

Each man's doubts are equally incompatible with continuation in their chosen career. Whereas Mr Prendergast (a clergyman) can't understand why God had made the world at all, Mr Peace (a psycho-analyst) can't 'find one shred of experimental or rational proof that the unconscious existed at all'.[16] By a doubtless intended irony, Peace decides at the end of the novel that he will enter the Church: 'It seems the best way out of my doubts.'[17]

*Holy Disorders* was greeted favourably by the press. Reviewed on the same day as Michael Innes' latest story *Appleby's End*, the *Daily Telegraph* reported 'both are incorrigibly highbrow with classical allusions on every other page and literary quotations by the score'.[18] The *Observer* said the novel was 'fantastic, 'literary' and contorted […] an academic, ecclesiastical free for all'.[19] The reviewer in *Time and*

13    Ibid., Chapter 3
14    Ibid., Chapter 5
15    Ibid., Chapter 2
16    Ibid.
17    Ibid., Chapter 15
18    *Daily Telegraph*, 25 January 1946
19    *Observer*, 3 February 1946

*Tide* assumed that Edmund Crispin was a don.[20] In a comment that was to become increasingly true of the later books, the *Sketch* regarded the novel as a 'social comedy with a focus in murder'.[21] *Tribune* was typical of most notices: 'there can be no real complaint against such a clever entertainment',[22] although, ominously, one or two reviewers were already finding Gervase Fen a little tiresome. Even Amis had kind words to say about the novel. Noticing a copy in his local library a few years after publication, he read the first few pages 'and to my great surprise found them very funny indeed'.[23]

During 1946 Montgomery made a friendship which was to play an important part in his career as a composer. Geoffrey Bush had been an undergraduate at Balliol for two years before the war. Having looked after difficult evacuated children for some of the intervening years, he returned to Oxford for two terms. Independently of each other Montgomery and Bush had made the acquaintance of Margaret Deneke, a North Oxford hostess and musical socialite who was distantly related to Mendelssohn. Deneke and her sister were great benefactors of Lady Margaret Hall, and in their recital room they held large parties to which distinguished people and, as yet, undistinguished undergraduates were invited. When Bush returned to Oxford, Deneke decided that it was time that Montgomery and he should meet.

She invited them both to Glyndebourne for the first performance of Britten's opera *The Rape of Lucretia* on 12 July. They became firm friends on the spot, despite their very different inclinations. Bush was left-wing, whereas Montgomery was right-wing; Bush was energetic, whereas Montgomery's disability left him disinclined to take exercise; Bush did not share Montgomery's adoration of Wagner. These differences of opinion did not seem to matter: 'We soon discovered that we had just the right mix of things on which we agreed – bridge, detection, Bing Crosby – and disagreed – exercise, politics, Richard Wagner – to form the basis of a lasting friendship.'[24] On the actual evening they were united by a dislike of the composer whose music they were hearing, 'Bruce because he owed nothing to Britten, I because I owed too much.'[25] Bush later changed his views, but Montgomery retained his dislike, not entirely on musical grounds. He did not care for the manner in which he considered Britten had established his position in musical life.

Although Montgomery later sought Bush's opinions on his music, at this time his development as a composer was still being supervised by Godfrey Sampson. Everything he wrote was shown to Sampson, who did not hesitate to give his opinion even if it was not immediately encouraging. Communication between the two was not always easy with Sampson moving around the country working in intelligence. With the flowering of Montgomery's literary career, Sampson enquired whether they could collaborate on an opera, with Montgomery acting as Hofmannsthal to Sampson's Richard Strauss. *Prunella*, a play by Granville Barker (1877–1946)

---

20   *Time and Tide*, 20 April 1946

21   *Sketch*, 20 February 1946

22   *Tribune*, 22 February 1946

23   Amis to Larkin, 10 August 1950 [LKA]

24   *An Unsentimental Education*, Bush, p. 18

25   Ibid.

and Lawrence Housman (1865–1959), was suggested as a subject. The pair learnt from Housman, brother of the poet A.E. Housman, that Barker was abroad and that they would have to wait his return for an answer as to whether permission might be given for them to use the story. The situation was further complicated by the fact that *Prunella* had already been turned into a musical play in 1904 by Joseph Moorat (1864–1938). By July 1945 they had been given permission to use the plot of *Prunella*, with the stipulation that the names of the characters must be altered. Within eighteen months, however, the scheme was dropped, mainly through their inability to agree on the nature of the libretto. Meanwhile, Montgomery was writing his own opera, *Tailor (of Shrewsbury)*. Initially, this was suggested as the basis for the collaboration with Sampson, but the latter did not care for the idea. An amount of this exists in manuscript, but it never progressed very far. What was written seems to have been subsumed into the later, also unfinished, opera Montgomery began with Kingsley Amis.

Other work was more successful. In 1947 Oxford University Press published *As Joseph was a-walking*, a carol for treble solo, SATB and organ (or piano), and *Fair Helen*, a song for voice and piano. In these works Montgomery kept up his habit of setting verse of ancient lineage. Both these pieces must count amongst his most successful, the former for its engaging melody and the latter for the manner in which Montgomery has matched the yearning expressed in the text. The carol is a simple strophic setting, its firmly diatonic melody giving Montgomery the opportunity to indulge his chromatic tendencies in the accompaniment, particularly in the last verse where he gives way to a sliding accompaniment in the manner of Peter Warlock. The use of false relations during the harmonisation of the descending phrase ('He neither shall be born', for instance) adds further variety to the strophic setting. Before publication Montgomery had to make sure that the accompaniment was playable on both organ and piano, but the use of lengthy tonic pedals rather suggests that it was intended for the former. *Fair Helen* has a wistful quality which is in keeping with the melancholy nature of the anonymous poem. Montgomery produces this by constant chromatic interplay between the languor of the vocal line and the restless sliding piano part; his liking for tonic pedals under shifting chords is again shown in the short introduction. He avoids a strophic setting, instead bringing back the music of the first verse at the end (the structure is ABCA) when there is some repetition of the text. The song begins and ends in E minor, with the central two verses modulating widely with a fast harmonic rhythm through many, sometimes barely related, keys (B flat major is reached at one point, for example), although it would be more accurate to say that these various keys are touched on as the modulations are in many cases transitory in the extreme. Despite this restless tonality, which the composer uses to considered dramatic effect, there is a flow and balance to the music which comes partly as a result of Montgomery's use of sequence ('O Helen fair beyond compare!' and 'Shall bind my heart for evermair', for example). He is also showing more development in his sensitivity to the text. In the first verse the vocal line soars as the poet thinks of his beloved ('I wish I were where Helen lies') and then sinks down as he considers her grave. The exultant opening of the second verse soars even higher ('O Helen fair beyond compare!') with the rapid harmonic rhythm of the accompaniment underpinning it, whilst the melody of the brooding third verse sinks to the lowest point in the song as the poet ponders his own death ('A winding sheet drawn over my e'en') with an appropriately slower harmonic rhythm in the accompaniment. As in *My joy, my life, my crown!* there is a telling use of the flattened 7th at the end of the first and last verses, giving the modal quality which is occasionally a characteristic of Montgomery's work. These two pieces show Montgomery's increasing sureness of touch with small-scale works and are well worth performing.

The remaining work published in 1947 was his first on a large scale, and one of only two works by Montgomery for full orchestra and choir. It was dedicated to the memory of Charles Williams, Montgomery's literary advisor at Oxford. *On the Resurrection of Christ*, for chorus and large orchestra, rejected by Oxford University Press in 1945, was subsequently accepted by Novello. The text is by William Dunbar (?1456–?1513), Scottish poet and priest, and deals with the victory of Christ and the Church Militant in a suitably bellicose fashion (it seems appropriate that Dunbar probably met his end at the Battle of Flodden). The orchestra is large, including a tuba, harp, four timpani and an impressive array of percussion.

Montgomery began composing the work at the end of 1943, and it was completed by September 1944: 'As many people seem to think it the best (or the least bad) thing I have done', Montgomery wrote when submitting it to Oxford University Press, 'I thought it might be worth while letting you have it.'[26] Norman Peterkin, the man responsible for Montgomery's music at Oxford University Press, sent it for opinion to Patrick Hadley, shortly to be appointed Professor at Cambridge but in 1944 a university lecturer and composer of some standing. The letter Peterkin addressed to Hadley is of some significance at this stage of Montgomery's career:

> I wonder would you care, and could you find time, to give me your professional opinion on a short choral work by a young composer sent to me and recommended. I find myself interested in it and in other music which has also been submitted by the composer, but I feel I should like to have the advice and opinion of a more experienced man in choral matters than I can claim to be.
>
> I might mention that there is no chance of accepting it for publication at present – it could only be taken on much later when conditions are better. But I find myself interested in this particular young man's music in many ways, and if I find my feelings supported by others it might be possible to give him some definite encouragement as to our taking it on after the war.[27]

In his reader's report, Patrick Hadley made various general and fairly damning criticisms of the work:

> But what it seemed to me he had failed to do was to find a satisfactory musical shape to his setting, viewed as a whole and not just in bits.
>
> What however seemed to me to be the most serious defect and the most prevalent and underlying one was rhythmical monotony [...] That bass, whether choral, orchestral or the two coincident is a fearful old plodder, don't you find?

---

26    RBM to Norman Peterkin, 14 September 1944
27    Norman Peterkin to Patrick Hadley, 2 November 1944 (OUP Archive)

Actually I didn't detect a great deal of imaginative resource either in the choral writing or, so far as one can judge from a reduction for pfte, in the score. It seemed to me just to plod along and to be lacking in those high lights so necessary to a choral-orchestral work [...] But I do think that he has not always made the most of them [the words].[28]

These faults were excusable to a certain extent. All of Montgomery's successful compositions so far had been on a small scale. This was his first attempt at a more substantial work which included orchestral writing. Unusually for Montgomery there is no date on the autograph of the full score, and so it is difficult to establish whether he made any changes to the work in the light of these observations before submitting it to Novello. Although it is unlikely that he would have completely rewritten such a piece, a comparison of the published score with Hadley's charges suggests that, if his criticisms were merited, revisions of some sort were certainly made. It may have been to this work that Sampson referred in a forceful letter in 1945. Advising Montgomery about orchestration, he noted that the flutes were too low, there was too much oboe, the full range of the clarinets was not used and the horn parts were not spaced satisfactorily. Sampson wrote that he

> had spent a considerable time over your score and I hope you're not going to be very much depressed over my criticisms, but I think they are necessary and I also think any other person, similarly placed, would say that same sort of thing. But please understand this. Scoring is a job that can easily be learnt, and you, of all people, only need to be told once (thank God!) in order to inwardly digest forever.[29]

Hadley's first point is of a lack of structural coherence. Whilst it is true that parts of the work have an episodic character, Montgomery treats each of the four verses in distinct ways and in the second half of the setting repeatedly brings back the opening line of the poem ('Done is the battle on the dragon black') almost like a refrain. Although the work modulates through a wide variety of keys, the tonic (E major) is rarely far away and there is a confident grasp of tonal structure. Hadley's charge of 'rhythmical monotony' seems harder to understand. At the start of the work the bass line certainly does 'plod' along, sometimes as a dominant pedal, but in a section in which Christ and his forces are marching against hell this is surely an appropriate and suitably descriptive musical device. There are other similar passages, and to lump these together and dismiss the bass as 'a fearful old plodder' is rather missing the point. Away from the bass line, Montgomery shows plenty of rhythmic variety. The 14 bar orchestral introduction, for instance, trades bars of 3/4, 3/2 and 5/4 with hemiolas much in evidence, and this continues when the chorus enters so that the inflections of the text are suitably pointed. When, for instance, 'The gates of hell are broken', Montgomery sets this with a long and angular melisma on 'broken'. Later in the work when he builds up the phrase 'The great Victor again is risen' by imitation, Montgomery alternates bars of 3/2 and 2/2 but he does so at different points in the phrase in different parts so that rhythmic interest is maintained; and to make the high soprano entry on 'risen' even more effective, Montgomery places

---

28    Patrick Hadley to Norman Peterkin, 26 December 1944 (OUP Archive)
29    Godfrey Sampson to RBM, 5 April 1945

a 7/4 bar immediately before it, which has the effect of a crucial half beat delay (in a fast section with a minim pulse). These are far from isolated examples of the methods by which Montgomery certainly injects rhythmic interest into the work.

Hadley's complaints of missing 'imaginative resource' in the choral and orchestral writing and a lack of 'those high lights so necessary to a choral-orchestral work' also do not stand up entirely to close scrutiny. There are plenty of sections which are dominated by a full choir texture but, again, this is a full-blooded poem. There are also many contrasting passages. Textures are constantly shifting: polyphony alternates with homophony, tenors work with basses, sopranos and tenors contrast with altos and basses. Single parts take the melodic lines. There are *a cappella* sections. Montgomery enjoys imitation, and this is particularly evident in the central section: 'And like a lamb in sacrifice was dight' has an elegantly arching phrase between soprano and tenor. There is plenty of evidence of an increasing command of word setting. The more obvious device of dissonances in the orchestra under 'The devils curse and wail with hideous voice' contrasts with passages such as the one in which his chromatically rising phrases underpin 'The great Victor again is risen'; Montgomery's readiness to alter metre for the sake of the rhythm of the text has been mentioned previously. The setting of the second verse ('He for our sake that suffered to be slain') which forms the central section, is slower and offers a calm oasis in this generally belligerent work (the music of Gerald Finzi comes to mind here). It also retains the flexible approach to time signatures and the sensitive approach to word setting whilst never losing its sense of flow. Montgomery is also sufficiently confident to set one of his later repetitions of 'Done is the battle on the dragon black' as a wistful and pianissimo reminder of the earlier bellicosity, and this just before the final onslaught.

Rather than having too few 'high lights', one might almost make the opposite observation that climaxes come along rather too often – a not unreasonable state of affairs given the energetic and euphoric nature of the text. Quite early in the work 'Our Champion Christ confounded has his force' is set to a descending phrase starting from a top B for the sopranos (on 'Champion'), with luscious suspensions in the lower parts and a further top B and a hemiola to reinforce the finish. In the central section 'Is like a lion risen up again, And as a giant rais'd him on height; Ris'n is Aurora radiant and bright' is set as a group of continuously rising phrases which breaks into full glory with a sudden modulation to B major at 'Ris'n is Aurora'. The conclusion of the work is suitably climactic as 'the field is won', and the final setting of 'Surrexit Dominus de sepulchro' (this phrase occurs at the end of each verse) with its bold dominant 7th on C in an E major phrase and its chromatically descending bass makes Christ's victory utterly convincing.

Despite his reservations, Hadley acknowledged that the composer 'had evidently been moved by the poem and had been fired to set it'.[30] Montgomery's friend Geoffrey Bush was more enthusiastic: 'I find it prodigiously impressive and exciting. It gives me the impression that the Resurrection and the Life meant something to you, and what is more, that you could express that meaning.'[31] There is certainly a commitment

---

30    Patrick Hadley to Norman Peterkin, 26 December 1944 (OUP Archive)
31    Geoffrey Bush to RBM, undated

about this setting and it contains, as Peterkin noted, passages 'which are moving and imaginative, harmonically interesting'.[32] Despite the defences put up against Patrick Hadley's criticisms, the episodic nature of *On the Resurrection of Christ* tends to support the view that Montgomery is more at home with short pieces where his ranging tonality does not have sufficient opportunity to suffocate the listener. The musical language which characterises Montgomery's works is becoming firmly established: the shifting harmonies, appoggiaturas and sequences, all imbued with his essential chromatic outlook, mix with a firm and extended grasp of modulation. There is an individual style emerging here from the 26-year-old composer. Despite his rebuff, Peterkin told Montgomery that 'only actual performance will decide whether it "comes off" as a whole',[33] and he suggested that the composer submit it to the BBC. 'I may do as you suggest and send the choral work to the B.B.C.', Montgomery replied, 'but think your analysis of its defects so true that I shall more probably consign it to oblivion. The compensation is that one learns a certain amount even from writing a bad piece of music.'[34] Following reassurance from Peterkin that he should not attach too much weight to one person's views ('The choral work is very far indeed from being a "bad piece of music" [...] There is a great deal in it I liked very much'),[35] Montgomery decided to give the work a second chance.

Despite its flaws this exciting work certainly deserves a hearing, but unfortunately it cannot be proved that the work has ever been performed. One imagines that it would be enjoyed by the more able choral societies even if the large orchestra might deter some from tackling it. *The Musical Times* was enthusiastic: 'The writing is thick with a "Delian" tendency, nevertheless there are many fine moments in this thirty-two page work. The composer has a distinct sense of word painting, and understands the capacities of the voice. It needs a good choir and orchestra. Given this, it should take its place in the modern school of choral writing.'[36] [At this point the position of *The Musical Times* in the reception of Montgomery's music should be clarified. The journal was produced by Novello, the same company which became Montgomery's major publisher, and its generally enthusiastic reviews of his music, although understandable and often merited, should be viewed in this light.]

About this time Montgomery became involved in sitting the Oxford B.Mus examination. In November 1945 he had asked Colin Strang, now back at Oxford after serving in the Essex Yeomanry, to find out details of what was required. In July 1946 Mary Brownrigg congratulated him on passing;[37] earlier the same month Sampson wrote using their Wagner code to note his delight that 'Weimar' (= Oxford) University had seen fit to confer its award.[38]

Sampson had suggested to Montgomery that he consider conducting as a career. In February 1946 he wrote that 'a little preparatory pushing and pulling of wires

---

32    Ibid.

33    Norman Peterkin to RBM, 22 January 1945 (OUP Archive)

34    RBM to Norman Peterkin, 18 February 1945

35    Norman Peterkin to RBM, 20 February 1945

36    *The Musical Times*, April 1948, p. 119

37    Mary Brownrigg to RBM, 20 July 1946

38    Godfrey Sampson to RBM, 7 July 1946

should soon get you settled in the rostrum'.[39] A few days later Sampson talked to Ernest Read[40] about Montgomery's prospects, and it was suggested that he should start as pianist and coach, 'a thing for which, I believe, you have a certain amount of experience'.[41] Montgomery did not care for the idea because he thought it would leave him little time for composition, but Sampson thought it would be the musical making of his protégé, reminding Montgomery that 'the master' (Wagner) wrote four of his music dramas whilst a Kapellmeister: 'I think you would find it stimulating in the extreme.'[42] The matter was not pursued, but Montgomery did become involved with directing music on a small scale. He took up Mary Brownrigg's invitation to the Summer School at Newburgh Priory in August 1945, where he conducted the choir and met Sydney Northcote (1897–1968), to whom he dedicated *Fair Helen*. Northcote, a small dynamic Welshman who had heard of Montgomery and wanted to meet him, was national adviser to the Carnegie United Kingdom Trust and spent most of his time encouraging amateur music-making. He became a useful contact for Montgomery. During the course at Newburgh they talked of a post which was vacant at the Carnegie Trust, that of drama organiser. Northcote was keen to promote Montgomery for the position, but it came to nothing:

> [Sir George] Dyson has made up his mind that only professional dramatists will do, so that my efforts are therefore in vain. However, this will not prevent us meeting fairly often and talking over things in a proper manner.[43]

Peter Oldham, a friend from Oxford days, told Montgomery what he knew of the affair:

> I heard of your attempt at getting the Carnegie Drama organiser's job – apparently you were very nearly successful. All the people I know were very much in favour, but someone at the top was not. Rather a pity, because the job is a very attractive one, although it would have left you rather too little spare time for your various other commitments.[44]

Montgomery had more success at the course. Some time afterwards Brownrigg wrote to him: 'You will be glad to know that [participants] have written to say that the most moving experience of the week was singing your anthem […] The schoolgirl element of the Course continues to call on me at the most inopportune moments and rave about YOU, and ask me quite unanswerable questions about your past life.'[45] He again helped on the course in 1946, this time in Bridlington. He was driven by Brownrigg from York to Bridlington and amused her by indulging in his superstition of spitting out of the car every time they passed a white horse.

---

39      Ibid., 17 February 1946

40      Ernest Read (1879–1965), educationist and pioneer of the youth orchestras, founding both the London Junior and Senior Orchestras

41      Godfrey Sampson to RBM, 20 February 1946

42      Ibid., 10 March 1946

43      Sydney Northcote to RBM, 26 September 1945

44      Peter Oldham to RBM, 23 May 1946

45      Mary Brownrigg to RBM, not dated

These courses were annual summer events, run by the East Riding of Yorkshire and intended for teachers from that area. Most of these teachers were musically very inexperienced. As it was just after the war there were not many such gatherings. Classrooms were often taken over for dormitories, and many of the people who came had not been away from home before. This seemed to encourage them, particularly the middle-aged women, into behaving strangely and larking around. Mary Brownrigg collected tutors she thought would fit this atmosphere. Montgomery was a breath of fresh air and joined in all the fun. Compared with many of the participants he had a refined accent, but because of his affection and gaiety no one though him pompous or over-clever. Although he did some conducting and accompanying, he was mainly engaged for his ability to lecture, particularly on twentieth-century music. An example of the type of thing he did was his advice for village organists: 'In the Benedicite don't feel you have to use the 2 foot stop for ice and snow.'[46]

Many of the students were Methodists and abstainers, but because they liked Montgomery so much they were willing to ignore, or failed to notice, his devotion to nearby public houses. After the morning session he and a few others would set off for the pub, the dinner ladies keeping lunch warm until the drinking party reappeared as pudding was being served to the others. Montgomery gave organ recitals, usually at 2pm, quite the worst time for him. When sober he was quite a decent organist. His pedalling technique was never terribly secure, though, and these post-prandial sessions could sometimes end in disaster. Brownrigg recalls a recital when she asked if he could finish the programme with something rather light and jolly. Montgomery clutched his head and said: 'Oh, God, that means a toccata!' The toccata was rather disastrous.[47]

*The Moving Toyshop*, Montgomery's third novel, was published in 1946. Julian Symons, writing in *Bloody Murder*, his masterly survey of crime fiction, regards it as probably Montgomery's best novel, and on publication the general view was that it was his best yet, particularly if the reader was after comedy. 'If you can laugh at Professor Fen you will like it, but heaven help you if you're expecting detection' was the exaggerated verdict of the *New Statesman*.[48] The setting is again Oxford, and the novel gets off to an intriguing start with a toyshop which does indeed appear to move overnight. This idea was suggested to Montgomery by Larkin during their Shropshire days:

> As it happened, I was working near Shrewsbury myself at the time, and unwittingly provided the genesis of the last named [*The Moving Toyshop*] by reporting that when I left his lodgings to catch the midnight train there was always one particular shop with its awning left down.[49]

Larkin's influence in the novel is suggested in other ways, too. Richard Cadogan, the character who notices the flapping awning, is a poet, and the lengthy oration Cadogan gives on poetry late in the book is a distillation of conversations

46    Mary Strang (formerly Brownrigg)
47    Ibid.
48    *New Statesman*, 20 August 1946
49    Foreword to *Fen Country*, Larkin

Montgomery and Larkin had on the subject (in 1963 Montgomery noted that Larkin had since modified these views 'to some extent').[50] As a result of these influences, the novel is dedicated to Larkin, 'in friendship and esteem'. A little of this discussion of poetry has previously been quoted in support of Montgomery's influence on the Movement, but Cadogan warms to his theme and expands on why he claims there is no poet-type:

'I think the only thing poets have in common is a kind of imaginative generosity of heart towards their fellows – and even then one can't be too sure, with people like Baudelaire and Pope and unpleasant little neurotics like Swinburne. […] poetry isn't the outcome of personality. I mean by that that it exists independently of your mind, your habits, your feelings, and everything that goes to make up your personality. The poetic emotion's impersonal: the Greeks were quite right when they called it inspiration. Therefore, what you're like personally doesn't matter a twopenny damn: all that matters is whether you've a good receiving-set for the poetic waves. Poetry's a visitation, coming and going at its own sweet will.

[…] 'As a matter of fact, I can't explain it properly because I don't understand it properly, and I hope I never shall. But it certainly isn't a question of oh-look-at-the-pretty-roses or oh-how-miserable-I-feel-today. If it were, there'd be forty million poets in England at present. It's a curious passive sensation. Some people say it's as if you've noticed something for the first time, but I think it's more as if the thing in question had noticed *you* for the first time. You feel as if the rose or whatever it is were shining at you. Invariably after the first moment the phrase occurs to you to describe it; and when that's happened, you snap out of it: all your personality comes rushing back, and you write the *Canterbury Tales*, or *Paradise Lost* or *King Lear* according to the kind of person you happen to be. That's up to you.'

'And does it happen often?'

In the darkness Cadogan shrugged. 'Every day. Every year. There's no telling if each time, whenever it is, mayn't be the last …. In the meantime, of course, one gets dull and middle-aged.'[51]

Cadogan's last and rather gloomy statement certainly rings true of Larkin. In one of the house-jokes, Montgomery makes sure that his dedicatee's name is contained in the novel: an abstruse essay left by an undergraduate in Fen's rooms must be by Larkin, 'the most indefatigable searcher-out of pointless correspondences the world has ever known'.[52]

The plot does not creak as much as some, although comedy still prevails. The Gollancz reader's report notes that Montgomery shows an 'airy unconcern for the reader's outraged sense of probability […] However, it is all put over with such verve that one is ready to accept pretty well anything. […] A thin plot, everyone agrees. But nobody cares.'[53] Fen can still be intolerant, but there are signs that he is mellowing slightly. Montgomery's frivolity remains rampant. It begins in a note before the novel starts:

---

50    RBM to Dr Bellinghausen, 18 March 1963
51    *The Moving Toyshop*, Chapter 12
52    Ibid., Chapter 10
53    Gollancz report (Gollancz Archive)

None but the most blindly credulous will imagine the characters and events in this story to be anything but fictitious. It is true that the ancient and noble city of Oxford is, of all the towns of England, the likeliest progenitor of unlikely events and persons. But there are limits.[54]

When deciding which way to turn in a pursuit, Cadogan decides to go left: 'After all, Gollancz[55] is publishing this book.'[56] Fen's devotion to the pub mixes with this trait:

'Well, I'm going to the police,' said Cadogan. 'If there's anything I hate, it's the sort of book in which characters don't go to the police when they've no earthly reason for not doing so.'
   'You've got an earthly reason for not doing so immediately.'
   'What's that?'
   'The pubs are open,' said Fen, as one who after a long night sees dawn on the hills. 'Let's go and have a drink before we do anything rash.'[57]

Montgomery's experiences as a schoolmaster also come under scrutiny:

'You've no idea what it is to be a schoolmaster. I've watched strong men go to pieces under it. It's a perpetual war. You can keep the boys off for maybe thirty years, but they get you in the end.'
   'It sounds terrible.'
   'It is terrible. You get older, but they're always the same age.'[58]

The plot again hinges on an apparently locked-room mystery (even the murderer refers to it as such at one point); there are plenty of suspects, but no one, it seems, could have been in the room at the right time.

Montgomery's style is no less literary. Authors of every type and age are mentioned or quoted. Cadogan's diatribe on poets passes over an enormous number of them in a few lines and during two periods of enforced inactivity Fen and Cadogan, as we have previously seen, play games of 'Detestable Characters in Fiction' and 'Unreadable Books'. In the course of an enthusiastic greeting after publication in America, the *New York Times* noted that 'Mr Crispin's erudition [American reviewers had great problems accepting this part of Montgomery's style] is not so obtrusive as it was in his earlier books, or perhaps it is merely obscured by the farcical antics of his characters.'[59] Montgomery's love of the poetry of Edward Lear works its way into the plot of the book (a newspaper advertisement put out by a solicitor refers to people – all of whom are suspected of the murder at one time or another – by the names of characters from Lear's poetry), and he takes the opportunity, via Fen, to defend

---

54    *The Moving Toyshop*, Note
55    The publishing house was well known for its left-wing sympathies
56    *The Moving Toyshop*, Chapter 6
57    Ibid., Chapter 3
58    Ibid., Chapter 4
59    *New York Times*, 28 December 1946

Lear's use of the same first and last lines in his limericks. The D.H. Lawrence-reading lorry driver is the local with the by now mandatory dropped aitches.

Montgomery had a fondness for chaotic *Boy's Own*-like chases in his later novels and there are two such pursuits in *The Moving Toyshop*. The second is near the end and leads to the final scene at the Botley fairground. This arresting conclusion (Larkin wrote that the 'runaway roundabout [...] came from an evening we spent at a fair'),[60] with Fen and the murderer on board an out-of-control roundabout, was bought from Montgomery by Warner Brothers in 1951 for modified use in Alfred Hitchcock's film of Patricia Highsmith's novel *Strangers on a Train* (in the novel the roundabout does not collapse as happens in the screen version).

Montgomery's admiration of Evelyn Waugh and his tendency of keeping up with the latest developments in music and literature come together in a scene which owes something to *Brideshead Revisited*, published in only the year before *The Moving Toyshop*. In a room furnished by the Uccello Martyrdom hanging over the fireplace, first editions scattered about the shelves and deep armchairs, an undergraduate (Adrian Barnaby) throws a party at which madeira, buttered scones and iced cake are consumed. One young man is pitied silently for referring to the madeira as sherry. Barnaby is lamenting the presence of sporting people, most of whom he did not invite ('who are all these *awful people*? They're talking about rowing. [...] My dear Charles, I know: *bumps* and things. Like a *phrenologist*').[61] Barnaby, glad to escape his own party, takes Mr Hoskins off to consult the local hypochondriac, a bed-ridden Welshman called Gower who speaks with all the caricature ('Look you, I am ill, now')[62] of the leader of the Llanabba Silver Band in *Decline and Fall*. These bright young men are not merely ornamental as they serve their purpose in the first of the two chases.

Music and musicians do not play a central part in this novel, but Montgomery still manages to work them in. There is a scene in the Sheldonian where Fen reduces a rehearsal of Brahms's *Requiem* to a shambles. He gains entry by claiming that Cadogan is Paul Hindemith, the German composer, and Montgomery enjoys himself by taking swipes at choral music and its executants ('the altos, hooting morosely like ships in a channel fog – which is the way of altos the world over').[63]

Richard Cadogan is Fen's assistant in this novel, with Mr Hoskins taking the more minor rôle that was occupied by Henry Fielding in *Holy Disorders*. Comedy plays a more important part in the story as a whole, and this gives Montgomery the opportunity to introduce Fen's motor car, a vehicle which has as many eccentricities as its owner and over which Fen displays a less than complete authority:

A red object shot down the Woodstock Road.
It was an extremely small, vociferous, and battered sports car. Across its bonnet was scrawled in large white letters the words LILY CHRISTINE III. A steatopygic nude in chromium leaned forward at a dangerous angle from the radiator cap. [...] It was evident

---

60    Foreword to *Fen Country*, Larkin
61    *The Moving Toyshop*, Chapter 10
62    Ibid.
63    Ibid., Chapter 5

that the driver had his vehicle under only imperfect control. He was wrestling desperately with the levers.

Fen makes various attempts to park it in the grounds of his college (St Christopher's), in the process laying waste to the flower beds and forcing the President of the college to retreat in panic.

> The car uttered a terrible shriek, shuddered like a man smitten with the ague, and stopped; after a moment it emitted its inexplicable valedictory backfire. With dignity the driver put on the brake, climbed out, and took a brief-case from the back seat.
> At the cessation of noise, the President had approached his window again. He now flung it open.
> 'My dear Fen,' he expostulated. 'I'm glad you have left us a little of the college to carry on with. I feared you were about to demolish it utterly.'
> 'Oh? Did you? Did you?' said the driver. His voice was cheerful and slightly nasal. 'You needn't have worried, Mr President. I had it under perfect control. There's something the matter with the engine, that's all. I can't think why it makes that noise after it's stopped. I've tried everything for it.'[64]

Fen's assessment of his driving is not shared by anyone else, and Lily Christine continues to backfire and make other strange noises (later she arrives 'clattering like saucepans at war').[65]

Montgomery was becoming acquainted with other crime writers. He had met J.I.M. Stewart ('Michael Innes') for lunch shortly after Stewart had returned from Australia at the end of 1945. 'I gathered that he was a young musician who had taken to writing detective stories', Stewart later recalled, 'and I'd like to think that I spoke up as one trade-fallen character to a considerably younger man in danger of the same thing. Not so! I must have been just dull and unresponsive – even when the young man thought to improve matters by ordering a second bottle of wine.'[66] With the enthusiastic greeting given to Montgomery's third novel and his position as one of the rising authors of the genre came an invitation to join the Detection Club, an association of the leading writers of crime fiction which met regularly for a dinner, usually at the Café Royal or Moulin d'Or in London. In May 1947 John Dickson Carr suggested his membership by letter:

> You may remember that some time ago – years, wasn't it? – I mentioned my intention of proposing you as a member of the Detection Club when it should come together again.
> Well, the club has come together. Your name has been proposed and enthusiastically accepted. This is just an informal line to ask whether you would like to join.[67]

Montgomery did join. He was proposed by Carr and seconded by Dorothy L. Sayers. Following his initiation ceremony where he promised in front of Eric the Skull always to play fair with his readers, he wrote to thank Sayers. She was glad

64    Ibid., Chapter 2
65    Ibid., Chapter 4
66    J.I.M. Stewart to author, 3 October 1989
67    John Dickson Carr to RBM, 3 May 1947

that he had enjoyed the dinner, making the point that the good thing about private club dinners was that there were no speeches and thus the members could move promptly to the club room to 'have more time for discussing clues and corpses'.[68] Montgomery became an enthusiastic member of the Club, keenly embracing its quirky traditions and, at the annual dinner, providing red carnations for the men and white for the ladies. Everybody liked him, and he became a particular favourite of Dorothy Sayers and Agatha Christie.

Early in 1947 Montgomery was best man at Godfrey Sampson's wedding. 'Your only duties, I believe', Sampson wrote, 'are to get me there on time, decently turned out and sober, and to be <u>sure</u> you have the ring.'[69] The ceremony took place at St James, Muswell Hill, on 29 March with only about a dozen people present. The reception lunch was at Claridges, 'at which, of course, you have to propose our health in cunning and well-turned phrases'.[70] Alas, Sampson died in June 1949 at the age of only 47 from malignant hypertension, a condition from which his brother died at the same age. There is no record of Montgomery's feelings on the death of the man who had done most to guide his musical development, although it is appropriate that Montgomery dedicated his most ambitious work, *An Oxford Requiem*, to Sampson's memory. He kept on friendly terms with Edwina, Sampson's widow, entertaining her in both Devon and London.

Any sadness Montgomery felt was not shown in his work. These years were his most hectic, and it was the time during which he saw his rising reputation as a composer and author firmly cemented. His working time was split evenly between writing and composing, with some socialising in between, but the sheer amount of music and stories he wrote during these years left little time for much else. Seventeen pieces of music were published during this period, as well as five novels and a collection of short stories. He was often called upon by the media, principally the radio, to discuss trends in music and crime fiction, and he also became involved in writing plays and adaptations for BBC radio. One play he wrote was *The Hours of Darkness*. 'I thought it on the whoale [sic] good, especially the ingenious main idea', Kingsley Amis wrote, 'but I couldn't forgive that cut-glass-facetiousness of the 'tec.'[71] One adaptation was of L.P. Hartley's story *The Killing Bottle*, for which Montgomery received a letter from its author praising the 'almost uncanny skill and insight you have shown in developing the characters according to my conception of them […] I wouldn't have believed that my story would have made such an exciting and closely-knit play.'[72] Despite this prolific work rate, he claimed, as he was to frequently later in life, that he was 'an indolent man'.[73]

His diaries show a regular stream of meetings, recordings, broadcasts and rehearsals, with visits to London, Detection Club dinners, music or talks on the BBC and the start of his film work the most common entries. Living with his parents in

---

68    Dorothy L. Sayers to RBM, 8 July 1947
69    Godfrey Sampson to RBM, 23 March 1947
70    Ibid.
71    Amis to Larkin, 1 January 1950 [LKA]
72    LP Hartley to RBM, 14 April 1950
73    *Evening Standard*, 10 December 1948

the comparative remoteness of Brixham meant that he was forced to travel a good deal to keep up his contacts, although he was involved in teaching at the Torbay School of Music in Paignton as well as conducting the Paignton Fairbairn Choir. By now he had become quite a celebrity in the South West and was frequently to be found giving talks to local societies on musical and literary matters, or even opening exhibitions. Montgomery continued to be involved at summer music schools all over the country. In August 1950 he attended consecutive courses in Hampshire and West Sussex. These occasions helped to publicise his music, and his attendance usually meant that at least one work of his was on the programme for the course.

Montgomery made the most of his trips to London, entertaining friends at his club (Authors') and meeting others at the International Musicians' Association, a new watering hole, referred to since by Kingsley Amis as 'the most drunken institution in the world.'[74] His convivial companions, including Amis, Malcolm Arnold (whom Montgomery would accompany regularly to the erotic entertainment at Soho's Windmill Theatre)[75] and Gerard Hoffnung, found the IMA congenial, and it is not difficult to connect these days of excess with Montgomery's later alcoholic problems. In 1955 Amis was introduced by Montgomery to John Dickson Carr at the IMA. Carr was capable of switching with great discipline between periods of very heavy drinking and complete abstinence. This meeting took place during a period of the latter. Soon realising what sort of place the IMA was, Carr announced: 'This is where I fall off the wagon with a resounding crash.'[76]

His twin careers meant that Montgomery was well-off, certainly in comparison with most of his friends. Larkin found him 'too rich and successful for the likes of I',[77] and after a visit to Brixham reported that 'his way of life is *not* mine'.[78] Montgomery was also extremely generous with both advice and money. 'Bruce gave me long lectures about taking sex too seriously, & money not seriously enough,' Larkin reported after a meeting London, 'in the intervals of taking his pulse & frantically stubbing out his current cigarette with the cry "I *must* give it up!" All in all he was very nice & certainly I am grateful for these glimpses of high life he gave me, as long as they don't come too often, even though they do make me feel like a *poule de luxe*.'[79] A visit to Amis in Swansea followed the same pattern. 'Bruce came for a very happy few days, in which he spent £55 on himself and me, and I spent perhaps £7 on myself and him. He was very good company.'[80]

This accounts for why Montgomery found himself periodically short of money and did not think twice about trying to borrow from his friends, a habit which persisted for all of his life. 'Bruce wrote today to borrow £100!' Larkin wrote in 1954. 'Sent him £50. Why he applies to me & not Kingsley. God only knows.'[81]

---

74    *Memoirs*, Amis, p. 74
75    *Malcolm Arnold: Rogue Genius*, Meredith/Harris, p. 196
76    Kingsley Amis, quoted in *JDC*, Douglas Greene, p. 370
77    Larkin to J.B. Sutton, 30 July 1950 [in *Philip Larkin*, Motion, p. 194]
78    Larkin to Eva Larkin, 1 January 1955 [in *Philip Larkin*, Motion, p. 246]
79    Larkin to Patsy Strang, 4 January 1953 [SLPL]
80    Amis to Larkin, 6 November 1952 [LKA]
81    Larkin to Winifred Arnott, 7 April 1954 [SLPL]

Shortly afterwards he did apply to Amis who was surprised that Montgomery needed £50 to tide him over a few weeks: 'Having had at least twice that amount given to me in kind by the old devil, I felt I couldn't very well refuse. But what in hell is the matter with him, or with his bank account? Is he keeping three homes going, or what?'[82] Having not been paid back four months later, Amis was not pleased: 'If he just cut down his smoking to three packets a day, and didn't drink before 12 noon, he could save my money in a couple of weeks. [...] I mean he never seems to have a book coming out. What does he live on? These films only pay £400, which, less tax, wouldn't support him for the time he'd take to write the music, would it?'[83]

Kingsley Amis recalled that at meetings of the two in London Montgomery would often pay for lunch without any return at all: 'I've got the money; I'd like a decent lunch, so let's have a decent lunch, and you mustn't mind if I pay for it.'[84] In 1947, Amis and his future wife met Montgomery. 'Hilly and I had a very good time with Bruce', he told Larkin, 'who spent a lot of money on us both; a dinner at White's cost £6.'[85] Amis admitted to some difficulties: 'He is very charming but I never really know what to talk to him about; it is always as if we talk of things that don't really matter to either of us. He said you were fed up with him; I contradicted this. I said he didn't like Ruth;[86] he said she didn't like him either. He has the most un-annoyingly assured and charming manner of anyone I know. But I wish he wouldn't keep telling me to marry Hilly, or that he wants to marry Hilly.'[87]

A little later, when Amis had in his turn done rather well out of his books and was living in Swansea, he was delighted to be able to pay his way. On Montgomery's first visit to Amis at Swansea he found (at each side of the fire) a table with a bottle of Gordon's gin, a glass and a 100 Player's cigarettes for each man. Amis's one regret was that he had been unable to find the brand of cigarette (Piccadilly) that he recalled Montgomery buying at the Randolph during their Oxford days. A subsequent visit with Peter Oldham was also drink-laden, according to Amis:

I have little to report on the visit, because almost as soon as they arrived I was drunk, and stayed drunk until, and indeed beyond, the time they left. For 48 hours afterwards I had a stomach-ache, engendered, I fancy, by fish and chips we had at a nasty café. It was 9 p.m., you see, and so we couldn't eat anywhere nice, you see. [...] Bruce trod on my Mozart horn concerto at one point, but after the drinks he had bought me I could hardly have said anything, could I? He left ½-bot. of gin behind for us, too.[88]

Montgomery had always been a heavy smoker, and little by little he was becoming a heavy drinker. Over the years Montgomery rarely showed the slightest inclination to give up alcohol, but he made frequent unsuccessful attempts to stop smoking. In 1952 alone his diary notes that he stopped smoking on 2 March but managed barely

82    Amis to Larkin, 8 July 1954 [LKA]

83    Ibid., 13 November 1954 [LKA]

84    Sir Kingsley Amis

85    Amis to Larkin, 6 February 1947 [LKA]

86    A girlfriend of Larkin

87    Amis to Larkin, 6 February 1947 [LKA]

88    Ibid., 30 July 1950

two weeks ('LAPSED!' booms his entry 13 days later). He had another go on 14 April, but this time it was only four days until he started again. On 29 September there comes a portentous announcement: '1200 Examination by Dr Snodgrass: told me I must give up smoking permanently.' Despite this warning, Montgomery did not manage to give up again until 11 October. This time his diary does not indicate how long he lasted.

If he had money Montgomery spent it, and he tended to spend on the best. He arrived for a visit to Amis in a new Jaguar, one of a great line of expensive cars he bought over the years. He was very proud of this particular model and its anti-creep device, which made the vehicle unable to go forward after using the foot brake until the accelerator was depressed, but he still felt able to let Amis' wife drive even though she gave him palpitations: 'I can't bear it,' he said to Amis. 'I have to shut my eyes. When I open them, something even worse is happening!'[89]

Montgomery also spent money on travel, particularly to Paris and Bayreuth. In July 1951, after a short visit to Paris en route, he drove with Peter Oldham, Colin Strang and his wife in Strang's elderly Daimler to the first Bayreuth Festival after the war. Germany was still an occupied country and the road was frequently crossed by US tank transporters. Because of the lack of tourists, the US soldiers assumed that any car would be driven by a German. At one point a soldier waved a pistol at them and told them to stop. Strang bellowed something rude at him out of the window and drove on.[90] Later in the journey they witnessed an accident and Montgomery urged them to stop and see if Patsy, Strang's wife and a doctor, could help. She refused, on the grounds that they might be late arriving at Bayreuth and miss the opera. Montgomery was not impressed by this.[91]

At their first breakfast in Bayreuth (they stayed in Beethoven Strasse), the party was disconcerted by the German version of a boiled egg, par boiled in a glass and consequently all runny. The thought of enduring this for future breakfasts was too much for them, and a demonstration of the English method was immediately given. They saw the entire *Ring* cycle and *Parsifal* (the first time the latter had been staged at Bayreuth since Hitler banned it in 1940), something of which the Wagner worshipper Godfrey Sampson would have thoroughly approved. They also wanted to pay their respects to Wagner in a more personal way and bought a wreath to place at his tomb. The gate to the tomb was unlocked for them by the custodian. They were surprised to discover that that the tomb appeared completely unkempt, as if nobody had visited it for years. Under the watchful eye of the custodian they trooped in in a self-conscious fashion, put the wreath down and stood twiddling their fingers whilst wondering what to do next. Eventually they backed out and left, leaving the custodian with the impression that the English were rather 'dotty'.[92] Of the trip, years later, Montgomery recalled 'driving across Europe in a decrepit car [...] We squabbled all the way but enjoyed ourselves immensely.'[93]

89    Sir Kingsley Amis
90    Colin Strang
91    Sir Kingsley Amis
92    Colin Strang
93    RBM to Emily Murphy, 3 October 1977

Around this time Montgomery visited Colin Strang, now lecturing at the Queen's University, Belfast. Philip Larkin was also working at the university, and Mary Brownrigg flew from Glasgow for the weekend. On Sundays the pubs were shut, so Montgomery insisted that Strang drove them all over the border into the Republic so that they could get a drink. When they were leaving, fog was down at Belfast airport. Brownrigg was terrified and frantically taking sickness pills whilst Montgomery continued imbibing, not at all drunk despite having been at it all day.

In May 1952 Montgomery managed to persuade the home-loving Philip Larkin, still based in Belfast, to visit Paris with him. They stayed at the Hôtel Madison near the rue Danton. Montgomery maintained that everything was much dearer than it was but, as Larkin recorded, still kept up a punishing schedule:

My chief emotion at present is one of horror at the amount of sleep I seem to be doing without. [...] On Friday night we drank till late, on Saturday we saw the Monet, drank what can only have been a bottle of champagne each in the Ritz bar and saw Benjamin Britten (this, to Bruce, was like being vouchsafed a vision of Martin Luther after years of devout Roman Catholicism), went up the Eiffel Tower (never again for me!), and at night after a luxurious meal went to a night club where Bechet was reputed to be appearing. This proved fallacious in fact, but we did hear Claude Luter's band, which I knew from records and was pretty exciting at times. To balance this we intend hearing *Salome* on Monday...always assuming we have enough money. Today we had better spend in the Louvre, which I am told does not charge on Sundays.[94]

---

94    Larkin to Patsy Strang, 26 May 1952 [in *Philip Larkin*, Motion, p. 223]

# Chapter 6

# 'It ought to go off all right': Music 1948–1950

Montgomery was now in the middle of the most productive period of his life as far as music and novels are concerned. In the next five or six years, he wrote a further four novels, a collection of short stories and more or less all of his most important concert music.

The year 1948 saw the publication of six pieces of vocal music. Two of the pieces are short unaccompanied partsongs for SATB. *Gather Ye Rosebuds*, to words by Robert Herrick (1591–1674), is an unremarkable strophic setting in F major. *Musical Opinion* called it 'gay, unpretentious, but effective'.[1] The relatively diatonic nature of the piece is unusual for Montgomery, although he cannot resist a quick swerve into A flat major at one point. The final line of each verse contains some pleasantly drawn out suspensions. With *I Loved a Lass*, words by George Wither (1588–1667), we are on more typical ground. The harmonic swerve, accentuated by considerable use of sequences, is in great evidence, as is a chromaticism that borders at times on being jazz-inspired, with augmented chords to the fore. *Musical Opinion* was not so welcoming for this piece: the critique referred to 'restless, melodically rather awkward music [...] Its constantly shifting harmonies make it a good test piece, but judged purely as music it is hardly convincing.'[2] The partsong has an astonishingly brief publishing history. On 8 June 1948 Novello wrote to Montgomery asking if he had a choral work suitable for the insert they included each month in the *The Musical Times*, 'the completion of which is an ever-present problem with us'.[3] He sent *I Loved a Lass* by return, and it was accepted the following day!

Novello also published two sets of *Four Shakespeare Songs*, for voice and piano. The well-known texts are all taken from the Bard's plays. With three other published songs (*Fair Helen*, *My True Love hath my Heart* and *Willy Drowned in Yarrow*) they represent the best of Montgomery and show him entirely at home as a miniaturist. Strong melodies and interesting harmonies combine to strong effect, and the relative brevity of each song ensures that he keeps his tonal wanderings under control. *Fair Helen* has already been described, but it is appropriate here to consider the remaining two songs although they were not published until a little later (*My True Love hath my Heart* and *Willy Drowned in Yarrow*). The choice of poems is typical: nine are Elizabethan texts; the remainder are Scottish verse, a consequence perhaps of Montgomery's maternal ancestry. His decision to set most

---

1   *Musical Opinion*, April 1949
2   Ibid.
3   Novello to RBM, 8 June 1948

of the songs strophically limits the opportunities for responding to the texts. Even so, Montgomery shows that he was well aware of the musical possibilities of the poems, as should be expected from one who was establishing himself at the time of their composition as a novelist.

'Full Fathom Five', the opening song in the first set of *Four Shakespeare Songs*, is through-composed. It has a plodding descending bass (one wonders what Patrick Hadley would have made of this), much in the mode of Holst's *Turn Back O Man* of 1916, and is unusually diatonic for Montgomery, although he makes great use of added 2nd, 6th and 7th chords. This subdued harmony makes even more effective his descriptive swerve from G major to E flat major for just three bars on the words 'sea-change into something rich and strange' with its accompanying rather shocking dissonances (given the harmony in the remainder of the song). G major is restored almost immediately, however, and the bells which are proclaimed towards the end of the text are reflected in the chiming left hand accompaniment and in the triadic melodic line.

'Come Away, Death' is a strophic setting. The sense of modality already glimpsed in *Fair Helen* is apparent again, the same E minor background clouded by a lack of D sharps. Montgomery also makes use of flattened thirds: firstly, at the modulation to B major ('I am slain by a fair cruel maid') where the vocal line causes a false relation with a D natural just two quavers before the piano plays the major chord; secondly ('My part of death no one so true did share it') the voice sings repeated B flats over G in the piano bass. These effects do much to convey the melancholy of the text. Montgomery makes use of another of his favourite devices when a chromatically descending three-chord phrase (B flat major, A minor, G sharp minor) is underpinned by a pedal B. In this song the strophic setting does not preclude word-painting. The second half of each verse of the text falls into a mood of despair, and Montgomery's music shifts away from E minor towards G minor using the devices described above. Certainly in the first verse the melody rises impressively at 'Fly away, fly away, breath'. Again, like *Fair Helen*, the song's melodic balance comes from the initial two phrases being partially sequential.

'O Mistress Mine' has further examples of the flattened leading note (here the third note of the vocal line) and the flattened third. The second half of each verse in this strophic setting contains a typically sweeping sequence. Unlike 'Come Away, Death', this time the modulation to the dominant (F major) at the half way point in each verse is uncomplicated by chromatic movement and is confirmed by a clear perfect cadence.

The first three songs in this set each have a characteristic rhythm (or rhythms) which helps to give each song unity. The last, 'Tell Me, Where is Fancy Bred?', relies less on rhythm but makes use of the relationship of a third to which attention has been drawn above. In the earlier songs E minor has shifted (the word conveys Montgomery's brief modulations) to G minor, G major has moved to E flat major; in 'O Mistress Mine' the first bar in the accompaniment has a shift from B flat major to D flat major (a similar shift happens at the start of each verse of the song), and this is imitated here with the first four bars of the piano part working their way through B flat major–D flat major–F major–D flat major. Although the song is notionally in F major, chords of D flat major figure prominently. The song also sets off as if to be strophic, and then towards the end of the second and last verse Montgomery introduces a coda, which serves to conclude both the individual song and the set as a whole. A luscious dissonance on 'Let us all ring Fancy's knell', formed by the dominant 13th of E major over an F natural, resolves to an F major chord. Almost immediately 'Ding, dong, bell' is sung to an augmented triad (as opposed to the major triad used by the bells at the end of 'Full Fathom Five'). This phrase is supported in the piano by a minor 9th chord on C sharp (as far as the ear is concerned this is again the D flat–F relationship) which also resolves to a chord of F major. And the final two chords of the song are ones of the dominant 7th of E major relaxing into F major again. These distantly related chords in sharp juxtaposition are another of Montgomery's fingerprints, and can be seen as his harmonic swerve reduced to even smaller proportions.

*The Musical Times* was positive about the songs and made similar observations:

> Bruce Montgomery's 'Four Shakespeare Songs' are happily without Tudorbethan preciosity; still more happily, each has a musical conception. (So much modern song-writing is mere formless declamation, supposedly in good taste because it does so little to the words.) An ostinato treatment serves 'Full fathom five' well, and is none the worse for reminding us of the second theme of Holst's 'Saturn'. For 'Come away, death' the voice has an easy melody, and could be sung unaccompanied, suggesting but one key; but an ingenious accompaniment makes the successive tonal shifts that impart the desired malincolia. A similar technique is used for 'Tell me, where is Fancy bred?'[4]

The second set of *Four Shakespeare Songs* begins with 'Take, O Take Those Lips Away', perhaps the most sincerely felt of all Montgomery's songs. This through-composed song has a restless harmonic rhythm and, like *Fair Helen*, there are many suspensions in the interplay between voice and piano. This song demonstrates the importance of the accompaniment to Montgomery's music: taken alone, the vocal line of 'Take, O Take Those Lips Away' is angular, but the flow of the harmonies gives the melody a smoothness it would otherwise lack. As in others of his songs, it is an indication of the control Montgomery has over his chromatic wanderings that he arrives back at the tonic without giving the feeling that this is an artificial move.

'When Icicles Hang by the Wall' is the most vibrantly rhythmic of Montgomery's songs. There is a variety within the accompaniment in this strophic setting that is missing from other songs, although after a syncopated introduction, which is used later under the voice, the piano settles for a time into a smooth chromatically sliding crotchet accompaniment. Montgomery's liking for chords moving by step over a pedal (and the dissonances this produces) is again demonstrated ('When blood is nipp'd and ways be foul') [Example 6.1].

This phrase also gives an example of the Montgomery swerve: the song is notionally in E minor (a favoured key, and here again the leading-note is usually flattened), yet for one bar the melody shifts into an enharmonic dispute with the accompaniment with a phrase built from an augmented chord. Appropriately, for a novelist who was often called erudite because of the unusual words he was fond of using, Montgomery often employs rarely used Italian terms in his music. This song is marked 'strasciando' (in a heavily slurred manner).

---

4    *The Musical Times*, September 1949, p. 325

**Example 6.1** *Four Shakespeare Songs* (Second Set): **'When Icicles Hang'**

'Who is Silvia?' has a broader, more sweeping melody than most of Montgomery's songs, and the harmonies are less dense than usual. In the third bar of each verse of this strophic setting there are examples of the harmonic swerve, which last for just two beats [Example 6.2].

**Example 6.2** *Four Shakespeare Songs* (Second Set): **'Who is Silvia?'**

The modulation in the melody from the tonic (F major) to F minor ('Holy fair, and wise is she; The heav'n such grace did lend her') is underpinned by such a harmonically mobile accompaniment that this otherwise unremarkable phrase is transformed, again showing how Montgomery's melodies rely for their effect on the harmonic accompaniment. In this song Montgomery makes great use of clusters of 2nd, 6ths and 7ths in the piano chords. The ending ('To her let us garlands bring') is marked *mf* with a diminuendo to *p*, an unexpectedly subdued conclusion given the triumph of the text.

The final song in this set, 'Under the Greenwood Tree', is also strophic. The vocal line again has modal influence (the song is in E flat major with a flattened leading note), and the accompaniment leaves the relative diatonicism of 'Who is Silvia?' well behind as Montgomery indulges again in sliding chromaticism. Nowhere is this better demonstrated than at the end of each of the two verses ('But winter, winter and rough weather') [Example 6.3].

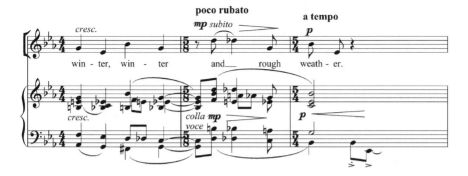

**Example 6.3** *Four Shakespeare Songs* (Second Set): 'Under the Greenwood Tree'

The skipping right-hand figure underneath 'Come hither' causes a quite blatant and, for Montgomery, unusual simultaneous dissonance between the E flat of the vocal line and E natural in the piano in the same register.

*The Musical Times* again summed up the general mood of the notices:

> [Montgomery] has also issued a second set of Shakespeare songs, which at first seemed to use a more advanced accompanimental texture and harmony, leaving the voice parts less interesting melodically than are those in the first set. One finds, however, that these songs are not to be judged by silent reading, and there are enough great songs (in Schubert alone, for example) to disprove the thesis that a good art-song needs a vocal part of great intrinsic worth. If one sets aside the first of this second set, 'Take, O take those lips away', Warlock's setting having made one pair of ears unwilling to accept any other modern one, this set seems even better than the first. It includes 'When icicles hang', 'Who is Sylvia?' and 'Under the greenwood tree'. A.H.[5]

*Musical Opinion* referred to Montgomery's success 'in giving rich musical impressions of the poems, rather than inevitable, spontaneous musical expressions to them' and regarded them as 'sincerely felt, pleasing and worthy of the fine singer and pianist they demand'.[6]

*My True Love Hath my Heart*, to words by Sir Philip Sidney (1554–1586), was published in 1949 and has perhaps the most memorable melody of any of Montgomery's songs. Although the flattened leading note again appears early on in each of the two verses of this brief work (later it is sharpened), this melody is otherwise diatonic and has a clear modulation to the dominant at the halfway point. Further tinges of modality occur when Montgomery again shows his disposition to avoid the leading note in the melody at the final cadence of each verse by approaching

---

5    Ibid.
6    *Musical Opinion*, March 1949, p. 301

the tonic via the submediant. The melody is able to stand by itself, and Montgomery lets it do so by providing a harmonically restrained accompaniment, with only a small and unexceptional amount of chromatic movement. The metre of the vocal line is more restless than usual, switching between 2/4, 3/4 and 3/8. In the first two lines of each verse these changes of metre coupled to the constant quaver syllabic setting and the pause at the end of each line give the song a flowing recitative-like quality which keeps the text firmly in focus. 'This is a straightforward song in ballad style, keeping just clear of commercial balladry' was the view of *The Musical Times*, 'and might serve well as an encore.'[7]

In 1952 the last of Montgomery's published songs appeared. *Willy Drowned in Yarrow* (to anonymous words) was composed as the second of *Two Scottish Songs* with *Bonnie Lesley*, but the latter was not accepted for publication. After the predominantly diatonic language of *My True Love Hath my Heart*, we are back in more typical Montgomery country. The first thing one notices about the piano introduction is that there is a typical harmonic swerve in bar 3, where the tonality switches from the tonic C major to a perfect cadence in C major via an implied perfect cadence in E flat major for just 3 beats (there are reminiscences of the organ interludes in *My joy, my life, my crown!* here). In form AABA, the vocal line again oscillates between the flattened and unflattened leading note in the A sections, where Montgomery uses his fingerprint of a sliding chromatic accompaniment. Section B ('The lav'rock there') is preceded by an abrupt modulation to D major, and the chromatic harmony of this section is often underpinned by the use of 2 bar pedals which lead to greater dissonance.

At the end of this section ('There Willy hecht to marry me') another of the fingerprints of Montgomery's music is shown. After a series of restless harmonic shifts, the tonality seems to clear by settling into a key for just a few beats before the harmony moves on again. But the highly chromatic language has not really quietened down, as the accompaniment moves through chords of G major (with added 2nds and 6ths) to D major via a dominant 13th on B flat. It is the vocal line which has set the impression of D major, and the feeling of the tonality clearing comes as a result of a slower harmonic rhythm (one chord every 3 beats rather than every beat as in the previous bars). This device serves to highlight the triumph of the text. Montgomery uses the piano symphony at the end of this verse to return to C major from D major via a perfect cadence in A flat major, a pause on an E major seventh chord which slides straight to a perfect cadence in C.

Although three verses of the four are treated strophically, Montgomery manages to inject variety. There is some word painting of the more obvious kind (is it coincidence that in the last verse the twice previously used melody rises and falls appropriately for 'She sought him up, she sought him down'?), and in the middle of the last verse, as if to make the most of the drama of Willy being found 'drown'd in yarrow', Montgomery inserts a short piano interlude as if to delay this discovery. At the end of the song, Montgomery augments part of the last phrase ('She found him drown'd in Yarrow') to cause a dramatic pause and dissonance on 'drown'd', with an augmented 7th chord which tries to resolve onto a dominant 7th of D major, but

---

7     *The Musical Times*, September 1949, p. 325

which is prevented from doing so by the B flat in the bass firmly refusing to drop to A [Example 6.4].

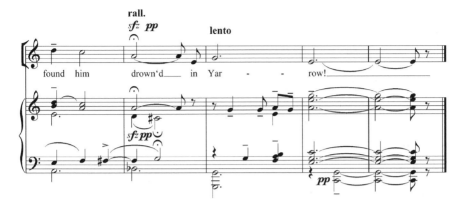

**Example 6.4 *Willy Drowned in Yarrow***

Two bars later the song concludes via an implied perfect cadence in C major. This song demonstrates, as much if not more than any of Montgomery's works, how his harmonic progressions are clouded by the addition of 2nds, 6ths and 7ths to many chords. When this tendency to densely textured chords is added to heavy chromatic movement, the sum is a complex language.

Thomas Armstrong particularly enjoyed this song. Writing in *The Oxford Magazine* following its first performance on 16 October 1949 with others of his songs at a concert of the Oxford Ladies' Music Club (where many of Montgomery's songs received their first airings), he gave a brief but considered view of Montgomery's work in this genre:

> The most striking quality of Montgomery's songs […] seemed to be warmth and naturalness of feeling. The composer has rare skill in the handling of words, and his settings are an unfailing joy in the matter of phrasing and cadence. If one had to choose out of all the songs a single item for special commendation it would be the deeply moving though simple setting of 'Willy drowned in yarrow' which was beautifully sung, as all the songs were, by David Galliver, with the composer at the piano. [8]

With this sort of ringing endorsement, it is not surprising that on publication the song was dedicated to Armstrong. *Bonnie Lesley*, its unpublished fellow (although available in the public domain),[9] is worthy of a brief mention. This is a strophic setting of words by Robert Burns (1759–1796), with the second of the three verses having different harmonies for short but effective sections. Montgomery's fondness

---

8    *The Oxford Magazine*, 3 November 1949

9    As Appendix 1 in David M.T. Whittle, 'Bruce Montgomery (1921–1978): a biography with a catalogue of the musical works' (unpublished PhD thesis, University of Nottingham, 1998)

for a tonic pedal underneath chromatically shifting harmonies opens the song, and is used again later in each of the three verses. This is the most overtly chromatic of all Montgomery's songs, and this feeling is generated by the constant interplay of sequences, suspensions and sliding harmonies, both within the accompaniment and between the voice and piano, over what is often a static bass. Apart from the triumphant descending phrase at the end of each verse, *Bonnie Lesley* has little of the melodic or expressive qualities of *Willy Drowned in Yarrow*, and in its concentration on a rather suffocating harmonic texture it also lacks variety. For those, if not other, reasons it is not entirely surprising that it failed to gain acceptance for publication.

Montgomery's songs are worthy contributions to the English tradition, along the route traversed by composers such as Peter Warlock, Roger Quilter and other members of the so-called English Musical Renaissance. They share some common features. There is a predisposition towards sixteenth-century or other ancient texts. The musical language is of a predominantly Romantic nature but with a personal idiom; Montgomery's debt to Warlock may be obvious, but it is not overwhelming, and there is still room for his own style to come through. Although Montgomery shows no interest in the folksong influence which others embraced, the hints of modality which have been noticed take us back, as with his texts, to an earlier period. In many ways Montgomery's songs are his most accomplished work and deserve a place in the concert hall.

Another piece published in 1948 was *Mary Ambree*, a short ballad for chorus and small orchestra. On its submission it was greeted with enthusiasm by Oxford University Press (Norman Peterkin felt that he might 'have a minor choral "find" in this little work').[10] Alternating rapidly in its five-minute duration between violence and tenderness, it certainly is, as *The Times* put it, 'good stirring stuff and not too difficult for a normal small choir to sing effectively'.[11]

*Mary Ambree* has an immediately engaging appeal. Montgomery himself referred to it as 'not a very serious affair',[12] and there is a tongue-in-cheek atmosphere most of the way through. The appeal is engendered by the marriage of robust music to a bellicose sixteenth-century text (from *Reliques of Ancient English Poetry*, edited by Thomas Percy in 1765) which tells of a legendary English heroine who was involved against the Spanish in the siege of Ghent in 1584. The appeal is increased by the frequent juxtaposition of this musical vitality with parody. Energy is generated by passages of a constant march-like crotchet rhythm and plenty of aggressive triplets in the orchestra coupled to scotch snaps in the chorus. Parody comes from exaggeratedly sentimental passages: the swooning phrase first used when brave Sir John Major is 'slain in her sight' (an example of a Montgomery harmonic swerve) is marked 'Dolorosamente', and the rising imitative phrase first heard at 'Was this not a brave bonny lass' is marked 'Affetuosamente (and with a touch of parody)' at its final deliberately elongated appearance.

Montgomery's word-setting is competent, with the work containing more rhythmic variety than is common in his choral pieces (scotch snaps and triplets are

10    OUP report dated 6 September 1946 (OUP Archive)
11    *The Times*, 21 January 1949
12    RBM to Oxford University Press, 19 July 1946

used to good effect in the vocal lines). What is certainly conveyed is the difference between the war-like outbursts over tramping crotchets and the sentimental sections where dotted and lombardic rhythms give way to a smoother and more sustained texture. Montgomery enjoys setting words such as 'betrayed' (a piquant false relation of a D flat over a chord of B flat major). The harmonic language is typically dense and shifting. A good example of this occurs at the phrase 'Now say, English captain' [at F in the vocal score] where a descending sequence is delivered over 16 beats [Example 6.5]. Montgomery's love of dense, clustered cadential chords is clearly seen at 'Mary Ambree' [shortly before G], where augmented intervals and added 2nds and 6ths stretch out the phrase [Example 6.6].

**Example 6.5** *Mary Ambree*

**Example 6.6** *Mary Ambree*

In accepting the work for publication, Norman Peterkin noted that the words 'are reflected admirably in a racy post-Stanford idiom to which Montgomery brings a harmonic flavour of his own. The vocal writing is bold & vigorous, & varied without being at all difficult.' It brought to mind Balfour Gardiner's *News from Whydah* and *Shepherd Fennell's Dance*: 'There is something of the same "English" atmosphere, the vigour and rhythmic urge, combined with an excellent melodic line & a personal flavour in the harmonic idiom.'[13] There is no doubt that *Mary Ambree* is one of Montgomery's most accomplished works. It again shows how much at home he was with shorter structures, albeit one that was on a larger scale than his songs and partsongs. The criticisms that Patrick Hadley made of *On the Resurrection of Christ*, predominantly about the structure and treatment of words, do not apply here.

By scoring the work for a small orchestra (originally there was no woodwind at all), Montgomery aimed the work at small choral societies with modest resources, and the work received a number of performances (including a BBC radio broadcast in 1949) – which makes its subsequent fate even more disappointing, and shows something of the problems that less well-known composers faced. In 1976 Montgomery discovered that someone who had been trying to arrange a performance of *Mary Ambree* with orchestra had been told by Oxford University Press that orchestral parts for the work were not available. In reply Montgomery vented his spleen:

> The overall answer is, I'm afraid, quite simple: all music publishers nowadays exist in a permanent condition of confusion and folly. [...] I write with some feeling, since I have recently had a great deal of trouble with music publishers, whose interest in promoting the music they publish has seemed to me over the last 25 years to be either negligible or totally non-existent. It is only thanks to the kindness and persistence of people like yourself that one ever gets a performance at all.[14]

On the same day he fired off a letter to the publishers demanding that a new set of parts should be made: 'At best', Montgomery wrote of the situation, 'it suggests an extraordinary muddle, and at worst, unethical behaviour [...] since under my agreement with you I have a financial interest in their hire, to destroy them without consulting me is wholly unwarranted.'[15] What he would have made of the current situation one can only imagine. Recent enquiries have revealed that the full score of *Mary Ambree* has also been mislaid by his publisher (full scores of Montgomery's works for hire were merely copies of the composer's manuscript). It is the only published work of his for which, it would seem, no full score survives – an inexcusable situation.

In addition to getting plenty of music published, Montgomery was getting quite a lot of it performed. An unpublished work, *Overture to a Fairy Tale*, received its first performance in February 1948 at the hands of the Torquay Municipal Orchestra. A further performance by the West Country Studio Orchestra was broadcast on BBC radio the following year. The circumstances of its composition are unclear, but it seems unlikely, given that it was completed two years previously, to have

---

13    Reader's Report, Oxford University Press, 6 September 1946
14    RBM to D.A. King, 16 July 1976
15    RBM to Oxford University Press, 16 July 1976

been a commission. It is an important piece in Montgomery's output, being the first of just three completed works for full orchestra, none of which were published, that are not linked to his later film work. In its ready adoption of the style that has come to be known as light music, not something it seems he had attempted before, it is easy to see why Montgomery was to find the composition of scores for similarly light films much to his liking. The music is immediately appealing, with a conveyor belt of abundant melodic invention (there are four major themes in its eight-minute duration). The orchestration is vivid and assured, and it seems that the scoring was increased for the actual performance, or perhaps, in the light of experience, for the later broadcast as a used set of parts in Montgomery's papers includes a second trumpet and three trombones which do not appear in the sole surviving score. The work contains many of the traits that were to mark his film scores. There is a transparency in the scoring with woodwind solos prominent, and these are often accompanied by a chromatically sliding counter-melody on another woodwind instrument or, more commonly, a horn. Montgomery is keen on violins in thirds, a technique much favoured by composers of light music. If the opening theme brings Elgar to mind (by both melodic material and scoring, the mixture of a descending sequence and the clarinet doubling the violins), the rest of the music is individual and in essence what we have come to expect from Montgomery, with chromatic inner-lines competing with descending sequences. There is, however, an easy charm about this work which is missing from his grander, more harmonically dense compositions such as *On the Resurrection of Christ*, and the film world was to benefit from Montgomery's ability to slip into this lighter style.

A piece which received a great deal of attention was *Christ's Birthday*, a setting of six carols for chorus, strings and piano which was published in 1948. It was used at a summer school in Berkshire run by Sydney Northcote in August 1948, but its first public performance was in November that year at a concert given in the Sheldonian Theatre by the Oxford Bach Choir. Although Thomas Armstrong conducted the rest of the programme (which included *Fantasia on Christmas Carols* by Vaughan Williams and *Before the Paling of the Stars* by Benjamin Dale, a composer with whom, stylistically, Montgomery had been compared), Montgomery was in charge for his own work. 'Provided the performers pay no attention to me', he wrote to friends in Amersham, 'it ought to go off all right.'[16] *The Musical Times* was again enthusiastic:

The last, a suite for chorus and string orchestra (including piano), was given its first performance, with the composer conducting. It is a refreshing work, interesting for choir and orchestra to perform, and shows sensitive approach to the six aspects of Christmas lore and thought contained in the poems. The composer's command of his forces was completely satisfactory and they obviously enjoyed his music. There was some particularly beautiful tone in the setting for sopranos of Wedderburn's 'Balulalow', and the choir's versatility was tested in the various moods of the four anonymous fifteenth-century poems used in the suite. 'Adam lay ybounden' had a vigour that contrasted well with the tensity of Montgomery's setting of 'There came Three Kings from Galilee'; there was a calm

---

16     RBM to 'Uncle Harry', a former neighbour of the Montgomerys in Amersham, 24 November 1948

beauty in the setting of 'A maid peerless'; and a jolly swing about the final poem 'Good, day, my Lord Sir Christemas', to which the orchestra responded with the best playing of the day. R.N.[17]

Described as a suite of carols for string orchestra and piano obbligato, *Christ's Birthday* is the second of Montgomery's published larger scale works for chorus and orchestra, although the orchestra in this case is relatively small. The piano is used sparingly, particularly for percussive effect. The six carols (all the words, with the exception of the first carol by the nineteenth-century Christina Rossetti are sixteenth century or earlier) show that Montgomery is still happiest dealing with short movements. His structures hold together well, despite the sometimes wide modulations. The work shows, perhaps, a greater willingness to experiment with dissonance as opposed to chromaticism, although the former is often the result of developing the latter.

'In the bleak mid-winter' begins with a string introduction which shows the nature of Montgomery's style and reinforces the impression that he is at his best with the discipline and structure of words to set. Dissonances at the semitone (what the *The Musical Times* referred to as the 'modern touch') suddenly clear to reveal a passage of descending melody with alternations between E major and minor that are a reminder of Vaughan Williams. Many of Montgomery's instrumental introductions in his choral pieces include a harmonic swerve shortly before the voice or voices enter, and this happens here. More usually this swerve ends with a return to the tonic, but here it is different: in a movement which begins and ends in E minor, the voices enter on a chord of E flat minor with an added 6th. Further on, the cadence on 'Jesus Christ' with its clustered chords and static bass shows that the influence of Delius is still in evidence [Example 6.7].

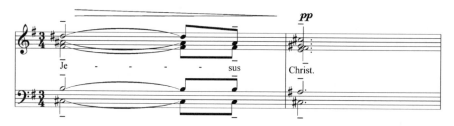

**Example 6.7 *Christ's Birthday*: 'In the bleak mid-winter'**

Any attempt to describe Montgomery's style has to accept that although he took much from English composers of the first part of the twentieth century, he forged his own voice by advancing his treatment of chromatic harmony. This is the essence of his style: added notes consistently cloud chords until the harmonic swerves lead away, and Montgomery's use of clustered chords even at this stage in his development shows why he found it congenial to write in a more popular language for some of the

---

17     *The Musical Times*, December 1948, p. 377

film scores he composed twenty years later. After all, the type of dense chromaticism written by Montgomery is very close to the style of chordings used by many jazz musicians. Indeed, there are two examples of blue note chords in 'In the bleak mid-winter': one on 'Frosty wind made <u>moan</u>' at the very beginning is used for its word painting effect (a dominant 7th with a minor 3rd at the top) [Example 6.8], and later ('In her <u>maiden</u> bliss') the same chord appears with the blue note acting as a rising appoggiatura.

The two most vigorous carols, 'Adam lay ybounden' and 'Good day, Sir Christèmas', bring the music of Walton to mind. The rhythmic vitality of 'Adam lay ybounden' is reminiscent of *Belshazzar's Feast*, a work we know Montgomery was particularly keen on during his Oxford years. An instrumental interlude which leads into 'And all was for an apple' turns a 3/4 bar into one of 6/8 by accenting the half beat, and the six bars which lead into 'Blessed be the time' in their use of rhythm and rests and their clash at the tone are a reminder of the orchestral sections in the Walton work.

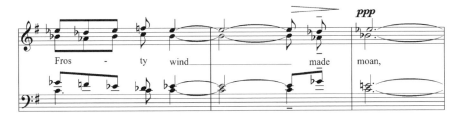

**Example 6.8** *Christ's Birthday*: **'In the bleak mid-winter'**

Montgomery's use of chromatic movement over a static bass is often seen in these carols. 'In the bleak mid-winter' contains an eight-bar pedal ('Angels and archangels') above which the violins descend by semitone steps over two octaves; the second carol 'Balulalow' (which Montgomery rejected late in his life as 'too Warlockian'[18] when writing to the conductor Sir Adrian Boult) has a dominant pedal in the bass for 20 of its 26 bars, and the remaining six bars have a tonic/dominant drone; 'There came three kings' also makes great use of shifting tonalities above a rarely changing bass. In 'Adam lay ybounden' a six-bar section makes much of the clash of a minor 2nd between the chorus and the instrumental pedal ('Ne had the apple taken been'). This dissonance at the semitone is much favoured by Montgomery: the shifts above the pedals in 'There came three kings' are characterised by this dissonance, and it forms the harmonic basis for the entire carol.

At other times Montgomery resorts to more mainstream writing for the voices. This happens particularly during unaccompanied sections. 'Our God, heav'n cannot hold him' in 'In the bleak mid-winter' is such an example, with use of 6ths, 7ths and contrary motion [Example 6.9]. 'A maid peerless' is particularly marked by this style, and these passages show that when Montgomery breaks away from his

---

18    RBM to Sir Adrian Boult, 27 March 1978

clustered harmony he often turns to the type of modality which is suggested by the flattened leading note, a tendency that has been noted previously. 'A maid peerless' demonstrates this: in a short movement which is based around F sharp minor, there is not a single E sharp until the penultimate bar of the concluding orchestral passage.

Perhaps more than any earlier work, the music of *Christ's Birthday* engenders a sense of atmosphere. The orchestral introduction to the first carol, 'In the bleak mid-winter', produces a sense of cold stillness by its semitone dissonances; the short, truncated, homophonic opening choral phrases and their staccato instrumental punctuations continue this mood, as does the static choral texture. When the snow falls, the imitative vocal lines become longer and smoother. The lullaby, 'Balulalow', rocks Jesus to sleep by its constantly lilting cross-rhythms in 6/8. The insistent and unresolved dissonances in the accompaniment to 'There came three kings', and its hypnotically repeated rhythm, continue the air of aridity from the start of 'In the bleak mid-winter'.

**Example 6.9** *Christ's Birthday*: **'In the bleak mid-winter'**

Three movements from the Oxford performance of *Christ's Birthday* were broadcast the following month on BBC Western Region. In that same month, December 1948, Montgomery and his friend Geoffrey Bush took the bold step of hiring the Wigmore Hall to secure London performances of some of their music, although Novello inserted an advertisement in *The Musical Times*, sold tickets, handled posters and were 'very pleased to act as guarantor for any loss on the concert to the amount of ten guineas',[19] which amount they were asked for following the concert. Bush has written of the evening:

> It was probably then, [at Montgomery's parents' house in Brixham] however, that we discovered we were both writing cantatas for Christmas. (Bruce's was called *Christ's Birthday*.) This led to the idea of our giving a joint concert of our music at the Wigmore Hall. Accordingly we engaged the Riddick Orchestra, enlisted Trevor Harvey as conductor, and conscripted other friends and colleagues to act as soloists, chorus and chorus-master. Everything had to be done on a shoestring: one three-hour rehearsal was all we could afford. (When in mid-session I got to my feet to query something with the conductor, Trevor turned round, uttered an abrupt 'no' before I could even speak, and went straight on with the rehearsal.) Pre-concert nerves – although we were not performing ourselves – induced us to drink large amounts of alcohol at the last minute without the slightest sedative effect. We need not have worried: hall and gallery were almost full, the performances

---

19    Novello to RBM, 27 July 1948

satisfactory, and all but one of several notices enthusiastic. When we appeared on the platform together at the end of the concert, the conductor's podium proved to be too small to hold both of us simultaneously: the sight of two composers trying to wedge each other in like a pair of sardines gave the audience some much needed light relief.[20]

Ruth Dyson played the piano in this performance and remembered, amongst other things, that:

> It was an exciting occasion but rather frustrating owing to the short rehearsal time and the very crowded stage arrangements. I played an upright piano I remember – the only time I have ever played that style of instrument on that particular stage and with the piano's squat bulky shape it was not easy to arrange myself so that I could both see the conductor and hear the cellos.[21]

Reviews of the work following the performance were enthusiastic, with *The Musical Times*, as always, leading the way: 'Each of the six pieces has its own distinct idea, and the musical means are there to articulate it.' The 'lines of composition and of harmony are more intensely drawn and the modern touch more apparent. But it is not laid on for its own sake.'[22] *Musical Opinion* thought the 'six enterprising and sensitive choral settings' were 'imbued with true lyrical inspiration and notable for ripe craftsmanship. They are as enjoyable to hear as they doubtless are to sing, and one – 'Balulalow' – is worthy of Warlock in its searchingly expressive harmonies and challenges comparison with his own version. The performances were all admirable.'[23] *The Times* thought *Christ's Birthday* harder to sing than Bush's work 'by reason of its chromaticism, which is occasionally reminiscent of Peter Warlock. But for the most part this composer has found a distinctive harmonic idiom of his own, which he uses with absolute certainty of effect. All six carols in the work are original – some of them strikingly so – and an excellent, vigorous performance made them the more telling.'[24]

The evening also contained the first concert performance of Montgomery's solitary published orchestral work, the *Concertino for String Orchestra*. Although not appearing until 1950, this three-movement work had been completed early in 1948 and accepted soon after by Novello. It had already been given a 'hilarious' broadcast performance by the BBC ('Hilarious, because the studio was opposite a pub called The Southampton Arms, whose boast was that they offered gin at a lower price than any of their competitors').[25] *Musical Opinion* was cautiously welcoming:

> There is an engaging simplicity of design and economy of material in each of the movements of this work, that makes for a ready understanding and appreciation, despite the composer's free use of dissonance. If the music rarely gets off the ground, it is always craftsmanlike, and its technical competence holds the interest. There are three movements,

20    *An Unsentimental Education*, Bush, pp. 18–19
21    Ruth Dyson to author, 4 March 1992
22    *The Musical Times*, January 1949
23    *Musical Opinion*, February 1949
24    *The Times*, 11 December 1948
25    *An Unsentimental Education*, Bush, pp. 19–20

a *Moderato quasi allegro*, which is mainly fiercely energetic, with some good contrasting sections; a flowing *Lento espressivo*, and a *Vivace ed energico*, which again has two main contrasting ideas, one explosively rhythmical and the other a cantabile melody finely developed.[26]

Geoffrey Bush, the dedicatee, had stronger views:

I sometimes wonder why Bruce called the piece Concertino, for in every respect – scale, ideas, technique – it is a major composition. Possibly he had been impressed by the fact that John Ireland had christened a work of comparably large ambitions *Concertino Pastorale*; and there are indications that Bruce had heard Ireland's toccata finale before writing his own. Despite that, Bruce's work is (in its own highly chromatic way) decidedly individual, and certainly deserves to become a regular part of the British string orchestral repertory.[27]

Although Montgomery's music can never be regarded as progressive, his free use of chromaticism (referred to as 'dissonance' by *Musical Opinion*) within a firmly tonal framework marked him as different from many other composers of his time. Even so, the most effusive notice of the concert came from C.G.R., also in *Musical Opinion*, who praised both Bush and Montgomery in terms which amount to a personal statement against what he viewed as the prevailing contemporary trends, and which are entirely in keeping with the characteristic conservatism of that journal:

More important than personal data is the music, and this proves beyond a shadow of a doubt that both men are outstanding talents. Neither has as yet forged an unmistakably personal style and idiom, but both appear to have saturated themselves in healthy influences, and it is refreshing to hear such *un*-contemporary work by living composers. Their music, indeed, is so good that neither would stand a dog's chance at the I.S.C.M. [International Society for Contemporary Music]. Both the Concertino of Montgomery and the Concerto of Bush are based, consciously or not, on well-known models, but are none the worse for that; both show an intimate knowledge of the medium, the writing is invariably effective, the harmonic scheme is perfectly suited to the fund of genial melodic invention, and if neither work says anything very profound and frankly aims at pleasing the ear and soothing the mind, then so much the better. Not every composer is intended by nature to become a great master, and unpretentious works of this order have a far higher expectation of life than the pseudo-profundities and pathological phenomena with which we have been surfeited for the last several decades. The two works are, in fact, most useful additions to a relatively limited repertory. C.G.R.[28]

With the exception of two works for piano, this is the only published piece by Montgomery which is purely instrumental. Its relatively extended movements give the opportunity to examine the composer's use of structure and development when away from the guiding hands of a text. Although the first movement gives the impression of a basic ABA form, this is not achieved by conventional means. There are three main thematic and rhythmic ideas. The opening 4 bars contain a dotted figure [Example 6.10] which becomes the dominant rhythm of the movement.

---

26    *Musical Opinion*, May 1951
27    *An Unsentimental Education*, Bush, p. 20
28    *Musical Opinion*, February 1949

**Example 6.10** *Concertino for String Orchestra*: **'Moderato quasi allegro'**

This is immediately followed by the first theme [Example 6.11] which is lengthened by sequence.

**Example 6.11** *Concertino for String Orchestra*: **'Moderato quasi allegro'**

A bridge passage based on Example 6.10 leads to a second theme [Example 6.12] which is also lengthened by sequence.

**Example 6.12** *Concertino for String Orchestra*: **'Moderato quasi allegro'**

After these statements, the music moves into a central development section in a rhapsodic vein which makes use of all three ideas. The movement comes to a recapitulation with the restatement of the first theme, but the second theme does not reappear.

Montgomery's increasingly restless chromatic style makes the tonality ambiguous. The music often shifts so quickly and abruptly that keys are rarely established, and he is swift to juxtapose sharp and flat keys. The first theme hovers in an unsettled combination of E and G minors and majors, the relationship at a third much favoured by Montgomery. The second theme wavers between A minor or major. When the first theme reappears at the end a third higher than at the start, the tonality remains ambiguous.

The second movement follows a similar path. There are two discernible themes [Examples 6.13 and 6.14] which share certain rhythmic characteristics, as do the two main themes in the first movement.

Again, the movement develops rhapsodically with particular emphasis on the broad second theme and the quaver–semiquaver–semiquaver rhythm which appears in both themes. To complete the movement, as in the first movement, the first theme but not the second is re-introduced. Tonally the movement is similar to the first, but at the arrival of the second theme Montgomery introduces the key signature of D flat major for most of the rest of the movement. This is an unnecessary if revealing device, as within five bars the music is again modulating freely.

**Example 6.13** *Concertino for String Orchestra*: **'Lento espressivo'**

**Example 6.14** *Concertino for String Orchestra*: **'Lento espressivo'**

The structure of the third movement also relies on three motifs, but this time the overall form is defined more conventionally. Here the opening predominantly semiquaver rhythm contrasts with the later rising triplet figure [Example 6.15], and the first part of the development section is an argument between these two ideas.

**Example 6.15** *Concertino for String Orchestra*: **'Lento espressivo'**

Later, another sweeping triplet figure [Example 6.16] is introduced and developed, often in imitation, over a marching and usually static bass. This time the recapitulation bears comparison with traditional sonata form: the semiquaver figure reappears on C sharp rather than on E (as at the beginning) but the passage which contains the triplet figure is repeated exactly as it was at the start of the movement. The coda is constructed from the semiquaver figure.

**Example 6.16** *Concertino for String Orchestra*: **'Vivace ed energico'**

Each movement, then, follows some type of ABA¹ pattern, with B developing material presented first in A, and A¹ restating some of the material from A. In conversation with his friend Geoffrey Bush, Montgomery was once struck by the notion that themes do not have to be developed in the manner of the Germanic tradition. This observation was a result of Bush's study of French and Russian music, and Montgomery should have drawn a similar conclusion from his admiration for the music of Delius. The *Concertino for String Orchestra* is evidence that this less formal treatment of material came naturally to Montgomery. Motifs and short themes lend themselves to the type of rhapsodic development he favours. Bush has drawn attention to the superficial similarity between the third movements of the work and John Ireland's *Concertino Pastorale* (1939). Although both movements open with a rapid single note figure, the progress thereafter of each shows their composers' difference of approach to structure. In Ireland's case the semiquaver rhythm continues without a break except for two solitary quavers for the entire movement. Montgomery soon leaves his motif behind and turns to new and contrasting material.

A closer look at many of the themes Montgomery uses in the *Concertino for String Orchestra* shows that in fact there is a cyclic link between many of them. The underlying melodic figure of a swooping rising phrase followed by descent can be seen in Examples 6.12, 6.13, 6.15, 6.16, 6.17 and 6.18, and Montgomery's habit of extending his themes by sequence only serves to underline this melodic tendency. Many of his themes in other works have this characteristic.

**Example 6.17** *Concertino for String Orchestra*: 'Vivace ed energico'

**Example 6.18** *Concertino for String Orchestra*: 'Vivace ed energico'

One or two other points need to be made about the work. Montgomery's use of tonality has already been mentioned. His use of free chromaticism is unconstrained here by any text. Because of his constantly changing tonalities, the harmonic swerves which are conspicuous in many of his vocal works do not stand out. Montgomery shows more harmonic daring than in previous works, and this was noted as a modern idiom by critics of the time. He was becoming particularly keen on the clash at the tone or semitone, whether between outer parts or within the harmony: sometimes this is over a static bass, as in *Christ's Birthday*, and at others it is within parts moving in parallel. Despite the ever-changing tonality, Montgomery still makes great use of static basses. The very start of the first movement and the central section of the third movement are examples of this. His use of the sequence is also much in evidence.

A last observation concerns Montgomery's use of rhythm. The *Concertino for String Orchestra* has a much greater feeling of rhythmic vitality than many of his pieces, particularly in the outer movements. This comes about through his changes of metre, with irregular bar lengths extending phrases, and through his contrasted figures. The struggle between the semiquaver figure and the later themes with their characteristic triplet figures which colours the whole of the final movement has been mentioned above, but the contrast in the first movement between the opening rhythmic figure [Example 6.10] and the more languid later themes [Examples 6.11 and 6.12] is just as important.

For a change *The Musical Times* was not completely won over after the first performance: the work 'left an impression of excellent writing coupled with an invention that had not quite hit upon the right ideas'.[29] *The Times* was slightly more encouraging: the work was 'skilfully constructed' and 'aims at saying something wholly new, and sometimes succeeds'.[30] Following a later performance, *Musical Opinion* accurately referred to the *Concertino for String Orchestra* as 'a graceful, flowing, three-movement work, well written, economical in notes and notable for a lyrical *lento expressivo* of imaginative warmth'.[31] This author believes it to be a fine work, one in which Montgomery plays to his strengths. Motifs are developed thoughtfully but without overstaying their welcome. The second movement, in particular, moves the listener with its thoroughly English mixture of pensive nostalgia.

Ruth Dyson, the pianist in the Wigmore Hall performance of *Christ's Birthday*, was responsible for the early performances of another work completed at this time. The *Suite in E minor* for piano, which remained unpublished, was not composed specifically for Dyson, but she played it first on a tour of Sweden in 1948 'where it was much liked'.[32] It was one of a number of Montgomery's works that were first performed at concerts given under the auspices of the Oxford Ladies' Music Society. These were organised and funded by Margaret Deneke, the German émigrée who had introduced Montgomery to Bush, and were held in her recital room at Norham Gardens. Like the Wigmore Hall concerts, they were further occasions when the music of both Bush and Montgomery was performed on the same bill (the latter referred to them in his diaries as 'Bushgomery' events). Regular soirees were held on Friday afternoons, social gatherings with an assortment of abilities, where original works could be given a first airing. 'Mr Montgomery, have you anything up your sleeve?' Deneke was heard to ask more than once.[33] On a later occasion, she delighted the assembled undergraduates as she played the piano by calling over

29    *The Musical Times*, January 1949
30    *The Times*, 11 December 1948
31    *Musical Opinion*, June 1951
32    Ruth Dyson to author, 4 March 1992
33    Colin Strang

their heads in her idiosyncratic English: 'Dr Watson,[34] will you come and turn me over?'[35] Before the Oxford performance of the *Suite* in 1949, Deneke had taken Dyson and her father, Bush and Montgomery for a grand lunch at an Oxford hotel. 'Miss Deneke was very vocal on the subject of Britten's "Let's make an Opera" which was new and which she had just seen. [...] She said little to my father and me, but remarked rather characteristically to us with a wave of the hand "I hope you don't mind if I talk to my friends." Geoffrey and Bruce must have been at least 30 years her junior at that time.'[36]

The *Suite for Piano* is notable for the signs of impressionistic colouring in its five movements (in 1946 Montgomery had written a work for piano entitled *Homage to Delius* which showed a command of the musical language of that composer), and for the fact that the last movement makes use of material that was apparently destined originally for the last movement of the *Concertino for String Orchestra*. Of her performance of the work at the Oxford Ladies' Music Society ('a smallish gathering usually but with some very august personages present – Ernest Walker[37] in his wheel chair and usually Dr Thomas (not yet Sir!) Armstrong'),[38] Dyson recalled one comment: 'When I reached the last bar of Bruce's work Thomas Armstrong's light but incisive voice came from the back of the auditorium; "WELL DONE Bruce!"'[39]

Another work to make its first appearance at a similar gathering was the *Concert Waltz for Two Pianos*, arranged by Montgomery specifically so that Bush and he could play it at Norham Gardens. This was in late 1949, but at a subsequent performance in February 1953 the audience was treated to it twice as a reward for having braved a snowstorm.[40] The waltz, published in 1952, was salvaged out of Montgomery's abandoned opera *Tailor (of Shrewsbury)* which he had begun to his own libretto in 1946 (in 1948 it was reported that Montgomery was 'working on an opera designed in the Wagner–Strauss tradition').[41] The surviving twenty or so pages of the vocal score share considerable musical similarities with the surviving 715 bars of the vocal score of *To Move the Passions*, an opera he started to write later to a libretto by Kingsley Amis. Although Montgomery was reported by Amis to have written about 15 minutes of the opera by April 1948 ('I only hope the bugger can compose; do you know?'),[42] this project also hit the buffers:

What he [Montgomery] failed to do, much to my own disappointment, was to write more than the first act (if as much) of a projected and fully planned grand opera to my libretto, *To Move the Passions* - the only libretto, I should guess, to have been written in the consonantal rhyme or chime Wilfred Owen used in poems of his like 'Strange Meeting'. It was to have been a costume piece set in the musical world of eighteenth-century London,

---

34    Sydney Watson (1903–1991), lecturer in Music at Christ Church
35    Colin Strang
36    Ruth Dyson to author, 20 March 1992
37    Ernest Walker (1870–1949), Hon. Fellow of Balliol College
38    Ruth Dyson to author, 4 March 1992
39    Ibid.
40    *Oxford Mail*, 9 February 1953
41    *London Musical Events*, October 1948
42    Amis to Larkin, 24 April 1948 [LKA]

with a plot about a decent middle-aged composer, a nasty pushy young composer, and the young ingénue they were both pursuing. Virtue and middle age were to have triumphed. Also featured were Three Critics, who sang in a stricter metre various platitudes about Nature and the poetical Imitation thereof derived from the course on Augustan literary theory I was giving in my lectures at Swansea at the time. Then, mysteriously, the project went cold, but the mystery was soon cleared up when Bruce revealed that he had 'had' to cannibalise the existing music for a film score that had been running late. (Not a *Carry On* film, I hope.)[43]

Amis' worst fears were quite conceivably realised. Given the similarity of musical material between the remnants of the two operas, it is worth noting that themes from the *Concert Waltz* appear in the score for *Carry On Constable* (1960) during a scene in which Constable Gorse (Charles Hawtrey) is riding a child's scooter. The grandness of the title of the *Concert Waltz* is certainly matched by the music. With its richness of harmony and flow of majestic harmonic and melodic ideas, this is a work that would grace the most opulent of occasions and settings. The flow of musical ideas stems almost entirely from Montgomery's penchant for harmonic sequences. This device dominates the work; the sequences are always chromatic, with the inevitable harmonic swerves, and with four hands at work Montgomery is able to indulge his predilection for a dense texture. *Musical Opinion*'s one criticism of this 'cleverly-written and melodious work' was 'that the thick chromatic harmonic texture is so unrelieved as to become rather cloying';[44] *The Musical Times* found the work 'nicely seasoned with romantic sentiment and rich chording'.[45] It is unusual in a work of this length to have six discernible themes, but here, because they are all so tightly sequentially bound, the work holds together in a seamless flow with interest carefully shared between the two players.

---

43    *Memoirs*, Kingsley Amis, p. 74
44    *Musical Opinion*, September 1952, p. 737
45    *The Musical Times*, March 1953, p. 123

# Chapter 7

# 'I still think it isn't half bad': Music 1951–1952

Montgomery's busy period continued with the first performance of his most ambitious work, *An Oxford Requiem*. It was commissioned by the Oxford Bach Choir to celebrate the Festival of Britain and performed with the London Symphony Orchestra under Thomas Armstrong in the Sheldonian Theatre, Oxford, on 22 May 1951. It was well received, with a particularly good notice from *The Times*:

> At a special Festival of Britain concert at the Sheldonian Theatre last night, Dr. Thomas Armstrong conducted the Oxford Bach Choir and the London Symphony Orchestra in the first performance of 'An Oxford Requiem' for chorus and orchestra by Bruce Montgomery, a young Oxford-nurtured musician whose work has already won him a London publisher and no mean reputation.
>
> Like that of Brahms, it is a protestant Requiem with its words taken from the psalms and the burial service, and even were there no inscription to the memory of a friend in the score, the music itself would betray that it was written under strong compulsion. It plays for only 30 minutes, but the imaginative flash which illumines each of the four movements burns all the brighter for this concentration. Alike in the piercing prayer for deliverance from the 'bitter pains of eternal death' (from the burial service) at the lowest ebb of grief in the third movement, and in the exultant climaxes of the second and fourth movements depicting the confident hope of the Christian believer, the music is as trenchant as it is moving. It is Montgomery's most considerable achievement to date; it confirms the suspicion that he is a composer with something of real significance to say.
>
> The choir [...] showed few signs of dismay at the Requiem's often exacting chromaticism.[1]

The reviewer from *Musical Opinion* made an interesting point about the effectiveness of Montgomery's chromaticism in performance:

> Mr. Montgomery's tendency to chromaticism is not so apparent in performance as it seems on paper, which means that he really has something of significance to write and that the means by which he achieves it do not matter.[2]

In terms of both duration and scale, *An Oxford Requiem* is Montgomery's largest published work. There are four movements, and the text, taken from the Psalms and the Burial Service, concentrates on the transitory nature of human life. The work is dedicated to the memory of Godfrey Sampson. There remains no documentary

---

1    *The Times*, 25 May 1951
2    *Musical Opinion*, July 1951, p. 525

evidence to reveal Montgomery's feelings on the death of his friend, but the music in the requiem is his most personal yet. His highly chromatic style is well-suited to conveying the anguish we must assume he felt. As in *Christ's Birthday*, he creates a genuine sense of atmosphere, particularly when his spare music reflects the emptiness of man's existence. This is particularly noticeable in the third movement, 'Man that is born of a woman', at the setting of the passage which ends 'deliver us not into the bitter pains of eternal death'; over a single sustained note in the orchestra the voices work initially in pairs in mostly open intervals, then together as the dissonance increases until 'pains' is pointed with a semitone clash a (compound) minor second. This is not the relatively cosy chromaticism of his earlier works but a direct and more developed response to the text. It is a continuation of the trend noted in *Christ's Birthday* for dissonances at the tone and semitone.

This use of dissonance is also shown at the very beginning, in the orchestral introduction to 'As for man, his days are as grass', the first movement. Over a pedal on B there is a series of dissonances, sometimes resolving, which builds up and concludes, immediately before the voices enter, with a sudden swerve to a chord of C minor. A similar shift happens at the start of *Christ's Birthday*. Within two beats there is a chord of E minor, the key suggested by the long dominant pedal. There is a similar occurrence at the start of the final movement: a broad melody ('Lord, thou hast been our refuge') sweeps over a rippling accompaniment until the swerve on 'one generation' [Example 7.1].

**Example 7.1** *An Oxford Requiem*: **'Lord, thou hast been our refuge'**

This time the harmonic device, in returning immediately towards the tonic of E major, follows the pattern of the swerves of Montgomery's earlier work. The whole work has a restless harmonic rhythm, often built over pedal points which serve to accentuate the dissonances. The third movement, 'Man that is born of a woman', is particularly rich in these effects. The quick rise and fall within motifs previously observed in the *Concertino for String Orchestra* is also evident in both first and second movements, particularly in passages of vocal imitation, and there is no reduction in his use of sequences to extend phrases [Example 7.2].

**Example 7.2** *An Oxford Requiem*: **'As for man, his days are as grass'**

Following one of these chromatic sequences ('a tale that is told', again in the first movement) Montgomery uses another of his favourite devices, a 7th chord, this time with an added 2nd, on which the tonality seems to rest for a moment after a lengthy passage of harmonic fluctuation [Example 7.3].

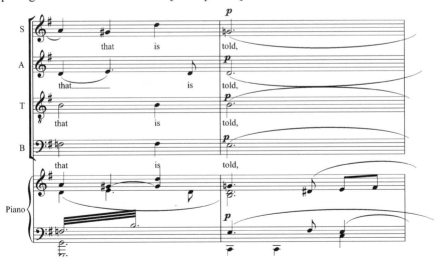

**Example 7.3** *An Oxford Requiem*: **'As for man, his days are as grass'**

The music grows more by the use of motifs and their development and sectional writing than by any clear-cut structure. The rhapsodic tendency noted in the *Concertino for String Orchestra*, another major work of his with extended movements, is also apparent here. On occasions ideas used at the start of a movement make a reappearance at the conclusion. At the end of 'As for man, his days are as grass', there is a reminder of the orchestral introduction as well as of another motif which appeared in the middle of the movement [Example 7.4].

The dirge-like orchestral figure which opens 'Man that is born of a woman' returns at the conclusion of that movement. The opening melody of the final movement [Example 7.1] is heard again towards the end of the whole work. Within each movement, however, the music tends to be sectional: an idea will be used, sometimes discarded thereafter or combined with another motif. The similarity of some of his motifs, with their quick rise and fall, as mentioned above, leads to a sense of unity. In the second movement ('But thou, O Lord, art my defender') a dotted motif is used in the orchestra [Example 7.5] to link together such passages.

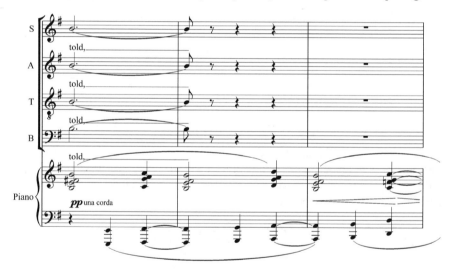

**Example 7.4 *An Oxford Requiem*: 'As for man, his days are as grass'**

Montgomery responds to the words in an intuitive rather than structured fashion, a habit he keeps under control more convincingly in small-scale pieces such as the songs than he does in the larger works. Montgomery's writing for voices is typical, with imitative entries commonplace [Example 7.2]. The personal element shows in his greater attention to the possibilities of the text. In the first movement he repeats the phrase 'so he flourisheth' three times, each time higher and louder over a strong underpinning bass, and orchestral murmurings highlight the phrase 'For the wind passeth over it'. The requiem as a whole exhibits a much greater sense of climax than many of Montgomery's works, with the second movement finishing in a rare blaze of triumph: 'In thy presence is the fulness of joy' builds up by constant repetition, and the setting of the final affirmative phrase 'and at the right hand there is pleasure for evermore' is made more impressive by the resolution to F major of a chord of E flat being delayed by a clash of cymbals on the strong beat. At the close of the whole work the orchestra has an imposing passage which leads into the final 'Amen': perhaps in homage to Sampson, the swooping melodic phrases and the rising chromatic upper line bring to mind Mahler and the late-Romantics, something of which the arch-Wagnerian dedicatee would surely have approved.

**Example 7.5** *An Oxford Requiem*: **'But thou, O Lord, art my defender'**

Three further smaller scale works appeared during this period. *To Phyllis*, a partsong for SATB and piano to words by Thomas Lodge (1558–1625) was published in 1950. Composed shortly before *An Oxford Requiem*, its relatively uncluttered textures are in sharp contrast to the larger scale pieces he was producing at the time. There is a charming simplicity about the vocal parts and their relationship with the piano in this essentially strophic setting. Many of the same comments are true of *Go, Lovely Rose*, a two part song with piano accompaniment which was published a year later. To words by Edmund Waller (1606–1687), the latter part of the central verse departs from the strophic setting in a passage whose tonal shifts bring to mind the dreamy atmosphere of *Serenade to Music* by Vaughan Williams (1938). An unidentified cutting in Montgomery's papers gives a further view: 'Its composer has the rare gift (today) of being able to write a melody and harmonies which verge on the sentimental yet, by a touch of innate good taste which marks the true artist's work, and sufficient subtlety to infuse technical skills with inner meaning, are redeemed from any hint of banality.'[3] *To Music*, a part-song for five male voices with words by Robert Herrick (1591–1674), was published in 1952. Composed for, and first performed by, the City Glee Club, it is hard to imagine that this is by the same composer as the previous two works. In place of the sweepingly melodious strophic

---

3    Unidentified cutting in Montgomery's papers, GB-Ob. MS. Eng. C. 3953

settings we have a curtly episodic through-composed piece which reacts vividly to the text in a sometimes quite harsh fashion. 'Those who like to explore mild shocks may enjoy the rather strained harmonies' was the verdict of *The Musical Times*.[4] Novello obviously liked it; when Montgomery sent the work for copies to be made for the first performance, it was accepted for publication before he had officially submitted it in the expectation that he would do so in due course.

The good impression Montgomery was making on the musical world was rising by the day, and his last major choral work, *Venus' Praise*, composed shortly after *An Oxford Requiem*, was soon accepted by Novello. The publisher asked Montgomery about the possibility of altering the title: 'It's all the fault of that ___ apostrophe. No one likes it, even after he has found out what it means.'[5] The title remained, even after a meeting. *Venus' Praise* is a setting of seven sixteenth- and seventeenth-century poems for chorus and string orchestra. It is Montgomery's most assured work; the deep feeling clearly expressed in *An Oxford Requiem* is developed in a more controlled manner. The seven settings show Montgomery at his best: he is able, in relatively short choral movements, to respond to the texts without the problem of his cloying harmonic style overstaying its welcome (towards the end of his life Montgomery claimed that *Venus' Praise* was written when he 'was young and romantic' and was 'like being ducked repeatedly in molasses').[6] Although the music is no less chromatic, it is more controlled both harmonically and structurally and contains his most sincerely felt work. It is clearly the most effective of his larger works, and it represents a peak past which it appears he was unable to progress, for a variety of reasons as we shall see later.

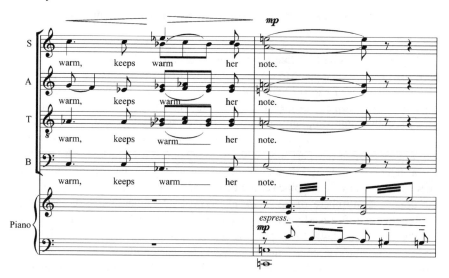

**Example 7.6 *Venus' Praise*: 'Ask me no more where Jove bestows'**

4    *The Musical Times*, May 1953, p. 219

5    Novello to RBM, 4 April 1951

6    RBM to David Shapland, 20 March 1976

'Ask me no more where Jove bestows' opens with a rising figure in the strings over a pedal which, typically, swerves for a bar or so before returning to the tonic of C major for the entry of the chorus. The song is through-composed until the second half of the third and last stanza where Montgomery brings back the music of the second half of the first stanza, an imposing rising passage which, despite its chromaticism, returns without artifice to the tonic at the end of both stanzas. A fingerprint progression of Montgomery's finishes each of the three stanzas: 7th chords on A flat move to C major, showing again his liking for the relationship of a third (major or minor) [Example 7.6].

The second half of the second stanza ('For in your sweet dividing throat') begins with vocal imitation, and this leads to a striking dissonance on 'She winters' as the fate of the nightingale is considered [Example 7.7].

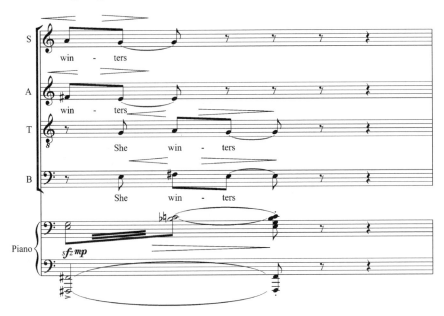

**Example 7.7** *Venus' Praise*: **'Ask me no more where Jove bestows'**

Reviewers were impressed by the depths of feeling Montgomery was able to produce in slow movements, and this is probably his most successful of that type in any choral work.

'Love for such a cherry lip' is more sprightly, but equally effective. Montgomery makes much of the refrain of both stanzas ('But they shall not so'), using one of the chromatic sequences that are such a feature of his work [Example 7.8].

This refrain (C) also includes vocal imitation ('None but I'). The first stanza ends in the dominant (E major), whereupon the opening string symphony (A) is repeated in that key. The second stanza opens in the dominant, set to different music (D): the refrain is repeated, also transposed, and it works back to the tonic, to conclude the movement with the opening symphony and a structure of ABCA$^1$DC$^1$A.

**Example 7.8** *Venus' Praise*: **'Love for such a cherry lip'**

'Whenas the rye reach to the chin' is a vigorous through-composed number with characteristic off-beat and cross-beat rhythms. Word painting is prominent: the vitality of the opening phrase ('chop-cherry, chop-cherry' is contrasted with the unresolved swooning dissonances of 'Strawberries swimming in the cream'. Towards the conclusion, the yearning sequence on the repeated 'She could not live a maid' is very effective.

'More white than whitest lilies far' is a through-composed setting. The rising choral phrases to the opening words are echoed in the course of the movement in string interludes, and this gives cohesion to the harmonic explorations. The strings add to the descriptive music: 'Or moonlight tinselling the streams' is signalled by a rapid violin scale rising to the heavens.

'Love is a sickness full of woes' is a strophic setting with some unusual modifications. The second stanza begins, as does the first, in the tonic of F sharp minor but soon modulates to repeat much of the music a tone higher. Almost as soon as the refrain is reached ('More we enjoy it, more it dies'), the music returns to the tonic and repeats the material of the first stanza, with a slightly extended last phrase to finish the movement. Rhythmically the setting is well contrasted. It opens with a vibrant figure whose accents realign two bars of 2/2 into 3 bars of 3/4. Off-beat rhythms (the string figure before 'A plant that with most cutting grows' brings to mind 'Adam lay ybounden' from *Christ's Birthday*) are set alongside passages of straight crotchets ('All remedies refusing', for example). The repeated drooping phrase for 'Heigh ho' with its attendant suspensions in the refrain does much for the ironic mood of the setting. The movement finishes with another of Montgomery's fingerprints: a quadruple appoggiatura which is held for some time before resolving on to a short final chord [Example 7.9].

'Weep you no more, sad fountains' is another example of Montgomery's expressiveness in slow movements. The opening choral phrase is again anchored by a pedal, and the dense chromatic style which the composer uses to set this poem takes until the start of the second stanza before it gives way to a relaxing passage in C major ('Sleep is a reconciling'). Montgomery responds directly to the text: the dynamic climax of each of the two stanzas is reached with mention of the sun, and in each case the melodic line rises to the climax. The movement has a satisfying structure: the words of the last four lines of each stanza are broadly similar and Montgomery sets them to similar music (the earlier part of each stanza is set to new material); and the short sliding string interlude between the stanzas is repeated, transposed, at the conclusion.

'Come, be my valentine!' is mostly through-composed, with only the very start of the third and final stanza using the same material as the start of the first stanza. Montgomery enjoys the possibilities of setting this exuberant text in 6/8 time, with plenty of skipping dotted and cross rhythms. The music contains many of his favourite devices: a very fast harmonic rhythm and plenty of sequences are the most prominent. Whereas the first and third stanzas are set without instrumental interludes, the central stanza contrasts by having frequent short passages for the strings. Before the last stanza, the strings also have, by the standards of the whole work, a quite lengthy symphony which ends with part of the shorter string passage which opened the movement. The last stanza is built on three of Montgomery's fingerprints: vocal imitation, sequences, and his love of repeating phrases or words to give emphasis. He sets the penultimate line 'and that shall be thy stock' twice, and to end he repeats 'Come' (from 'Come, be my valentine!') a further five times to bring the whole work to a suitably imploring conclusion.

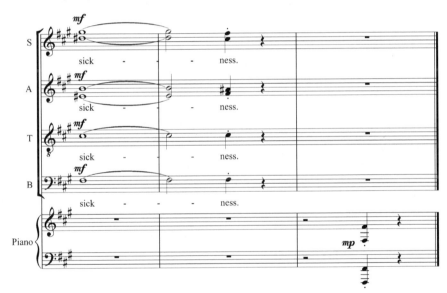

**Example 7.9** *Venus' Praise*: **'Love is a sickness full of woes'**

The first performance was in April 1951 when Montgomery and Geoffrey Bush again hired the Wigmore Hall, this time for a concert of music connected with spring which included the latter's *Summer Serenade* as well as *Venus' Praise*:

Both were settings of old English poems, but otherwise they had little in common. Bush's idiom is the more spontaneously conceived and immediate in its appeal, Montgomery's the more searching; Bush succeeds in scherzo-like mood, while the best of Montgomery emerges in a slow movement; in short, whereas Bush's fancy is light and effortless, Montgomery can touch deeper springs of feeling. The conductor, Mr. Trevor Harvey, successfully concealed his own predilections, and brought his customary sympathy, integrity, and vigour to bear equally on the two works. The strings of his newly-formed London Classical Orchestra, however, like the singers of the South London Bach Society, found 'Venus' Praise' considerably the harder to bring off [...][7]

Montgomery shared these reservations about the choir: 'The concert was marred by a decidedly inadequate choir', he wrote to his sister Sheila, 'but G. and I managed to enjoy it in spite of that. We collected a nice notice from The Times and a thoroughly nasty one from The Manchester Guardian which said our music was far too old-fashioned to be any good. We're not unduly cast down, however. There was quite a fair-sized audience, which seemed to like it all.'[8]

Much was made in the press of the way Bush and Montgomery appeared to be working in tandem, although their relative merits were assessed rather differently:

If the two composers could cooperate in a single composition, as they have been known to do in the writing of detective fiction, what excellent music would result. For Bush, whose innate, facile musicianship would enable him to dissolve even a railway timetable into song, knows the secret of the scintillating vocal scherzo, while Montgomery, of more searching mind, has much of real worth to say in a slow movement.[9]

The comment in *Musical Opinion* concentrated less on their differences, but made its point more aggressively:

We may well wonder why Messrs. Bush and Montgomery appear to seek each other's company in programmes and which of them, as it were, sets the pace: if one writes a Christmas Cantata, the other writes a similar work; if Bush writes a string Divertimento, Montgomery responds with a Concerto; one song cycle follows another, and so on. Unless they are going to join forces *a la* Tin Pan Alley, it would surely be artistically saner and healthier if each were to develop his own individuality along entirely separate paths? One report, however, avers that they collaborate in the writing of detective fiction, so perhaps their ultimate aim is to become the first Siamese twins of serious music.[10]

The references to their writing detective fiction together came as a result of 'Who Killed Baker?', a short story on which the pair had collaborated in 1950. It was published at the time in the *Evening Standard* and appeared subsequently in *Fen Country*. Montgomery and Bush were members of The Carr Club, as Montgomery always called it, or The Carr Society, as it was properly titled. This was a group of four friends and had been formed during a session in a public house near Oxford in December 1944. Inspired by John Dickson Carr's *Appointment with Fear* radio plays, it met irregularly and informally to tell detective stories for which solutions had to be proposed by the members. After Montgomery joined the Detection Club,

7      *The Musical Times,* June 1951, pp. 276–277

8      RBM to Sheila Rossiter, 30 April 1951 (copy in author's collection)

9      *The Times*, 27 April 1951

10     *Musical Opinion,* June 1951

he and Carr became drinking partners and he often stayed overnight with the Carrs at their house in Hampstead.[11] The members of The Carr Club were delighted when Montgomery persuaded Carr to attend one of the meetings. Carr's widow recalled that her husband received 'a mysterious letter (penned by Crispin) inviting him to face danger, and daring him to go by train to the meeting at the King's Arms pub in the village of Ockley, Surrey. He was delighted to accept.'[12] Carr was 'exceedingly friendly, unpretentious, convivial – he seemed to enter fully into the spirit of the occasion, making an attentive listener to the contributions of others.'[13]

Other meetings took place on Dartmoor, near to Montgomery's home, when the members of the club would take a cottage on the Hartland Estate. Montgomery outlined the plot of *Love Lies Bleeding* on one of these occasions. After their first Wigmore Hall concert, Bush, Montgomery and the other members of the Carr Club retreated to a hotel in Burnham on Crouch where they spent a riotous weekend telling stories. Bush recalled that the bill was something like Falstaff's: accommodation £5, drink £25.[14] After another meeting, Montgomery was hard pressed for ideas for a series of short stories he was writing for the *Evening Standard*, and Bush offered him the storyline of a tale he had told to the club. As in their compositional styles so carefully delineated by *The Times* after their most recent Wigmore Hall concert, there was a clear division of labour in 'Who Killed Baker?': the story was by Bush, and the writing was by Edmund Crispin. It has a clever plot and is told in Crispin's most elegant and amusing style.[15]

Montgomery also composed two pieces for military band during this period. Through meetings at the International Musicians' Association [IMA] he had become acquainted with Lieutenant C.H. ('Jiggs') Jaeger, the conductor of the Band of the Irish Guards. *Heroic March* and *Flourish for a Crowning*, a slightly misleading title for what is a relatively substantial piece, were both commissioned, the latter for the coronation of Elizabeth II. Both received broadcast performances. Given Montgomery's lack of familiarity with military bands, Jaeger himself scored *Heroic March*. Score and parts do not appear to have survived, and the only source of the work is a 78 r.p.m. recording held in Montgomery's papers. By the time Montgomery composed the *Flourish* in 1952 he felt able to orchestrate it himself. It was good practice, because a few years later he composed his score for the film *Carry On Sergeant* entirely for military band.

Two other works deserve a mention. *Amberley Hall*, a one-act ballad opera for three characters, piano and string quartet to a libretto by Kingsley Amis, was commissioned by the Arts' Council and scheduled to be performed at the Festival of Britain by Intimate Opera in Notting Hill Gate in the summer of 1951. Various magazines, including *Vogue*, announced as much, but the work appears never to have reached a performable condition despite Amis' recollections:

---

11    Douglas Greene
12    *John Dickson Carr*, Greene, p. 307
13    Ibid., quoting Geoffrey Bush
14    Geoffrey Bush
15    Ibid.

In fact we actually completed, as far as I could tell, a one-act chamber opera to be called *Amberley Hall*, another costume piece. There were only three characters, a lady, her husband and her aspiring lover. It had one dramatic twist I still think was jolly clever, whereby the lover wants to get caught somewhere near getting his way and the husband doesn't want to know, so the latter stands impassively in front of the necessary screen while the lover thumps and clumps away behind it. It was never performed that I heard of.[16]

Letters from Amis reveal the troubled gestation of the opera. 'We had a nice time with Bruce', he wrote to Philip Larkin, 'who gave us even more food and drink than usual. We fudged out an opera plot, which seems quite adequate, thought it'll have to be done rather quickly. He says we ought to make £20 each at the worst. [...] We arranged a plot involving 5 characters, and quite neatly tied up it was. Crippen[17] now postcards me to the effect that the arts council want 4 characters.'[18] More changes happened a month later: 'I heard from Bruce by the way that the Farts Council want 3 singers now, not 4 and not 5. He suggests I go to London to help talk things over. [...] He says he is 'half-inclined to cry off' [...] I'm not.'[19] A further six months later there were more problems:

the most noteworthy event of my stay in Oxford was being told by Bruce that the men have thanked us very much for that singing thing [...] but they can't do it, you see, because there's not enough singing in it, do you see, and they thought there would be more of that, you see, and 'we're not actors, you know' [...] none of it was my fault. The point was that B. had had too little time to set all the words BECAUSE HE WAS WRITING FLITHY FLIM [sic] SCORES AND STING-KING STORIES FOR THE POPULAR PRESS, and asked them if we could do a ballad opera. They said yes, because they thought a ballad opera meant song then six lines of conventional dialogue then duet then eight lines of c.d. then song, do you see. Our idea was the same, except that we read '150' for 'six' and '200' for 'eight'. They didn't like that. At least I hope that's what it was and not that they thought my dialogue too bad to do. Next year perhaps we shall re-do it with singing all through but I'm still despondent.[20]

Montgomery agreed that the work had been turned from 'an opera with spoken dialogue' into 'a play with songs'.[21]

A few years later, when interest was revived by an opera company in New York, Montgomery claimed that the opera, 'a mildly scandalous burlesque set in England in the 18th century',[22] was two-thirds complete with three numbers out of eight yet to be completed. It had been 'put aside owing to the exigencies of earning a living'.[23] He also claimed that the libretto required 'drastic pruning' as it was 'deliberately written over-length'.[24] The work was never completed, and it was the third of Montgomery's

---

16    *Memoirs*, Amis, p. 74
17    Amis' name for Montgomery, a pun on his pseudonym Crispin
18    Amis to Larkin, 17 December 1950 [LKA]
19    Ibid., 8 January 1951 [LKA]
20    Ibid., 12 June 1951 [LKA]
21    RBM to Mr Austin, 10 May 1951
22    RBM to Richard Flusser, 21 December 1959
23    Ibid.
24    Ibid.

attempts at opera to end inconclusively. The fourth was more successful. Although not published until 1962, *John Barleycorn* was composed almost ten years earlier. The history of its gestation makes an interesting tale:

> In 1962 Novellos belatedly published Bruce's *John Barleycorn*, an elaborate opera with spoken dialogue intended for amateur performance. This – like my own *The Blind Beggar's Daughter* (1952) – was the consequence of getting mixed up in the machinery of Dr Sydney Northcote. [...] Most of Sydney's working life was given over to the enthusiastic promotion of amateur music-making, and in the course of this he had devised a wonderfully inexpensive method of widening the repertoire of contemporary operas suitable for performance by young people. First, a competition for librettists was held; the prize for the six winners was a promise that their libretti would be set by a professional composer. Six composers were then commissioned; as a commissioning fee they were each supplied with a free libretto. This scheme – conceived in a flash of pure genius – was thirty years ahead of its time; today it would be an answer to prayer for a government which believes that The Arts Should Support Themselves And Not Be A Drain On the Taxpayer.[25]

The competition was organised by the advisory committee of the National Council for Social Service, and the resultant works were intended for use in schools. *John Barleycorn*, like *Amberley Hall*, is a ballad opera which for publication Novello wanted suitable for 'higher grade schools [...] as well as amateur societies'.[26] The work had been turned down by Oxford University Press in 1958 on the grounds that short operettas for schools were not a paying proposition.[27] Novello had also originally rejected the work before having a change of mind. The libretto was written by Mary Fairclough, an artist and author of children's books from Bristol. The west country setting of the action appealed to Montgomery, and the libretto gave him plenty of scope to introduce various musical styles into the opera, as Elizabeth Poston noted in her review:

> *John Barleycorn*, a Ballad Opera in 3 acts (8s 6d) with libretto by Mary Fairclough and music by Bruce Montgomery, is scored for a moderate orchestra; alternatively, it can be performed with horn, percussion and string quintet or string orchestra and piano; or with one piano, or two. The voices cover the full range, and the chief tenor parts need a more experienced singer. The rest of a biggish cast is well designed to give scope to all, including those who can't really sing, and the chorus does not exceed fairly unexacting 4-pt.
>
> The plot is an original affair of English harvest and symbolical and fantastic corn characters, of whom the Three Girls are quite an invention, providing two of them with an opportunity for disc-crazy teenagers to get their favourite styles out of their systems. In general, I find the conception of the opera of more interest than most of the music, though this is always adequate. The work's strength is in the variety it offers, and in some exciting writing for percussion (piano included) which will give young school players a splendid chance. Its weakness in production, I suspect, will be the Mummerset required of the farm characters. The dances should be highly effective, and the whole is out of the ordinary.[28]

---

25    *An Unsentimental Education*, Bush, pp. 21–22
26    Novello to RBM, 8 March 1962
27    Oxford University Press to RBM, 2 November 1958
28    *The Musical Times*, November 1962, p. 782

There is a wide variety of basic musical styles within the opera. For three of the thirteen numbers Montgomery uses traditional tunes. These he generally treats diatonically, although the harmonic swerve is occasionally brought into the accompaniment. For a further number ('9: Old Uncle Tom Cobley') Montgomery wrote his own melody in the style of a traditional tune. Omitting short sections, three main numbers remain. '5: The Three Hungry Girls' and '11: The Three Girls' are quite closely linked musically, the character of each of the girls (the same three appear in each movement) being delineated by the style in which they are intended to sing. The one who stands out is the Black Girl, whose music is a mixture of blues and spirituals, a style in which Montgomery seems quite at home. '5: The Three Hungry Girls' begins with a typical Montgomery device, a rising and falling phrase which is treated in imitation [Example 7.10]. This motif appears frequently in the course of the opera.

**Example 7.10** *John Barleycorn*: **'The Three Hungry Girls'**

The major number is '7: The Corn-Dance'. It is one of the longest, and certainly the most varied, of any single movement Montgomery composed. As the opera was intended for performance in schools, it is appropriate that plenty of scope is given here for percussion instruments to be used, and the number opens in vigorous fashion. When John Barleycorn begins to sing, the style is immediately familiar. Sequence-like figures are abundant [Example 7.11] and intricate chromatic suspensions are frequent between the vocal line and accompaniment.

The many characters are given striking material, and the conflict between the Corn-children and the Corn-maidens on one side and the Wind-serpent and Flood-serpent on the other is dramatic and musically convincing. Attention has previously been drawn to Montgomery's penchant for setting texts from the seventeenth century, not infrequently of a religious nature. Here for once he has a contemporary and secular libretto which demands rapid changes of mood, and he sets it with relish. Motifs are worked into the drama and there is a genuine sense of climax. Towards the end of 'The Corn-Dance', John Barleycorn sings a passage in which Montgomery shows that, given the appropriate text, he is capable of writing in a wistful romantic manner [Example 7.12].

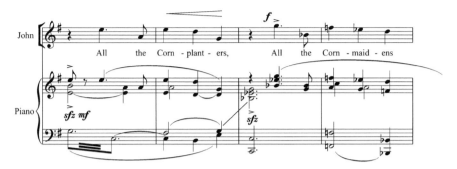

**Example 7.11 *John Barleycorn*: 'The Corn-Dance'**

Given Montgomery's interest in both opera and drama from his Amersham and Oxford days (*The Case of the Gilded Fly* and *Swan Song* are two of his novels which deal with such subjects, and if it had not been for Sir George Dyson he might well have become drama organiser for the Carnegie Trust in 1946), it is unfortunate that he completed only one of his attempts at a stage work. *John Barleycorn*, even in its relatively restricted scope, shows that the marriage of drama and music was much to his liking. In one of the few comments that survive on his own musical work, Montgomery told his librettist: 'I still think it [*John Barleycorn*] isn't half bad.'[29] Despite this view, the work did not receive its premiere until 1968 at Wellsway County Secondary School in Keynsham, Bristol, near Fairclough's home. She and Montgomery attended the performance, the former hinting afterwards that it left something to be desired: 'They really did do well, those kids, given the circumstances and the ____ pianist.'[30]

Although *Venus' Praise* was the last of his major choral works to be published, Montgomery did compose one more. Written for the Glasgow Choral Union (whose conductor, Charles Cleall, was an old friend), *The Century's Crown* was scored for chorus and orchestra to a text by Kingsley Amis. When Montgomery, an ardent conservative and monarchist, approached Amis to write the poem, he found that his friend did not have entirely the right political views to approach a work that was intended to celebrate the forthcoming coronation:

> What will be hardest I think is the 'personal stuff about E[lizabeth]', because the kind of personal stuff that leaps to my mind about her isn't quite the sort of stuff that would be appropriate to public, or even to any, delivery. Still, something will of course be fudged up.[31]

---

29    RBM to Mary Fairclough, 22 February 1962
30    Mary Fairclough to RBM, 8 August 1968
31    Amis to RBM, 23 October 1952

**Example 7.12** *John Barleycorn*: **'The Corn-Dance'**

Amis had some reservations about his poem. He hoped that it would stand as a poem in print as well as being sung or on a concert programme. 'I console myself', he told Montgomery, 'by thinking you wouldn't set it if it were a positively bad poem.'[32] The last line of the poem ('Certitude, glory, peace, the century's crown', a list of hopes for the new reign) prompted letters between Amis and Montgomery, culminating in the former giving his advice on the musical setting:

> iv) the Century's Crown. This is an example of 'poetic ambiguity'; the last line suggests
> a) four different things arranged in ascending order of importance; b) three things summed
> up as together being equivalent to the century's crown; c) certitude and glory, and peace-
> which-is-the-century's-crown. The 'main meaning' is that most naturally suggested by the

---

32     Amis to RBM, 2 December 1952

construction, viz. meaning a). I suggest therefore a grouping something like Certitude-woomp-woomp-bash-bash-glory-woomp-woomp-bash-bash-BASH-peace-woomp-woomp-bash-bash-BASH-BASH-the century's crown. Okay old man? Title? Music for the Queen or Bum bum bum would be nice, too.[33]

The work was first performed with the Scottish National Orchestra in St Andrew's Halls, Glasgow, on 3 June 1953 in a concert that also included the second concert performance of Walton's *Coronation Te Deum*. Charles Cleall admired *The Century's Crown*:

> The work lasted about fifteen minutes, and was beautiful: colourful; romantic; highly effective, and superbly orchestrated. Glasgow Choral Union loved it, and sang it with elan; and The Scottish National Orchestra liked it so much that, the score not having arrived in time for the orchestral rehearsal, they meekly followed my direction in both orchestral and choral rehearsals and the performance from memory of the vocal score alone (not that I told them that: the vocal score was well cued orchestrally), and played it with bravura. The audience revelled in it; and it got a stinging dismissal from the critics, who seemed totally unable to realize its perfect suitability for a concert in honour of the newly-crowned Sovereign.[34]

By no means all the critics were as negative as 'M.B.' in the *Glasgow Herald*: 'It is an undistinguished and uninspired work with an irritatingly indiscriminate use of the percussion at the beginning – and seems to have little to commend it.'[35] Don Whyte, in the *Scottish Daily Express*, called it 'a tuneful panegyric [...] The voices sung of heraldry, the orchestra lingers in a rich sunset of solo violin and cor anglais. Delius, one feels, is never far from the composer's thoughts.'[36] One or two made the point that they would have liked to have judged the work after a better performance. Although Amis was not present, giving as excuse 'money, and the thought of travelling in Coronation week',[37] Montgomery had a small team of supporters in tow, including his mother and father, as Philip Larkin reported:

> Tuesday we (Colin [Strang], Bruce & I) spent mainly in the Central Hotel: we listened to some of the [Coronation] service on a portable in Bruce's room, then descended to the American bar. About twenty to one a porter or waiter came in, and said 'She's crowned', so we had champagne, & drank a silent toast, or at least I did: the others just drank. About 2.30 we started lunch, wch ended at a qr to 4, & we then returned to Bruce's room to sleep.[38]

When it came to the performance, which he just managed to catch before boarding his boat to Belfast, Larkin followed the example of the *Glasgow Herald* in drawing attention to Montgomery's use of percussion:

---

33    Ibid.

34    Charles Cleall to author, 3 January 1989

35    *Glasgow Herald*, 4 June 1953

36    *Scottish Daily Express*, 4 June 1953

37    Amis to Larkin, 26 May 1953 [LKA]

38    Larkin to Winifred Arnott, 3 June 1953, [SLPL]

Tonight [...] I just managed to hear Bruce's *Ode* at the St Andrew's Hall, leaving as he was struggling onto the platform to take a bow, or many bows: gosh! what a racket he does like making with the loud cymbals, and he had the choir yelling its head off, or heads, but it was certainly thrilling & I must write & tell him so.[39]

Much as Charles Cleall had enjoyed the performance, he found afterwards that Montgomery's love of conviviality had not diminished:

Bruce had asked that younger members of the Choral Union attend a party in their honour after the performance: a happy occasion, marred for me only by the fact that, unknown to me, every time I looked away from my tonic water, Bruce laced it with gin; so that I ended the evening by following my door-key round with stupefaction as Mary's aunt (with whom I stayed during my first year in Glasgow) opened the door at the very moment that I began to insert my key. Mary's aunt did not notice the key (which was never seen again), but did notice my condition, and commented on it as though I were wholly culpable; despite the fact that I was unaware of having taken alcohol.[40]

---

39     Ibid.
40     Charles Cleall to author, 3 January 1989

## Chapter 8

# 'The home of lost corpses': Novels 1947–1948

After the success of his first three novels, Gollancz awarded Montgomery another three-book contract. The first in this series, *Swan Song*, was published in 1947, keeping up his record of one novel a year. The notices were the customary mixture. The *New Statesman* referred to its 'rollicking badinage', mentioning in particular that the methods of murder 'are a wild contraption, reminding us of Mr Dickson Carr at his worst'.[1] The *Daily Express* echoed many of the comments about previous novels: '*Swan Song* is a good novel first, a puzzle-solver second.'[2] The most positive review appeared in the *Daily Telegraph*: '*Swan Song* will establish Mr Crispin's reputation in this class of fiction. He is witty as well as intelligent.'[3]

The story is again set in Oxford, and revolves around the relationships contained in a visiting opera company. The setting gives Montgomery free range to indulge his musical interests. The novel opens with a scathing attack on singers:

> There are few creatures more stupid than the average singer. It would appear that the fractional adjustment of larynx, glottis and sinuses required in the production of beautiful sounds must almost invariably be accompanied – so perverse are the habits of Providence – by the witlessness of a barnyard fowl.[4]

The opera being produced is Wagner's *Die Meistersinger*, and Montgomery goes to town with the opera, its composer and their wider implications. As we have seen, Montgomery experienced the rise of Nazism at first hand during his trip to Germany in 1937, and the relevance of the many passages in the novel which deal with the alleged links between Wagner, Hitler and Nazism was increased by being published so soon after the end of the war. The leading tenor of the company, Adam Langley, gives a homily about Wagner and Nazism:

> 'It's a highbrow axiom,' Adam explained, 'that Wagner was responsible for the rise of Nazism. If you want to be in the fashion you must refer darkly to the evil workings of the Ring in the Teutonic mentality – though as the whole cycle of operas is devoted to showing that even the gods can't break an agreement without bringing the whole universe

1    *New Statesman*, 8 November 1947
2    *Daily Express*, 7 February 1948
3    *Daily Telegraph*, 15 August 1947
4    *Swan Song*, Chapter 1

crashing about their ears, I've never been able to see what possible encouragement Hitler can have got out of it.'[5]

The producer of the opera is Karl Wolzogen, a Wagner-adoring German-Jew whose pidgin-English is liberally littered with German phrases. He has a more intimate experience of the problem:

> When the Nazis came I was too old for their ideas, and I hated that such fools should worship the *Meister*. I had preferred that they banned his performances. So I worked here, and then there was the war, and fools said: 'Because Hitler is fond of Wagner we will not have Wagner in England'. Hitler was also fond of your Edgar Wallace, with his stories of violence, but no one said that they were not to be read.[6]

In a passage of unusual seriousness (and also topicality) for Montgomery, a sad portrait of the producer and the conditions he left behind in Germany is painted. For its rarity value in Montgomery's novels, it is worth quoting at length:

> Karl Wolzogen climbed on to a bus at Carfax which took him to Headington. From there he walked towards Wheatley – a small, thin, stooping figure, trudging along with his hands thrust for warmth into the pockets of a disreputable overcoat. He had had that overcoat for so long that he had completely forgotten when and where it had been bought. Somewhere in Germany or Austria, certainly. He paused to examine the grease-stained tab sewn inside one of the cuffs. Friedrich Jensen, Wettinerstrasse 83D, Dresden. He remembered now – remembered, too, that there had been a girl who lived in the Wettinerstrasse, a dark girl, perhaps a *nachgedunkelte Schrumpfgermane*, or perhaps with Jewish blood. In the latter case, what would have happened to her? She had had no use for opera. '*Das alles ist altmodisch*,' she had said. But he was old-fashioned too. As he grew older he lived more and more in the past. It meant that the end was not far off, and he was sufficiently satiated with living to be indifferent. Except perhaps for the loneliness which had come as a reward for his exclusive devotion to music, the world had given him only what he desired of it. He had reason enough to be content.
>
> A passing labourer wished him good afternoon, and glanced at him with quick, sharp curiosity when he replied. They distrust us, he thought. They distrust the Germans, and one can't blame them. But they don't realize that we distrust them, too. Dresden in ruins ... The opera-house gone: no longer any refuge for the shades of Weber, Wagner and Strauss. But Strauss was alive. He was at Garmisch. He had had an operation. Perhaps he would welcome a visit from someone with the same background, the same memories, as himself ... Were there still pigeons on the *Brühlsche Terrasse*? The long, thick black poles at the corners of the Post Platz, each surmounted with its tiny gold swastika, would have been taken down. No loss ... Hot chocolate in a restaurant in the Neu Markt, and Frieda listening in insolent silence while he talked of the opera. One evening she had admitted him to her bed. He had been clumsy, it had been a failure, but that hardly mattered now, any more than three years of near-starvation during the slump mattered. He would have enough to eat until he died ... [7]

---

5    Ibid., Chapter 3
6    Ibid., Chapter 18
7    Ibid., Chapter 21

Fen also talks of Nazism, in connection with his qualms about the ethics of pursuing the murderer of an unappealing character (in *The Case of the Gilded Fly* he expresses similar doubts as to whether he should present the police with the evidence confirming that the death of the unpleasant Yseut Haskell was murder and not, as the authorities believe, suicide):

> But none of us has the right to assess the value of a human existence. All must be held valuable, or none. [...] And the evil of Nazism lay precisely in this, that a group of men began to differentiate between the value of their fellow-beings, and to act on their conclusions. It isn't a habit which I, for one, would like to encourage.[8]

Montgomery also allows Fen to speak more generally about Wagner and art:

> 'As Puccini said, we're all mandoline-twangers in comparison with Wagner. *Pace* W.J. Turner.'
>
> 'W.J. Turner,' said Fen dreamily, 'thinks *The Flying Dutchman* is Wagner's best opera.' He made trumpeting noises, vaguely reminiscent of the overture to that work. 'But as for *Meistersinger* – apart from *Henry IV* it's the only thing I know which convinces one of the essential nobility of *man*; as opposed to *Macbeth* and the Ninth Symphony, which are really about the gods.'[9]

There is a particular episode in *Swan Song* which shows Montgomery's breadth of reading, and it was one that caused the Gollancz libel lawyer some concern. In the bar before the first performance of *Die Meistersinger*, a group of 'Young Intellectuals' are discussing the work:

> 'Cecil Gray says, you remember, that it's [Meistersinger] a great hymn to Germany's achievement in art and war.'
>
> 'There's only one mention of war in it,' said the dark-haired girl, ' and that's where Sachs says at the end that if Germany's ever defeated her art won't recover from it.'
>
> They gazed at her with great dislike.
>
> 'Surely, Anthea, you're not maintaining that you know more about Wagner than Cecil Gray does?'
>
> 'Yes,' said the dark-haired girl simply, 'I am. But of course if you interpret Sachs' remark as a great hymn to German achievements in war, you're capable of believing anything.'[10]

The lawyer claimed that this passage could hold Gray, a rather combative music critic, up to ridicule and contempt, and Montgomery was asked for his justification. As always, he was ready for some philosophical jousting:

> The Cecil Gray remark (which I've slightly paraphrased but not misrepresented) comes from his <u>History of Music</u> (Kegan Paul, 1944), p. 204:

---

8    Ibid., Chapter 18
9    Ibid., Chapter 14
10   Ibid., Chapter 22

In his (Wagner's) <u>Meistersinger</u>, which is primarily a glorification of German civilisation and a hymn in celebration of its triumphs in the fields of both art and war, he speaks, etc...'

While the only reference to war in the entire text of <u>Meistersinger</u> is (Act 3, sc. 2, Jamiesons's translation):

<u>Sachs:</u>	'Beware! Ill times now threaten all;
	If we Germans should even fall
	In thrall to any foreign land.
	No prince his folk will understand,
	And foreign mists will blind our eyes,
	And o'er our German land will rise:
	The art we own were lost for ay,
	Living in German song today.'

Gray's assertion is thus demonstrably false. He quotes nothing in support of it (there is nothing <u>to</u> quote), and I am responsible for linking it up with Sachs's remarks.

I leave you to judge if the passage ought to be changed. It might perhaps be strengthened by substituting Gray's exact words – 'a hymn to Germany's triumphs'... instead of 'a great hymn to Germany's achievements'... I don't particularly want to rewrite this passage, but if you think it necessary, even in view of the facts stated above, I will do so.[11]

This detailed answer was immediately accepted. In the same correspondence there is a smaller but (in the light of critics' suspicion that Montgomery had used elements of some of his acquaintances as the basis for characters, particularly Fen) equally important riposte to the lawyer's request for an assurance that he had not made any allusions which might be considered derogatory of living people:

For the rest, none of the characters has the same name as any of my friends and acquaintances. I trust that Mr Rubenstein's rather sinister final paragraph does not refer to me. I have never attempted to describe, or allude to, any actual persons in any of my books.[12]

There are observations on the collaboration of Strauss and Hofmannsthal as a result, perhaps, of Sampson's promptings on his and Montgomery's future work. He also parades his knowledge of more recent work in a parody of *Peter Grimes*, Britten's opera, which had been first performed only two years before the publication of *Swan Song*:

The tuba-player arrived, unpacked his instrument, and began making a sound like a fog-horn on it, while the rest of the orchestra chanted 'Peter Grimes!' in a quavering, distant falsetto.[13]

As Montgomery was struggling with at least one operatic project at the time, it is appropriate that one member of the operatic cast, Boris Stapleton, is also an

---

11	RBM to Gollancz, mis-dated 18 January 1947, actually 18 February 1947: (Gollancz Archive)

12	Ibid.

13	*Swan Song*, Chapter 14

aspiring composer of opera. Montgomery does not miss the chance to mention the problems he faces: 'virtually the only way to get a new opera put on is to be a multi-millionaire'.[14]

The book is noticeably less frivolous than his previous efforts, with Fen continuing to calm down, and this was remarked upon in the *Observer*: 'Mr Edmund Crispin has steadied down a bit [...] some of the members of the opera company visiting Oxford [...] behave quite like ordinary people.'[15] The main comedy of the book is provided by Charles Shorthouse, an absent-minded composer of operas, and his formidable paramour who calls him 'The Master' and shields him against his will from any interruptions to his work. She also runs his household to the extent that he has little idea of what is happening. Charles Shorthouse is the brother of Edwin Shorthouse, a fine singer but disagreeable character, who is the first victim of the novel. Edwin is a constant and lustful pursuer of women, 'and his resemblance to the gross and elderly roué of Strauss's opera [Ochs in *Der Rosenkavalier*] was sufficiently remarkable for it to be a subject of perpetual surprise in operatic circles that his interpretation of the role was so inadequate'.[16] Charles is constantly attempting, by almost any means, to get his own operas performed (in some ways he is a comic caricature of Wagner), and tells Fen that 'the question really was whether Edwin's *voice* or Edwin's *money* was going to be more useful to me in producing the *Oresteia*'.[17] Having decided that the money was more useful, he admits that he intended to 'sacrifice' his brother – but someone else got in first. At the inquest into his brother's death, and the possibility that it was suicide, Charles Shorthouse claims that Edwin's obsession with women might be 'included in the definition of madness':[18]

'The whole of our family is more or less unbalanced.'
'But can't you give some instance to show that your brother was unbalanced?'
'He refused to finance the production of my *Oresteia*.'[19]

There is more familiar territory. Montgomery makes reference to Sir Henry Merrivale, one of Dickson Carr's detectives (when writing under the rather transparent pseudonym of Carter Dickson), Mrs Bradley and Albert Campion (the sleuths of Gladys Mitchell and Margery Allingham). Fen rather surprisingly claims that these detectives are more able than he, but this is low-key in comparison with earlier novels. The only in-joke is when Fen, sitting in the Bird and Baby, suddenly announces: 'There goes C.S. Lewis [...] It must be Tuesday.'[20] The Bird and Baby was the local name for the Eagle and Child, and it was in this pub each Tuesday that the 'Inklings', a literary group made up of Lewis, Tolkien and others, including Charles Williams, used to meet for a discussion. Fen co-opts a journalist as his assistant, and a few characters from previous novels make a reappearance, amongst

---

14    Ibid., Chapter 3
15    *Observer*, 24 August 1947
16    *Swan Song*, Chapter 2
17    Ibid., Chapter 10
18    Ibid., Chapter 17
19    Ibid.
20    Ibid., Chapter 8

them Sir Richard Freeman and a batty old don called Wilkes. Lily Christine III, 'creating a din like a gang of riveters on Clydeside',[21] continues her erratic progress along the Queen's highway. This time it is the stage-doorkeeper Furbelow who drops his aitches, and there are two romances which blossom instantly.

The tone of the novel is less openly erudite. The prose is not so littered with quotations or with words which send the reader scuttling to the dictionary. The book does not suffer from this; in many ways it gains. Most of the characters may not be as memorable, but the writing is still lively, the plot, despite its 'wild contraption', is more assured and the denouement has a pleasing symmetry.

Both *Love Lies Bleeding* and *Buried for Pleasure* were published in 1948. The former became one of Montgomery's favourites. Its basis was a short story he had once read to a Carr Club meeting on Dartmoor and which he extended at the suggestion of Gollancz. Like his previous novels, *Love Lies Bleeding*, which is dedicated to the Carr Club, uses a milieu with which Montgomery felt at home. Murders are committed in a midlands' public school, Castrevenford, around the time of the school play, *Henry V*, and a lost play by Shakespeare becomes involved later in the novel; Montgomery's brief teaching career at Shrewsbury School and his love of setting poetry from the sixteenth and seventeenth centuries are used here.

The setting gives Montgomery the chance to indulge in a few swipes at the qualities necessary in educational establishments:

> The framers of the Education Acts have little use for such dominies as Mr Etherege; but in this, as in so many other things, they are grossly impercipient. The fact is that every large school requires an *advocatus diaboli* – and at Castrevenford Mr Etherege occupied this important post. He was flagrantly lacking in public spirit. He never attended important matches. He was not interested in the spiritual welfare of his boys. He lacked respect for the school as an institution. In short, he was impenitently an individualist. And if, at first sight, these characteristics do not appear particularly commendable, you must remember their context. In a school like Castrevenford a good deal of emphasis is necessarily laid on public spirit, and the thing is liable to develop, if unregulated, into a rather dreary fetish. Mr Etherege helped to keep this peril at bay, and consequently the Headmaster valued him as much as his more stern dutiful colleagues. His divagations from the approved syllabus were the price that had to be paid, and its evils had in any case been minimized by the removal from his time-tables of all work for important examinations.[22]

Fen has been asked, as a last-minute substitute, to give away the prizes at the school's Speech Day. The Headmaster claims that Fen should be an interesting speaker: 'In fact, my only fear is that he may be too interesting. I'm not quite sure that he's capable of the sustained hypocrisy which the occasion demands.'[23]

In a reference to *The Moving Toyshop*, Fen says: 'I was irresponsible and carefree in those days […] I've sobered up a lot since then, and become nostalgic, which is a sign of diminished vitality.'[24] This is an accurate assessment of the trend that has been noticed over the past few novels, but it hardly means that Fen – as a waspish

---

21     Ibid., Chapter 10
22     *Love Lies Bleeding*, Chapter 2
23     Ibid., Chapter 1
24     Ibid., Chapter 9

individual – is a spent force. When someone observes that there has been a great deal of crime at Oxford recently, Fen asks them whether they have read Matthew Arnold: 'Oxford is proverbially the home of lost corpses',[25] a statement that was doubtless met with approval some fifty years later by the television audiences for the highly successful adaptations of Colin Dexter's Oxford-based crime novels featuring Inspector Morse. When a young lady tells Fen that she has followed all his cases, he is greatly pleased: 'That's more than Crispin's readers manage to do.'[26] Fen shows greater humility than normal at times; even though he has a good deal of self-esteem, we are told that 'he habitually regarded it with a detached and mocking eye'.[27]

Although there are fewer signs of gratuitous frivolity and of Crispin's usual bizarre characters, his in-jokes remain. The English master is called Mathieson (after Muir Mathieson, a sign of Montgomery's future work as a composer of film scores); he is 'an untidy, heavily-built man of middle age, clumsy in his movements'.[28] Du Cann, a contemporary of Montgomery at Oxford, and Peterkin, his music editor at Oxford University Press, are names for other members of staff. The musical fun continues with a carpenter by the name of Mr Taverner[29] whose assistant, Mr Tye,[30] is a 'diffident, shambling, overgrown youth'.[31]

The immaculately-spoken Mr Taverner is given an impressive introduction in the *Beacon*, the landlord of which is the character favoured in this novel with the dropped aitches:

Apart from his carpenter's clothes, which were stained with paint and impregnated with sawdust, Mr Taverner resembled a superior butler. His face was fleshy, of an ochre hue, with pouches beneath the eyes; and his body was shaped like a pear. A Johnsonian portentousness emanated from him. The wooden floor creaked beneath his substantial weight. A chisel projected from his breast-pocket. He wished the company good morning in a mellow, rotund parsonical voice. Then he moved with a measured and dignified tread to the bar. [32]

In Crispin's vein of eccentric non-humans is Mr Merrythought, an elderly bloodhound of singular habits and the most memorable animal since the linguist parrot in *The Case of the Gilded Fly*. Mr Merrythought, 'liable to homicidal fits',[33] is introduced to Fen early on:

The dog was a large, forbidding bloodhound, on whose aboriginal colour and shape one or two other breeds had been more or less successfully superimposed. He stood just inside the doorway, unnervingly immobile, and fixed Fen with a malevolent and hypnotic stare.[34]

---

25    Ibid., Chapter 3
26    Ibid., Chapter 11
27    Ibid., Chapter 11
28    Ibid., Chapter 2
29    John Taverner (c.1490–1545), English composer
30    Christopher Tye (c.1505–?1572), English composer
31    *Love Lies Bleeding*, Chapter 9
32    Ibid., Chapter 9
33    Ibid., Chapter 3
34    Ibid.

He makes regular appearances in the course of the novel, trying to climb tables and walls and appearing at various times self-righteous, dazed and comatose. Like Ellis the tortoise in Montgomery's last novel, *The Glimpses of the Moon*, Mr Merrythought has a predilection for eating pansies. He is also the first animal who is not a mere decoration of the plot. When Fen goes in search of a missing girl in dense woods who may have left a trail of blood, the expertise of Mr Merrythought's breed is called upon. He also helps to save Fen from the murderer's gun:

> But he [the murderer] had reckoned without Mr Merrythought. He had reckoned without Mr Merrythought's recurrent homicidal fits. The labour and excitement of the evening had clearly had a baneful effect on Mr Merrythought's constitution, for now, enraged beyond belief, he was foaming at the mouth, growling, yelping, and capering monstrously, with his eyes bloodshot and the hair standing up along his spine like a porcupine's quills.[35]

Despite apoplexy abolishing his 'normal physical limitations',[36] the dog is shot in the course of the struggle. Having saved Fen, he meets his end beneath a distant tree:

> He had fought like a gladiator, but now he could do no more. He did not whimper; he growled softly to himself. And in this fashion, irate, suspicious, and undaunted to the last, he waited for death.[37]

Two characters, Daphne (the mandatory young lady described as always in idealistic terms) and Mr Plumstead, fall in love with great rapidity, and the novel ends with the inevitable chase. Lily Christine leads this, 'leaving a train of devastation and ruin' in her wake as she rattles 'vociferously down the drive'. Her usual signs of 'disaffection' develop into 'open mutiny'[38] as she grinds to a halt at a vital moment – but then she is up against a Hispano-Suiza.

The *Birmingham Post* was enthusiastic about the novel: 'Previously his plots have been so freakish that the mind was staggered, not puzzled; the writing inclined to be precious. All this has been toned down and the feeling that here is, after all, a relaxation not to be taken too seriously, adds the final touch.'[39] Ralph Partridge in the *New Statesman* made a point about Crispin's erudition: 'Edmund Crispin establishes himself as our leading exponent of "Third Programme" detection. He is not ashamed to address his readers on the assumption that they are his equals in education and intelligence.'[40]

*Buried for Pleasure* finds Gervase Fen following his latest enthusiasm and standing for Parliament in a rural constituency. When asked early in the novel why he wishes to enter parliament, it appears that he is not entirely sure:

---

35    Ibid., Chapter 13
36    Ibid.
37    Ibid.
38    Ibid., Chapter 15
39    *Birmingham Post*, 6 April 1948
40    *New Statesman*, 12 June 1948

Even to himself Fen's actions were sometimes unaccountable, and he could think of no very convincing reply.

'It is my wish,' he said sanctimoniously, 'to serve the community.'

The girl eyed him dubiously.

'Or at least,' he amended, 'that is one of my motives. Besides, I felt I was getting far too restricted in my interests. Have you ever produced a definitive edition of Langland?'

'Of course not,' she said crossly.

'I have. I've just finished producing one. It has queer psychological effects. You begin to wonder if you're mad. And the only remedy for that is a complete change of occupation. [41]

Fen stands, of course, as an independent, and we are told that 'his programme, in so far as it was ascertainable at all, leaned rather to the Right than to the Left'[42] (Montgomery was of a strongly conservative disposition himself). As polling day draws closer and the possibility of his election grows, Fen begins to realise that he no longer wishes to enter parliament:

A whole-time preoccupation with democratic politics, he rapidly discovered, is not easily imposed on a humane and civilized mind. In no very long time the gorge rises and the stomach turns. And, the prospect of five years spent trooping in and out of lobbies, crying 'Oh!' from back benches, arguing in committee rooms, corresponding with crazy constituents, and suffering without protest that which the House of Commons supposes to be wit – all this […] Fen was beginning to find inexpressibly dispiriting. He had money of his own: he had been a Professor at Oxford for nearly ten years; he had felt that a change of occupation would be good for his soul. And he now saw with belated clarity that he had been mistaken.[43]

Fen believes that by insulting the electorate at his final meeting he can ensure there is no possibility of election. He sets to the task with enthusiasm in a lengthy speech, claiming that 'the English have no more political good sense than so many polar bears':

'For some days past I have been regaling this electorate with projects and ideas so incomparably idiotic as to be, I flatter myself, something of a tour de force. […] [My] inane basic principles […] have included, among other laughable notions, the idea that humanity progresses, and that fatuous corruption of the Christian ethic which asserts that everyone is responsible for the well-being of everyone else. Such dreary fallacies as these, expounded by myself, have been swallowed hook, line and sinker. And I am bound to conclude that this proven obtuseness is not unrepresentative of the British people as a whole, since their predilection for putting brainless megalomaniacs into positions of power stems, in the last analysis, from an identical vacuity of the intellect.'

In urging his would-be constituents to abstain entirely from voting in the election, Fen gives his reasons:

---

41    *Buried for Pleasure*, Chapter 1
42    Ibid., Chapter 15
43    Ibid.

'Do not allow yourselves to be cajoled into supposing that political apathy is dangerous. Dictators such as Hitler, Mussolini and Stalin are raised to power, not by apathy, but by mass fanaticism. [...] A contemporary French writer – whose name I shall not mention, since you are probably too stupid either to recognize it or to remember it – has pointed out with unanswerable logic that men adopt ideas, not because it seems to them that those ideas are true, or because it seems to them that those ideas are expedient, but because those ideas satisfy a basic emotional need of their nature. Now what emotion – I ask you – provides the chief motive power of the politically obsessed? [...] the reply to my question is in the monosyllable hate. Never forget that political zealots are people who are over-indulging their emotional need of hatred. [...] it is the lust to defame and destroy. Let no such men be trusted. [...]

'I intended to talk for a long time about the effects which endemic envy and hatred, masquerading as public-spirited interest in politics are producing in this country; but I now find that I am tired of looking at your rather plain faces, so I shall not do so. In conclusion, I may as well add, however, that if you take my advice you will not go to the polls at all tomorrow. The politicians will not like this, because your indifference will be an affront to their sordid trade; but you must not let that worry you.

'That is all I have to say.

'Now go home and think about it.'[44]

They do, and still Fen gets elected – by one vote. He later admits that 'the delights of invective rather ran way with me there'.[45] Extraordinarily, just over twenty-five years later, one Norah Buckley, attempting to make her entry into local politics as a councillor in Richmond Upon Thames, asked Montgomery if she could make use of Fen's address. He had no objections, but warned her that 'in real life, your voters may not be as gratified at being insulted as the voters in my book are'.[46] Nothing daunted, Mrs Buckley used the speech and reported that it was received with polite applause. Like Fen she won the vote.

One hopes, however, that she did not suffer the same post-election fate as Fen: much to his pleasure but the chagrin of Captain Watkyn (Fen's agent, who spends most of his time grappling mostly unsuccessfully with an unreliable campaign van and its even more unreliable public-address system), they have overspent on their permitted election expenses and Fen is disqualified. The rakish Watkyn is also a keen betting man, something he had in common with Montgomery who kept an account with his local betting shop with little apparent success. Towards the end of his life he told Dick Francis: 'Have just lost £50 on the hurdlers. Horrible creatures!'[47]

In *Buried for Pleasure* Montgomery's characters are perhaps at their most bizarre yet, with the usual assortment of half-witted rustics as well as a genuine lunatic on the loose. The latter is Elphinstone, an escapee from the local asylum with more neuroses than might be thought possible, whom Fen first encounters rushing across the road wearing only pince-nez and who is responsible for the demise of the murderer at the end of the novel. The leading comic turn in many ways is the non-doing pig, the latest in Crispin's line of animals.

---

44    Ibid., Chapter 19
45    Ibid.
46    RBM to Norah Buckley, 15 January 1974
47    RBM to Dick Francis, 29 November 1977

She [Myra] indicated the pig. 'Did you ever see anything like him?' she asked.

'Well, no, now you mention it I don't think I have.'

'I've been cheated,' said Myra, and the pig grunted, apparently in assent. 'I like a young pig to be nice and pink, you know, and cheerful-like. But him – my God. I feed him and feed him, but he never grows.'

They meditated jointly on this phenomenon. A passing farm-labourer joined them.

''E don't get no bigger, do 'e?' he observed.

'What's the matter with him, Alf?'

The farm-labourer pondered. ''E'm a non-doer,' he diagnosed at last.

'A what?'

'Non-doer. You're wasting your time trying to fatten 'im. 'E'll never get no larger. Better sell 'im.'[48]

The creature refuses to grow, and all Myra's attempts to move it elsewhere are stymied by the pig's homing instinct. The chase at the end of the novel involves motor cars, one of which is baulked by the pig returning from yet another attempt by Myra to rid herself of it, a previous one having failed when the pig throws itself off the back of a lorry: 'Along the exact centre of the lane, its head bandaged but its homing instinct unimpaired, trotted the non-doing pig, making resolutely for "The Fish Inn".'[49] At the end of the novel, when The Fish Inn is accidentally demolished, the non-doing pig is rewarded for its fidelity to Myra by meeting its maker under the rubble. Montgomery's animals, despite their amusement value, are not always treated well. The Dalmatian in *The Moving Toyshop*, like Mr Merrythought in *Love Lies Bleeding*, is gunned down, and now the pig is flattened. Quite why Montgomery felt it necessary to deal in this way with them is not obvious. There may be some evidence in his claim to have an antipathy towards dogs, although he was an enthusiastic keeper of cats.

Crispin's lingering interest in the supernatural is demonstrated by a rector whose residence harbours a particularly active poltergeist. This is, however, very much a comic poltergeist which hurls from the rectory, amongst other articles, 'pebbles, a comb, a box of Nuits d'extase, books, soap, a reproduction of the Sistine Madonna, a cushion, the detachable top of a small prie-dieu, a vase of flowers, a jade elephant, and a pair of white woollen bed-socks'.[50] Montgomery includes a socialist Lord (who proposes marriage rather rapidly), a writer of 'complicated, lurid and splendidly melodramatic'[51] detective fiction (Mr Judd, who writes under the ludicrous pseudonym of Annette de la Tour) and an echo of Evelyn Waugh's *Decline and Fall* ('lay interest in ecclesiastical matters is often a prelude to insanity')[52]: 'Elphinstone went to the University. There he undertook the study of philosophy, politics, and economics – and our records show […] that an interest in these subjects often leads on to total madness.'[53] There is more than a hint of *Cold Comfort Farm* at times.

48  *Buried for Pleasure*, Chapter 3
49  Ibid., Chapter 21
50  Ibid.
51  Ibid., Chapter 4
52  *Decline and Fall*, Evelyn Waugh, Chapter VIII
53  *Buried for Pleasure*, Chapter 13

Three other things remain to be said about the novel. Blackmail features prominently, and the views Montgomery gives to one of the policemen are a distillation of his own, spoken of to his friends:

> 'Sentimental claptrap about blackmail – 'the meanest of crimes' and that sort of conventional jabber – I haven't normally much use for. If a man has committed a crime and got away with it, then I cannot see that another man who extorts money from him as the price of silence is one half as disgusting, morally, as a thug who savages an old woman in order to steal her life's savings. But where it's blackmail for a mere fault – and even more for a fault for which the wretched victim can't be held responsible – then I agree, it's nauseating.'[54]

The plot hinges on deafness and lip-reading, and Montgomery explained how this idea came to him: 'I have a niece who is deaf, and it was my interest in her early problems about lip-reading and speaking which suggested the plot of the book.'[55] Later authors have also used this idea, including Colin Dexter, himself with hearing difficulties, in *The Silent World of Nicholas Quinn*.

*Buried for Pleasure* also sees the first appearance of two in his novels of Montgomery's cheroot-smoking Detective-Inspector Humbleby of New Scotland Yard (the other is in *Frequent Hearses*). Humbleby, 'a neat, elderly mild-looking man with a round red face and a grey Homburg hat tilted forward over his eyes')[56] acts as a sober counter-balance to Fen, although he is not averse to literary quotation himself. He is particularly important in Montgomery's short stories, and we shall hear more of him later.

Notices of the novel were enthusiastic, particularly Anthony Boucher in the *New York Times*:

> After a few early chaotic attempts, he's learned by now how to juggle Wodehousian farce, social satire and a strictly constructed detective plot, keeping all three balls glinting through the air so adroitly that they form one delightful pattern [...] absolute and unalloyed delight.[57]

---

54    Ibid., Chapter 8
55    RBM to G. Smith, 14 May 1968
56    *Buried for Pleasure*, Chapter 11
57    *New York Times*, 17 March 1949

# Chapter 9

# 'Mania for needless impostures':
# Novels 1950–1953

Two further novels brought to an end this productive phase of Montgomery's career. Continuing his habit of placing stories in settings of which he had experience, *Frequent Hearses* (1950) concerns the murder of a film starlet, and most of the action takes place within the hot-house atmosphere of a film studio. Montgomery had composed his first film score in 1948. He loses no time in making fun of his friend Geoffrey Bush, who had recently decided that the frenzied schedules of composing for films were not for him, and other prominent composers, including John Ireland, are also mentioned in passing. There is a vivid description of how composers for films are expected to submit to the conventions of the screen as well as to keep their natural inclinations under control:

> Judy [...] was in Sound Stage Number Two, listening while the Philharmonia Orchestra, under Griswold's direction, rehearsed and recorded the score for *Ticket for Hell*. Upon the screen in front of her two lovers, bereft of their sound-track, mouthed preposterously at each other; in the sound engineer's glass-fronted control-room, behind her, the composer sat complacently imbibing through a substantial loudspeaker the noises he had contrived. The ticker on the wall spelled out the seconds; Griswold, with headphones adjusted and a cigarette in his mouth, glanced rapidly and continuously from the players to the score to the ticker to the screen; and music appropriate to its erotic context – susurration of strings, plangency of French horns, the oily sweetness of tubular bells and the aqueous ripple of harps – filled and overflowed the room. Not a bad score, Judy conceded: in his concert works Napier was a somewhat acrid modernist, but like most such composers he unbuttoned, becoming romantic and sentimental, when he was writing for films.[1]

Later, when praised for his score, the composer tries to play it down:

> 'For heaven's sake,' said Napier, visibly pleased, 'don't judge me by this stuff.'
> 'That's what all you composers say. [...] On the day one of you admits that his film score is the best thing he's ever done, the Music Department will take a week off and get plastered by way of celebration.'[2]

Fen remains less offensively ebullient than in the earlier novels and acknowledges this himself: 'As I get older [...] I get less resilient and more predictable. It depresses me sometimes.'[3] At some points, in terms of pre-eminence, he plays second string

---

1    *Frequent Hearses*, Chapter IV, Section 1
2    Ibid.
3    Ibid., Chapter I, Section 6

to Humbleby, who this time appears from the start of the novel. Humbleby, with his cheroot and Homburg, is described as looking like 'a prosperous and engaging commercial traveller with mild pretensions to culture';[4] he is able to trade blows with Fen about the works of Henry James and to introduce his own quotation from Voltaire. The pair play off each other: at one point Fen tells Humbleby that he is 'unbelievably dense';[5] Humbleby, generally less caustic than Fen, gets his own back later by telling Fen to 'Get on with it [...] and don't ramble so much.'[6]

Erudition is not missing: Fen has been called in as literary advisor to a projected fatuous film about Alexander Pope (the novel's title is taken from the poet's *Ode to the Memory of an Unfortunate Lady*) and it gives Montgomery many opportunities for literary references. The tone of the novel is less comic than *Buried for Pleasure*, and there are fewer outrageous characters. One of them, Bartholomew Snerd, is a furtive blackmailer with remarkable principles:

> It was a rigid law with him never to make an excessive demand and never to make more than one, and it was doubtless this wise and temperate plan which kept him immune from retribution. Indeed, it had developed, as time went on, into something very like a principle of ethics; *unfair*, or *ungentlemanly*, were the terms in which Mr. Snerd would have stigmatised any attempt to take the pitcher a second time to a previously plundered well; and his attitude to his victims, once they had acceded to his demands, was a kindly, paternal tolerance.[7]

Another is an 'old, improvident-looking'[8] communist butler with the absurdly inappropriate name of Primrose:

> 'They'll see you,' said the butler, with the air of one whose good news is much against his inclination. 'They'll see you now.' He observed that Humbleby was removing his hat and coat. 'Chuck those down anywhere. And get a move on, will you? I've got other things than you to attend to.'
>
>     'Until I choose to be ready, you most certainly haven't,' said Humbleby.
>
>     'Bossy, aren't you?' the aged creature snarled. 'You just wait till the revolution, that's all. That'll finish you and your sort.'
>
>     'There is not going to be any revolution.'
>
>     'No, I don't think so either,' said the butler unexpectedly.[9]

Reminding us of Philbrick, Evelyn Waugh's rough-and-ready butler in *Decline and Fall* who is constantly asking people 'I expect you wonder how it is I come to be here?',[10] Primrose asks Humbleby: 'You're saying to yourself: "Now, 'ow does it come about that a straightforward chap like old Syd Primrose works for a lot of

---

4    Ibid., Chapter I, Section 2

5    Ibid., Chapter II, Section 1

6    Ibid., Chapter V, Section 3

7    Ibid., Chapter II, Section 4

8    Ibid., Chapter III, Section 2

9    Ibid.

10   *Decline and Fall*, Evelyn Waugh, Chapter VII

degenerate capitalists like the Cranes?'"[11] Humbleby deals with Primrose by telling him that he looks 'like some ghastly relic left over from the earliest origins of the Fabian Movement' and gets rid of him by suggesting he reads *'The New Statesman* or something'.[12]

Lily Christine, now described as 'exceptionally strident and dissolute-looking',[13] has been patched up after her accident at the end of *Love Lies Bleeding* and manages to make a short, but noisy, trip. She carries Fen by night to the maze at Lanthorn House where the slow but atmospheric chase of the novel takes place. Montgomery's growing regard for the plot was noted by the critics. *'Frequent Hearses* runs on more formal lines than any previous Crispin',[14] was one comment, and another lamented his own previous remarks:

> I railed against his undergraduate cleverness, but now that he writes a straightforward crime story without the sparkling digressions and slapstick repartee of his earlier books, I am sorry, as it were, that I spoke.[15]

One character in the novel sparked an unintentionally hilarious correspondence which, had it been foreseen, would have had the libel lawyer mopping his brow in trepidation. It also shows how even the most careful of novelists can be caught out by someone with a ridiculously thin skin and suspicious mind. In *Frequent Hearses* Montgomery refers to 'Gresson, a diminutive, futile Cambridge don whose task it was to advise on the history and sociological background of Pope's period'.[16] For the absurdity and pomposity to be appreciated properly, the letters need to be quoted in full. Victor Gollancz received the following from a Mr F.S. Salisbury who, to judge from his extraordinarily spidery hand, must have been quite elderly:

> I am in the habit of reading detective stories as a relaxation from the rather exacting studies which occupy most of my time.
> One of the your books –'Frequent Hearses' by Edmund Crispin – deprived me of my recreation this week-end. I disliked the tone of the book and discarded it after a few chapters. But my chief reason for writing to you is to call attention to the introduction on pp. 59ff. of a vulgar, dirty-minded person named Gresson who is described as a Cambridge history don.
> As a graduate and member of the Senate of the University I protest most strongly against this deliberately insulting attribution.
> I am also personally acquainted with a distinguished young Cambridge history lecturer (whom I see from time to time at meetings of one of the learned societies I belong to, of which we are Fellows & present or past members of the Council) whose name is closely similar to that used in the book. The only difference by which identity might be merely masked is that of a vowel sound in the middle.

---

11   *Frequent Hearses*, Chapter III, Section 5
12   Ibid.
13   Ibid., Chapter IV, Section 5
14   *New Statesman*, 4 March 1950
15   *Sketch*, 1 February 1950
16   *Frequent Hearses*, Chapter I, Section 6

PS. I regret that this particular volume came from the local library and I have to return it to possible further [indecipherable word] instead of putting it behind the fire.[17]

Victor Gollancz took much pleasure in replying:

I was delighted by your letter. I shall send it to 'Edmund Crispin' who is in the habit of writing detective stories as a relaxation from the rather exacting studies in musical composition which occupy most of his time – in the hope that he will turn it into a humoresque.

It is possible that you may have run across 'Mr. Crispin' without knowing it: I imagine that he is a member of quite a number of learned societies, though too young, I think, to be a past-member of any council, or even a member of the Senate of the University of Oxford, of which he (like myself) is a graduate.[18]

Gollancz, having signed himself to Mr Salisbury 'Doctor of Laws Honoris Causa', also wrote to Montgomery:

Please see the enclosed (and return it to me, and don't forget to return it). I am sending you the original (together with a copy of my reply) as I think the hand-writing will amuse you as much as the letter. The poor old buffer must be about 150.[19]

Montgomery's reply to Gollancz suggested a way future problems of this sort might be avoided:

Thank you so much for letting me see this. Oh dear, is all I can say: Oh dear. Your reply is most pleasing, and the only fly in the ointment would seem to be the existence of a Cambridge history don with a name resembling 'Gresson'. If there is a Grisson, Grosson or what not, I hope Mr. Salisbury doesn't sick him on to sue; also, I'm sorry, having of course intended no malice to any man. In future, I think I shall distinguish my characters by means of numbers: names are too risky.[20]

The matter was not yet finished. Gollancz's light-hearted reply enraged the humourless Salisbury to even greater comic heights:

I am not impressed by the high-horsey manner of your letter. Neither of us, I am sure, will desire a continuation of this correspondence, but there remain one or two things that need to be said.

It was with some distress, but I am afraid not altogether with surprise, that I learned the Oxonian source of the book which occasions you such pleasure.

As my previous letter made clear I am zealous for the honour of my university, but I hope as a sportsman. The passages I complained of are not sportsmanlike: they touch honour. You class yourself by approving them (honoris causa? presumably a variety of it made in Oxford).

17    F.S. Salisbury to Victor Gollancz, 5 March 1951 (Gollancz Archive)
18    Victor Gollancz to F.S. Salisbury, 7 March 1951 (Gollancz Archive)
19    Victor Gollancz to RBM, 6 March 1951 (Gollancz Archive)
20    RBM to Victor Gollancz, 10 March 1951 (Gollancz Archive)

I have always put Cambridge first, as of course your letter does decisively in another way, but I have not therefore learned to besmirch Oxford. That would require a cad with an inferiority complex.

Of my two closest friends of the younger generation, both of whom I have known from their childhood, and both of whom won the Military Cross in the war, one (now prominent in the world of music) was at Cambridge; the other, who had Oxford antecedents, went there with my complete approval, and I have reason to be sure he would not have done so otherwise. He represents the best spirit of Oxford, of which I think you know little.

I am minded to increase by one more copy the sales of your anonymous mud-slinger from the Isis, and keep it with this correspondence as a sure reminder that honour and breeding begin to wither from one of their ancient haunts.[21]

And there, it seems, the matter rested. Montgomery also had trouble with a reader who complained that the cockney dialect he used in the novel was all wrong. 'You're right, I think, in suggesting that I haven't got a very good ear for dialect,' he wrote in reply. 'As regards the talk of the cockney girl you mention, that was taken from life during a visit to Ealing Studios round about 1948. I'm sorry that what the girl actually said doesn't fit in with your preconception of what she ought to have said.'[22]

*The Long Divorce* was published in 1951, and it finished a period in Montgomery's life. His next (and final) novel did not appear until 1977. Fen poses as a Mr Datchery, having been called in to help by Colonel Babington, the local Chief Constable. Mr Datchery is the name of a character in Dickens' unfinished novel *The Mystery of Edwin Drood*. Late in the novel Babington complains about Fen's 'mania for needless impostures'.[23] He may well do so, but Montgomery's readers are accustomed to such literary pleasantries: a Henry Fielding appears in *Holy Disorders*, and in *Buried for Pleasure* a policeman called Bussy masquerades, unsuccessfully with Fen around, under the name of Rawdon Crawley, a character from Thackeray's *Vanity Fair*. Although not literary, Harry James, the landlord of the Whale and Coffin in *Holy Disorders*, is likely to be a tribute to the American bandleader, given the exposure to jazz Montgomery received from Larkin at Oxford.

The trend of the past few novels continues: Fen works in tandem with the local police rather than co-opting one of his friends. He may not be quite as irascible as he was in the early stories, but he is still capable of exploding, even at Babington, when he thinks fit ('I'll be damned! [...] Of all the unscrupulous misstatements').[24] A description of Fen earlier in the novel sums him up well at this stage:

To say that Mr Datchery had not in the meantime been idle would be slightly disingenuous, for he was by nature a volatile man, readily distracted by trifles from any business which he happened to have in hand, and he had never found in total activity the tedium which proverbial wisdom ascribed to it.[25]

---

21    F.S. Salisbury to Victor Gollancz, 9 March 1951 (Gollancz Archive)
22    RBM to Mr Hope, 5 August 1970
23    *The Long Divorce*, Chapter 16
24    Ibid.
25    Ibid., Chapter 6

Mention has been made previously of Montgomery's social satire, and in *The Long Divorce* he makes a good deal of the values of the new residents in the village. It was something he was concerned with himself in the 1960s when he moved to a rural location (towards the end of the century a possessor of these attitudes became known as a *nimby* – 'not-in-my-back-yard'):

> It [Cotton Abbas] was essentially a residential village for members of the cultured upper middle class – intelligent company directors, fashionable portrait painters and so forth – who needed to be within reach of London but who could dictate their own time of arriving there; and it was they who had been responsible, at some sacrifice to themselves, for preserving the village's amenities. They had restricted new building, and dictated its style when it proved inevitable; they had sat in judgement on inn-signs; they had pestered the Vicar to remove the Victorian pews from the great church, and had paid for better ones to replace them; they had supervised restoration and rebuilding; by titanic wrangling they had brought into being a by-pass to divert main-road traffic from the village's broad and airy street; they had ordained a minimum bus service from Twelford, and stringent anti-charabanc laws, in their determination to keep trippers at bay.[26]

In another swipe at a subject dear to his heart, Montgomery refers to a character 'who had started making money before penal taxation made the accumulating of it impracticable'.[27]

Many of his narrative tendencies are evident: there is a chase, this time to rescue a possible suicide from a railway bridge; young lovers still take only one glance, it seems, to fall hopelessly in love and only a few moments more to propose marriage, and there are a handful of the usual characters including an 'ostentatiously sabbatical'[28] religious fanatic called Amos Weaver. Like Mr Merrythought in *Love Lies Bleeding*, this novel's curious animal plays an important part in the denouement. Lavender is a cat whose unpredictable behaviour leads Fen to credit it with seeing Martians at every turn:

> Though beautiful, the cat Lavender did seem to be not very bright; it moved about with the hypnotic air of the feeble-witted, and unlike most of its species was scarcely able to take a step without knocking something over, so that at intervals, whenever its ramblings brought it in the vicinity of a clock or a vase, Colonel Babington closed his eyes and went rigid until the danger had passed. 'I can't think,' said Mr Datchery, 'why you allow it to walk along the mantelpiece like that.'[29]

The cat's freedom to walk where it likes and to send ornaments crashing to the floor saves Fen and his associates from the gun-wielding murderer, like Mr Merrythought in *Love Lies Bleeding*.

Peter Rubi, a rather dull and self-righteous young Swiss psychologist (Fen opines that 'a woman trapped naked with him on a desert island would run no more intimate

---

26    Ibid., Chapter 7
27    Ibid., Chapter 13
28    Ibid., Chapter 11
29    Ibid., Chapter 6

risk from his company than the risk of death from boredom')[30] is keen to bring up the subject of Evelyn Waugh:

> The girl Runcible in *Vile Bodies*, she is the great contemporary symbol of dissociation in our modern world. She drives the car in the race; it swerves from the course; she dies ... I have written an article about this in the *Neue Züricher Beobachter* which has been praised by many of the best critics.[31]

Penelope, a girl with a crush on Rubi, gives what one imagines is closer to Montgomery's view:

> 'I admit,' she said carefully, 'that some of his [Rubi's] ideas about other subjects seem a bit odd. For instance, that book he was talking about – *Vile Bodies*. He told me I ought to read it, and I did, but the only thing about it I could see was that it was *funny*.'[32]

The relatively restrained tone of the novel, though, continued Montgomery's trend of cutting back the frivolity in his stories. This led to certain comments. 'At his best, Mr Crispin can be witty', wrote the *Sketch*, 'but often, too often, he is no more than waggish.'[33] Without the same level of farce as in previous books to distract them, the critics concentrated on the plot: 'The story has too many loose ends', was *Time and Tide*'s verdict, 'let's hope he gets hold of a better subject next time.'[34] The *New Statesman* held a similar view: 'His ingenuity, however, is never at fault; and as a feat of detective jerry-building *The Long Divorce* must be warmly commended.'[35] More fulsome praise lay elsewhere. Roy Fuller regarded it as 'one of its undoubtedly talented author's best'[36] but was outdone by the triumphant *Birmingham Post*: 'It is a brilliant book.'[37]

Before Montgomery went into an extended publishing hibernation, a collection of his short stories appeared in 1953. This was appropriate, because the only crime writing he produced over the following few years were further short stories which appeared in the national press. *Beware of the Trains* contains 16 tales, all but two of which feature Professor Fen who is usually assisting Detective-Inspector Humbleby. With one exception all the stories had originally been published in the London *Evening Standard*. The notice in the *Times Literary Supplement* pointed out the main drawback to this:

> *Beware of the Trains* [...] contains some clever and amusing tales: they would have been better still had not the limitations of space imposed the need to cast them in a strictly

---

30    Ibid., Chapter 2
31    Ibid., Chapter 1
32    Ibid.
33    *Sketch*, 1 August 1951
34    *Time and Tide*, 25 August 1951
35    *New Statesman*, 15 July 1951
36    *Tribune*, 10 August 1951
37    *Birmingham Post*, 3 July 1951

anecdotal form. The development of character and situation possible for Conan Doyle, who had some 5,000 words to play with, is inevitably denied to Mr. Crispin.[38]

The problem of constriction was made worse by an occasional lack of newsprint at the *Evening Standard* which forced Montgomery to prune the stories even more. Although Montgomery's short foreword notes that 'the great majority of [the stories] have been substantially revised and rewritten',[39] he still does not have sufficient space to include many of the odd-ball characters that characterise his novels. As a consequence, the stories have a comparatively sober mood. The foreword also demonstrates Montgomery's view of what detective fiction should be, and it was one that he would increasingly propound in his capacity as a critic as the years progressed. 'All of them [the stories] embody the nowadays increasingly neglected principle of fair play to the reader – which is to say that the reader is given all the clues needed to enable him to anticipate the solution by the exercise of his logic and common sense.'[40] Much will be made later of Montgomery's growing lack of sympathy with the direction the crime novel began to take, and it is significant that his parting shot in published form for almost twenty-five years should contain this barb. Because of the limitations of space, he is forced to give most attention to the plot – and these range widely. He usually concentrates on apparently small details such as the position of a bolt on a door, the difference between the speed of sound and light, or the condition of a typewriter ribbon; Fen also likes to show that things are not always what they seem. Such compression does not favour locked-room type plots, although 'The Name on the Window' includes musings on the subject:

'Gideon Fell once gave a very brilliant lecture on The Locked-Room Problem, in connection with that business of the Hollow Man; but there was one category he didn't include.'

'Well?'

Fen massages his forehead resentfully. 'He didn't include the locked-room mystery which isn't a locked-room mystery, like this one. So that the explanation of how Otto got into and out of that circular room is simple: he didn't get into or out of it at all.'[41]

The occasional story occurs after dinner, Fen holding court with various acquaintances in attendance whilst the port is passed round, rather in the manner of P.G. Wodehouse's Oldest Member tales. In one of these, 'The Quick Brown Fox', Fen seizes the opportunity to lecture on the difference between criminals in real life and detective fiction:

'Just the same,' he [Wakefield] said, irrupting on a discussion whose origin and purpose no one could clearly remember, 'detective stories *are* anti-social, and no amount of sophistries can disguise the fact. It's quite impossible to suppose that criminals don't collect useful information from them, fantastic and far-fetched though they usually are.

---

38    *Times Literary Supplement*, 10 April 1953
39    Foreword to *Beware of the Trains*
40    Ibid.
41    *Beware of the Trains*, 'The Name on the Window'

No one, I think' – here he glared belligerently at his fellow-guests – 'will attempt to contest *that*. And furthermore –'

'*I* contest it,' said Gervase Fen; and Wakefield groaned dismally. 'For all the use criminals make of them, the members of the Detection Club might as well be a chorus of voices crying in the wilderness. Look at the papers and observe what, in spite of detective fiction, criminals actually do. They buy arsenic at the chemist's, signing their own names in the Poisons Book, and then put stupendous quantities of it in their victims' tea. They leave their fingerprints on every possible object in the corpse's vicinity. They invariably forget that burnt paper, if it isn't reduced to dust, can be reconstituted and read. They spend, with reckless abandon, stolen bank-notes whose serial numbers they must know are in the possession of the police ....

'No, on the whole I don't think criminals get much help from detective stories. And if by chance they *are* addicts, that fact by itself is almost certain to scupper them, since their training in imaginary crime – which as a rule is extremely complicated – tends to make them over-elaborate in the contriving of their own actual misdeeds; and that, of course, means that they're easy game.[42]

It is also appropriate at this point to consider in tandem *Fen Country*, his second set of short stories, which, although not published until after his death, consists almost entirely of stories written at around this time. The few that did not originally appear in the *Evening Standard* were published in *Ellery Queen's Mystery Magazine* in the USA or in *Winter's Crimes*. Only one story had not previously appeared in print. Unlike the tales in *Beware of the Trains*, these stories were not revised at all and are as a consequence even more compressed. Of the 26 tales, Fen appears in 17 and Humbleby in eight. They appear together in just six. The stories and the type of plots are similar to *Beware of the Trains*, although certain subjects recur. Linguistic clues solve two cases, as do the switching of telephone lines and the close observation of dust. Montgomery manages to introduce music into one of the stories, as he does in 'Lacrimae Rerum' in *Beware of the Trains*, a case in which Fen demonstrates that it *is* possible to commit the perfect murder (one of his friends had been postulating that such a thing cannot be, as without discovery it cannot be proved to exist). Switched characters and deafness both occur in two stories, with Montgomery making further use of the condition of his niece as he had in *Buried for Pleasure*. Much is made of things not being what they seem, particularly in terms of time. The ingenious 'Who Killed Baker?', plot by Montgomery's friend Geoffrey Bush but written up by Montgomery, hinges on the ability to ask the right question. The author's view of blackmail, previously observed in *Buried for Pleasure*, makes a further appearance in 'Man Overboard'.

A characteristic of Montgomery's work is Fen's view of justice (blackmail is of course a part of this). We have already seen that in two of the novels he has his worries about handing over information to the police that might help to convict a person for the murder of a disagreeable character. In two of the stories in these collections he tells Humbleby not to worry that the culprits have evaded justice:

'Justice?' Fen reached for his hat. 'I shouldn't worry too much about that, if I were you. Here's a wife who knows her husband killed her brother. And here's a husband who knows

---

42    Ibid., 'The Quick Brown Fox'

his wife can by saying a word deprive him of his liberty and just possibly – if things didn't go well – of his life. And each knows that the other knows. And the wife is in love with the husband, but one day she won't be any longer, and then he'll begin to be afraid. And the wife thinks her husband is in love with her, but one day she'll find out that he isn't, and then she'll begin to hate him and to wonder what she can do to harm him, and he will know this, and she will know that he knows it and will be afraid of what he may do …

'Justice? My dear Humbleby, come and have some dinner. Justice has already been done.'[43]

A similar conclusion is reached in 'Shot in the Dark' in *Fen Country*.

In many ways, the three stories in *Fen Country* that have no detective stand out for more than that single reason. 'Cash on Delivery', the sole previously unpublished story, has perhaps Montgomery's most calculatingly unpleasant villain, a contract killer who is willing knowingly to murder the wrong person so that he can claim his fee and reach his getaway route before the body is discovered. Montgomery makes clear what sort of person we are dealing with in the tale's opening lines:

Max Linster was degenerate in the stricter sense of the word: I mean that he really had had something substantial – education; a good heredity; a stable, by no means poverty-stricken background – to degenerate from.[44]

'The Pencil' is another unpleasant tale, in which a character charged with blowing up the boss of a rival group of villains succeeds only in doing the same to himself.

The outstanding tale in *Fen Country*, however, is the impressively titled 'We Know You're Busy Writing, But We Thought You Wouldn't Mind If We Just Dropped in for a Minute'. Written in 1969, this longer than average short story is based on Montgomery's irritation at being interrupted in his work and is in many ways a self-portrait at that time:

I am forty-seven, unmarried, living alone, a minor crime-fiction writer earning, on average, rather less than £1,000 a year.

I live in Devon.

I live in a small cottage which is isolated, in the sense that there is no one nearer than a quarter of a mile. […]

I am a hypochondriac, well into the coronary belt.[45] Also, I go in fear of accidents, with broken bones.[46]

These interruptions get in the way of his character, a Mr Bradley, as he attempts to finish work that will placate his bank manager. When he is visited unexpectedly by some people he does not like, he murders them, manages to make it look as if they

---

43    Ibid., 'Otherwhere'

44    *Fen Country*, 'Cash on Delivery'

45    A phrase Montgomery also used when piling into a taxi with Brian Aldiss, Kingsley Amis and Harry Harrison after a rather 'jolly and bibulous' lunch at the Café Royal in honour of the launch of *Billion Year Spree* by Aldiss on 15 June 1973: 'Oh, well chaps, we're just entering the coronary belt, you know' [Brian Aldiss]

46    *Fen Country*, 'We Know You're Busy Writing, But We Thought You Wouldn't Mind If We Just Dropped in for a Minute'

have disappeared without trace – and admires his harvest cabbages the following autumn ('you can't beat nicely rotted organic fertilizers').[47] It should be a chilling tale, but Montgomery as always brings out the lighter side, although it is written in a very different manner to his other work. The story was written in rather a hurry after he was very close to a deadline. 'I've done it,' he told friends. 'I've written a story out of sheer desperation. It's all about ME and it might come true one day, if I get desperate enough.'[48]

---

47    Ibid.

48    Joan Bagley to author, 20 June 1990

# Chapter 10

# 'A genuine unforced enthusiasm':
# Films 1948–1962

Despite his growing success as an author and composer of concert music, Montgomery had already embarked in a small way on a further career as a composer of background music for films. Given his wide-ranging interest in contemporary artistic developments, this was a logical development of his musical talents. He had always been very keen on the cinema. We already know that he took Muriel Pavlow to see *The Wizard of Oz* at least four times at the Odeon at Rickmansworth. During his time at Oxford Montgomery loved going to the cinema and made a point of seeing *The Lady Vanishes* every year with Colin Strang. He was also very keen on Disney's *Fantasia*. In the notes for a talk on film music he gave later in life, Montgomery explains how his fascination with the scores began:

> From about the age of ten I went regularly every Saturday afternoon to the Regent at Amersham, sitting rather grandly in the Shilling Seats, for which I paid what was mysteriously advertised as a half price of eightpence.
>
> As I got older, I went to the pictures more and more. In a very amateurish way, I was also interested in music. So when in 1935 the Regent at Amersham got hold of a new British film called 'Things to Come', I went and saw it five times in the same week. For the first time an important composer[1] had been asked to write background music for a picture, and for the first time a reasonably serious attempt had been made to <u>fit</u> the music to the picture, carefully and in detail.
>
> I had day-dreams about how nice it would be if ever I could work on films, but I honestly never thought I should.[2]

Montgomery first looked for film work in 1946, and Sydney Northcote, whom he had met through his work at summer schools in Yorkshire, used his contacts in the film world. A letter from London Film Productions, whose chairman was Sir Alexander Korda, to Northcote showed some promise:

> Many thanks for your letter regarding Bruce Montgomery. Actually we have had to delay the film with the cathedral music background until the summer as it will obviously call for a number of exteriors. So I may get in touch with you about him later.[3]

Nothing came of this film, but within two years Montgomery had his first commission. As was common with first scores, it was for a short picture, of only

1    Arthur Bliss (1891–1975), English composer
2    Untitled notes: GB-Ob. MS. Eng. c. 3969, fols. 39–53
3    London Film Productions to Sydney Northcote, 13 December 1946

36 minutes duration, in this case a film called *Which Will Ye Have?* (also known as *Barabbas the Robber*). The production company was G.H.W. Productions, which was later responsible for a good number of Montgomery's films including the *Carry On* series. This score consisted of eleven music sections lasting almost 14 minutes in total. It is not clear exactly how Montgomery became involved in scoring this picture, but towards the end of his life he noted that he was introduced into film music through John Hollingsworth, a conductor known to some friends of his parents,[4] and this seems likely given that Hollingsworth conducted this score.

Unlike Geoffrey Bush, who 'swore never to undergo such an ordeal again'[5] after completing his second film score at much the same time, Montgomery found the hectic pace of film work more to his liking, at least initially. In *Frequent Hearses*, his sixth novel, he makes fun of the difficulties experienced by Bush in a passage which was to mirror his own later problems:

> Miss Flecker was saying 'Well now…' when the telephone rang. 'Damn,' she said. 'Excuse me… Yes, put him through… Good morning, Dr Bush – Geoffrey, I should say… Triple woodwind? Well, I imagine it might be managed; I'll ask Mr Griswold…. It'll be the Philharmonia, yes.' Dr Bush crackled prolongedly. 'No measurements for reels four and five yet? All right, I'll nag them…. Yes, I know you can't be expected to write a score if you haven't got any measurements…. No, there's not the least chance of postponing the recording; you'll just have to work all night as well as all day… Have you sent any of the score to the copyists yet? … Well, you'd better get on with it, hadn't you?… See you at the recording…. No…. Certainly not. Good-bye.'
>
> She put down the instrument. 'A composer,' she explained soberly, like one who refers to some necessary but unromantic bodily function.[6]

Composing music for films appealed to Montgomery for various reasons. Cinema was a long-standing interest of his, and the opportunity to combine this interest with his work as a composer proved irresistible. In his concert music Montgomery shows that he is at his best with short movements. In essence he was a miniaturist, and for this reason film scores suited him. Sections within the films for which Montgomery wrote the scores rarely last as much as three minutes, and are usually considerably shorter. He did not need to concern himself with developing material, although he sometimes did: much more important was that he conveyed the intended mood. For someone who was also a writer of detective novels, the puzzle of composing music to fit action, particularly in the comedy films in which he came (reluctantly) to specialise, was one that appealed to him. To fit this action with a section of music which also had its own musical integrity was an even greater challenge. The style of music which such films demanded came easily to Montgomery. There was no pressure on him to be fashionable or experimental. He could compose in his own richly romantic language without fearing critical comment; and for a composer who was not a household name, the knowledge that his music was going to be performed and recorded immediately was a further incentive.

---

4     RBM to Sheila Bush (Gollancz Archive), 1 April 1977
5     *An Unsentimental Education*, Bush, p. 23
6     *Frequent Hearses*, Chapter 1

There is no evidence to suggest that Montgomery had made any particular study of film music before he began work in this field. It appears that, like his detective fiction and to a certain extent his concert music, his grasp of the genre developed out of an intelligent interest. He had been impressed by the manner in which Bliss had made a 'reasonably serious attempt to fit the music to the picture, carefully and in detail',[7] and it is this philosophy which characterises his own work.

John Hollingsworth also conducted Montgomery's second score, another short film, *This is Britain: Love of Books*, produced by the Crown Film Unit in 1951 under the auspices of the Central Office of Information. Hollingsworth was assistant to Muir Mathieson (1911–1975), a conductor who specialised in film work. In 1934 Mathieson had been appointed musical director of London Films, and it was he who had engaged Arthur Bliss to compose the score for *Things to Come* following a recommendation from H.G. Wells. By the time of Montgomery's third short film, *Two Hundred Million Mouths*, a film financed by the Mutual Security Agency, Mathieson was conducting the recording session, and he was responsible for the execution of many of Montgomery's early scores with such orchestras as the London Symphony and Royal Philharmonic. Mathieson had a high regard for Montgomery's work, on one occasion referring to him as 'one of the most gifted young composers of film music I know'.[8] The pair spent a considerable amount of time together and took part in broadcasts discussing film music. Montgomery occasionally stayed the night at Mathieson's farmhouse close to many of the studios. One of Montgomery's few non-film compositions in the 1950s, *Variations on a Harrow Theme*, written on a theme supplied by the winner of a composition competition organised by the Education Committee of the Harrow Urban District Council to celebrate the coronation of Elizabeth II, was commissioned by Mathieson and given its first performance in Harrow by the London Symphony Orchestra conducted by him in June 1953 with the composer in attendance. There is a nice touch during the finale of the work when some of the melodies by the runners-up in the competition are introduced to meet the winning theme. In 1952 Montgomery wrote the score for another short film, and this time the commission came from British Transport Films. Originally named *North and West* and *Highland Journey* before being released as *Scottish Highlands*, the film explores the glories of this region of Britain. Muir Mathieson conducted the score with the London Symphony Orchestra, and the 23 minutes of music covers all but the whole film. It gave Montgomery the chance to react to differing scenes, from the grandeur of Ben Nevis to the locomotive speed of the West Highland Line.

After five short films, Montgomery was finally given a full-length feature in 1953. Set in Nova Scotia, *The Kidnappers* involves an immigrant Scottish family. A couple are forced into bringing up their young grandsons after the boys' father is killed by Boers in South Africa. The stern grandfather is in a dispute over land with a local Boer, and a tragic conclusion seems unavoidable until the boys find the missing baby of the Boer's family and look after it without telling anyone. When they are found out, the subsequent court case leads to a reconciliation. The score shows that Montgomery already had a sure touch. Completed in a month, the

---

7  Untitled notes: GB-Ob. MS. c. 3969, fols. 39–53
8  *Record Mirror*, 8 February 1958

38 minutes of full orchestral music, played by the Royal Philharmonic Orchestra under Mathieson, support the action admirably. Grand climaxes mix with delicate underscoring, and Montgomery demonstrates his ability to make sure that his music does not overwhelm during dialogue by cutting down both scoring and musical interest at these points. His style is richly romantic, and although there are still signs of his harmonic swerves and chromatic sequences, these are far less prominent than in his concert works. The music is more firmly melodic, and there is an assured grasp of orchestration. Montgomery's scoring is vivid; as in his concert orchestral works such as *Overture to a Fairy Tale*, woodwind solos frequently take over from the full orchestra, and sliding horn lines often accompany the melody. Montgomery always regarded this picture highly, considering it later 'a delightful film which still gives him pleasure to look back upon [and the score] his most satisfying achievement as a writer of film music'.[9] It was also a successful film: the two child actors were given special Oscars for their performances.

*Scottish Highlands* and *The Kidnappers* both have scores which are infused with Scottish folk idioms. In 1954 Montgomery made concert pieces out of the two scores, the only adaptations he made from his film work. *Scottish Aubade*, based on *Scottish Highlands*, was written for a quite large orchestra whereas the shorter *A Scottish Lullaby*, based almost entirely on the Gaelic melody 'O Can Ye Sew Cushions?' which Montgomery used in *The Kidnappers*, is for chamber ensemble. Both works received broadcast performances on the BBC, most notably in 1956 by the Bournemouth Symphony Orchestra conducted by Charles Groves. Neither work was published, although *A Scottish Lullaby* was rejected in 1966 on the grounds that an original work would be considered more appropriate after the Managing Director of Ascherberg, Hopwood and Crew, having heard his score for *The Truth about Women* (1957), invited Montgomery to submit any unpublished light music for consideration.

In 1954 Montgomery composed a score which was to set his film music career very firmly along a particular path. The picture was Rank's *Doctor in the House*, and it was a great commercial success. It was also the first major film to bring his name to public attention, as well as being the first comedy for which he wrote the music. This latter point is particularly important. Of the thirty or so feature scores Montgomery composed in the period 1954–1962, the great majority are for comedy films. He was responsible for a further three scores for films in the *Doctor* series, and the first six in the cycle started by *Carry On Sergeant*.

Starring in *Doctor in the House* were some of the rising actors of the British film industry, such as Dirk Bogarde, Kenneth More and Donald Sinden, as well as Montgomery's old flame Muriel Pavlow. The producer/director pairing of Betty Box and Ralph Thomas were also beginning to make their mark. Ralph's brother Gerald, later to direct the *Carry On* films and others which Montgomery scored, worked on the film as editor. As Montgomery later noted, this did not lead to any guaranteed success:

---

9    *Herald Express*, 22 February 1960

I was called in once to write the background music for what was at that time quite a new type of film comedy. Seeing the run-through, I myself thought it was pretty grim, but on talking to the producer and the director I found that both of them were genuinely very unsure in their minds about its prospects. They liked it; the questions was, would anyone else? As it turned out, they needn't have worried, because the film, 'Doctor in the House', made a profit of somewhere in the thousands percentage area.[10]

Writing to Philip Larkin at the time he composed the score, Montgomery presents a slightly different view of his 'most lucrative job' since last writing: 'It's really a very funny picture: the first picture I've had to do with for which I've been able to feel a genuine unforced enthusiasm.'[11] As with Kingsley Amis' fears about the fate of music from *To Move the Passions*, Montgomery also confessed to having used the music from a song Larkin and he had written a few years previously:

> I felt very nostalgic during the music recording, because one of the dance numbers I've put in it is our old friend of Shrewsbury-Wellington days, <u>Now Let's Talk About Love</u>. There's no one to sing it, unfortunately – it's just background to Kay Kendall in a restaurant scene – so you won't be getting any money, I'm afraid. But I'm quite well in with Francis Day & Hunter these days, so we might try publishing it, yes? (For pseudonymous purposes, how about music by James Dixon, lyrics by Christine Callaghan?)[12] It needs a bit of polishing, one way and another, so be prepared to think about it when we do at last succeed in meeting.[13]

For this quite 'new type of film comedy' Montgomery composed a quite new type of score, establishing a style which would serve him well in a number of similar films over the coming years. In music that is in many ways very different from his previous work, there remain some of his fingerprints. The boisterous title music has prominent high horns, with the main theme in the brass beneath rapid, scurrying violin passagework, and there is a more pompous sequential section which hints at the ceremonial music of Elgar and Walton. Passages from these titles are reintroduced later in the film. Shorter sections start with woodwind trills accompanied by the harp and make use of swooning, sliding strings; rasping brass interjections accompany moments of drama; pizzicato lower strings plod about, and these sections often end on unresolved chords. Montgomery is much given to woodwind solos with little or no accompaniment, particularly on the clarinet and bassoon (the latter sometimes finishes sections unaccompanied). He enjoys using the clarinet in its lowest register, often with trills, and occasionally he uses a pair in thirds higher up. The xylophone appears from time to time, although not as much as it does in later scores. Violins on their own often rush about. The short final section swells up in romantic fashion and Montgomery allows himself to fall back into chromatic sequences. Even if Kingsley Amis rather exaggerated when he observed that the score 'might have attracted more attention than it did if a technical defect had not seen to it that the music

---

10   From notes for a lecture on films (GB-Ob. MSS. Eng. C. 3967–8)
11   RBM to Larkin, 13 February 1954
12   Characters in *Lucky Jim*, Kingsley Amis (1954)
13   RBM to Larkin, 13 February 1954

itself remained practically inaudible throughout',[14] it is true that this accomplished score with its appropriate underlying sense of irony is not well served overall by the balance of the soundtrack.

Montgomery was aware of the style he worked in and outlined it in notes he made for a talk on composing for films:

> Comedies mean perpetual allegros, with staccato-dots and great belts of semi-quavers and a very large number of pages of bustling full score to each interminable minute of playing time (aeroplane pictures give much the same sort of trouble, but in those, after the commotion of the take-off, you can at least settle down eventually to some huge bawling eroico tune above the cotton wool of the white cumulus formations). No, for a film-composing ergophobe like me, heavy drama is the thing: swingeing slow recitative passages for unison strings, with emotive intervals and much crescendoing and diminuendoing, written out just once on the first violin stave with the direction 'same as 1st vlns' on the second violin, viola and cello lines. Love-stuff is nice, too, and so are naval ships leaving harbour on a mission; whooping upward glissandi on horns for the ships' hooters – a device also useful for ferocious hunting dogs (see *Walküre*, First Act) in historical pictures.[15]

Some of these can be seen by examining the music he composed in response to the music measurement sheet reproduced below. It is from the score for a maritime comedy, *Watch Your Stern*, which Montgomery composed for Peter Rogers and Gerald Thomas in 1960. This particular section (3M1: that is, the first music section in the third reel of the film) lasts for 2½ minutes and accompanies action in which there is only one character, Blissworth. There is no dialogue and the only speech during the section consists of very occasional remarks from Blissworth to himself. The music takes the place of words in commenting on the action.

|  | Ft | Time |
|---|---|---|
| Music starts as Blissworth takes hold of wire | 0 | 0 |
| Pulls plug from wall | 3 | 2 |
| Starts working on plug with screwdriver | 8 | 5⅓ |
| With a puff of smoke and a bang Blissworth blows a fuse | 10 | 6⅔ |
| Porthole cover falls and hits Blissworth on head | 11 | 7⅓ |
| Holding head with one hand, sucking fingers and complaining bitterly, he moves away from porthole | 14 | 9⅓ |
| Sits down | 26 | 17⅓ |
| Puts burning fingers in glass of gin | 31½ | 20⅔ |
| Sucks gin from fingers | 36½ | 24⅓ |
| Spits gin out | 37½ | 25 |
| Sees plan of torpedo on table, Blissworth forward to inspect it | 46 | 30⅔ |
| Cut to L/S Blissworth getting up from chair and taking plan from desk | 51 | 34 |
| Blissworth to self 'That's it' (pointing out error in plan) starts | 69 | 46 |
| 'That's it' Blissworth to self ends | 72 | 48 |
| Blissworth starts drawing on plan | 75 | 50 |

---

14    *Memoirs*, Amis, p. 73
15    From notes for a lecture on films (GB-Ob. MSS. Eng. C. 3967–8)

'There, damn fools. Oh, what have I done?' Blissworth to self.

| | | |
|---|---|---|
| Dialogue to self continues | 84 | 56 |
| He starts frantically rubbing out alterations on plan | 92 | 1:01⅓ |
| In picking up plan he knocks a glass of gin over it | 98½ | 1:05⅔ |
| Takes handkerchief from pocket and starts mopping gin from plan | 107½ | 1:11⅔ |
| N.B. Camera pans Blissworth to bathroom | | |
| Cut to Blissworth entering bathroom | 130 | 1:26⅔ |
| He wrings out sodden handkerchief | 132 | 1:28 |
| Hangs it over electric fire to dry | 140½ | 1:33⅔ |
| Cut to Blissworth entering cabin | 148 | 1:38⅔ |
| Picks up plan | 153½ | 1:42⅓ |
| Blissworth enters bathroom carrying plan | 163 | 1:48⅔ |
| Hangs plan in front of fire | 171 | 1:54⅓ |
| Blissworth enters cabin from bathroom | 184½ | 2:02⅔ |
| Brushes remainder of gin from table | 188 | 2:05⅓ |
| N.B. Starts generally tidying up cabin | | |
| Picks up refrigerator plan | 201 | 2:14 |
| Cut to insert refrigerator plan | 203½ | 2:15⅔ |
| Cut to Blissworth, an idea strikes him | 206½ | 2:17⅔ |
| Puts plan on table where other plan was originally | 216 | 2:24 |
| Music ends as door click is heard off and Blissworth reacts | 225 | 2:30[16] |

Not all these individual timings needed specific pointing, but there are enough to demonstrate the skill required to compose an appropriate length of music which holds together.

Montgomery had what he referred to as his 'slapstick and cod formula'.[17] Elsewhere he calls it his '"Carry-On" bag of tricks'.[18] He makes great use of the possibilities of flutter-tongued muted brass. The rasp which accompanies the porthole cover striking Blissworth on the head (at 7⅓ seconds) is vivid, as is another when Blissworth knocks over a glass of gin (1 minute 5⅔ seconds). When Blissworth writes frantically (50 seconds) he is accompanied by a rushing motif on the xylophone; when he attempts to erase this writing (1 minute 1⅓ seconds) the strings scurry about. At 2 minutes 17⅔ seconds an idea strikes Blissworth; Montgomery has a single sforzando note high on the vibraphone ring out above the orchestral writing. This is the musical equivalent of the light bulb which often appears in cartoon films above the heads of characters who have been visited with a great scheme.

Many of these same fingerprints can be seen in his score for *Carry On Nurse*. One of Montgomery's most assured sections in any film is 4M2. Here there are three motifs which are linked into a seamless flow. The first is the use of flutter-tongued muted brass to accompany burning catheters; the second is the use of scurrying strings whenever people are seen frantically attempting to tidy the ward ready for Matron's inspection; the third is the portentous use of the 'Carry On' theme [Example 10.1] in the tuba [Example 10.2] as Matron is seen marching menacingly towards the ward.

16    Music measurement sheet 3M1: GB-Ob. MS. Eng. c. 3968, fols. 212–257
17    RBM to Eric Rogers, 10 May 1962
18    RBM to Peter Rogers, 26 March 1962

**Example 10.1 *Carry On Nurse*: Section 1M1**

The action switches constantly and swiftly between these three scenes, and Montgomery's music matches it step for step with an astonishing facility. The autograph for this section shows Montgomery's extraordinary attention to detail. He notes with arrows above the strings what action is taking place, and every bar has the culminative timing of the section written above it. Marks of articulation and expression are also extensive, with most notes qualified in some way. Crescendo marks are so exact as to extend often over no more than a quaver. Matron's tuba melody is marked 'molto pomposo'. All this is typical of his scores, and Montgomery's attention to detail added to the pressure of time he fell under when composing for films.

**Example 10.2 *Carry On Nurse*: Section 4M2**

The section above builds to a clearly ironic orgy of brass, in the manner of *Tannhaüser* or *Lohengrin*, as Matron finally arrives in the ward. Montgomery had few problems introducing frivolity into his scores. The author of light-hearted detective novels found it natural to bring this tendency to his music. Towards the end of *Carry On Nurse* (8M2) Montgomery introduces snatches of the drinking song 'Landlord, Fill the Flowing Bowl' when various inebriated patients are moving furtively around the hospital; in the title sequence for *Watch Your Stern* there is a reference to 'What Shall We Do With a Drunken Sailor'; in *Carry On Teacher* (2M4) Miss Alcock, the PE mistress, attempts to pull on shorts that are too small for her to the strains of the 'Song of the Volga Boatmen' ('O, heave-ho!'). He was not averse to throwing in reminiscences from other composers. 'Brass, when you get to the bit from *The Planets*', he was once heard to say, 'play it very loud.'[19]

Montgomery made use of motifs when appropriate. Mention has previously been made of his use of the 'Carry On' theme in *Carry On Nurse*. Montgomery wrote

---

19   Douglas Gamley

this theme as a march for the title music of *Carry On Sergeant*, the first film in the series, and in various arrangements, not all by Montgomery, it was used for the title sequences of the first six *Carry On* films. In another section of *Carry On Nurse* (1M2A) the theme is varied in a different way [Example 10.3]. Towards the end of *Carry On Teacher*, (10M4A) a contrasting passage of the march becomes the subject of treatment [Examples 10.4 and 10.5]. A stirring brass motif in the title sequence to *Watch Your Stern* is used during the film when the admiral makes an appearance. We have already seen how in one of Montgomery's early films, *The Kidnappers*, the score makes frequent allusions to the Scottish song 'O Can Ye Sew Cushions?'

Reference to this point has been mainly to Montgomery's later comedy films. This is because they are the most successful films with which he was involved and the ones in which he established his reputation. More importantly, the sources for them have usually survived. As far as his other scores are concerned, it is not possible in a handful of cases even to view the pictures for which he wrote the scores. But there are sufficient films to show (and almost half of his scores were not comedies) that Montgomery was capable of modifying his usual style, if not all of the characteristics, to compose in most veins demanded by directors.

**Example 10.3** *Carry On Nurse*: **Section 1M2A**

**Example 10.4** *Carry On Nurse*: **Section 1M1**

**Example 10.5 *Carry On Teacher*: Section 10MA**

By the late 1950s Montgomery was writing an average of four scores each year. In 1957 Larkin received a letter which began: 'Mr Montgomery is frantically busy on a new picture, but has asked me to tell you – '.[20] These scores include thrillers such as *Guilty?* and *Eyewitness* (both 1956). Montgomery wrote a suitably tense score for the latter; the inclusion of a nerve-jangling motif on the musical saw in the orchestra for the title sequence sets the mood for the following film. *Guilty?* has a dramatic title sequence, with plenty of brass and percussion under a sustained and soaring string theme. The dissonance is controlled but dominant. He makes more use of atmospheric effects, with high shimmering strings and interpolations on the vibraphone. Other fingerprints remain, such as sliding horn counter-melodies, unison unaccompanied violins and woodwind solos. The style is similar in *The Brides of Fu Manchu* (1966). Montgomery wrings some hideous dissonances out of the orchestra to accompany the hideous behaviour of the characters on screen. In contrast, the title music for *Twice Round the Daffodils* (1962) has a broad string theme of enormous passion coupled with a luscious orchestration that would not appear out of place in the most romantic of films [Example 10.6].

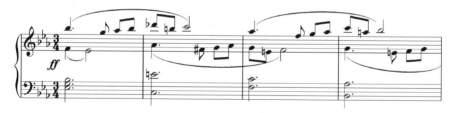

**Example 10.6 *Twice Round the Daffodils*: Section 1M1**

There was the incidental music, but not the songs (they were composed by Lionel Bart), for *The Duke Wore Jeans*, a 1958 musical starring Tommy Steele. This reduced contribution suited Montgomery; although he did not think much of the film, it was at least 'exceptionally well paid, and also not so hectic and burdensome as they mostly are'.[21] In the same year Montgomery wrote the score for *Heart of a Child*, a tear-jerker involving a boy and his dog set in the Austrian Tyrol during the Second World War. There is a bold romantic theme which perfectly fits the storyline,

20    Larkin to Judy Egerton, 28 May 1957 [SLPL]
21    RBM to Geoffrey Bush, 30 January 1958

and Montgomery later explained some particular scoring: 'It's a great big gloomy dog and I have written solo 'cello music to depict it. The boy's music is on solo clarinet.'[22] Muir Mathieson was very impressed by the score. He was not the only one who felt this way: after the recording the orchestra burst into spontaneous applause, an unusual tribute for a composer.[23] Mathieson also thought that there was the basis for 'a brilliant sonata for clarinet and 'cello',[24] and Montgomery indeed later claimed to have 'made a short, self-contained piece out of the boy-and-dog music',[25] but nothing of this has survived.

His next score after *Heart of a Child* was *Carry On Sergeant*, the first of a series of films which has earned a special place in the history of British cinema. It was directed by Gerald Thomas and produced by Peter Rogers; Montgomery had composed the music for this pairing's first film, *Circus Friends*, in 1956 and had been recommended to them by both Betty Box (Rogers' wife) and her brother Sydney.[26] The film had actually begun life as a treatment of *The Bull Boys* by R.F. Delderfield (1912–1972), a story about ballet dancers and an army defector which was far from being a comedy. Sydney Box had suggested it to Rogers and Thomas, thinking it might transfer well to the screen as a comedy set in the army. Gerald Thomas, himself not long out of the army, was very interested. Various writers were approached, including Eric Sykes and Spike Milligan, but it was Norman Hudis who wrote the final screenplay. Rogers and Thomas took the treatment to a company called Anglo-Amalgamated which agreed to a low budget of £70,000. *The Bull Boys* had never been a popular title for the project, and during the shooting Stuart Levy, one of the directors of Anglo-Amalgamated, suggested *Carry On Sergeant* as a title, an attempt to cash in on the success of *Carry On Admiral*, a comedy released in 1956 by an entirely different production team.

In keeping with the subject matter, Montgomery composed the entire score for military band. He had some previous experience of writing for this ensemble through the commissions from his friend Lt. Jaeger of the Band of the Irish Guards for *Heroic March* and *Flourish for a Crowning*. Even so, in March 1958, some months before he needed to write the music, Montgomery asked the BBC Library if he could borrow full scores of arrangements by Gerard Williams for the BBC Military Band so that he could familiarize himself with the style.[27] The soundtrack was recorded by the Band of the Coldstream Guards conducted by Montgomery. He wanted a guitar in the instrumentation and felt he had to explain its inclusion: 'I ought perhaps to mention that one of the things we want to record is the sound of a guitar string breaking: needless to say the player will be fully compensated (including if necessary hospital bills) for producing this effect!'[28]

---

22    *Evening Standard*, 6 February 1958
23    *Western Morning News*, 31 January 1958
24    *Record Mirror*, 8 February 1958
25    RBM to Brian Doyle (Rank), 2 March 1958
26    Sydney Box (1907–1983), producer
27    RBM to BBC Library, 25 March 1958
28    RBM to Major Douglas Pope, 3 May 1958

Although *Carry On Sergeant* was, of course, a great success (it was the third top grossing film in the UK in 1958), it nearly ground to a halt after Thomas showed the rushes to the film's distributors and they failed to raise as much as a smile. The final result was a tribute to Peter Rogers' editing. Montgomery scored the next five in the series, and for the title music they all used versions of the march he had composed for *Carry On Sergeant* (he later claimed that 'it was intended to be the sort of thing a not very intelligent Army bandmaster might have written round about 1900; but unfortunately I'm stuck with it for this whole series of pictures').[29] Montgomery arranged it for full orchestra for *Carry On Nurse* (1959) but, as was his habit, sent it to Eric Rogers[30] when Peter Rogers suggested that a version in the style of Ted Heath or Geraldo would be appropriate for *Carry On Teacher* (1959): 'It's pretty intractable, but I feel that if anyone can make a free symphonic-pop version of it, you can.'[31] This version was also used for *Carry On Constable* (1960) and *Carry On Regardless* (1961).

Montgomery's greatest achievement in his film work came in 1961 with the release of *Raising the Wind*. Not only did he compose the score, but he also wrote the story and screenplay. The film is a comedy set in a music college, and Montgomery used the *Doctor* films as his model. Montgomery had been working on the idea for some time, initially with an enthusiastic Sydney Box. In May 1957 he sent the 'bare-bones plot-summary'[32] of the screenplay to Box, but later in the year was giving the reasons why the script was not yet completed:

> a) Keeping the 'Doctor' films out of my hair; b) the fact that a music student's life has no distinctive stages in the way that a medical student's has; c) the fact that, except for people who are going to be schoolteachers, the examinations are of no professional importance; and d) the fact that, music teaching being such a grim business, there are no standard jokes on the subject, combined with the further distressing circumstances that the jokes I've thought up myself don't seem to me to be very good.[33]

At the very end of the year Box received the screenplay, with a note from Montgomery in which he refuses to apologise for its obvious 'debt' to the *Doctor* films 'as I believe something on those lines was what you wanted'.[34] By May 1958 Box had persuaded Peter Rogers to take an interest in the project and was encouraging Montgomery to meet with him to discuss it. Two months later Rogers poured cold water on the possibility of producing the film; this did not deter Box, but prompted him to announce that he would do it if no one else would. By early 1959, however, Rogers had changed his mind, and in March he paid Montgomery £1,500 for both the screenplay and the as yet unwritten score. 'I'm delighted that you should think "OH, MUSIC" [the project's working title] worth buying', Montgomery wrote to

29    RBM to Eric Rogers, 11 April 1959
30    Eric Rogers (1921–1978), composer
31    RBM to Eric Rogers, 11 April 1959
32    RBM to Sydney Box, 8 May 1957
33    Ibid., 2 September 1957
34    Ibid., 30 December 1957

Rogers, 'and look forward immensely to watching you make a sow's-ear-into-a-silk-purse transformation of it.'[35]

Events started to move faster. Rogers was soon suggesting genres for the title music (a piano concerto at first, then a five-finger exercise jazzed up, neither of which was eventually used), and the script was revised. In April 1960, following an enquiry from Rogers asking about progress, Montgomery replied that Rogers had told him to delay the work until he had finished the score for *Doctor in Love*. Montgomery claimed that Eric Sykes helped a little with the revision,[36] although later Sykes could not recall this,[37] and Montgomery also took the advice of his old friend John Maxwell: 'In the end I used hardly any of your detailed suggestions for the film script, but they did have the valuable effect of getting my own mind on the move again, and everyone now seems to feel pretty well satisfied with the final product.'[38] Gerald Thomas, the director, clearly fell into this category: '[I] must tell you I have put on several pounds in weight through laughing. I congratulate you on a really good piece of work both technically and dialogue-wise.'[39] Montgomery approached another old friend, Thomas Armstrong (now Principal of the Royal Academy of Music) to ask if Rogers and Thomas could visit the Academy before shooting started: 'Needless to say, they wouldn't be aiming to produce anything like a replica of the Academy, but rather to get the general "feel" of the place.'[40] The London Philharmonic Choir was asked to provide the singers for the film and was immediately enthusiastic: 'Our difficulty will be to select 60 from the many volunteers.'[41]

*Raising the Wind*, as the film was finally called ('Couldn't be more fatuous, but one has no control over these things', he later wrote)[42] was a labour of love for Montgomery. He was involved in every aspect, even appearing briefly as the conductor of *Messiah*, and he gave the impression of enjoying the experience more than anything else he did in films.[43] At one point he was going to play the piano himself, particularly as he had recently joined the Musicians' Union, but in the end he engaged Douglas Gamley to do it. Gamley not only had to play the first few bars of Beethoven's *Hammerklavier Sonata* with a bicycle chain laid across the wires ('bicycle chain will be supplied by us'),[44] but also had to play Chopin's *Revolutionary Study* with only his hands visible on the screen. Gamley suggested that a concert pianist should be brought in to play it better. 'That's why I want you to do it,' Montgomery told him. 'I want you to play it slightly faster than you can. I won't put your name on the credits, but I want it to be just not quite good enough.' Gamley practised a great deal and completed one perfectly good take which could

35    RBM to Peter Rogers, 20 March 1959
36    *Herald Express*, 10 October 1960
37    Eric Sykes to author, 14 May 1993
38    RBM to John Maxwell, 2 December 1960
39    Gerald Thomas to RBM, 4 July 1960
40    RBM to Thomas Armstrong, 4 February 1961
41    London Philharmonic Choir to RBM, 20 February 1961
42    RBM to John Maxwell, 20 September 1962
43    Gerald Thomas
44    RBM to Douglas Gamley, 8 March 1961

have been used. Montgomery, however, insisted on one more take at a speed he tapped out which was just too fast for an accurate performance. The result is very amusing: a brash, self-confident fellow sits down and blunders through the piece.[45] Montgomery coached both Kenneth Williams and Leslie Philips to conduct so well that the latter received a round of applause from the players. The orchestra, the Sinfonia of London, an ensemble with which Montgomery had worked many times and which was assembled specifically for film work, enjoyed the shooting so much that they did not need Montgomery's apology for having to take Rossini's *William Tell Overture* ridiculously fast.[46]

Montgomery's screenplay makes use of certain stock characters. Eric Barker plays an absent-minded composer, whilst James Robertson Justice more or less recreates his role of Sir Lancelot Spratt from the *Doctor* films in what seems to be an affectionate send-up of the notoriously acerbic conductor Sir Thomas Beecham (1879–1961) who coincidentally died shortly before shooting began. The link with the *Doctor* films is made even closer by the use of the same buildings (University College, Gower Street, London) for the exterior shots of the fictitious music college as are used for the exterior shots of the equally fictitious St Swithun's medical school. Montgomery also made use of anecdotes from his friends. The incident where a craven string ensemble leaves a rather prissy music society in the lurch was based on a story about his own student days that Eric Coates (1886–1957) once told Montgomery when they were together at the International Musicians' Association.[47]

*Raising the Wind* had an encouraging success at the box office. One reviewer claimed to know why: 'What makes this film a cut above several others turned out to the same formula is the fact that someone in on the deal (I suspect Mr Bruce Montgomery, a professional composer [...]) really knows a good deal about music. There is a devastating analysis of how to write a pop tune [...] and an equally devastating demonstration of how professional musicians can spike a conductor they don't like.'[48] Montgomery never had any such problems as a conductor. He knew what he was doing and the players respected him as a musician, although he did not have as great an authority over the orchestra as someone such as Eric Rogers because he did not have as violent a temper. After he threw a party for the Sinfonia of London following the recording for *Raising the Wind*, Montgomery was told that 'warm and friendly feelings [...] are always felt for you, whenever we are working together'.[49] He hired a room at Pinewood for the party, and the accent was on drink. A party he had thrown for the Sinfonia after an earlier film had been similarly rowdy. Douglas Gamley had been out of the country at the time: 'Terrible tragedy you were away,' he was told by the orchestra's manager on his return. 'Wonderful evening. Can't remember anything about it.'[50]

45    Douglas Gamley
46    Peter Rogers
47    RBM to Josephine Bell, 5 October 1961
48    Peter Green in *John O'London's*, 31 August 1961
49    Sinfonia of London to RBM, 10 February 1962
50    Douglas Gamley

Montgomery helped to promote *Raising the Wind* in various ways, amongst them travelling to Norwich to be interviewed on Anglia Television in October, and going to Dublin in November with two members of the cast for the Irish premiere. Although Gerald Thomas felt the musical setting was a little erudite, the same company might have produced Montgomery's sequel, a script provisionally entitled *Lowering the Tone*, had it not been too busy with other projects.[51] Some of the characters from *Raising the Wind* survived, and the screenplay concerned a new music festival in a midlands' town with all the southern/northern prejudices on show. A 'muck and brass' mayor tries to wreck the festival with the help of the local paper and succeeds in turning it into a disaster. Following the denouncing of the mayor, however, the organisers of the festival live to fight another day. Montgomery quite liked it: 'The new script is making me laugh quite a reasonable amount', he informed Peter Rogers, 'and I hope it'll do the same for you.'[52]

Despite the problems that eventually overwhelmed his film music career, Montgomery gained a reputation as a very able composer. Malcolm Arnold, himself the composer of over eighty scores, has claimed that Montgomery was regarded 'very highly'[53] in the film world. The director of the *Carry On* films, Gerald Thomas, has said the same.[54] We have already seen that after the recording of Montgomery's score for *Heart of a Child* in 1955, the orchestra gave him the rare tribute of a spontaneous ovation.[55] Douglas Gamley, who helped Montgomery complete some of his scores, thought him a wonderful craftsman with an excellent technique. A sequence in *Carry On Cruising* illustrates Gamley's point: a character does handsprings all along the deck, with irregular timings, and Montgomery manages to catch them all in the music. This ability to point the action was one of his particular gifts. It explains why he was, for a time, so much in demand for comedy scores. From 1958 he also conducted all his scores.

Alas, his success was not destined to last much longer than *Raising the Wind*. For a number of years Montgomery had been becoming less and less reliable at producing scores under the demanding schedules imposed and expected by film companies. As early as 1955, when composing for a film called *Cartouche*, he had to summon help to complete the work. Philip Martell, the musical director for many of Montgomery's early films and a great admirer of his work, suggested Douglas Gamley, Muir Mathieson's assistant. When Gamley arrived at Montgomery's Brixham house, having travelled down from London to receive instructions for the single lengthy section he had to compose, almost the first words he heard from Montgomery were: 'Of my last six major features, I have failed to complete five.' Gamley thought this almost a statement of Montgomery's working methods, the verbal equivalent of the sashes worn by people who are members of an order.[56] He played Gamley some

---

51   Peter Rogers
52   RBM to Peter Rogers, 11 December 1961
53   Sir Malcolm Arnold
54   Gerald Thomas
55   *Western Morning News*, 31 January 1958
56   Douglas Gamley

acetates of his previous scores ('which were very good, marvellous')[57] so that the idiom was clear, but told him little about the film. They spent most of the day talking about music in general, finding they had many likes and prejudices in common.

At around the same time, Montgomery was quoted in a magazine about the problems he had when composing the score of a short film, *A Prince for Cynthia*, in 1953:

> 'The important part of the dream, very romantic, very rich,' says the composer, 'was exactly the kind of writing I did best and most easily. I settled down to it at once. Three days later I hadn't thought of a single note which seemed to be the slightest good. I had sat at the piano, I had ridden on tops of buses, I had gone to the local bar for several drinks, and none of these things had produced the right tune for Cynthia.' [Montgomery went to see Mathieson, played him several ideas, one of which Mathieson liked.] 'It's a sad, sighing tune, high up on the strings'. Muir Mathieson remarked 'Use it on the titles too, all the strings on it, with the trombones holding the harmonies.' 'So I really built a whole score on this particular tune, Cynthia's theme, which comes in over and over again and reaches a climax, of course, on the kiss.'[58]

A glance at Montgomery's film list shows that as time goes on the number of different companies by whom he was engaged dwindles until it is only G.H.W. Productions, the makers of the *Carry On* films, which is employing him. Gerald Thomas, who worked with Montgomery as closely as anybody, remembers that they kept on using him because he was such a nice person and the music he actually completed was so good. He seemed like a professor or academic, not quite of this world. Thomas did not ask or expect him to behave like others in the profession. Peter Rogers knew that Montgomery did not like deadlines. He knew what he had to do, but was too lazy to do it, 'like a landscape gardener who didn't want to do the weeding'.[59] Rogers had the impression that Montgomery would much rather be at home in Brixham so that he could pop down to the pub in his carpet slippers.

Because of Montgomery's approach, there was often a panic on the day of the recording. A copyist was usually in the backroom writing out parts for Reel 7 whilst Reel 1 was being recorded. Montgomery was often late for recording sessions. Thomas reached the point when he used to tell the musicians that the recording was due to start at 10 a.m. whilst Montgomery was given the impression that it started at 9 a.m. He would arrive in a terrible sweat at 9.55, apologising profusely, and Thomas would be able to say rather curtly, without actually being annoyed or delayed, that they had better make a start.[60]

Others were not so forgiving. As Montgomery's reputation spread throughout the industry, he was gently dropped by some of the companies who had used him previously. A case where he badly let down his employers came early in 1960. Towards the end of the previous year Montgomery had been contracted by Cavalcade Films to be composer, conductor and orchestrator for a film called *Follow That Horse*.

57    Ibid.
58    *The Sound Track* (USA), August/September 1955
59    Peter Rogers
60    Gerald Thomas

The recording sessions were booked to start on 11 January, but nine days before Montgomery called them off, having composed only a few of the required sections. Another composer was called in, and it seems that none of Montgomery's music was used. In a letter to Cavalcade Films, Montgomery blamed himself 'very much for having let you down as a result of (in effect) biting off more than I could chew'.[61]

Peter Rogers, producer of the *Carry On* films, experienced this unreliability in another context. Having listened to Montgomery complain that no one commissioned composers any more, Rogers asked him if he would compose a 'cello concerto. With friends at the BBC, Rogers thought he might be able to arrange a performance at the Promenade Concerts. When Montgomery agreed, Rogers immediately wrote out a substantial cheque. In 1963 Montgomery was writing to Rogers and letting him know that now his domestic problems were 'mercifully smoothing out a bit [...] I shall, of course, carry on (if you'll forgive the phrase) with finishing the 'cello concerto.'[62] On a visit to Dartington for the summer school, Malcolm Arnold was shown a few fragments of the work which included the main theme and told that 'it's only going to be in one movement'. Arnold offered to finish the concerto but was never given the opportunity.[63] Many years later Geoffrey Bush told Kingsley Amis that he thought Montgomery had written 'two chords on the spot and [...] never another note'.[64] Bush later recalled Montgomery sending him a scribbled motif ('nothing as extensive as a theme') for his inspection in a letter.[65] Rogers never saw anything of the concerto, nor did he get his money back. Beyond two sketches of four bars' length there is nothing to indicate that Montgomery made any serious attempt to compose the work.

Montgomery's film work came to an abrupt end in 1962 when he precipitated a similar crisis with the music for *Carry On Cruising* as he had for *Follow That Horse* in 1960. He wrote very little of the required score in time for the recording sessions, and both Gamley and Eric Rogers, the latter having previously helped Montgomery with popular style arrangements, had to be summoned to rescue the situation. Gerald Thomas claims that no conscious decision was made not to use Montgomery again,[66] but Peter Rogers remembers differently. He felt that Montgomery had let them down professionally and found it unfair that the composers who had done most of the work on *Carry On Cruising* had not received the credit.[67] Douglas Gamley met Rogers at Pinewood Studios shortly after this episode and found him still very angry, to the extent that he had already asked Eric Rogers to compose the scores for future *Carry On* films. Gamley was told that he would have been asked to write them if Peter Rogers had seen him before meeting Eric Rogers, such was his determination to drop Montgomery.[68] Montgomery may have seen that the writing was on the wall.

---

61    RBM to Thomas Clyde, 12 February 1960

62    RBM to Peter Rogers, 11 October 1963

63    Sir Malcolm Arnold

64    Amis to Larkin, 15 February 1982 [LKA]

65    Geoffrey Bush to author, 14 August 1990

66    Gerald Thomas

67    Peter Rogers

68    Douglas Gamley

In 1960 he had written to his literary agent to arrange a meeting: 'With the picture business decaying momently, I must meet you soon and pick your brains about how best to make money by writing; I feel a definite need to go on keeping myself in the style to which I'm accustomed.'[69]

*Carry On Cruising* was the last straw for the only director/producer pairing who were still standing by him. Thomas and Peter Rogers never employed Montgomery again, and it is ironic that the commission for the one remaining film for which he composed the score, *The Brides of Fu Manchu* in 1966, came about at the last moment as a result of the indisposition of the contracted composer. A few months after *Carry on Cruising*, Thomas wrote to Montgomery: 'Peter and I have decided to have a change with the music on *The Iron Maiden*, which I am sure you will appreciate. Don't be too depressed, we still love you.'[70] Relations between the three men certainly remained outwardly cordial. They kept in touch, particularly over wine. 'The hunt for White Musigny continues,' was Montgomery's rallying cry to Peter Rogers in 1965.[71] Two weeks later he reported partial success: 'White Musigny seems to be like white crows, completely unobtainable. A useful merchant has, however, offered me Corton Charlemagne and Meusault-Blagny, both of 1962, both shipped by Louis Latour.'[72]

---

69     RBM to Peter Watt, 12 September 1960
70     Gerald Thomas to RBM, 17 August 1962
71     RBM to Peter Rogers, 10 March 1965
72     Ibid., 26 March 1965

**1  Domus, RBM's childhood home**

**2  RBM in 1925, aged 4**

**3 Olive, RBM, Robert Montgomery, Elspeth, Sheila and unidentified man at Hayling Island, August 1928**

**4 RBM at his piano in Rock Hill House, *c.*1950**

5  RBM composing at his piano in Rock Hill House, *c.*1950

6  Jeni Turnbull, RBM, Mrs and Mr Turnbull at the Crown and Thistle, Abingdon, New Year's Eve, 1954 (*Jeni Turnbull*)

7    Sinfonia of London dinner at ISM Club, *c.*1957. RBM on nearest table, 6th from right, looking away from camera. Others present include Muir Mathieson and Malcolm Arnold, on top table, respectively 5th and 6th from left. (*James Brown*)

8  RBM with his parents and Nora, *c.*1960

9 RBM with Elspeth, Sheila and Nora at Rock Hill House, August 1960

10 RBM's brief conducting appearance in *Raising the Wind*, 1961 (*Canal+ Image UK*)

**11  RBM with his mother and Mr C.A. Warnford, assistant manager of the ABC Cinema, Torquay, at a showing of *Raising the Wind*, 1961**

**12  Week Meadow (*author*)**

13  Brian Aldiss, Kingsley Amis and RBM at the British Science Fiction
Association Convention, Bull Hotel, Peterborough, April 1963 (*Brian Aldiss*)

14  RBM with Desmond Bagley at Week Meadow, *c.*1970 (*Joan Bagley*)

15  RBM with Ann outside Week Meadow on their wedding day, 19 February 1976

# Chapter 11

# 'Complicated by downright panic':
# Films 1958–1962

A number of issues are raised by Montgomery's involvement in film work. Why, for instance, did composing scores dominate his work in the 1950s to such an extent? The answer to this question is money. Before the 1950s Montgomery had made a modest income from his concert music, and although his detective novels had been fairly lucrative, he discovered that film work brought in the money. Film scores, he told an American friend in 1962, 'even now pay better than books and consequently appeal to my innate instinct for getting relatively large sums of money in return for absolutely small amounts of work'.[1] Montgomery used film work as an excuse for not writing concert music 'by saying he had to go on writing film music to pay his taxes'.[2] Even if the payments he received as composer and conductor were not always vast, performing rights for successful pictures usually made the work thoroughly worthwhile. Some companies gave their composers only 50 per cent of the performing rights, but Peter Rogers felt they deserved 100 per cent. These rights were worth having. In 1958 Montgomery suggested to the director Sydney Box the unusual approach that he might consider composing for nothing the scores for 78 television films Box was intending to shoot that year if he could have the considerable performing rights fees which would result.[3] In 1959 he wrote to his friend, the author Brian Aldiss: 'I'm currently composing music for four films in unbroken succession; you don't happen to know of a cure for the love of money, do you?'[4] When Peter Rogers made a quip about the £500 Montgomery was paid for scoring *Carry On Teacher*, he retorted with: 'Still, even though I am being overpaid, I did do a bit of work on it somewhere back in the lost years of my youth.'[5]

The ample financial rewards also brought their responsibilities and irritations. In 1958 Montgomery had arranged a trip to Jamaica, which was to be part holiday and part research for a story commission. He cancelled it when offered a film score at the usual short notice, only to discover a little later that the film (*Anna*) had been abandoned. He told a friend in 1959 that he was suffering from 'too much money in the bank (this [...] is delusory, since most of what I have is ear-marked for tax: but it's demoralising none the less'. In the same letter he also reported that he was

---

1     RBM to Anthony Boucher, 27 June 1962
2     Amis to Larkin, 15 February 1982, reporting a conversation with Geoffrey Bush [LKA]
3     Sydney Box to RBM, 25 August 1958
4     RBM to Brian Aldiss, 12 November 1959
5     RBM to Peter Rogers, 11 July 1959

'currently being ground between the upper and nether millstones of two overlapping film jobs'.[6]

In tandem with his steadily growing income went an awareness of, or at least an uneasiness about, the nature and value of his work. Talking about Montgomery, Geoffrey Bush told Amis that writing film music was 'V. demoralising; the speed you have to work at means you put down the first thing that comes into your head *all the time*'.[7] Peter Rogers felt that although Montgomery enjoyed the income from films, the work was rather beneath his talent.[8] Whilst composing the background music for *The Duke Wore Jeans*, Montgomery referred to it as 'rather lower than most in aesthetic content, but exceptionally well paid'.[9] His clearest opinion of the level of music expected for broad comedy came when he was in trouble over completing the score for *Carry On Cruising* and explaining to Douglas Gamley what was required:

> The very opening of the picture, at which point (in theory) no one yet knows it's going to be a comedy [...] calls for some sort of tweet-tweet music on flutes (you'll realise what you've let yourself in for when I say that if we did a parody of Beethoven's Minuet in G it would have everyone rolling uncontrollably in the aisles).
>
> The chief thing to remember about the score as a whole is that YOU CAN'T POSSIBLY BE TOO VULGAR AND OBVIOUS. I mean, if 'Funiculi Funicula' weren't copyright, that would be the ideal thing to use for the Italian sequence. Anyway, put your highbrow instincts into cold storage for the duration.[10]

Over the phone he told Gamley: 'You must understand that this is not the moment when you make your name as the great film writer. You have got to write a lot of rubbish.'[11] The letter to Philip Larkin in 1956 previously quoted is especially revealing: 'There's still time, I suppose, for me to switch to some pursuit more highly esteemed than either film music or detective fiction – but should I be any good at it if I did? And what would become of the big cheques I so much enjoy receiving?'[12]

His tune had certainly changed on the financial rewards. Whilst composing the score for *Raising a Riot* in 1954 he told his parents that 'the film is going ahead tolerably well, but it's been exceptionally trying, in one way and another, and really will, I think, be my last: writing is not only more profitable but also a more gentlemanly occupation – less like jungle warfare'.[13] Early in his film career Montgomery discovered that his talents were not quite what he imagined. When he once remarked to Muir Mathieson that he thought he was particularly good at romantic music, Mathieson 'said I wasn't, that I rambled far too much harmonically, and that in fact the thing I was really good at was comedy!'[14] His type-casting as a composer of music for comedies irritated him. 'Heavy drama, pathos and love stuff

6     RBM to Evelyn Smith, 12 October 1959
7     Amis to Larkin, 15 February 1982 [LKA]
8     Peter Rogers
9     RBM to Geoffrey Bush, 30 January 1958
10    RBM to Douglas Gamley, 10 March 1962
11    Douglas Gamley
12    RBM to Larkin, 19 June 1956
13    RBM to parents, 28 October 1954
14    *The Sound Track* (USA), August/September 1955

are what I'm temperamentally suited for,' he informed Philip Martell. 'Consequently I never get anything but comedies and thrillers.'[15] Just as he was starting the score for *Doctor in Love* in 1960 Montgomery told Geoffrey Bush 'I'm mortally sick of comedies.'[16] When he complained to Malcolm Arnold that he was never asked to score big films for companies such as Twentieth-Century Fox, Arnold told him that it was because the *Carry On* films had never been popular in the United States.[17] He certainly had no illusions about the sort of work he was involved in. His letters are rich with references: 'I can't say I was very thrilled with the picture, but still, it's a job', he wrote about *Raising a Riot*;[18] 'a bottom-of-the-barrel Ronald Shiner comedy' was his verdict on *Keep it Clean*;[19] *Cartouche* was dismissed as 'a feeble romance'.[20]

The clearest indication of how Montgomery saw his career as a film composer can be seen in a passage from his last novel, *The Glimpses of the Moon*, which was published in 1977, the year before he died. Montgomery was very fond of including caricatures of his friends in his detective novels, but these rarely go further than brief references. Here, as Geoffrey Bush has noted, the character of Broderick Thouless is 'mutatis mutandis […] a portrait of Bruce himself':[21]

> For more than a decade now, Broderick Thouless had resentfully specialised in monsters.
>
> For him, type-casting had set in with a highbrow horror film called *Bone Orchard*, a Shepperton prestige production which against all probability had made a profit of over a quarter of a million pounds. By nature and inclination a gentle romantic composer whose idiom would have been judged moderately progressive by Saint-Saëns or Chaminade, Thouless had launched himself at the task of manufacturing the *Bone Orchard* score like a berserker rabbit trying to topple a tiger, and by over-compensating for his instinctive mellifluousness had managed to wring such hideous noises from his orchestra that he was at once assumed to have a particular flair for dissonance, if not a positive love of it. Ever since then he had accordingly found himself occupied three or four times a year with stakes driven through hearts, foot-loose mummies, giant centipedes aswarm in the Palace of Westminster and other such grim eventualities, a programme which had earned him quite a lot of money without, however, doing anything to enliven an already somewhat morose, complaining temperament. A bachelor of forty-six, he existed in an aura of inveterate despondency, lamenting his wasted life, various real or imagined defects in the luxurious large bungalow he had built himself, the slugs among his peas, his receding hair-line, taxes, the impossibility of getting decent bread delivered, the Rector, jet aircraft, the deterioration in the taste of Plymouth gin ('It's a grain spirit now, you see') and a whole manifest of aches and pains, some of them notional, others the inevitable consequence of smoking too much, a sedentary life, mild obesity, not being young any longer.[22]

15    RBM to Philip Martell, 8 July 1960
16    RBM to Geoffrey Bush, 29 March 1960
17    Sir Malcolm Arnold
18    RBM to parents, 28 October 1954
19    RBM to Larkin, 6 November 1955
20    Ibid.
21    *An Unsentimental Education*, Bush, p. 24
22    *The Glimpses of the Moon*, Chapter 3

More or less everything in this passage is true of Montgomery's own career, and even though he is mocking his own type-casting as a composer for comedy films, the horror score has a parallel. As Montgomery spent the best part of twenty years writing *The Glimpses of the Moon*, it is difficult to know exactly when he wrote this section. But if one assumes that the age he gives Thouless (46) is a fairly accurate description of his own at the time, he would have written it around 1967. In 1966 he composed the score for his last picture, *The Brides of Fu Manchu*, and noted: 'Round about 1908 they'd have considered the noises I made daring, definitely daring.'[23]

There was a further attraction for a composer of film music, especially for one who was struggling to get performances of his concert music. A film score was guaranteed a performance, and with orchestras of the calibre of the London Symphony and Royal Philharmonic being used, there was no need to worry about the level of difficulty. This had repercussions on his more serious work. When Geoffrey Bush asked Montgomery to contribute a work for amateur orchestra to a series he was editing for Novello, he found it very difficult: 'My great trouble, of course, is that the picture business has got me into the way of composing for tip-top players, with the result that I'm finding it almost as difficult to jack myself down technically as to jack myself up artistically.'[24] He failed to produce a piece for the series.

As to why Montgomery eventually became unemployable by the film industry, the main problem, that of failing to complete scores punctually, has already been mentioned. Despite his considerable output of books and concert music in the 1940s and very early 1950s, Montgomery rarely found composing background music easy. The demands of the industry are high. Typically, he would have about three weeks after viewing the fine cut of the film to complete the score, which could be anything between 30 and 50 minutes of music. In 1956, for the film *Circus Friends*, the first picture which Peter Rogers and Gerald Thomas made together, Montgomery began work on 21 June and completed the score on 15 July, although some was recorded on 11 July. The total of all the music sections came to slightly under 40 minutes. In the same year his score for *Checkpoint*, a Rank Organisation film, was composed between 6 and 28 August and lasted for just over 30 minutes. All but one of Montgomery's scores were for full orchestra, and this required a constant and relentless application to produce a certain number of minutes of music each day.

The composition of music for comedies has some demands that are not faced when writing for other types of films. The pointing of comic moments ('mickey-mousing' as it is known in the profession) requires great precision, not only in the composition but also in the execution in the recording studio. Montgomery's ability here has already been mentioned in connection with his work on *Carry On Cruising*. Music sections for comedy rarely require simply a certain amount of rather general background music. As we have seen, the music measurement sheets given to the composer specify exact times during a section when some piece of action calls for a highlight in the score. Thus, a composer can rarely develop an idea for more than a few seconds before he has to switch to another mood, or interrupt the flow for some effect or other. Indeed, one of the skills Montgomery possessed was to knit all these

---

23    RBM to Geoffrey Bush, 21 May 1966
24    Ibid., 14 August 1961

demands into a continuous flow of music which had its own integrity if taken away from the action. The biggest compliment most film composers believe can be paid to their music, and it was one Montgomery often repeated, is that the audience should not be aware of the score whilst watching the picture. If the music overwhelms the action, except, of course, for deliberate dramatic purposes, the score has not done its job properly.

These considerations mean that writing one minute of background music for a comedy film is very different from writing one minute of general atmospheric background music. It was a challenge that Montgomery found initially 'much to his taste', as we have seen.[25] It helped that his early films were short and thus required comparatively little music, but as he graduated to full-length features the demands grew.

One problem Montgomery appeared to have was a lack of confidence in his own ability. He never really thought he was good enough.[26] He had previously shown this in regard to his novels and concert music, despite the considerable success he achieved with them. Gerald Thomas thought some of this might have stemmed from laziness. Montgomery did not sell himself and seemed unambitious, being content to appear occasionally at the studios. He lived in Devon, a long way from the work, whereas most composers lived near the studios and were easily available.[27] He almost always asked another composer (usually Eric Rogers, sometimes Ken Jones) to compose any sections which called for music in a popular style (dance music, for instance). For *Too Young To Love* in 1960, a film dealing with teenagers, Ken Jones composed more of the music than Montgomery. 'I felt a bit guilty about leaving the "pops" to someone else', he wrote to the director, Muriel Box, 'but I'm not terribly up to date in these matters and I felt it was essential to have them absolutely authentic.'[28] This meant that Montgomery wrote less than half the music for a film which required relatively little in the first place. Similarly, when Peter Rogers suggested that the title music for *Carry On Teacher* needed to be in a jazz style, Montgomery sent the march he had originally composed for *Carry On Sergeant* to Eric Rogers. But Montgomery *was* capable of writing and arranging in a lighter style: his title music for *Watch Your Stern*, with its brash brass scoring and syncopated rhythms, is very much the sort of work he would have expected back from Eric Rogers, as indeed was the case when Montgomery wrote the title melody for *Please Turn Over* (1959) but passed it to Rogers for arrangement. Much of this reluctance must be put down to Montgomery's combination of laziness and a lack of confidence.

Both Douglas Gamley and Gerald Thomas have suggested that because of his lack of confidence Montgomery panicked easily,[29] and this could be why he called in other composers when things were not going well. Towards the end of his film career he certainly appeared a changed man, finding the work more difficult than ever and showing signs of stress. One should note his use of the expression 'manufacturing

---

25    *An Unsentimental Education*, Bush, p. 23

26    Gerald Thomas

27    Ibid.

28    RBM to Muriel Box, 1 December 1959

29    Douglas Gamley

the *Bone Orchard* score' in his description of Broderick Thouless in *The Glimpses of the Moon*. Correspondence around the time of *Carry On Cruising* shows this. Only ten days before the recording sessions were due to begin, Montgomery was writing to Eric Rogers: 'There's a bit of panic about "Carry On Cruising" owing to the fact that they need about twice the usual amount of music written in about half the usual time.'[30] He asked Rogers if he could write certain sections, including one which had to merge into one of his own, meaning that Rogers had to tell him what key he was finishing in. On the same day he wrote a similar letter to Gamley in which he said that his own ideas were 'coming horrible sluggishly'.[31] We have also seen that he was very particular over the detail on his scores, and this did not help him keep to deadlines.

In the end, as we know, Montgomery failed to produce most of the music for *Carry On Cruising*. Whilst Gerald Thomas wonders if this was because he was getting lazier and did not want the responsibility any more, Montgomery's letter of apology to Peter Rogers suggests the state into which he had worked himself:

> I'm so sorry about 'Cruising'. I'd hoped that my 'Carry On' bag of musical tricks was good for a lifetime, but on this occasion its contents were frantically difficult to dig out, and not too good a quality anyway. Less metaphorically, I found that each day's work was producing only about a third of the essential quota, with the result that in the end brain-fag and disappointment were complicated by downright panic. I can only apologise, and hope that what I did get written was at any rate adequate.[32]

By way of contrition, he refused any part of his fee. 'As you know', he wrote to his copyist, 'there have been a lot of comedies in the last two or three years, and my subconscious (or something) seems to have suddenly rebelled against doing another; it'd be nice, financially, to be a musical sausage-machine, but if one isn't, one isn't.'[33] Answering Eric Rogers' enquiry about his health (there seems to have been an understanding that he had not been well), Montgomery was even more explicit:

> All that really happened was that my slapstick-and-cod formula (which I've been using in other pictures besides the 'Carry On' series) went stale on me, from too much use in the last four years, at a time when I had to grind out three minutes playing time a day; the result was that I had to fight for every bloody bar, and got more and more behind schedule, and eventually panicked. I didn't actually go around telling everyone that I was Queen Elizabeth, but there's a fair chance I should have if I'd had to go on. Anyway, I'm much better now, and am trying to work out a new sort of approach to the music for film comedies, one which I hope will feel less like trying to roll a huge stone up an unending hill.[34]

The sadness was, though, that now his reputation for not completing scores was well known throughout the industry,[35] he would never get the chance to try this new

---

30    RBM to Eric Rogers, 10 March 1962
31    RBM to Douglas Gamley, 10 March 1962
32    RBM to Peter Rogers, 26 March 1962
33    RBM to Wilfred Puttick, 27 March 1962
34    RBM to Eric Rogers, 10 April 1962
35    Douglas Gamley

system – if indeed he ever found one. As a composer of film scores it is for comedies that Montgomery deserves to be remembered. We have seen that leading figures admired his brilliance at pointing the action. With his involvement in both the *Carry On* and *Doctor* series, Montgomery was writing for some of the most successful British comedy films of his time, and although he eventually fell out of favour, his achievement was to set the style for the scores of these types of pictures.

In addition to a perceived laziness and lack of ambition, there were other contributory factors to Montgomery's decline as a film composer. These can be put under the general heading of illness. From birth Montgomery had never been constitutionally particularly strong, and during the period of his film work his health deteriorated. He was a chain smoker, thinking nothing of getting through 80 cigarettes a day. The stains this habit caused on the walls and ceiling of the room he occupied in his parents' house in Brixham led to its frequent redecoration. The bone problems first manifest in the congenital deformity of the feet with which he was born had begun to worsen, and he suffered increasingly from osteoporosis. He also began to be troubled by a condition called Dupuytren's Contracture which affected the webbing of his right hand and made it difficult for him to write and to play the piano. None of these problems, bad enough on their own, was helped by his increasing addiction to alcohol. From Oxford days he had been a fairly heavy social drinker, but the 1950s saw a considerable increase in his consumption. Towards the end of the decade he was writing to Geoffrey Bush to suggest a summer school to avoid losing touch with his friends: 'Activities would be drinking, eating, drinking, talking, drinking, women, etc, and we might also spend some of our time in the local pubs.'[36]

The film industry certainly played a part in Montgomery's slide towards alcoholism. Montgomery found it difficult to drink at Brixham. His father was a strict non-conformist who disapproved of alcohol, and empty bottles had to be smuggled out of the back door. Consequently Montgomery spent a great deal of time in local hostelries, sometimes staying a night or more. The Imperial Hotel in Torquay was a favoured haunt, and he could spend up to a week there. On the day his father died in 1962, the family had to search local public houses to find him. These attempts at concealment were not necessary when he was away from home at the studios. Drinking was rife in the film world. In 1956, after Montgomery had already been on a drinking binge for a few days and was looking 'distinctly shaky', he met up with Malcolm Arnold at Pinewood Studios and the pair went off for a further two nights' carousing.[37]

Gerald Thomas was aware of Montgomery's drinking, but felt that it did not affect his work. Peter Rogers often had to help Montgomery because he was so 'bloody drunk',[38] and was not impressed by the long lunches with expensive wines on which the composer insisted when he was at the studios. Montgomery usually needed a drink to get him onto the rostrum for a recording session (Eric Rogers similarly required a couple of large whiskies before he would conduct). Dutch courage also

36    RBM to Geoffrey Bush, 14 June 1959
37    *Malcolm Arnold: Rogue Genius*, Meredith/Harris, p. 196
38    Peter Rogers

helped him sometimes to get as far as sitting down with Peter Rogers and Thomas to discuss the music for a film. Even the lonely and daunting business of sitting down with a blank sheet of paper to begin a score could be helped by a generous dose of alcohol. Yet other composers managed: Eric Rogers, for instance, drank more than Montgomery but could be relied upon to produce his score on time.[39]

Montgomery's over-reliance on alcohol caused other problems such as unpunctuality. At 9 o'clock one morning Gerald Thomas received a telephone call from someone at whose house Montgomery had called to ask directions to Pinewood Studios, information when sober he would certainly not have needed. When Thomas asked after Montgomery, he was alarmed to discover that the composer had been given a brandy because he had worked himself into a terrible state at the prospect of being late.[40] It is difficult to tell whether Montgomery's problems in finishing scores were caused more by his lack of ambition than by his incipient alcoholism. The most likely answer is that one led to the other: as Montgomery grew tired of the work load and responsibility that film scores demanded, he drank in an attempt to ameliorate the pressure he felt under. It began the downward spiral that was responsible for his fatally unproductive last years.

39     Gerald Thomas
40     Ibid.

# Chapter 12

# 'Much engrossed with Doom': Anthologies 1954–1966

Montgomery's detective novels, the production of which had been almost annual in the preceding years, came to an abrupt halt with the publication in 1951 of his eighth, *The Long Divorce*. By early 1955 Victor Gollancz was getting a little restive about a novel, provisionally titled *Stratagems and Spoils*, for which he had given Montgomery an advance in September 1954 on the understanding that it had only to be typed. This was the first shot in a campaign by Gollancz which took twenty years before it finally wrested Montgomery's ninth and final novel out of him. By the end of 1957 Montgomery had abandoned *Stratagems and Spoils* and was engaged on another story, *Judgement in Paris*. This began life as a novel set in a Paris hotel involving a beauty competition and shenanigans about oil rights (at one point it was subtitled *Oil or Nothing*). It changed into a murder story, with Miss Scotland as the victim and the oil rights replaced by a Physics Congress. Gervase Fen is present in Paris receiving an honorary degree at the Sorbonne. The papers connected with *Judgement in Paris* are some of the few that survive from Montgomery's novels, so the brief glimpse they give of his working methods is valuable. There are extensive notes for the plot, in the form of a pencilled conversation with himself. 'Try this,' he writes after one possibility throws up difficulties; 'Start again' is the instruction after a dead-end is reached. 'BAD BASIC FLAW [...] DAMN!' is a more forceful and typical rejection of an idea. The initial typescript of the first seven chapters is copiously annotated and amended, and a further typescript of the same chapters remained unaltered. This, it seems, was as far as the novel progressed.

Dissatisfied with the 'interminable consultation' film work involved and looking forward 'to some sort of work in which I've only myself to consult',[1] Montgomery told his publisher that the new novel would be ready within six months. Over a year later there was still no sign of the manuscript. '[*Judgement in Paris*] has been giving a certain amount of trouble,' he wrote to Gollancz. 'The plot requires very deft handling if it's not to seem grotesque, improbable, and faintly distasteful, and consequently I feel I must work it over carefully before letting it loose.'[2] He made it clear that film work was to blame for his lack of progress. The book's next deadline, July 1959, came and went. Eventually *Judgement in Paris* met the same fate as *Stratagems and Spoils*. 'I wrote more than half of it before realising that the plot was over-complicated, and in patches downright absurd. I shall have to start again from

---

1    RBM to Victor Gollancz, 10 December 1957
2    Ibid., 21 April 1959

scratch, I'm afraid.'[3] Little further progress was made on the long-promised novel for some years.

Yet, despite this inability to produce a novel, Montgomery's reputation was still sufficient for him to be pursued by a major publisher. In 1956 he agreed a contract with Collins to produce three detective novels under his pseudonym after he had completed his existing contract with Gollancz. As this contract had a further two books outstanding, there was no likelihood of the books for Collins appearing in the near future. Because of this, Montgomery's agent Peter Watt, although keen for financial reasons on the new contract but fearful that details might leak out to Gollancz, suggested that Montgomery did not sign until he was in a position to fulfil his obligations to Collins. Watts' advice went unheeded. Montgomery signed for Collins in April 1956, but the agreement was cancelled in 1959 because of his continuing failure to complete the Gollancz novels.

Montgomery's work aroused interest elsewhere. In September 1960 Alfred Hitchcock instructed Paramount Films' London office to get him copies of Montgomery's novels. One imagines that, having used the Botley Fair sequence from the conclusion of *The Moving Toyshop* at the end of his screen treatment of *Strangers on a Train* by Patricia Highsmith, Hitchcock was keen to see what else Montgomery had written. Nothing came of Paramount's interest, but Hitchcock directing a Crispin novel with a score by Montgomery would have made an arresting career move for the composer.

What demonstrates the extent to which films dominated his creative life during this period is that not only did Montgomery fail to complete a novel, but that he also wrote only one piece of concert music. This was a motet, *At The Round Earth's Imagin'd Corners,* which was published by Novello in 1958. Commissioned by Cecil Cope, an old friend of Montgomery and the conductor of the Exeter Elizabethan Singers, it was first performed by his choir in Exeter Cathedral at the Devon Festival of the Arts during the summer of 1957. Setting a typical piece of verse, this time a sonnet by John Donne (1572–1631), Montgomery reacted to the drama of the text in a more vivid fashion than he had in earlier choral works. Many of his stylistic fingerprints are still evident (static basses, sequences, vocal imitation and tonal shifts), but the music is more angular, more openly dissonant and less romantic than his earlier work. There are many alternations between compound and simple time, much syncopation and many abrupt dynamic changes. Montgomery sets the text in a sectional through-composed structure. This gives him scope for word-painting: strident dissonances characterise the phrase 'All whom war, dearth, age, tyrannies, Despair, law, chance, hath slain', with a particular emphasis on the last word [Example 12.1], but there is little attempt to develop any of the ideas in the first section.[4]

---

3     RBM to Hilary Rubenstein, 25 September 1961
4     Geoffrey Bush once told Montgomery that there was no need to develop themes. They were both indoctrinated by being brought up in the Germanic tradition, but Bush had studied French and Russian music and found that they did not bother. Montgomery was very struck by this notion. (Geoffrey Bush)

**Example 12.1** *At The Round Earth's Imagin'd Corners*

The second section ('But let them sleep, Lord') returns to more familiar Montgomery territory, a warmer harmonic style with imitation but still treated in sections. There are examples of his liking for clearing the chromaticism by alighting onto 7th chords [Example 12.2].

**Example 12.2** *At The Round Earth's Imagin'd Corners*

At first glance the work can, in the words of Erik Routley, appear to be 'a terrifying composition. To the eye, or on the piano, it appears and sounds so disastrous that I can only hope all its goodness is revealed in unaccompanied performance. It is highly chromatic and full of strange and graphic discord, and probably very difficult to sing.'[5] The work's apparent difficulty led Montgomery to report that Cecil Cope 'nearly had a stroke when I sent him the MS'.[6] Cope's wife, however, told the composer that the choir had thoroughly enjoyed singing his exciting setting,[7] and there is no doubt that Montgomery's music matches the text, from the strident aggression of the first part to the atmospherically peaceful conclusion. It is an indication that Montgomery was moved to set the text in a highly descriptive and personal fashion, and the piece requires a competent choir. There are signs, particularly in the harmonically daring first section, that Montgomery was making some move towards developing his style. It is unfortunate that there are no other works from the remaining 19 years of his life to show whether this development would have been sustained.

The only other completed music Montgomery composed during these years was mostly commissioned by the BBC in Bristol. There was title and incidental

---

5    *British Weekly*, 26 September 1958

6    RBM to Lionel Dakers, 3 June 1958

7    Mrs Cecil Cope to RBM, 10 April 1958

music for *Look*, anchored by Peter Scott and one of the earliest television natural history programmes, as well as incidental music for a radio dramatisation of *The Woodlanders* by Thomas Hardy. In 1954 Montgomery also managed to write some incidental music for *Joyce Grenfell Requests the Pleasure*, a revue. This was a new and, as it turned out, isolated departure for him. He had been involved in the project since the previous year, meeting with the director, Laurie Lister, and an old friend from Oxford, Donald Swann, at the Royal Court Theatre to discuss the music. Initially called *Cash on Delivery*, Montgomery's contribution seems to have been intended to accompany a musical representation of his short story of the same name, published posthumously in *Fen Country*. As with his film work, the score was not ready on time so Bill Blezzard, Grenfell's musical director, 'cobbled' something together until Montgomery's score was ready.[8] Following rehearsals the score was immediately revised and renamed *Perfidia*. The sketch involved Grenfell and three dancers and remained part of the show in both London and New York.

There were one or two schemes which failed. The first was the completion of the one-act opera *Amberley Hall* which he had partly written, in collaboration with Kingsley Amis, in 1952. An American opera company showed some interest in the work towards the end of 1959 but took the matter no further. Another scheme with Amis which never saw the light of day was a musical on the apparently unpromising subject of beauty queens. It appears that the libretto by Amis was to be based on Montgomery's aborted novel *Judgement in Paris*.[9] Although Amis recalled the project never progressing further than a series of conversations in bars, word leaked out, deliberately or otherwise, and with Amis' reputation high as a result of the enormous success of his first novel *Lucky Jim* and with Montgomery's reputation still high as a detective novelist and film composer, interest was shown. 'We hope our show will be a change from the little, tinkling and rather unsophisticated musicals that we have seen on the West End stage recently,' Montgomery was quoted as saying by the *Evening Standard*. 'Ours will be on a bigger scale and in, we hope, the Cole Porter, or Rodgers and Hart tradition.'[10] Sydney Box enjoyed reading the framework on which they proposed to construct the musical. Peter Rogers, having read the press announcements, wondered whether it was the same show that he had commissioned Montgomery to write.[11] In February 1958 Chappell and Co. made an unsolicited offer to discuss the possibilities of publishing the work. At that stage Montgomery had to admit that the show was not very far advanced, which made it all the more remarkable that within a month the *Western Mail* was announcing in error that 'Mr Montgomery has just completed a musical show in collaboration with Kingsley Amis.'[12] In the same month Montgomery visited Amis in Swansea where 'Bruce and I did some work on our musical, which it now seems I shall have to try and write. Feel nervous about this, as if I'd contracted to write pornography for a posh, limited-

---

8     Bill Blezzard
9     RBM to Peter Watt, 11 September 1958
10    *Evening Standard*, 11 November 1957
11    Peter Watt to RBM, 15 November 1957
12    *Western Mail*, 12 March 1958

edition, aristocrats' press.'[13] Like most of his non-film music projects at this time, little more was heard of the musical.

Montgomery had been very impressed by Amis' first novel. 'You were quite right – of course, of course, about <u>Lucky Jim</u>,' he wrote to Larkin. 'It's a wonderful book, and what interests me about it is that it's not only stupendously funny, it's a great many other things as well – an unexpectedly rich and many-sided job. […] God, how I laughed. Queer, isn't it, to think that a friend of ours should have written such superb stuff. Talk about entertaining angels unawares.'[14] Not long afterwards he was equally delighted with Larkin's new poetry collection and willingly subscribed to the first edition: '[I] congratulate you – a bit belatedly, but <u>really</u> sincerely – on having produced a book as moving and impressive as <u>The Less Deceived</u>.'[15] A little later he amplified his views: 'Do you know what I think? I think those poems of yours are <u>bloody good</u>, and was saying to that Amis fellow that I thought that in five years or so you'll probably be having quite a considerable vogue.' Having made one or two minor criticisms he goes on to praise the majority of the poems. 'One curious thing about you as a poet is that you're almost the only contemporary I know of who takes naturally, and of strong personal volition, to the traditional subject-matter of poetry – love, death, nature; you are also, I should add, the only one irresponsible enough to ruin beautiful lines of verse with shouts of <u>Stuff your pension</u>! (it's Shakespeare's beautiful line I'm talking about, not yours).' He finishes with 'How nice it is to be a friend of a really Fine Poet.'[16] Montgomery knew that his friends were in the ascendancy.

Despite the stagnation of his creative work outside films, Montgomery's career did branch out in another significant direction during the 1950s. Early in the decade he attended a party with Amis and Larkin at All Souls' College, Oxford, in the rooms of Lionel Butler (later Principal of Royal Holloway College). There he met Charles Monteith, a barrister and a great admirer of Montgomery's novels. The pair found that they shared an interest in science fiction. Montgomery's introduction to the genre had come in 1947 when a friend sent him some stories, and he had been hooked ever since. A year or two later Monteith joined Faber, and at an early editorial committee he suggested that the company should expand their series of short story anthologies to include one of science fiction.

The genre was at a low ebb. In Britain science fiction had come almost to a standstill because the stories being written were a pallid imitation of what was available in America. In the very early 1950s British publishers discovered science fiction on lists in the USA and used to dash over, buy a few books, have a few drinks with their friends and dash back again. Some bought back publishers' lists, either entire or in chunks, assuming that what sold in the USA would sell in Britain. Most of this was ill-advised and the books did not sell well.[17]

---

13    Amis to Larkin, 15 March 1958 [LKA]

14    RBM to Larkin, 13 February 1954

15    Ibid., 27 December 1955

16    Ibid., 9 January 1956

17    Brian Aldiss

To add to the problems, few distinguished authors had anything to do with science fiction and there was little to suggest any immediate market to encourage a publisher. Because of this the Faber board was distinctly lukewarm about the idea (the sales manager was openly hostile), but the daring Monteith knew that in Geoffrey Faber he had a fellow enthusiast. To his delight the idea was approved. In the first instance Monteith turned to Angus Wilson[18] as prospective editor. Wilson was sufficiently interested to discuss the project, but in the end he decided that it would take up too much time. It was then, early in 1954, that Monteith recalled his earlier conversation at All Souls. Montgomery's reputation as Edmund Crispin was very high at this time so the Faber board had no objections to him as editor. Montgomery was immediately enthusiastic, and it took little time for a contract to be agreed.

The work on Montgomery's part, which he did under his pseudonym, consisted of reading a vast number of short stories, which he liked, and of writing a number of letters to authors and publishers to ask permission to use their stories. The correspondence was rather irksome, but it did give him the opportunity to become acquainted with writers he admired. Monteith was delighted with the anthology, particularly with Montgomery's introduction which he thought highly intelligent and very stylishly written. He also felt that it genuinely succeeded in getting across to the reader why Montgomery felt so excited by this genre of writing.[19] When *Best SF* was published, shortly before Christmas 1954, the critics felt much the same. Angus Wilson in *The Spectator* may have had one or two minor quibbles about the selections, but he was full of praise for the 'excellent introduction'.[20] Brian Aldiss, to become a leading author in the genre and a good friend of Montgomery, was equally satisfied: 'To read and recommend this book is a pleasure. Here is a volume to take away the unbelievers [...] as stimulating as any of the stories is the introduction by Edmund Crispin, the editor.'[21] Douglas Newton in *Time and Tide*, although like Wilson not entirely happy about the stories, was even more enthusiastic about Montgomery's main contribution, claiming it 'probably the most perceptive comment on science-fiction which has so far been published, at any rate in this country'.[22]

This much-praised introduction contains Montgomery's most developed essay on the general state of science fiction, with only occasional references to the stories he had chosen. He begins with a definition of the genre as he sees it:

A science-fiction story is one which presupposes a technology, or an effect of technology, or a disturbance in the natural order, such as humanity, up to the time of writing, has not in actual fact experienced.

He qualifies this by observing that at one extreme some stories may deal with subjects which are 'not much more than a camera-eye view of contemporary reality' such as industrial relations in an atomic power plant; at the other some may 'degenerate into goblins'.

18     Angus Wilson (1913–1991), novelist
19     Charles Monteith
20     *The Spectator*, 11 February 1955
21     *Oxford Mail*, 10 March 1955
22     *Time and Tide*, 2 April 1955

The great bulk of science-fiction, however, remains faithful either to the technical hypothesis and its attendant consequences, or else to the cosmic upheaval – the act of God rather than of the physicists – with all *that* implies: it is a distinctive, restricted variety of the Tale of Wonder, the age-old voluminous literature of 'If'.

The most common inventions are space and time travel, atomic hand-weapons, mechanical brains in robots, defensive force-fields and devices for inducing telepathy. Disturbances in the natural order have included 'such disparate menaces as aberrant comets, automotive vegetables, collisions between planets, and giant octopuses off the sea-coast at Brighton'. Montgomery notes that although most science fiction is set in the future, authors can set their tales in the present or remote past if they write about races other than the human.

Having defined his genre, Montgomery realises that if this were the sum total, 'it would no doubt deserve the derision with which the stupider of the intellectuals are already, on occasion, condescending to favour it.' He goes on to claim that science fiction is 'by and large easily the least 'escapist' type of fiction currently available.'

> What at first appears to be an opiate is in fact, to anyone capable of cerebration at all, a heavy dose of amphetamine sulphate. What looks like a simple dream is in the long run, to all mankind everywhere, of the most urgent and immediate moment.

He makes the case that this non-escapist aspect is 'an overtone rather than a fundamental', not necessarily intended but there nonetheless. 'For in the simplest analysis, a science-fiction story is a straightforward Tale of Wonder, aiming to astonish and awe and delight its readers by recounting prodigies and marvels.' He claims that this is the most universal appeal of science fiction for humans who, becoming easily bored by predictability, are eager to be carried away by departures from the norm, in the same way that the 'most universal and enduring appeal of Moby Dick probably depends on the fact that it's a jolly good yarn about a chap going after a whopping enormous whale'.

Whilst not keen on humour in science fiction, because it usually ends in facetiousness, Montgomery lists what he considers the four greatest defects of the genre at a time when it is still at its early stages (he compares it to the state of detective fiction in the 1920s): it does not make the most of its material; its jargon appeals to a clique; there is a 'stuffy monasticism' in the sense that women rarely appear and normal relations between men and women are almost non-existent; and the characters are of little interest in themselves. This last sin he again compares with detective fiction, noting the difficulty writers have if their characters become too interesting and take over the story.

Montgomery realises, though, that these are not the sins that most critical commentators associate with science fiction. He answers the charge that a lot of the genre is badly written by firstly agreeing ('just as a lot of epic poetry would be illiterate and badly written if the sales of epic poetry equalled those of science-fiction') and then by asserting that this is not the fault of the genre. He responds to the further charge that the science is pseudo-science by again comparing it with detective fiction (whose 'crimes are artificial compared with crimes in real life') and by stating 'the penetrating observation sometimes heard in lunatic asylums, that the beef doesn't taste very much like mutton today'. Critics who hold these views are encouraged to abandon science fiction and read technical journals instead.

Montgomery's last, and most lengthy, refutation is against the charge that science fiction is overwhelmingly pessimistic. He agrees that it is 'much engrossed with Doom', but by no means all of it. Eight out of the 14 stories in his collection, for instance, end in some sort of catastrophe, a proportion he thinks typical of the genre. He justifies this by observing that science fiction 'is sceptical about *man*'. It cannot, for instance, trust him to invade or colonise other planets without brutality, or investigate other worlds without causing disaster. 'In a word, science-fiction has rediscovered Original Sin.' Its subject matter makes this inevitable. It is better, he says, to consider such things than to ignore them, even if that leads writers to have to 'endure the easy sneer and the superficial gibe for some time to come'. He ends with a blast:

> The inexorable condition laid down by science-fiction's subject-matter will remain, however: readers will continue to have their noses rubbed in ethics and politics and sociology – not to mention religion – and to find the process enthralling, regardless of what the critics may say. And in my belief, the world will be just that modicum the better, and the prospect before us just that modicum more hopeful, because of it.[23]

The success of the first anthology led to further ones in the series; *Best SF 7*, the last, appeared in 1971. All of them received good notices, and Montgomery's introductions continued to be regarded as vital parts of their success. Robert Conquest, reviewing *Best SF 2*, echoed most critics with his view that 'Mr Crispin's introductions are the most intelligent and illuminating writing on sf to appear in this country.'[24] By the time of the fifth anthology in 1963, the series was so highly regarded that one critic was moved to announce: 'An appearance in the Faber "Best SF" series is analogous to being picked for a test match.'[25]

The anthologies also provoked a lot of correspondence in which Montgomery often gave away more of his views. 'My knowledge of the sciences is hopelessly inadequate; my knowledge of mathematics is non-existent,' he wrote to Hugh Heckstall-Smith. 'In reading sf I have, however, found a frail bridge for what little I know about the humanities to the nothing I know about science.'[26] He admitted that he preferred the 'sf of ideas', and went on in his evangelical mode:

> Experience so far has suggested that scarcely anyone under the age of 40 is easy with the stuff even – or especially – in its most trivial forms. A fair number of us have been trying for a long time to persuade the <u>cognoscenti</u> that although this might not be Major Art, it still isn't wholly negligible. Very satisfactory, therefore, to find someone not only of your generation, but of your intellectual calibre too, contributing to rescuing us eccentrics from the miserable slough into which we've commonly supposed to have fallen.[27]

---

23    Introduction to *Best SF*
24    *The Spectator*, 8 March 1957
25    Ian Blake, *Irish Times*, 13 July 1963
26    RBM to Hugh Heckstall-Smith, November 1963
27    Ibid., 11 January 1964

In a letter to Isaac Asimov he discussed the problem of trying to write an introduction for an anthology aimed at a different level (*The Stars and Under*):

> Incidentally, this school anthology requires me to say, in an Introduction, in very simple terms, just what SF is and why. I'm not sure that even you could do that – not infallibly, I mean; as for me, the job is giving me nightmares. In practice, in the end, I find I'm getting back to the old 'What if' thing; but the nightmares still burgeon handsomely when I try to define all those unavoidable qualifications.[28]

The importance of Montgomery's anthologies has to be seen from the impetus they gave to the development of the genre. In the early 1950s readers of science fiction felt rather like members of a secret movement. They thought themselves better informed about the future of the world than most people, and this appealed to Montgomery and others from his Oxford days. During these years, young authors such as Kingsley Amis and Robert Conquest began to write about the genre in influential publications, and with more established literary figures (amongst them C.S. Lewis and Angus Wilson) in support, science fiction began to be taken seriously as well as coming into fashion. Montgomery's anthologies were the first such publications, and 'were crucial in establishing valid critical standards'.[29] An indication of the esteem in which he was held came in 1962 when Montgomery was asked to be guest of honour at the convention of the British Science Fiction Association at Harrogate. On this occasion he was unable to accept, but he took up the offer the following year in Peterborough and hoped that the fans were 'young, female, nubile',[30] whilst admitting that because of the bungalow he was having built he had to do 'a terrible amount of <u>work</u> at the moment in order to avoid landing in Cary Street'.[31] He asked for a quiet room at the hotel, but acknowledged that if certain of his friends, including Brian Aldiss and Harry Harrison, 'turn out to be too near by, and an unduly disturbing influence, then providing they have enough beer and blondes, I'll resign myself to not being able to beat them, and I shall join them instead'.[32] Montgomery clearly enjoyed the social side of the convention. He remonstrated with Robert Conquest for his absence: 'You ought to have come to Peterborough: not all that much in the way of girlies, but a hell of a lot of fun in every other way (e.g. there was <u>never</u> a moment in any twenty-four hours at which <u>someone</u> didn't have at least a couple of bottles of scotch in his bedroom.'[33] The memories were still vivid two months later: 'In future we must all try to keep off pickled eggs eaten in derelict East-Anglian pubs. I like to think that it's them I'm still suffering from, rather than all that Scotch.'[34] Referring to another convention, he reminded Brian Aldiss that

---

28   RBM to Isaac Asimov, 2 September 1965
29   *Trillion Year Spree*, Aldiss, p. 628
30   RBM to Brian Aldiss, 21 September 1962
31   Ibid.
32   RBM to British Science Fiction Association (BSFA), 23 February 1962
33   RBM to Robert Conquest, 19 April 1963
34   RBM to Harry Harrison, 15 June 1963

'Jim's [J.G. Ballard][35] non-linear stuff may be the SF of the future, but there'll always be one strictly linear aspect to these pow-wows – namely the bee-line to the nearest bar.'[36]

A report in the *Guardian* said that Montgomery gave 'a succinct and stimulating address' which dealt mainly with the dangers the genre faced as it became more popular. It had become 'a fashionable new hunting ground for the literary highbrow' and authors of other genres were 'jumping on the bandwagon and writing poor versions of what had already been done'. He claimed that science fiction had made an important contribution to twentieth-century writing: 'It had absorbed into the literary imagination the post-Darwinism idea of evolution, of man as merely a small part of a greater universe and not the end product of creation.'[37] Montgomery claimed that he had taken most of his speech from his own introduction to *Best SF 5* and 'I made a lot of it up as I went along.'[38] Clearly he was highly regarded: within three years he became President of the Association, after a short hiatus when it was discovered that he had to be elected rather than appointed. Writing to the members, he put forward his manifesto:

> I'm hoping that during my Presidency B.S.F.A. will not only keep its energy, its high standards and its sense of fun, but will also allow for the fact that the Association can no longer resemble a close-knit party on an alien planet, devoted to keeping intelligent, fascinating jellyfish happy. Whether we like it or not, the reinforcements are even now coming down from the skies. And we shall have to learn from one another – they more from us, no doubt, than we from them; still, we should be wrong, I think, to assume that just because they are newcomers, they have nothing worthwhile to offer. [...] It's not my business, but as an ordinary member I do hope B.S.F.A. will adjust itself, however painfully, to bringing in science fiction's big new recent audience for what in the long run will make (both) for more enjoyment and for more power.[39]

As someone who had done more than most to galvanize this 'big new recent audience', this was a subject close to his heart. He remained as President until his resignation in 1970.

Despite claiming on occasions that he never wrote a word of science fiction himself, a letter that he wrote to Brian Aldiss suggests the opposite:

> Incidentally, I have recently produced my own first number in the SF department; a peculiar story which analyses the instability of dictatorships and offers a simple, practical, make-it-in-your-own-backyard remedy guaranteed to keep any reasonably intelligent dictator effortlessly in power for as long as he lives.[40]

The novel he had written at Oxford (which was set in the future and began with the sinking of a passenger liner after it had struck an undetected mine left over from

35    J.G. Ballard (b.1930), English novelist
36    RBM to Brian Aldiss, 28 May 1968
37    *Guardian*, 15 April 1963
38    RBM to BSFA, 26 April 1963
39    *Vector*, 1965
40    RBM to Brian Aldiss, 9 May 1957

the war) also fits into this category.[41] Montgomery was certainly involved with a later attempt to write a composite science fiction novel. At the first SF Film Festival in Trieste in 1962, Aldiss, Kingsley Amis and Harry Harrison had an original idea about cannibalism and tried to enlist Montgomery and J.G. Ballard on to the project.[42] Nothing came of this, but three years later a lunch was called at the Café Royal during which Montgomery, Aldiss, Amis, Ballard and Harrison discussed a similar project, provisionally entitled *Virus From Venus* or *An Antic Disposition*. The basic idea was of a manned space ship returning from Venus with a virus that burns out human intelligence and leaves its victims retarded. The only people immune to it are the mentally sick, and the only other defence is alcohol in the blood stream, meaning that 'a sane person's only hope of surviving it is to stay permanently pissed'.[43] The space ship returns to Venus in an attempt to find an antidote manned by a crew of drunken and insane geniuses. The antidote has severe side effects, including paralysis. Civilisation begins to crumble. A second expedition finds a kinder antidote and peace returns.

There were numerous discussions by letter about alterations to the plot. In one Montgomery suggests that as the birth control pill is thought to delay the menopause, and therefore ageing, women in the story might live to 120 whereas men die at the usual age, thus creating a progressively more feminine world.[44] There were also frequent disagreements. Initially, the idea appears to have been to write two chapters each. Aldiss offered to write the first chapter, hoping that this might excuse him further involvement, and Montgomery offered to follow on from Aldiss's 'kick off'.[45] Meanwhile, Montgomery was trying to persuade another leading science fiction writer to join the enterprise:

> I telephoned John Wyndham. He was nervous about his capacity to collaborate, but I said so were we all. He was interested, I thought, and glad to be asked: slightly baffled (because I couldn't give him much detail) but by no means stand-offish. We left it that further developments should be communicated to him, without obligation on either side. And this, I'd say, is fair enough. I personally think he'd do all right, if he did join in.[46]

Around the time of the Peterborough convention in 1963, Kingsley Amis said 'there will be a lot of argument' over the project,[47] but unfortunately (much to the disappointment of science fiction lovers, one suspects) nothing came of it.

Another point needs to be made about Montgomery's new position as an increasingly respected critic. Although in the past he had made occasional appearances on radio, television and in the press as a commentator on matters concerning music and, particularly, detective fiction, these anthologies marked a new departure for

---

41    Sir Anthony Jephcott to author, 25 June 1990
42    Brian Aldiss
43    RBM to contributors, no date
44    Ibid., 1 May 1965
45    Ibid., 4 June 1965
46    Ibid.
47    *Daily Express*, 16 March 1965

him. His constructive and thoughtful encouragement of Philip Larkin's early poetry during the war years in Shropshire is an example of the early flowering of this critical ability. As his own creative powers waned, he found a niche from which, during the remaining years of his life, he became one of the most influential critics of detective fiction.

# Chapter 13

# 'I've become an Immobilist': 1950–1962

It was not only Montgomery's career that was changing. During the 1950s his personal life also underwent a radical change. Since his years at Oxford, Montgomery had been a convivial and enthusiastic socialite. He was always keen to become involved in societies and to get to know the people of importance in the different spheres of his world. As a member of the Detection Club he frequently attended its monthly meetings at the Café Royal, talking about philosophy with Dorothy L. Sayers and taking part in the high-spirited plays the club staged from time to time. One, *The Adventure of the Paradol Chamber*, written by John Dickson Carr, was a parody of Sherlock Holmes, with Cyril Hare[1] as Holmes, Sayers as Mrs Hudson, Carr as the French Ambassador and Richard Hull[2] as Watson who turns out to be Moriarty. Larkin was once his guest and recalled ending up 'in some unknown alley with Bruce & Dorothy Sayers drinking orangeade'.[3] Montgomery got on particularly well with Sayers: 'I remember many happy occasions, after Detection Club meetings', he wrote to an American fan, 'when she and I sat in the clubroom talking about detectives and detective fiction, and about a great many other things as well.'[4] Michael Underwood[5] recalled Montgomery and Sayers 'engaged in a deep philosophical discussion which was so far over my head as to be totally incomprehensible'.[6] Living close to Agatha Christie in Devon gave him the opportunity to entertain her: 'We did enjoy our evening so much,' she wrote after one such occasion. 'Everyone was such fun – and such a superb dinner – still regret not being able to find room for the Brie! Bachelors certainly know how to live […] shall look forward to seeing you this summer.'[7] His drinking bouts with another crime novelist, John Dickson Carr, occasionally assumed Herculean proportions:

> Those were the days, weren't they? – when, e.g., I fell drunkenly asleep on Christianna Brand's[8] ample bosom in a taxi, and she had the greatest difficulty in shifting me; when you and Tony Berkeley[9] and I indulged in maudlin confessions of our sexual preferences one late afternoon in the Mandrake Club; when I tried, after four bottles of champagne and

---

1     Cyril Hare, pseudonym of Alfred Clark (1900–1958), detective novelist
2     Richard Hull, pseudonym of Richard Sampson (1896–1973), detective novelist
3     Larkin to J.B. Sutton, 20 May 1950 [SLPL]
4     RBM to Mrs Bagley, 12 May 1963
5     Michael Underwood, pseudonym of John Evelyn (1916–92), detective novelist
6     Michael Underwood to author, 10 October 1989
7     Agatha Christie to RBM, 2 May (year unknown)
8     Christianna Brand (1907–1988), detective novelist
9     Anthony Berkeley, pseudonym of Anthony Berkeley Cox (1893–1971), detective novelist

two of brandy apiece to fight a duel with you in your Hampstead flat with (unbuttoned) foils; when your splendid little Holmes parody [see above] was mounted with the utmost grandeur, and a stunning cast, at the Detection Club; when I had to prevent you, at the I.M.A., from attacking single-handed six R.A.F. men whom you conceived (I don't know whether correctly) to have said something derogatory about you; and many, many other things, in other places, on other occasions.[10]

Another time Montgomery had to borrow money off Carr to sustain a drinking session; 'A couple of years ago I went on a similar bust in Copenhagen', Carr told Montgomery, 'and I had to cable my bank-manager.'[11] He also drank with Michael Ayrton;[12] welcoming him on his return from a trip to Mexico, Montgomery hoped 'that we can get in some hard drinking fairly soon after you've arrived back'.[13]

He continued to meet other convivial musicians at the IMA, such as Malcolm Arnold, Gerard Hoffnung and Major 'Jiggs' Jaeger, for whose Band of the Irish Guards Montgomery had composed two pieces. Montgomery, Arnold and Jaeger lunched there on one occasion with Geoffrey Bush and, having bribed the waiter to bring them another bottle after closing time, discovered (when Arnold asked apologetically if he could have another brandy) that they had been in all afternoon and the club was open again for the evening.[14] 'We were at the IMA all that evening', Montgomery wrote about another session there in 1957, 'vaguely attempting to nursemaid Malcolm [Arnold], who had come off the water-wagon with a colossal bump. Eventually Gerard Hoffnung succeeded in shooing him home to Sheila.'[15] Montgomery was also a member of the Savile and Authors' Clubs. He used these bases for his frequent trips to London for film work during this period. Another haunt was The Bull at Gerrard's Cross, this being particularly convenient for Pinewood Studios.

He met with old friends. In 1954, following a party at All Souls, Oxford, he spent a rather dissipated couple of days in London with Amis and his wife. Amongst other activities he entertained them to lunch at the IMA with Malcolm Arnold, after which Amis admitted to being 'so pissed I could hardly speak [...] and found myself in a pub, advancing towards Harry Hoff,[16] Bruce and C.P. Snow[17] sitting in a line. Hoff greeted me by saying "Here's Amis, but too drunk, I see, to say much."'[18] Montgomery decided to accompany Amis for another drinking spree on the train back to Oxford and rebuked him 'for tipping the waiter 9d instead of 1s'.[19] The pair

10    RBM to John Dickson Carr, undated, held by Douglas Greene (USA)
11    John Dickson Carr to RBM, undated
12    Michael Ayrton (1921–1975), artist
13    RBM to Michael Ayrton, 12 February 1959
14    Geoffrey Bush
15    RBM to Dusty Buck, 30 June 1957
16    Harry Hoff (1910–2002), civil servant and novelist both under his real name and as William Cooper
17    C.P. Snow (1905–1980), novelist and government scientist whose first and last novels were detective stories
18    Amis to Larkin, 14 March 1954 [LKA]
19    Ibid.

then carried on drinking in the Randolph Hotel where Montgomery revealed to Amis 'that he proposed to write a novel about the events of the past two days – drinking with me and the others in London. Rather thin, I thought and think it would be, though I didn't say so.'[20] In 1956 Amis met up with Montgomery again: 'He [Montgomery] was in very good form, telling me about the starlets he takes out to dinner (Jackie Lane, Shirley Ann Field, et al.), and introducing me to John Dickson Carr. I got too drunk too soon to remember very much about the encounter.'[21]

'I visited London & spent some time with Bruce, who seemed good fun', Larkin wrote in 1957, 'but very keen on establishing his ascendancy in what might be called "matters of the heart": however, he stood me several huge meals that nearly finished me. [...] Bruce took me to "Les Ambassadeurs" where many luminaries of the cinematograph world were to be found.'[22] A month later Montgomery met with Larkin and Amis in London, the first time they had done so for about ten years. Larkin was curiously impressed by his friends: 'They have left double gins now & gone onto champagne cocktails, & sign the cheque at the end of the session, no sordid passing of money. We got on fairly well, but Kingsley has less and less conception of talking *to* you: you are simply an audience [...] Bruce seemed curiously modest & gentlemanly beside him.'[23] The following year Montgomery visited Amis in Swansea where he was 'in very good form. The 4 of us, including my pa, played scrabble and Crip[24] got the worst score every time. He took it very well. On the Saturday he took us in his Jaguar (which has 3 "cigar-lighters" protruding from various parts of the interior coachwork) [...] B. and P. [Peter Oldham] played some piano duets which sounded like a sort of classical bop.'[25]

It was around this time that a further incident showed Montgomery's acquaintance with important figures. He was dining with Muriel Pavlow and her husband at The Ivy restaurant. Muriel told him that she adored the novels of John Wyndham. Montgomery asked if she would like to meet Wyndham and went out to telephone him. It was getting on for midnight when Wyndham appeared at the nightclub they had gone on to, looking slightly bemused and giving the impression that he had got out of bed to join the party. At a previous lunch Muriel had become aware that Montgomery had a drink problem, although her instincts in this direction were not always accurate. She had appeared in a film with Robert Newton[26] some years previously and, on her own admission, must have been the only person in the British Isles not to realise that Newton had a similar inclination.[27]

Montgomery was always very keen on luxury. He spent a good deal on cars, particularly Jaguars, and stayed in the best hotels. His residence at The Crown and Thistle in Abingdon in 1954/55 is typical of this, although his attempted dalliance

---

20   Ibid.
21   Ibid., 25 June 1956
22   Larkin to Richard and Patsy Murphy, 8 July 1957 [SLPL]
23   Larkin to Patsy Murphy, 4 August 1957 [SLPL]
24   Amis' name for Montgomery (short for Crippen, itself coined from Crispin)
25   Amis to Larkin, 15 March 1958 [LKA]
26   Robert Newton (1905–1956), actor
27   Muriel Pavlow

with Jeni Turnbull, the daughter of the couple who managed the pub, doubtless did nothing to make him leave. When she moved to work in London, Montgomery hired a Rolls Royce and escorted Jeni and her mother around the city. He had to have the most expensive of everything, whether it was champagne or the restaurant at which he dined. Whenever Montgomery lunched at the Athenaeum with the American writer and critic Jacques Barzun, he would always order plovers' eggs, saying that they were rarely found on menus.[28] Money went through his hands like water. It was as if he lived a hermit-like existence when in Devon and saved up his conviviality for trips to London.

The move to Abingdon had come about as the start of a failed attempt to find a home of his own so that he could get on with his novel after he found it increasingly difficult to live with his parents. 'I took one look at Oxford on arrival', he wrote to them in September 1954, 'and decided it was altogether too tiresome and noisy and crowded to live in for more than a few days.'[29] Initially he settled on the Queen's Hotel in Abingdon which was quiet, modest, comfortable and 'surprisingly cheap for a long stay'.[30] He could rent a room with a piano locally if a film score came along, and the manager found him a room to work in at other times. His initial intention was to stay until Christmas and then look for a house or flat: 'I've no intention of living a hotel life for longer than I need.'[31] Two weeks later, however, he had changed his mind after the food at the Queen's failed to match his expectations, and he decided on a move to the Crown and Thistle: 'This is a much more quiet and luxurious place than the Queen's, and correspondingly more expensive; but the food is first-rate, they can give me a little sitting room of my own, and there's no traffic and other noise at nights, so I'm sure the extra cost will be well worthwhile.'[32]

The Crown and Thistle was an old pub that had become more of a hotel and restaurant. It was painted pink, had two little bars and a cobbled courtyard with willow on one side and wisteria on the other. It was popular with the locals as well as with people from Oxford. Before long Montgomery was well settled in, being served breakfast in bed and waiting for a hired piano to be delivered. He was about to start the score for *Raising a Riot*, a feature film the rushes for which he just been shown, but was still aiming to look for a house and a housekeeper after Christmas. The delivery men could not get the piano up the stairs to Montgomery's rooms, so it was put into a small modernized barn at the back of the hotel which was used only for dances on a Saturday night. These occasions were well known in the district, with undergraduates from Oxford and local people flocking to them. Mrs Turnbull played records and kept a watching brief over guests and daughter; at other times a jazz band from Oxford might play. Montgomery spent most of his time during these dances in the bar, but would stomp in from time to time with a drink and sit at a table with the Turnbulls. Because of his feet he did not dance much. At quieter times he would sit and play jazz on the piano, not for show but quietly for himself.

---

28    Jacques Barzun to author, 14 February 1990
29    RBM to parents, 11 September 1954
30    Ibid.
31    Ibid.
32    Ibid., 25 September 1954

Despite it being early on in his work for films, Montgomery was already threatening to give them up, claiming a different financial return than he did in his later years: 'The film [*Raising a Riot*] is going ahead tolerably well, but it's been exceptionally trying, in one way and another, and really will, I think, be my last: writing is not only a more profitable but also a more <u>gentlemanly</u> occupation – less like jungle warfare – and one can always compose <u>other</u> things.'[33] The next day he was asking his parents for a loan of £50 to be repaid when his film fee arrived. He was realising that he had moved away from home at an awkward time and his financial position was now 'a bit tight'.[34] To make matters worse, he also had a bout of fibrositis. He continued to make economies: the piano was taken away, he gave up his sitting room and converted the bedroom into a bedsit. 'The management have been extremely kind to me all along,' he informed his parents. 'They're a very good type of people, a middle-aged couple, (he an ex-Cambridge man) with a shy and charming 23-year-old daughter whom I'm getting <u>rather</u> fond of! She teaches art in an Abingdon girls' school, and also works three days a week in the Ashmolean Museum in Oxford, and is, I believe, very much the sort of person you would approve of my getting fond of.'[35] Jeni Turnbull claimed that the girls at the convent school were 'fiends' and made her mother and Montgomery laugh one day when she came home and, rarely for her, announced that she must have a drink.[36]

Montgomery soon became part of the family. Mrs Turnbull, an outgoing woman who enjoyed taking people under her wing, loved his willingness to show off (she enjoyed going to the film studios with him and meeting stars of the time such as Leslie Phillips); she also loved his sense of humour and the party atmosphere that permanently surrounded him. Mr Turnbull was a steadier, more conservative person and Montgomery appreciated their differing characters. Indeed, they were similar in temperament to his parents. After the bar closed at night he would join the Turnbulls in their large sitting room and have another drink or a cup of tea and talk for hours. Montgomery never took over the conversation, but was amusing and worth listening to. He was not intimidating, despite his obvious intellect, and everyone felt included in the conversation.[37] For someone with his increasing tendency to excessive drinking, staying in a pub was not a good move. He gave the impression even at this stage that he was well on the way to becoming an alcoholic. His hands shook and he had a rather heightened colour. He would come down from his room in the morning and have to have a drink quite early – usually gin and tonic. He would invariably be the first one in the bar, greeting the staff with a large smile and looking 'rather like a hamster'.[38] If he had been working on the film score in the barn, Montgomery would come into the bar, smoke, beat time and wave his hands around very intensely. In contrast to his time at Oxford he did not seem much concerned about his appearance; previously he had been a fancy dresser with an immaculate hairstyle, but now there

---

33    Ibid., 28 October 1954
34    Ibid., 29 October 1954
35    Ibid., 6 December 1954
36    Jeni Turnbull
37    Ibid.
38    Ibid.

was sometimes ash down his front and he occasionally had a rather rumpled look. Jeni Turnbull recalls a characteristic view of him squinting to avoid the smoke from his cigarette as, with nicotine-stained fingers, he flicked back his hair after it had fallen over his forehead. His smoking and drinking were both social habits, and he used them to overcome his initial shyness and to break down barriers. To Jeni he seemed rather a lonely person. He told her that when he went home to Brixham he was not at all gregarious and did not see anyone for ages.

Montgomery did not eat sensibly, particularly if there was plenty of conversation in the bar. Mr Turnbull often tried to persuade him to have a meal, but Montgomery was a great talker, saying that he would come in a moment but continuing to chat. He got on well with the other locals; he was very easy-going and personable, and he appreciated that they were down-to-earth and friendly people. Both Turnbulls and locals did not let him get away with being too highbrow and he did not come across as snobbish – but he could take people down a peg or two if they merited it.

Montgomery attended the New Year's Eve party which had horse-racing as its theme with Colin Strang and his girlfriend, and early in the New Year he was doing his best to encourage the friendship with Jeni even though it was already having its ups and downs: 'On Thursday Jeni and I went up to Town for the first performance of a new ballet by Malcolm Arnold, with a supper party afterwards: all very jolly. There's no engagement in the offing yet! As a matter of fact Jeni and I had something of a quarrel at the beginning of the week, and although we're friends again, we're treating one another rather cautiously at the moment.'[39] The quarrel might have been caused when Jeni persuaded a rather reluctant Montgomery to go swimming with her. He had to borrow a swimming costume from the assistant manager of the pub, only to find that it was riddled with moth holes. This appalled him. The occasion was made worse by the fact that although a good swimmer, he was very self-conscious about his feet. Jeni also did not care for Montgomery's use of the endearment 'poppet' which was fashionable at the time.

In February, whilst Jeni was suffering with pneumonia, Montgomery was seeing some of his friends. He was best man at Peter Oldham's wedding, something for which he had little enthusiasm (although he had composed the *Bridal Procession* for the occasion), and Kingsley Amis stayed at the Crown and Thistle. A few months earlier Montgomery had visited Amis, reporting that 'Hilly [Amis' wife] and I got sick simultaneously and took to our beds, while Kingsley pattered about the house grumbling at having to fetch us things.'[40]

Montgomery's stay at the pub did not last much longer. Living there was an expensive business, and the ready availability of alcohol was a constant distraction. Although Mr and Mrs Turnbull were quite heavy drinkers themselves, they had a steadying influence on him. They were aware of his problems and warned Montgomery that he should leave if he wanted to get on with his career. A few months later he confessed to having to work rather hard

39    RBM to parents, 8 January 1955
40    RBM to Larkin, 6 November 1955

retrieving the situation caused by my incredibly idle and extravagant residence at Abingdon. That's a place I've now left, by the way: as a matter of fact I left it last April, returning here [Brixham] to find relations with my parents so vastly improved in my own favour that I had no incentive to leave again, and here I've stuck ever since and shall probably go on sticking; though I must admit that the general shaking-up Abingdon gave me was probably a good thing.[41]

Montgomery had spent a good deal of effort on women in the past to little effect. Nothing had come of his ardour with Muriel Pavlow, and now nothing came of his relentless pursuit of Jeni Turnbull. He expended an enormous amount of energy in the chase but did not get very far. He liked to have someone to go out with, usually to dinner where he could drink. He took Jeni to a Detection Club dinner where the snob in him came out as he mixed with well-known people. She also accompanied him to the IMA, on one occasion being carried by Malcolm Arnold up and down the very dignified staircase in a rather undignified manner.

Jeni was fond of him but did not find him physically attractive. Many people, including Turnbull herself, were of the opinion that Montgomery would have liked to marry her, but to her it seemed that he chased women because it was something he felt he ought to do, perhaps as a cure for his loneliness. He was not really interested in it except as a romantic ideal. He liked to think of himself as a womaniser and his sense of sophistication would have been increased if other people saw him as a womaniser, but he was simply not cut out for it. In comparison with his intellect, Montgomery's relationships with women were never of the same level. He was playing a game. This could well account for the idealistic portraits of eligible young women he draws in his novels. There was a juvenile streak in him (he would make jokes about Jeni's many other admirers, for instance), and his drinking did not help matters either.[42] 'There are times when I think I'd be happier without sex,' he wrote in 1956.[43] With his male friends he talked a lot about women because it was the thing to do, but he was incapable of bringing a relationship to a resolution, perhaps because he did not want to be seen as ordinary in any way.[44] These judgements reinforce the impressions we have received about his earlier relationships with women, and they are ones that will be repeated later.

Back with his parents, Montgomery was soon embroiled in film work and telling Larkin that 'Nothing, like something, continues to happen here in Brixham with monotonous regularity; I mean I'm not in a position to write to you that I've taken the veil or moved house or contracted a liaison or anything.'[45] He told Larkin that he found his visits to the Amis household bizarre:

Yes, I know what you mean about the Amises not worrying: their modus vivendi strikes me as being altogether slightly strange – in the sense of alien, incomprehensible. Now that I've stayed with them twice, I shall take with me, on the next occasion, (a) an ashtray,

41    Ibid.
42    Jeni Turnbull
43    RBM to Larkin, 17 January 1956
44    Jeni Turnbull
45    RBM to Larkin, 11 April 1956

(b) a wastepaper basket, (c) an alarm clock, (d) a goblin teasmade, (e) an electric torch, (f) clotheshangers, (g) two extra pillows, and (h) a bedside lamp: also, now I come to think of it, extra towels, a private bathroom and a variety of spiked, bullet-proof armour for domestic animals; oh, and earplugs for the radiogram … That sounds thoroughly unkind, too, when they're always so affable and keen for one to be there; it's just that one feels that asking for any of these things would be to burden their consciences and their understandings more than could reasonably be borne. And of course I'm immensely fond of them both, and find K a terrific stimulant.[46]

He also met Amis in London for a lunch 'at which he ate a great deal of shellfish terribly slowly' and they went on 'in the afternoon to drink in a Soho cellar-club and listen with unanimous lack of pleasure to a lot of Armstrong discs. I've recently unfitted myself for the company of decent folk by taking a liking (heavily qualified, but still a liking) for Ted Heath.'[47]

The picture we gain of Montgomery in 1962, just after the failure of his score for *Carry On Cruising*, is not a good one. It is of a composer of film music who has been gradually eased out of the more than comfortable living he had been making; it is of a composer of concert music who has completed only one piece of serious work in almost ten years; it is of an author of detective novels who has not completed one book during the same period. The only aspect of his career in which his reputation was rising was that of an expert on science fiction, but this was not earning him much of a living. The change in his personal life is also dramatic. Having started and spent much of the decade as a dilettante socialite, he turned gradually into a rather morose semi-recluse. 'I've become an Immobilist (following Nero Wolfe),[48] and never seem to get to see anyone these days,' he complained to Brian Aldiss.[49]

In 1964 Montgomery wrote a revealing letter to Philip Larkin:

a)   my father died a year ago last October;
b)   my mother, who'd been getting a bit difficult well before he died, got extremely difficult afterwards, when I was left living alone in the house with her; so that in March of last year I was forced to move out and take a small furnished flat in Totnes;
c)   these unhappinesses having affected my work, I found myself booted out of my corner of the picture business;
d)   lacking prescience, I'd none the less embarked on building myself rather an expensive new house; and –
e)   I reacted very inferiorily to all this by taking quite seriously to the bottle and getting near – though not, I hope, quite over – the verge of genuine alcoholism.
But just recently things have calmed down a bit, and seem to be improving.[50]

The death of his father and the awkwardness of his mother may have had something to do with the immediate problems he faced with completing the score

---

46    Ibid., 17 January 1956
47    Ibid., 11 April 1956. Ted Heath (1900–1969), English bandleader
48    The corpulent housebound detective of Rex Stout (1886–1975)
49    RBM to Brian Aldiss, 5 July 1962
50    RBM to Larkin, 26 March 1964

for *Carry On Cruising*, but they cannot be held responsible for his increasing unpunctuality before it.

As we have previously seen, Montgomery's career to this point is marked by the fact that he was, in the best sense of the word, an amateur, but one who managed to make a very good living. He never planned his career: he fell into it. His first detective novel came about as a result of an enthusiasm after he had read *The Crooked Hinge* by John Dickson Carr; he started composing concert music, but had little formal musical education; his film music started as a result of his interest in the cinema; his series of science fiction anthologies came about entirely as a result of his love of the genre. Yet he was successful, startlingly so in many ways. His first novel, *The Case of the Gilded Fly*, was accepted immediately for publication whilst he was still an undergraduate. His first published music appeared in 1944, the year after he graduated and in the same year as *The Case of the Gilded Fly*. By the time he was 32 years old he had eight novels and 21 pieces of music in print. His film career quickly got into gear, and he was soon composing for some of the most popular comedies of the time. The excellent reviews his science fiction anthologies received have been quoted.

So what went wrong? His health certainly deteriorated. Osteoporosis and Dupuytren's Contracture were natural developments of the bone problems with which he had been born, but Montgomery did nothing to help them by smoking and drinking to excess. The change in his character can be traced to these health problems, encouraging the gloomy moods which increasingly possessed him. Perhaps his domestic circumstances also contributed to this: the aura of sophistication he had been eager to project to his girlfriends could not have been helped by the fact that he was still living with his parents, although this was certainly advantageous for him financially.

Work had also, for the first time, become irksome to him. The early music and novels had been dashed off at an impressive rate. Work now became exactly that: it was no longer good fun. Montgomery had previously been able to write for a certain part of the year and relax for the rest of it. Interviews with him are littered with references to his love of doing as little as possible: 'I'm a lazy person essentially, and of a sedentary habit,' he wrote towards the end of his life.[51] During the 1950s Montgomery felt that he was having to turn into a professional, and he did not like it.

Montgomery's career had progressed in waves: novels and concert music in the 1940s, film music in the 1950s. The reasons for his mental and physical state in 1962 are many, but the demands of film work must take the largest share of the blame. For the first time in his life, Montgomery found himself under pressure. He had to work to very short deadlines. A lot of people were affected if he did not produce the score on time. His own livelihood was at stake if he did not produce the score on time. In short, he had responsibility, something he did not care for. His already worsening health was not improved by his increasing reliance on alcohol. From about 1957 onwards he had a standing prescription for tranquillisers and sleeping pills without which he found it almost impossible to survive.

---

51    *The Armchair Detective*, Spring 1979

The hard professional film world has a lot to answer for in Montgomery's demise. It may have helped to make him, by 1962, a fairly wealthy man. It also caused a crisis in his creative life from which he never really recovered.

# Chapter 14

# 'A sort of slack sabbatical': 1962–1976

Whereas the earlier parts of Montgomery's creative life break down into more or less clearly discernible periods during which he worked in particular genres, the last fifteen years of his life are more a catalogue of missed opportunities. The decline was as rapid as had been his early success. In many ways the zenith of Montgomery's career came in 1961 with the relative success of *Raising the Wind*, the film for which he wrote both score and screenplay. He might have been largely forgotten by this time as a composer of concert music, but his stock remained high as a detective novelist and he had more yet to contribute to the world of science fiction. At this stage he had few financial worries.

This did not satisfy Montgomery. He had always given the impression that he regarded writing detective novels and composing film music as lucrative diversions. Witnessing Amis and Larkin establish themselves as literary lions unsettled him. He had always wanted above all else to be taken seriously as a composer, and now he had the time for this work he was in no position to do anything about it. Threatening to finish writing detective stories ('fair browned off with this tec stuff, I am'), he told Larkin that he could not make his mind up what to do instead: 'there are times when I think it might be quite a good thing to give up writing altogether and concentrate on composing instead, but I doubt if I shall ever have the courage for that.'[1] In the remaining years of his life, Montgomery composed very little indeed. 'I am more and more giving up composing in favour of writing,' he wrote in 1976.[2] He rarely seemed to know where his greatest talents lay.

The only music of his published after 1960 was the ballad opera *John Barleycorn* which he had composed eight years previously. The work was published in vocal score in August 1962. Montgomery spent the early weeks of his freedom from film work arranging the full score of the opera. Apart from a piece for organ, *Bridal Procession*, apparently written for the wedding of a friend's daughter in November 1963 but which is actually more or less identical to the *March for Organ* Montgomery had composed for another marriage in 1947, Montgomery's only other completed musical work in these years were two scores of incidental music. The first was for his own radio play *Merely Players*, a BBC commission. The Drama Department had started the ball rolling in January 1964 by asking for a script dealing with 'a day in the life of a practising musician in London'.[3] By September, in keeping with his reputation at the end of his film career, Montgomery was already apologising for missing a deadline: 'Frankly, combining light-heartedness with solid information

---

1     RBM to Larkin, 9 January 1956
2     RBM to Lloyds Bank, 1 April 1976
3     Terence Tiller (BBC) to RBM, 17 January 1964

with some sort of dramatic storyline hasn't been easy – and it's only recently that I've hit on what I hope may be the right formula.'[4] The play proved to be a satirical semi-documentary comedy-drama about a 'representative, if perhaps abnormally lively, day in the life of a professional violinist'.[5] Montgomery's incidental music for the production was recorded by the BBC Midland Light Orchestra with Carmel Kaine, a young Australian, as the soloist and the composer conducting. The whole was broadcast on the Third Programme at the end of January 1965 and it was received favourably, with Kenneth Thompson in *Musical Opinion* particularly impressed: there were 'some hard things said about conductors' and the play was 'garnished with some glorious witticisms'. It was 'an unusual and most delightful musical entertainment. […] The entire production was beautifully managed, and I only wish it had been longer.'[6]

The second score was Montgomery's final film work, for a picture called *The Brides of Fu Manchu*. He had his old mentor Philip Martell, who conducted the score, to thank for being asked. The irony of this was that, after all Montgomery's problems with punctuality, he was called in at the last moment to write this score after the contracted composer, Johnny Douglas, dropped out. 'It's a rush job', he wrote,[7] but it seems that the intervening four years had not made him change his spots: 'The film-music war has escalated',[8] was his reaction as the work became serious. Although the cue sheet for the film credits all the music, almost 30 minutes' worth, to Montgomery, he wrote to thank and pay Douglas Gamley for his help.[9] He also sent Martell £30 to cover the cost of the three extra violins he required in the orchestra.[10] One thing he had learned, though, was to ask for changes in his contract so that if the publisher no longer wanted the score it was to return to Montgomery 'finally and absolutely'.[11] It is unlikely, though, that it did return to Montgomery as it is not to be found in his papers. After the years of complaining that he was only asked to score comedy films, in his last film (he claimed it was his fiftieth,[12] but in fact the total was nearer forty) he was at last given full rein to indulge in a more contemporary style, with plenty of dissonances and oriental percussion. Even so, there are plenty of unmistakeably Montgomerian passages in which he reverts to his tried and trusted style.

With concert music apparently out of the question, it was an ideal opportunity for Montgomery to complete the crime novel he had been promising Gollancz for the best part of ten years. 'It'll be a relief to revert to work which can be done without interminable conferences and consultations,' he told fellow author Roy Vickers,

---

4    Ibid., 15 September 1964
5    *Musical Opinion*, March 1965, p. 349
6    Ibid.
7    RBM to Harry Harrison, 6 April 1966
8    RBM to Harry Harrison, 30 April 1966
9    RBM to Douglas Gamley, 28 July 1966
10   RBM to Philip Martell, 26 May 1966
11   RBM to Tristram Owen (Fu-Manchu Films), 21 May 1966
12   RBM to Jacques Barzun, 6 April 1966

taking a swipe at the film world.[13] In 1963 he was writing confidently to Anthony Boucher about his plans:

> I don't know if you've noticed, but people's detectives tend to follow the life-line of their creators; so also with Fen. I'm not going to age him, or any tiresome nonsense of that sort, but I'm afraid he's bound to be a little less effervescent than he was when I was in my twenties. Luckily, however, I've still got a few ideas for orthodox detective plots, and I'm going to go on pushing those hopefully out for as long as the market will stand it; so that Fen – although now, like myself, in querulous middle-age – will, I hope, have something to occupy him for a few years yet.[14]

At least Fen was still in the picture. The previous year Montgomery had admitted that the thought of killing him off had passed through his mind,[15] as it had even earlier: 'Haven't decided yet whether to kill Fen; better keep him in reserve, perhaps, for emergencies, if not for old times' sake', was how he had worded it.[16] His indecision might have been influenced by overhearing Agatha Christie and Dorothy L. Sayers at a Detection Club meeting agreeing that they were sick of their detectives.[17] Montgomery was also being pursued by Clayton Rawson, the Managing Editor of *Ellery Queen's Mystery Magazine* in New York, for more short stories: 'At the moment, Crispin short stories are notable rather for the brilliance of their basic ideas, than for their author's willingness to get down to the really hard part,' Montgomery told him. 'Still, there are a few plots rattling around in my skull like peas in an empty gourd.'[18] Rawson had written his request when hemmed in his office by several thousand screaming Beatles' fans. Montgomery needed no encouragement to give his views on the matter: 'As regards the Beatles, you can keep them: isn't there some Federal or State law whereby they can be put behind bars for a few years for provoking orgasms in female minors? If not, the US isn't the splendid civilisation I'd always imagined it to be.'[19]

By 1965 his plan for *Judgement in Paris*, the novel on which he had supposedly been working for the best part of eight years, had been dropped, and on 17 December Montgomery met Victor Gollancz for lunch at the Savoy where he promised to deliver a novel in two months. Gollancz was so delighted by this undertaking that he cancelled Montgomery's previous three-novel agreement and gave him an immediate £500 advance, though he was careful to let the author know that this was 'a special case, and not to be a precedent'.[20] A few days later Montgomery was already suggesting *The Glimpses of the Moon* as a title ('the corpse in my story is revisiting them, and in another sense so am I').[21] In March 1966 Montgomery broke

---

13    RBM to Roy Vickers, 6 March 1958
14    RBM to Anthony Boucher, 25 August 1963
15    RBM to Jan Broberg, 17 December 1962
16    RBM to Larkin, 17 January 1956
17    MS. Eng. C. 3918
18    RBM to Clayton Rawson, 16 September 1964
19    Ibid.
20    Victor Gollancz to RBM, 17 December 1965
21    RBM to Victor Gollancz, 23 December 1965

his leg and was given an extension on the novel until the end of April. Early in May Livia Gollancz was chasing him. By November 1966 the publisher was sufficiently confident of the book's progress to announce it in its list of forthcoming publications. Montgomery's reputation as Edmund Crispin was high enough for advance orders of 2,300 copies to be taken, and that figure did not include London.[22] But none of this encouraged Montgomery sufficiently to complete the novel at that time.

Almost a year later Livia Gollancz's patience was clearly approaching breaking point. She wrote to Montgomery demanding to know whether he had scrapped *The Glimpses of the Moon*: 'I feel that perhaps the time has come to resolve the whole question.'[23] Montgomery replied with alacrity, claiming that the book was two-thirds complete and would take only another three weeks to finish. He offered to pay back the advance. None of this worked either. In 1969 he reported that 'The new Crispin is about two-thirds gone, and seems the same mixture as before. I don't seem to have matured in any way.'[24] A year later he was 'on the final agonising stages of my bloody novel. God almighty, how I detest writing! However, now that film music has petered out, there seems nothing else for it.'[25] Later that year the situation had not changed: 'The novel remains stuck about two thirds of the way through, but I'm going to make a tremendous attempt to finish it in the next three weeks, an enterprise roughly comparable with trying to knock out Cassius Clay, with a single blow, when he's all alert and ready for you. My trouble with writing remains what it always was, namely that I'm no good.'[26] Three years later he admitted to

getting a bit low financially, so shall have to discipline myself a bit. The Penguin Hugh Kingsmill, in its brief biography, says: 'After his second marriage he gave up work completely and devoting himself to writing.' Ah, Christ, if only it weren't work! But I sit in the middle of my stagnant novel, and for twenty minutes at a time can think of nothing (not just nothing interesting: nothing at all) for any of the characters to say or do next. 'He lit a cigarette ...' But practically no-one smokes nowadays.'[27]

As late as April 1976 Montgomery was telling Philip Larkin that

Chapter Eleven of Glimpses has had me rolling in the aisles at my own wit, but unfortunately I now have to get on with Chapter Twelve and try to find some rational explanation, within the nexus of the plot, of all the little bits and pieces I put in because I thought at the time they were amusing. This is not the way to win the CWA's Golden Dagger.[28]

Despite his difficulties in finishing this novel, other opportunities were presenting themselves. Early in 1965 Sydney Box asked Montgomery to write two thrillers under another pen-name which would be published in one paperback by a company with which he was involved. By October Box was suggesting that Montgomery

---

22    Gollancz Archive
23    Livia Gollancz to RBM, 16 March 1967
24    RBM to Larkin, 16 August 1969
25    Ibid., 3 April 1970
26    Ibid., 10 September 1970
27    Ibid., 10 April 1973
28    Ibid., 10 April 1976

should write a novella, offer it to Gollancz as his next novel under his agreement with them, and then give it to Triton, Box's publishing company, if Gollancz deemed it too short. Before long Montgomery decided that Box's rates were not good enough and abandoned the idea.

In the previous decade Montgomery had signed a contract to write detective novels for Collins which was cancelled when it became clear that he was incapable of completing the books that were due for Gollancz. Even so, Collins only finally admitted defeat in trying to lure Montgomery in 1969. By then, though, he was already negotiating with Macmillan to produce thrillers under his own name. 'With money from film music beginning to run low', he told Larkin, 'I'm having to make serious arrangements to become a Writer again – you know, two or three books a year (God!). Luckily, Macmillans have offered me a fat contract (advance of £2000 on each book) to turn out thrillers for them under my real name, so it won't all have to be the old Crispin malarkey, though of course I shall be carrying on with that as well.'[29] In 1972 a report in *The Spectator* suggested that Montgomery was likely to remove his Crispin books from Gollancz. Livia Gollancz wrote to Montgomery asking for clarification, and he was quick to reply:

> I should perhaps add that whatever the 'Spectator' may imagine, George Hardinge and I are most certainly not engaged in a sort of running conspiracy to remove Crispin from the Gollancz list. More than twenty years ago (!) George told me that I'd be welcome at Collins if I wanted to leave you; but nothing came of that. More recently, as you know from Michael Horniman (he having asked you to modify your option on my next book, which you very kindly did), I signed a contract to write a novel for Macmillan under my own name. I should emphasise, however, that George has made no overtures at all regarding the Crispin books, and that I shouldn't have dreamed of succumbing even if he had. In short, I can assure you categorically that the Crispin books are yours for as long as you want to continue publishing them.[30]

The fact that Gollancz was so keen to retain Crispin says a good deal about his popularity as an author, twenty years after the publication of his previous novel. It also says a good deal about Gollancz's patience, given that there was still no sign of his next book at the time. Gollancz's enthusiasm for his work was such that the company had been keen to bid against Macmillan for the novels under Montgomery's own name as well as being willing to offer him another three-book contract after *The Glimpses of the Moon*. The contract with Macmillan had been signed in December 1969 and it was intended on publication of the first novel to reveal that Crispin and Montgomery were the same person, although this was hardly a secret.

From his papers it is clear that Montgomery made some attempt at planning and writing at least one of these novels. *What Seems to be the Trouble?*, set partly in a doctor's surgery, was the most advanced. The story concerns two writers: one, Arthur Messenger, is an impecunious author of vast biographies (his current work on Dr Barnado has the infant making its first appearance on page 218); the other, John Prout, is a poet. They were at Oxford together, live ten miles apart, and cannot

---

29    RBM to Larkin, 24 November 1969
30    RBM to Livia Gollancz, 16 January 1972 (Gollancz Archive)

bear one another. They are commissioned, by the drunken Sir Aylwin Slaughter of publishers Ogden and Wain, to write a crime story together. Sir Aylwin is in hospital with broken legs and delirium tremens (rather close to home for Montgomery) and is part of the medical link, although two unbalanced doctors are also involved. Both authors want different types of detective for their story, and it appears that most of the novel was to be taken up by their mutual antipathy. The existing manuscript (46 pages) suggests that the book was to have many of Montgomery's traits, including names of his friends (the wives of the main characters are named after a former girlfriend of Montgomery and Kingsley Amis' wife). The poet in the story is 'in the very likely event of Larkin's panicking, the next Poet Laureate',[31] and there is a savage attack on VAT and on Ted Heath, the Prime Minister for some of the time the book was being written (he is called a 'monomaniac mugwump').[32] There are extensive notes about Montgomery's own doctor's surgery, including the décor, furniture and details of key holders. The tone of the novel was more basic than his previous work, with a greater emphasis on sex. In April 1978 Montgomery got as far as sending the first section of the book to his typist and there is a breakdown of the planned 37 chapters.

Its intended successor, *Make Red War Redder*, an anti-communist tract described by Montgomery as 'an armchair spy story',[33] made very little progress. The political slant of this planned novel was hardly a surprise. Montgomery had never passed through a left-wing phase like some of his friends (Amis, for instance), and his conservatism had grown with age. Towards the end of 1977 he told Julian Symons that he was having great fun buying red Christmas cards for leftists and blue ones 'for chaps like me'.[34] A few years earlier his fears about a planned trip to the continent had been divulged to Larkin: 'Can already visualise the swarthy, whiskered countenance of the demented son of the Prophet who will skijack us. Can also visualise trying to make myself understood in a country where "everybody speaks English". However, I suppose one mustn't let one's xenophobia get completely out of hand. (Mustn't one, mustn't one? WHY EVER NOT?)'[35] On another occasion, following statements critical of American foreign policy, he joined with a number of prominent figures in signing a letter to the *Daily Telegraph* putting the opposing view, lest 'Kenneth Tynan[36] [...] and an odd assortment of actors and actresses should go on being assumed by the Americans to represent intelligent British opinion'.[37]

Montgomery was also planning a novel called *Spotcheck*. It was to have a legal theme, based on the premise that with a jury of nine unanimity is essential:

> That, in a way, is what the following story is about. But for it, a juryman who disagreed with the majority, and was thoroughly obstinate in the matter, would never have been

---

31    Draft for *What Seems to be the Trouble?*
32    Notes for *What Seems to be the Trouble?*
33    RBM to Larkin, 1 September 1977
34    RBM to Julian Symons, 9 December 1977
35    RBM to Larkin, 10 September 1970
36    Kenneth Tynan (1927–1980), critic
37    *Daily Telegraph*, 21 January 1967

found dead in the jury-room, the back of his skull caved in by a vicious blow from an iron poker which even Dick Shepphard, the highwayman, would have regarded as antique.[38]

This introduction is as far as the novel got, although Montgomery did make notes on juries and courts.

There was some literary work which Montgomery did complete, all of it under his pseudonym. The work of editing seven anthologies of science fiction short stories for Faber continued until 1971. There were also two collections of science fiction stories designed for use in schools. For the first of these, *The Stars and Under*, Montgomery took steps to see if his introduction was suitable for its intended audience:

> My own schoolmastering days having ended 20 years ago, I did find it difficult to gauge whether I was striking the right level or not. In fact, I gave it to read to the (average-intelligent) 15-year-old of a neighbour, who in turn showed it to two of his classmates, and their unanimous opinion was that it was not too complicated, but too simple! However, they may possibly have been referring to the tone rather than to the content.[39]

Interspersed with these were other anthologies, of detective, murder and terror stories. Crispin's anthologies continued to be widely praised, and authors of repute were only too pleased to have their work included. 'I shall be very pleased and flattered if I can appear in one of your Best SFs again,' John Wyndham wrote.[40] Isaac Asimov was 'honored' to be approached for one of his stories.[41] For the school anthologies Crispin was warned to be careful as a previous attempt by Brian Aldiss had been abandoned. 'The limitations are that sex and violence should be avoided – that's where Brian came a cropper, I fear,' Charles Monteith (Montgomery's editor) wrote.[42] Montgomery found no difficulties over this: he did not 'see that there need be any great difficulty about avoiding sex and violence in the contents. In fact, my own experience has been that the problem with SF is to find sex and violence.'[43]

Montgomery's most regular work during this period came after he succeeded Julian Symons as crime reviewer for the *Sunday Times* in 1967. This was in some ways a strange move for someone who had never had much time for critics: '[Montgomery] resents the existence of the practice of critical writing,' Amis had reported as far back as 1952.[44] Montgomery and Symons had very different views of the detective story. Montgomery favoured the orthodox mystery with clues for the reader and deplored the use of psychology: Symons was more broad-minded on at least the latter. Welcoming Montgomery as his successor, Symons acknowledged their differences: '[*Criminal Records*][45] must have infuriated you at times in the past. Now I shall expect you to infuriate me – but there is nobody whose views about

38    Introduction to *Spotcheck*
39    RBM to John Oliver (Faber), 14 June 1967
40    John Wyndham to RBM, 11 September 1962
41    Isaac Asimov to RBM, 12 October 1964
42    Charles Monteith to RBM, 24 July 1964
43    RBM to Charles Monteith, 29 July 1964
44    Amis to Larkin, 6 November 1952 [LKA]
45    The crime review section in the *Sunday Times*

crime stories I am more eager to learn or regard with more respect, as I think you know.'[46] Symons certainly read the column:

> I liked very much your view of reading detective stories as a sort of therapy, rather similar to […] a couple of hours in the gym. 'Feeling much fitter after my session with Crofts this morning.' 'Yes, I had a good workout with Sayers myself.' Your views explain my physical feebleness. Work outs with Highsmith are strength-sapping affairs.[47]

The respect worked both ways: in 1971, after Montgomery had read *Bloody Murder* (Symons's masterly survey of crime writing) for Faber, he was asked to contribute the section on Symons himself. Symons had suggested Montgomery to Faber as a reader because he thought the book should be read by someone whose views did not coincide with his. Apart from one or two small quibbles ('that I'd given too much praise to Patricia Highsmith and been unfair to Sayers'), Montgomery's enthusiastic seven or eight page report 'was the best – and best-written – reader's report I've read. He began by saying something like "This is far from what a reader's report should be…" and then wrote what was in effect an elegant little essay on the book.'[48]

Montgomery was a good critic but found that the work took up 'a tremendous amount of reading time'.[49] In the ten years he wrote *Criminal Records*, he encouraged many promising authors who were in the early stages of their careers. When sent *Shroud for a Nightingale* by the then relatively unknown P.D. James, he was taken by her ability to mix imaginative literature with detective fiction. Many years later the by now established James reinforced her invitation to the launch of her novel *Death of an Expert Witness*:

> There is no one whose encouragement and criticism has meant more to me than yours (the more so because of my great respect for you as a writer) and it would be lovely to have the chance to say a personal 'Thank- you'. You have been kind to me from the beginning and it was your generous review of 'Shroud for a Nightingale' which gave me the breakthrough which I needed and which seemed so long in coming.[50]

Ruth Rendell wrote to Montgomery in similar vein in 1970 telling him that 'your two reviews, so generous and enthusiastic, have made me really happy and give me a confidence I sometimes lack'.[51] He welcomed Colin Dexter's first novel (*Last Bus to Woodstock*), having decided to review it in the paper rather than give the requested pre-publication 'puff'; he was pleasant about Jeffrey Archer (*Not a Penny More, Not a Penny Less*) in the same issue: 'a neat job of catharsis, written by a victim of similar shenanigans […] pacy, often amusing'.[52] He enjoyed Dick Francis: his notice of *Smokescreen* introduced his own equine experience: 'Hippophobes

46    Julian Symons to RBM, 3 February 1967
47    Ibid., 11 July 1972
48    Julian Symons to author, 4 March 1992
49    RBM to Fritz Leiber, 12 February 1972
50    P.D. James to RBM, 20 October 1977
51    Ruth Rendell to RBM, 28 April 1970
52    *Sunday Times*, 10 October 1976

(I myself was kicked on the head by a horse at the age of four, and have never felt the same about the creatures, or indeed been the same, since) nevertheless are usually greatly addicted to Mr Francis's horsey thrillers. [...] even the worst Francis is a lot better than the best of most other thriller writers, and this is far from being the worst.' Replying to Nicholas Freeling's letter of thanks for a good review, Montgomery acknowledged the difficulties of such curt notices. There was space only for a short description and 'a value judgement [...] I'm afraid that a good many of these brief notices do in fact read much too like impertinent school reports'.[53]

A reply he sent to Martin Russell is typical of his approach: 'As regards praising them [Russell's books], praising good books is, after all, one of the things I'm paid for. No need, therefore, for any words of gratitude – welcome though they are.'[54] In declining P.D. James' invitation to the launch of *Death of an Expert Witness*, he made a similar point: 'I can assure you that I never encourage anyone whom I don't think is genuinely good. So the credit is all yours.'[55]

Montgomery was a stickler for accuracy, and this did not always go down well with authors. Reviewing John Gardner's *Madrigal*, Montgomery referred to 'errors [...] abundantly in evidence'.[56] Gardner wrote asking for clarification. By this time Montgomery had lent his copy to a friend and had to make his points from memory. Even so, he managed eighteen errors (mostly concerned with French and German spelling and accents, and Ben Jonson spelled as Johnson), 'and I think it fair to say that if I went through the book I could more than double it. [...] I did feel, however, that since your book makes rather a point of knowledgeability, the mistakes in it were far too numerous.'[57] Gardner was not placated, claiming that these were typographical errors which had not been corrected from his galley proofs, and should have been stated as such. On another occasion Montgomery's review of *Passport for a Pilgrim* by James Leasor claimed that the book contained 'the usual helpful hints on how to set about sexual congress'. This mystified Leasor, as he knew that the book contained no sex whatever. Montgomery had to admit that he had been in hospital and had not seen the proofs into which a phrase from another review had been accidentally transferred. A correction was duly put into Montgomery's next column. Once, when responding to suggestions by Jack Lambert, the literary editor of the *Sunday Times*, that some of his choices were out of the ordinary, Montgomery wrote: 'Do I detect a faint dissatisfaction with my choices? [...] They aren't, of course, always the same as other people's [...] I've never come to feel that I'm unduly the odd man out. I do confess, though, to the weakness of hating to review a bad book by a big name to the exclusion of a better book by someone less well-known.'[58]

He lived up to this last claim when avoiding a clash with an old friend. 'Oh Lor',' he wrote when agreeing with Larkin about Kingsley Amis' detective novel, *The Riverside Villas Murder*:

---

53    RBM to Nicholas Freeling, 18 May 1971

54    RBM to Martin Russell, 15 September 1974

55    RBM to P.D. James, 31 October 1977

56    *Sunday Times*, 24 September 1967

57    RBM to John Gardner, 28 September 1967

58    RBM to Jack Lambert, 16 June 1975

Entirely between ourselves, I was sent it for review, but hastily returned it. [...] its detection is very poor indeed: young wives constructing catapults and launching gliders at their lovers' heads, Jesus, what next? Even in the thirties, it would have made the members of the Detection Club blink. [...] As to 'elliptic', you're right enough about that: elliptic, in the upshot, almost to the point of unintelligibility, I'd have said. [...] Nasty words, admittedly, about such an old friend. But was greatly taken aback by K.'s failure to do better.[59]

He was no more impressed by a later attempt: 'The trouble is, he [Amis] rather fancies himself as a detective writer, and unless we're all very careful he'll end up writing nothing else.'[60]

In June 1972 Montgomery started a three month sabbatical. For five years he had been ploughing his way through an average of 40 books a month, and told his editor that 'to read a book a day for you – which is what it amounts to – does leave one in increasing ignorance of what is going on elsewhere in the literary world'.[61] In the Christmas Book section in 1974 he was very happy to recommend Larkin's recently published *High Windows*: 'True, I dislike "The Old Fools" – a cruel poem; and true, I have some doubts about Larkin in his demotic mood, complete with four-letter words. But the rest is pure gold., For a 42-page book £1.40 is a lot to pay, but I wouldn't grudge a penny of it. Where contemporary verse is concerned, Larkin remains incomparable.'[62] Following the death of the Poet Laureate, Cecil Day-Lewis, in 1972, Montgomery had championed Larkin as his successor. 'You for Laureate?' he asked. 'Have been dispassionately considering the possibilities, and you're easily the most suitable. Auden is an American, a queer, a wartime scarperer; Betjeman's too old and rachitic and mad. Spender's a posturing ninny. Graves is always in Majorca. Plomer (a Daily Telegraph suggestion) – well, words fail me. Yes, you for Laureate.'[63] It was Betjeman who got the nod.

Away from reviewing, this period of Montgomery's life continued with missed opportunities and promises which were unlikely to be kept. With the exceptions already mentioned, he made little effort even to begin new musical work. One project which had tantalising prospects was a planned opera to be written with Anthony Burgess,[64] based on the latter's *The Eve of St Venus*. Montgomery had met and first discussed the scheme with Burgess at the Cheltenham Festival of Literature in 1965, where they both participated in a discussion on 'The Future of Science Fiction' with Brian Aldiss. Burgess, like Montgomery a composer as well as author, wrote a few months later to say that he would approach the BBC about the opera if Montgomery was still eager to go ahead. Montgomery replied that his broken leg had put him back and he had to earn some money, so it might have to wait until later in the year: 'But

---

59     RBM to Larkin, 10 April 1973
60     Ibid., 4 August 1975
61     RBM to Jack Lambert, 8 June 1972
62     *Sunday Times*, 1 December 1974
63     RBM to Larkin, 29 May 1972
64     Anthony Burgess, pseudonym of John Wilson (1917–1993), novelist and composer

I'm still very keen. I still think that television would be a very good medium.'[65] The intention was that Burgess would be responsible for the libretto and Montgomery for the music. It would have been fascinating to see how the two refrained from interfering with each other's work, but unfortunately nothing more was heard of the project.

The lengthy saga of *The Glimpses of the Moon* dominated Montgomery's literary work of the time, but at least that was finished eventually. Apart from *Merely Players* and one or two talks and small pieces, most of the work Montgomery was offered by the BBC came to nothing, although a television version of *The Moving Toyshop* was screened in 1964 (he had 'splendid red-carpet treatment' at the viewing).[66] 'The sound-radio adaptation of Toyshop struck me as being almost as sodding awful as the book itself', Larkin was informed, 'but the T.V. version is enormously better.'[67] He thought it might lead on to something: 'There's […] a chance, I think', he told a sister, 'that they may give me a series of my own, more or less by way of replacing Maigret.'[68] The *Daily Telegraph* had one view of the production: 'To compress any novel into an hour's television is asking a great deal. To compress "The Moving Toyshop" was well nigh impossible.'[69] The *Guardian* took another: 'This academic thriller bounced merrily along.'[70]

The advent of independent television provided further opportunities for a man in Montgomery's line of work. In 1959 he had bought shares in the fledgling Westward Television syndicate which applied successfully to run the station in Montgomery's home area. There was talk of him being a director at one point, but nothing came of it. A few years later Sydney Box tried to get him involved in his syndicate which was applying for one of the London stations. Montgomery was immediately enthusiastic and listed his special interests:

a)   Scripts or ideas for plays and serials – in part, SF, thrillers and light comedy;
b)   Composing and, if required, music-directing background music, signature-tunes and so forth;
c)   Specially designed 'musicals', more or less equivalent to the one-act play;
d)   Specially designed small operas, preferably light in character, but a bit more ambitious artistically than a 'musical' would be (I mention this because with Kingsley Amis as librettist and myself as composer I've recently been working on a thing of just this sort).

    I should certainly be prepared to work on at least one special television programme each year; and since the medium is so interesting, it would obviously be worth while to do something more than that, if invited.[71]

This project also failed to progress, but Montgomery was still in demand as a commentator. For independent television he interviewed Ngaio Marsh ('I thought

65    RBM to Anthony Burgess, 6 April 1966
66    RBM to Audrey Keir Cross, 14 February 1964
67    RBM to Larkin, 26 March 1964
68    RBM to Sheila Rossiter, 14 February 1962
69    *Daily Telegraph*, 31 March 1964
70    *Guardian*, 31 March 1964
71    RBM to Sydney Box, 30 October 1963

your interview [...] was pleasantly relaxed and to the point', was the producer's verdict),[72] although in transmission it was truncated because the previous item had overrun. The usual stumbling block to writing for broadcast was money. The BBC often demanded to see some of the work before making a final offer, and Montgomery was not prepared to spend time on something which ultimately might not be commissioned. This happened, for example, in 1968 over a play called *A Dream for Old Gentlemen*. It had also happened some years earlier over a proposed adaptation of *Beware of the Trains*. A production company at Shepperton had been interested in the project, 'but as they wanted me to write a further pilot, with the same detective but with an Oxford background to interest the American market, and moreover were not proposing to pay me anything for doing this, I am afraid I dropped the matter'.[73] Writing a dramatisation for the television, he was soon apologising for having to revise it: 'I'm very feeble at doing things to order and have consequently got myself into a bit of a muddle.'[74]

Montgomery always had another excuse, which was that he was in the process of completing a novel. In 1968, almost eight years before he finished *The Glimpses of the Moon*, Montgomery was commissioned to write a mystery play for *Saturday Night Theatre*. He told the script unit at the BBC that he could not start the play for another three or four weeks because he was 'toiling over the last stages of a novel'.[75] Although this play was never completed, Montgomery suggests that it was to be called *The White Knight*. This is almost the same title as the novel Montgomery was intending to dedicate to Jacques Barzun, the American musicologist and writer on crime fiction. In 1969 Montgomery was writing to Barzun claiming that

> owing to a quirk of publishing, the book dedicated to you (WHITE NIGHT, written under my real name) looks like coming out a few months after THE GLIMPSES OF THE MOON (by Crispin), which I'm finishing off now; but there won't be a great deal in it, so I hope you won't mind – hope too that WHITE NIGHT, when it does appear, will succeed in foxing you: whatever its other merits or demerits, I think it probably has the most cunningest whodunit plot that I've up to now managed to think of.[76]

The following year, after a bout of illness, Montgomery was letting Barzun know that both books were now delayed until 1971, with *White Night* due to be published as the first under his agreement with Macmillan. By 1973 there was still no sign of either book:

> Me, I've been very lazy for the past two years – a sort of slack sabbatical – and have consequently got a bit behind-hand with everything. 'The Glimpses of the Moon' is virtually complete; but both 'White Night' and 'What Seems to be the Trouble?' (a crime comedy rather than a detection story proper) are to some extent languishing. I hope to

---

72    Guy Verney to RBM, 31 May 1960
73    RBM to Sydney Box, 1 May 1957
74    RBM to ABC Television, 10 January 1961
75    RBM to Guy Vaesen, 13 February 1968
76    RBM to Jacques Barzun, 14 November 1969 (Columbia University)

get on with them soon, however – and indeed must, so as not to join the ranks of what I believe nowadays are called the underprivileged.[77]

Nothing appears to have survived of either *White Night* or *White Knight*. It seems unlikely, given the similarity of the titles, that the two pieces were unconnected. Perhaps the titles give some clue to Montgomery's cunning plot.

---

77    Ibid., 6 November 1973

# Chapter 15

# 'A full scale replica of Chatsworth': 1962–1976

Despite the difficulties he faced in later life, Montgomery was very comfortably placed in 1962. The income from films and books meant that he had few financial worries, and he was sufficiently optimistic to have a bungalow built to his own specification in Week, a hamlet near Dartington, just a few miles from Brixham. The death of his father and the subsequent erratic behaviour of his mother forced his hand. He had looked at other sites, including one in Broadhempston close to where his secretary Ann Clements lived ('I was very much impressed with the beauty and peacefulness of the place'),[1] but by early 1962 he had decided on Week and had engaged as architect Arthur Grayson, from Wincanton in Somerset. The residence which emerged from the plans (called Week Meadow) was a large one, with three bedrooms, two bathrooms, a studio, staff quarters and an atomic fall-out shelter. This latter was entirely at Montgomery's whim, and he let Grayson know that he did not want its existence generally known: 'I quite agree with you that my bolt-hole had perhaps better be referred to as a cellar.'[2] Montgomery had bought the land for £800 and had expected the house to cost £8,500, but the tenders ranged from £12,453 to £13,824. Eventually the contract was given to T. Brook and Co. Ltd of Totnes. Montgomery managed to reduce the cost to £10,465 by changing the roofing materials and making other small adjustments. Even so, with the sudden ending of his film work the financing of the bungalow became difficult: 'I've also been earnestly engaged in economising', he wrote to the London doctor who had been responsible for prescribing tranquillisers during his film days, 'for the purpose of building a house which, though not particularly vast or luxurious, appears to be going to cost me about as much as if it were a full scale replica of Chatsworth.'[3]

Montgomery had arranged a mortgage for the expected cost of the project, but he was forced to try and arrange a further loan of £1,000 from his mother. She agreed, but later changed her mind: 'As so often happens with elderly people', Montgomery wrote to Robert Thairlwall, his mother's solicitor, 'she is a little apt to change her mind at short notice, without consultation or warning.'[4] His mother was causing Montgomery other problems. She was 'so cross at my going away and living on my own', he wrote to his sister Elspeth, 'that nowadays nothing I either do or say can ever possibly be right, let alone reliable.' Rock Hill House was sold and Montgomery's

---

1    RBM to Arthur Grayson, 1 November 1961
2    Ibid., 24 January 1962
3    RBM to Dr Israel Feldman, 7 April 1962
4    RBM to Robert Thairlwall, 16 May 1963

mother moved into a nursing home. The financial side of this needed to be sorted out and Montgomery advised caution: 'The fact is', he continued, 'that mother has been going about accusing me of being not only drunk and disorderly but unscrupulously rapacious as well.'[5] It was not long before the boot was on the other foot. Nora, Montgomery's eldest sister, wrote to report that the matron at the nursing home had said that their mother was 'rapidly getting worse [...] She will probably shortly have to be moved to a place where she can be more confined and that that she was drinking very heavily which they could not control.'[6] Montgomery did borrow £500 from his mother's account to help his house building but made sure that it was paid back with interest. He had a conscience about this, for three reasons: 'First, about being pretty comfortable myself; secondly, about being the only unmarried one; and thirdly, about having had to leave her to herself in the last months at Brixham.'[7]

Building at Week started on 10 September 1962, but delays (notably in the electricity supply) meant that the house was not completed on schedule. 'My domestic problems are mercifully smoothing out a bit', Montgomery wrote to Peter Rogers in October 1963, 'and I'm hoping to get into my new house (eight months overdue!) by Christmas or thereabouts.'[8] In November he was able to tell Harry Harrison that 'the new house has suddenly speeded up like a Max Sennet comedy'.[9] Having moved out of Rock Hill House and put his effects into store, he spent a month living at his secretary's house and then took a flat in Totnes.

It was a surprisingly dreary flat for someone with Montgomery's tastes. It is likely he took it because he knew he would not be there for long and because it was conveniently sited at the top of the narrow High Street. It was furnished with everyone's cast-offs, dark, miserable and 'depressing in the extreme'.[10] It was on the first floor above two shops, and a narrow staircase went up to it from the street. There was a sitting room and two bedrooms. He had no piano or books, giving him the excuse to complete little work in his time there. In November 1963 his life was made intolerable as the two shops beneath the flat were knocked into one, but after he moved out it transpired that he had been making enough noise of his own. Inviting his former landlady to visit Week, he apologised to her, not only for some damage, but also for 'an occasional noisy party which you've been kind enough not to refer to, but which must, I know, have disturbed you; I can only hope that these weren't too frequent.'[11] At the start of January 1964 he announced that he was going to the far end of Cornwall and did not intend to return until he knew that Week was finished.[12] He was finally able to move into his new house on 28 January 1964. It took only a few months before he was complaining about its drain on his finances: 'And so long as I stay in this infra-palazzo', he wrote to Harry Harrison, 'I've bloody little hope

5     RBM to Elspeth Slaughter, 22 June 1963
6     Nora (RBM's eldest sister) to RBM, 4 July 1966
7     RBM to Sheila Rossiter, 14 February 1964
8     RBM to Peter Rogers, 11 October 1963
9     RBM to Harry Harrison, 26 November 1963
10    Audrey Stock
11    RBM to Miss Beer, 11 September 1964
12    RBM to Joan Harrison, 11 January 1964

of putting by enough to ferry me over the prostatitis stage [...] Admittedly, the drink will probably have killed me off long before then. But suppose it <u>doesn't</u>: what's going to become of me then.'[13] He was already mentioning the possibility of finding a smaller house: 'Grand luxe tends to be a bit expensive, I'm finding.'[14]

As we have seen, Montgomery's decline can be put down to two main causes. The first one can be covered by the general heading of illness. The physical problems with which he had been born gradually became worse, and by the 1960s he was having considerable trouble with osteoporosis. Shortly after he moved into Week there was a scare about his lungs, a worrying development for someone who smoked up to eighty cigarettes a day:[15]

I got back yesterday with a clean bill of health, though the alarms and excursions which led up to it were a bit unnerving. The first lot of X-rays were said by Dr. A. (and also by the radiologist) to show a shadow on one lung. Two days later there was a second more detailed lot of X-rays, which Dr. B. said showed nothing at all. Two days after that, Dr. A., re-appearing, said that he still wasn't quite sure, and that I ought to see a chest specialist (Dr. C.). Two days after <u>that</u>, Dr. C. gave me a good going-over, pronouncing eventually that I was suffering from nothing worse than a slight case of smoker's cough; but this, of course, had to be confirmed a day later still by Dr. A. – who meanwhile had scared the pants off Ann by telling her privately that he was 'very worried indeed' about me. I need hardly say that Ann kept this to herself until the whole nonsense was over.[16]

He had also written to his mother without mentioning his stay in the nursing-home, and did not propose to do so 'or she'll imagine that in an alcoholic stupor I married a Sister or a Matron or a nurse, or even a wardmaid'.[17] A more specific problem for a composer was the crippling of his right hand, a condition called Dupuytren's Contracture. By the early 1960s this affliction made any sort of writing very difficult for him. The manuscript of his *Bridal Procession*, written for the wedding of Jennifer Keir Cross in 1963, shows this clearly. The signature at the end of his typed letters is sometimes almost illegible, and compares very badly with the immaculate hand in which his earlier music is written. It also 'made normal piano playing impossible',[18] something which not only distressed him but was also a severe handicap for a composer. He had surgery to correct this more than once, but it was never entirely successful. His doctor was convinced that Montgomery used this as an excuse for not composing any more.[19]

Both of these physical problems, however, were dwarfed and exacerbated by the developing alcoholism which became appreciably worse after the film world closed its doors to him. In early 1963 he was having to write to his agent Peter Watt after an incident at the Bull Hotel, Gerrard's Cross:

---

13    RBM to Harry Harrison, 25 August 1964
14    Ibid.
15    Joyce Sims to author, 1 September 1980
16    RBM to Sheila Rossiter, 8 August 1963 (copy in author's collection)
17    Ibid.
18    RBM to Ian Copley, 4 October 1967
19    Audrey Stock

I'm much ashamed of myself for not having written sooner to apologise for letting you and all the family down over that lunch party at the Bull: do please ask Prue and Alexandra to forgive me. I was in a fine old state, that day we met: <u>I know what hit me</u>, all right, but still have no idea why the quantities involved should have been so innocuous on other occasions and so disastrous on <u>that</u>. I don't imagine I shall be hearing from the BBC Talks Department again for a long, long time.[20]

He could ill afford to upset potential employers. As the problem became worse, he made little attempt to hide it. 'I cower in my study, drinking rather heavily,' he wrote to one friend.[21] On another occasion it was responsible for a loss of memory: 'Champagne and Burgundy mixed, in quantity, at midday, unaccompanied by anything very substantial in the way of food, seem to have had a deleterious effect on my memory. I can't recall whether I was going to send you a record of Reger's Hiller variations, or a record of Reger's Mozart variations, or a score of the Mozart. The result is that you'll shortly be confronted with all three.'[22] He was also something of a hypochondriac. In 1967 he went to stay with Brian Aldiss and his wife Margaret near Oxford. After a heavy evening's drinking they all staggered off to bed. In the middle of the night Montgomery began to call out weakly 'Margaret! Margaret!'; he thought he was dying and asked for a doctor. In reality he was feeling a little under the weather. The next day he cut short his stay and insisted on going home. Aldiss went with him on the train to make sure that he arrived safely.[23]

The only journal of Montgomery's which has survived (apparently the only journal he ever kept) follows the first few days of 1966. It is a vivid document. He is clearly trying to cope with his twin demons of alcohol and tobacco, but for someone who had to generate income by freelance work it makes very grim reading:

<u>2 January</u>
Hangover. Day in bed. ½-bot. sherry, about 20 fags. Read endless travel-and-holiday newspaper supplements […] Futile day.
<u>3 January</u>
[…] nothing accomplished. Must have read, but can't remember what. Must have drunk a bit, too. Again futile.
<u>4 January</u>
Rang Anthony Burgess in p.m., talked a bit about 'Eve of Saint Venus' opera. Plan to see him in London some time after Feb: 2nd. Much too much drink.
<u>5 January</u>
Gave up smoking, God help me. No drink all day, either. (No work, either). Reading Ngaio Marsh's 'Swing Brother, Swing' – poor, and if she's going to write about jazz bands, why the hell can't she find out something about them? 'Tympanist', indeed […] To bed, smug and cleanly […] Ann treating the corn on my right foot, but it remains a bugger.

20    RBM to Peter Watt, 29 March 1963
21    RBM to Harry Harrison, 27 February 1964
22    RBM to James (surname unknown), 12 February 1961
23    Brian Aldiss

6 January

Halo intact all day. [Did some gardening] Zombie-like, totally unaware, lighting of cigarette, but put it out hastily [...] Time I did some work though: 'An SF Reader'? Yes, that.

7 January

Crossword one word short; am making too much of an issue of it [...] (appetite good, conscience active, bloody marvel I am).

8 January

Very little to drink. No smoking. No work or letter writing, either: <u>disgraceful</u>. In p.m. driven by Ann to see Doctor in the House in Paignton. Music unimpressive – too finicky, too much modulation; nice that it's still earning me a bit, though [...] Ann tucked me up and then switched all the lights in the hall on and off, several times, before leaving. That's my girl.

9 January

If I can write in this diary without smoking, as evidently I can, then obviously I must equally well be able to manage letters and work. So no more shilly-shallying, please. Get on, on, I say, on.

Bad fit of blues at lunchtime, so slept all afternoon.

10 January

[referring to letters]

NINE IN ALL!

AND ALL WITHOUT SMOKING!!

SIXTH RECORD-BREAKING DAY!!!

11 January

Literally nothing accomplished on own. General financial situation considered: £75 in black, but that will be eliminated by end of week, I fear [...] Slight tendency to want to go back on the booze. Must crack down on this.

12 January

Fed up with keeping crossword record [...] No work.

13 January

Quite gratuitously started smoking again. Also, at lunch-time, had too much of the hard stuff. Crazy [...] No work; you bugger, you.

14 January

Still smoking. Too much liquor at lunch-time. [...] then I became alcoholically surly, and took it out disgracefully on poor Ann [...] No lunch, or work, or anything much but that nastiness. Bad, bad, very bad; sickening.

15 January

Still smoking. Still too much of the hard stuff. Under its influence, dictated the beginning of an 'I Hate to Garden' book [...] Another blank, silly day.

16 January

No smoking.

17 January

Smoking again [...] Some drinking. [...]

18 January

Tons of cigarettes, gallons of scotch: disgraceful. Lunch hour spent at Cott [Inn] (so no lunch). Ugh, ugh, spent too much money. [...] No work.

19 January

No smoking; 2 sherries before dinner. No work. [...] From now on, Ann will come when summoned, instead of regularly; and I feel that in some obscure way this may help. Very odd, though, considering I'm so fond of her.[24]

A letter to Philip Larkin later the same year makes his health problems clear: 'I followed up my broken arm of two years ago with an even nastier leg-break this year, and lost my nerve, took to the bottle, etc.'[25] It was this explosive combination of brittle bones and alcohol which accounts for Montgomery's frequent and sometimes lengthy stays in hospital. He always had an excuse for these breaks, whether it was the result of slipping on the dining room floor whilst going to open a window after the soup course or tripping on a path in the dark, and the breaks gave him an excuse for taking it easy on the work front. 'I'm in plaster up to the shoulder,' he told Larkin in 1964. 'This means that for all except inessential purposes I'm more or less out of action till the end of June; v. trying, and although I do my best to dictate immortal prose, it's a long business, specially irritating because I can't write in corrections on the typescript, but have to get someone to do it for me.'[26] In 1966 Larkin told a mutual friend that Montgomery was now 'pretty well an alcoholic, looked after by a middle-aged secretary'.[27]

Whilst he was living in the flat in Totnes, Montgomery had a visit from Brian Aldiss and Harry Harrison, another writer of science fiction. They were late arriving and found Montgomery ensconced in the pub, chatting with the local bookseller. 'This calls for triples all round!' cried Montgomery. After the drink, Montgomery gave his guests the choice of a 'bit of cold buffet' at home or a hot meal in the pub. They decided on the latter. When they left the pub, Montgomery decided that he was too drunk too drive, so he asked Harrison to take the wheel of his Rolls Royce. Harrison was rather alarmed at the prospect of driving a Rolls, but was assured by Montgomery that he would soon get the idea. After they had gone down a few country lanes, Harrison said:

'Bruce, is this the petrol gauge?'
'I believe it is, Harry.'
'Well, it's in the red, Bruce.'
'Oh, what do you think that implies?'
'I think it means we're nearly out of petrol.'
'Well, perhaps we'll come across a garage down here.'

In a remote Devon lane, this was an unlikely eventuality. Even more unlikely was the chance that any such garage would be open in the early hours of the morning, as indeed it proved when they found one and hammered unsuccessfully on its doors.

'Oh, well', said Montgomery, 'we're nearly home now. My secretary will pick it up in the morning. She's used to this.'

---

24    Diary for 1966
25    RBM to Larkin, 2 October 1966
26    Ibid., 22 April 1964
27    Larkin to Monica Jones, 15 November 1966 [in *Philip Larkin*, Motion, p. 368]

His visitors left quite early the next morning for Wiltshire and, feeling rather ragged, went in to say goodbye to Montgomery. His bed had curtains around it; a trembling hand came out, reached for the whisky glass and took it back inside. It was as they left that Aldiss and Harrison discovered that the 'bit of cold buffet' had been in fact a full-scale meal which was still laid out for them. This whole visit had been typical of Montgomery's way of underplaying life.[28] Aldiss recalls him buying jeroboams of whisky and promptly throwing away the stopper: 'It makes it easier of access.'[29] On another occasion he said: 'I like these bottles [jeroboams]; they give me a feeling of security.'[30] In 1970 Larkin visited Montgomery, his first visit to Week: 'He seemed to be well set up, though a stern drinking bout on the first day left him more corpsed than I on the second – odd, that. I thought lushes were supposed to take any amount of drink.'[31]

The mostly revealing document about Montgomery's medical history is the extraordinary application he made for the restoration of his driving licence. In 1977, his last having expired in 1965, Montgomery had been refused a licence on the grounds that his health was such as to make him a likely source of danger on the road. Montgomery sent his doctor's medical report to the medical advisor at the Department of Transport. This report, by Dr Shapland, lists an extensive medical history, beginning with Montgomery's 'left sided congenital talipes-equino-varus' which left him walking with a limp and having to pause when walking as little as 100 yards. It refers to the fracture of his wrist in 1965 and the fracture below his left knee which he suffered the following year. The two operations to cure his Dupuytren's Contracture in 1968 and 1974 had disappointing results. In September 1968 Montgomery dislocated his left shoulder and fractured his left femur in a fall, 'but his general condition was such that it was not until a few days later that his left femur was treated. [...] His convalescence from this procedure was interrupted by an episode of delirium tremens.' After this he was helped by a consultant psychiatrist. In the autumn of 1971 there was an episode of paroxysmal tachycardia, and three years later he was treated for alcoholic hepatitis. In September 1975 he was again in hospital for complications arising from a cirrhotic liver: 'After a predictably stormy convalescence, he made a good recovery.' In February and July 1977 he was admitted again, 'both times with acute liver failure'. The report concludes: 'This is a man with a lengthy, chequered, history of severe trauma, and latterly of liver failure.'

After this catalogue of illness it might be expected that the application was difficult to support, but the report comes to the conclusion that Montgomery's disability would not make him a source of danger. When the question of whether Dr Shapland would be willing to give evidence in court is raised, he states: 'I would be a little hesitant in doing so, however, since I could not conceal from the bench the facts concerning the long-standing alcoholic basis of his recent liver complaints, if Opposing Counsel were to ask me about them. These facts might, in my opinion,

---

28    Brian Aldiss
29    Ibid.
30    Charles Monteith
31    Larkin to Robert Conquest, 19 June 1970 [SLPL]

well sway the Magistrates' opinion against him.'[32] The application was refused in June 1978, despite Montgomery sending the Department of Transport a telegram two days previously in which he claimed that 'much business has been lost to me personally and to the nation through your dilatoriness'.[33]

Montgomery makes frequent references to his problems in letters. 'As to being on the wagon', he wrote to Brian Aldiss in 1972, 'me, I haven't had a drink for three months now (well, not to put too fine a point on it, it was getting a bit much), and am proposing to stay that way for another nine. After that, we'll see.'[34] Two months later, though, Amis reported that 'Bruce threw up a bit in the bar at the Crime Club dinner on Thursday.'[35] In 1975 Montgomery told Larkin that 'I got myself to the verge of cirrhosis of the liver last Christmas, and had to spend 5 weeks in hospital, so now am teetotal from fear.'[36] Following a visit to Devon, Larkin reported that Montgomery was 'on the wagon'.[37] He had occasional visits to Moorhaven, a cross between a hospital and an asylum on the moor above Ivybridge, to see if its strict and unpleasant regime could curb his addiction.[38]

Montgomery's health problems made work very difficult, of course, but they also contributed to his increasingly bitter character. Reaching the age of 50 did not help. 'One is mistily poised between experience and the inevitable ultimate fading (well, fairly inevitable: with writers it often doesn't occur) of energy and intellect,' he informed one correspondent.[39] 'The point is that not getting on with earning the living has thrown me into a state of semi-paralysis which has spread, octopus-like to absolutely every other sphere of activity,' he told another.[40] Even before this age he had spent a good deal of his time firing off letters of complaint. In 1962 he vented his spleen at the Eagle and General company following a visit by one of its agents when Montgomery was attempting to arrange a non-cancellable sickness and accident policy.

> He [the agent] has now telephoned me to say that you are not prepared to consider issuing any such policy for a person of my profession. May I respectfully suggest that before sending your agents to people who have not asked for them, you revise your advertising matter in such a way that we shall none of us – and especially myself – be put to trouble and expense in following up offers from you which for no apparent reason turn out to have no substance in them?[41]

In 1964 he had found the towel rails in his new house to be defective; 'I ought perhaps to say that even with the kitchen towel rail turned off, the domestic hot

---

32   Medical Report by Dr David Shapland, 15 May 1978
33   Telegram to Department of Transport, 14 June 1978
34   RBM to Brian Aldiss, 1 March 1972
35   Amis to Larkin, 7 May 1972 [LKA]
36   RBM to Larkin, 20 June 1975
37   Larkin to Anthony Thwaite, 23 August 1975 [SLPL]
38   Sheila Rossiter
39   RBM to Henry Gibbs, 19 June 1973
40   RBM to Evelyn Smith, 27 February 1962
41   RBM to Eagle and General, 1 October 1962

water continues to be rusty,' he wrote in complaint. 'I suppose, in order to get clean hot water, I could turn off all the towel rails; but in that case there seems very little purpose in having them.'[42] When it was suggested that he could find the fault himself, he became very angry: 'I'd be surprised if, having been sold an equally expensive motor-car comparably defective, the vendors were to tell me to take it to pieces and advise them about what the trouble was.'[43] The problem was eventually solved.

Montgomery also crossed swords with most of the organisations with which he had been closely and amicably connected in the past. His membership of the Composers' Guild had helped him. During his years in films, Montgomery had often personally challenged the production company to cancel that part of his contract which gave the company, not the composer, certain rights over the music. In 1957, along with Malcolm Arnold, Sir Arthur Bliss, Eric Coates, Ralph Vaughan Williams and a number of others, Montgomery signed a resolution against 'the unilateral action of the British Film Producers' Association in attempting to compel composers to assign the property of the composer (such as publication, recording and performing rights)'.[44] These composers intended to refuse to sign such contracts in the future. The following year Montgomery was writing to Francis Chagrin, the Convenor of the Film Sub-Committee, expressing his and other film composer's dismay regarding the new contract 'increasingly foisted upon them. I mean, of course, the tendency of distributors to mulct the composer of up to 50% of his performing rights, while offering nothing but a highly dubious publishing arrangement in return.'[45] The reply from the Guild announced its intention to produce a draft form of agreement; by 1960 the BFPA had withdrawn its percentage claim and agreed that the composer was obliged only to record the music for the film.

Just as Montgomery's film work was drawing to a close, the Guild decided to raise its subscription. Instead of the previous £3.10s maximum on the 10 per cent levy on each composer's performing rights, it was to be raised to £5 (making a total of £6.10s with the basic subscription). Montgomery objected. He wrote noting that the other professional organisations to which he belonged (the Society of Authors and Crime Writers' Association, for example) did not charge even half this amount for membership. 'The new rate of subscription seems to me inordinate, and I must regretfully ask you to accept my resignation from the Guild.'[46] The Guild took this seriously. Malcolm Arnold, a good friend, was summoned to persuade Montgomery to remain a member. By referring to the work the Guild had done in the past, and claiming that the subscription compared favourably with the Musicians' Union, Arnold persuaded Montgomery to reconsider, even though the membership rate was shortly to rise again: 'Since it's you that's asking, I'll certainly stay on for the time being […] though I feel bound to say that the recent proposal to increase the

---

42    RBM to Buswell and Sons Ltd, 11 May 1964
43    Ibid., 7 July 1965
44    Composers' Guild material, 2 November 1957
45    RBM to Francis Chagrin, 1 August 1958
46    RBM to Stephen Dodgson, 17 June 1961

subscription still further dismays me rather.' The Guild was relying presumably on Montgomery being unable to 'resist a personal appeal from an old friend'.[47]

But the matter was not finished. Towards the end of 1965 the Guild proposed raising the performing rights levy to a maximum of £20. Montgomery could not be at the Annual General Meeting, but made it clear that he wished to vote against this 'quite inordinate and unconscionable'[48] increase. At this stage a good deal of Montgomery's relatively small income came from the performing rights fees from his film work, so he was reluctant to lose any more of it than necessary. When the increase was passed, he resigned from the Guild immediately. Wilfred Josephs wrote back asking him to reconsider, mentioning that the Guild had to raise either the subscription or the levy because it was in straitened financial circumstances. Whilst acknowledging the good work the Guild had done in the past for composers of film music, Montgomery launched into a condemnation of general policy:

> At the same time, I'm thoroughly dismayed, I'm afraid, at the lack of elementary financial caution implicit in some of our more recent, and less direct, enterprises. For example, from this morning's post I learnt that the Guild is underwriting half of the loss on a symphony concert. I'm afraid it seems to me that a Society with less than 300 members, many of them by no means well-off, just can't afford to do such things, any more than it can afford to organise loss-making 21st birthday parties, regular hob-nobbing with Russians, and various other extravagances which may be secondarily valuable but which, even allowing for the increased PRS levy, we shall never be able to pay for. As regards my own resignation, I feel, to be frank, somewhat uneasy at continuing to belong to a body whose financial policy has become optative rather than practical. A Composers' Guild bankrupt by lavish good intentions will be bankrupt none the less.[49]

Montgomery's support for his literary societies fared little better. In 1978 he resigned from the Society of Authors when it changed its status to a trade union:

> I'm afraid I have no wish to be a trades union man, i.e. even the humblest private in the battalions (and not such big battalions at that, constituting only a minority of the country's workers) of those who so frequently use their power irresponsibly and without proper democratic procedures. These will not get the smallest support from me, and despite your circulars suggesting that the minority should follow the wishes of the majority in the Society of Authors, I don't feel that I can bring myself to do this.[50]

Of more importance for what they show about his views on detective fiction are his relationships with the Detection Club and the Crime Writers' Association. In 1976 Montgomery was upset at the way in which Julian Symons succeeded Agatha Christie as President of the Detection Club. With a handful of other senior members of the Club, Montgomery was approached to suggest a list of possible candidates for the position. Amongst his favourites were John Dickson Carr, Michael Gilbert, Michael Innes, Ngaio Marsh and Symons. However, when it came to the AGM

---

47    RBM to Malcolm Arnold, 4 August 1961
48    RBM to Composers' Guild, 11 November 1965
49    RBM to Wilfred Josephs, 31 June 1966
50    RBM to Brian Aldiss, 16 May 1978 (Society of Authors' Archive)

(which Montgomery had been unable to attend) only the name of Symons came up, and he was duly installed. Montgomery, in a minority of one, was of the firm opinion that there should have been a postal ballot. 'Much as I respect you', he wrote to Symons, 'it never occurred to me that you would be the sole contender. [...] You have support from me which will be unswerving, in spite of a tiny bald patch on one of the tyres.'[51] In the same letter Montgomery also made it clear that he was not at all happy about the changing nature of the membership.

Montgomery's support for Symons was genuine. Despite his differences with the new president over the direction of crime fiction, he had actually proposed Symons for membership of the club as far back as 1951 but had himself been outvoted on the grounds that Symons did not write true detective stories.[52] He had tried again two years later, this time successfully. As one of the conservative members, Montgomery's worries were that Symons, of more progressive views, might attempt to change some of the Club's best traditions. His fears were partly realised. One of Symons' first moves as president was to abandon the loyal toast to the Queen, which seemed to him ridiculously formal for so small a group. Montgomery disapproved. 'I want the loyal toast back,' he said to Symons. He had always taken the Club with 'charming seriousness',[53] and the whole apparatus of the Club by which crime was treated as a serious game was very attractive to him. He did not want this apparatus tampered with.

The original idea of the Club had been 'to stop people propounding imbecile plots in appalling English', and now Montgomery felt that it had become 'to all intents and purposes, a thriller-writers' Club'.[54] He did not resign, though, as he did from the Crime Writers' Association in June 1976 when what he considered 'a preposterous and inept pastiche',[55] *The Seven Per Cent Solution* by Nicholas Meyer, was awarded the CWA Gold Dagger prize. It did nothing to curb the esteem in which he was held: in early 1978 he was elected an honorary life member of the Association. Before that he had shown that he was not always short-tempered. In 1967, reading an obituary of his publisher Victor Gollancz, he was rather alarmed to find himself described as among Gollancz's 'earlier' detective authors. He was soon writing a tongue-in-cheek letter to the editor of the Crime Writers' Association newsletter:

Good Lord, what is this? I know it's a long time since I wrote a book. Still, being shoved back among the Gollancz archetypes comes as a terrible shock. Now, Miss Britton, please attend a moment. I may look a bit older than I ought to (owing to carrying slightly too much weight). But the fact remains that in 1936, when Gollancz published that young fellow Michael Innes's first whodunit, I was still (myself) at that stage of thinking it interesting, if odd, that girls bulged at the front.[56]

---

51   RBM to Julian Symons, 23 November 1976
52   Julian Symons
53   Julian Symons to author, 4 March 1992
54   Ibid.
55   RBM to Duncan Kyle, 8 June 1976
56   RBM to Anne Britton, 1 March 1967

By this time, though, his membership of all these associations, musical and literary, had ceased to be as important to him as they had been when he was earning considerable amounts of money from his writing. As a reason for his lack of work, illness can be joined by fashion. None of Montgomery's output was ever fashionable, in the sense of following contemporary trends. His music, mostly published in the 1940s and early 1950s, looked back to a style more in keeping with what English composers had been composing some twenty years previously. His detective novels also belonged to an earlier era than the one in which they were written. Lack of sympathy with contemporary trends in those genres in which he had once been successful led to many problems from which Montgomery suffered in this last period of his life.

# Chapter 16

# 'Slightly low water': 1959–1970

As well as his problems with illness, Montgomery's finances became increasingly insecure: 'I'm on the brink of a financial crisis myself,' he noted in 1965.[1] His lucrative film work dried up just at the moment when he had committed himself to the building of his relatively expensive bungalow, and although performing rights from the films and royalties from his novels continued to come in on a regular basis, there was a limited amount of new work and his income was considerably less than what he had been used to. Montgomery did not help himself. His addiction to alcohol was a costly business; in 1970 his account at Victoria Wine in Totnes regularly reached at least £50 each month (a year later it was occasionally as much as £87) in addition to large bills at the Cott Inn, his local hostelry. Montgomery was a frequent visitor there, particularly at lunchtime. He would start with several pink gins or very dry sherries and then proceed to the dining room for his favourite meal of steak and kidney pie. This would usually be accompanied by a bottle of Lafitte 1952 or Latour 1953, the meal costing 7s.6d (38p) and the wine £3.17s.6d (£3.88). Invariably he would drink only half the bottle, the remainder being sent to the kitchen for cook – who would much rather have had a pint of draught Bass.[2] After living extravagantly for many years Montgomery found it difficult to economise. Writing to Jacques Barzun in 1973 to explain why he was unlikely to visit the United States, one of many times he put off the trip, Montgomery said: 'I realise that I ought to pay you a return visit, by coming to New York, but for the present finances forbid (I could afford an Economy Flight, but first, I detest flying, and secondly, I detest economy).'[3] We have seen how difficult he found any constructive work during this period and cannot be surprised if prospective employers thought twice before they commissioned anything from him.

The state of his finances led him to borrow considerable amounts of money, particularly from Arthur Hooker, his accountant. These were formal arrangements and Montgomery was as reliable as he could be over repayments. In early 1975 he suffered three months' illness, with five weeks in a nursing home, and told Hooker that 'inevitably it's set me back a bit financially, and I'm therefore very much afraid that I shan't be able to continue repaying your kind loan until August'.[4] He did manage to send the previous quarter's interest. Hooker, with his mixture of concern and practical good sense, was an ideal accountant for Montgomery.

---

1    RBM to John Maxwell, 11 December 1965
2    Nigel Shortman to author, 23 October 1989
3    RBM to Jacques Barzun, 6 November 1973 (Columbia University)
4    RBM to Arthur Hooker, 17 April 1975

In part his difficulties were the result of being a freelance and never being quite sure when payments would be made into his bank. 'A sound and reputable firm of paperback publishers has recently agreed to re-issue seven of my books', he wrote to his bank manager in 1964, 'half of the advance being payable "on signature"; but although the matter is settled, I have no means of knowing whether the amount concerned will arrive tomorrow, or next month, or even three months from now.'[5] Towards the end of his life Montgomery enlarged on his financial situation:

> I have had an overdraft of ceiling £4,000 for some 20 years now; and if you are agreeable I should like to continue with it. It was granted me in the first place partly because of the inevitable fluctuations in my income from authorship and composition (though over a period of, say, five years, this has averaged out well enough); and partly because by no means all publishers and editors can be relied on to make due payment at all promptly, even when the work has been completed, delivered and is actually in print. Apart from my somewhat brighter prospects for the future, therefore, my overall financial situation remains much as it has been for 20 years or so.[6]

Income generated by foreign editions of his novels, in at least thirteen languages, was something he relied on, claiming that two-thirds of his income came from export: 'In importing foreign currency without the expenditure abroad of British currency to offset it, I should say I was the equivalent of at least a couple of dozen British Leyland workers!'[7] This income, though, was not always easily available; in 1968 he and his bank spent some time trying to work out how he could get his hands on some royalties from Poland without actually having to go there. Some years earlier he had gone to Madrid just to spend the money earned from Spanish editions of his novels; he had stayed at the Ritz and been amused by taking a taxi driven by someone called Jesus.[8]

As early as 1968 he was considering remortgaging the house (his accountant was vehemently against this), and Kingsley Amis had been approached to stand as guarantor for a further bank loan. In the same year, having unsuccessfully attempted to borrow from Malcolm Arnold, he was lent some money to pay back when he could by Muriel Box, one of his old film world contacts. Five years later his accountant was registering concern over the financial situation with Montgomery acknowledging that he was 'in slightly low water'.[9] In 1976 he received a loan of £200 from the Society of Author's Contingency Fund, which was paid back after his death; in the same year he wrote successfully to Larkin asking if he could lend him £250: 'Bruce has been in my ribs for a small loan […] So he is recovering fast,' Larkin told Amis.[10] Larkin's approach was businesslike, noting on Montgomery's letter: 'I sent cheque on 6 April with request for acknowledgement & a promise to repay at 1½% per

5     RBM to National Provincial Bank, 19 September 1964
6     RBM to Lloyds Bank, 3 July 1975
7     Ibid., 21 January 1976
8     Jeni Turnbull
9     RBM to Arthur Hooker, 15 February 1973
10    Larkin to Amis, 13 April 1976 [SLPL]

month interest.'[11] By November Montgomery had paid it back, thanking Larkin for 'helping me over a sticky patch'.[12] Unfortunately, these demands became so frequent that Larkin asked his secretary not to put Montgomery's telephone calls through.[13] It did not help that Montgomery, as he confessed to his bank, was 'quite shockingly ignorant about business and financial matters'.[14] It was a constant struggle. There were times when he was trying to call in loans he had made: 'I'm in very low water and need every penny I can get,' he told a friend who owed him £195.[15] In October 1975 he managed to get a relatively modest refund when he was able to attend only part of the Crime Writers International Congress in London, apologizing for 'troubling you over so small a matter, but unfortunately, in these difficult times, one has to be a bit careful about money'.[16] Much of this money was needed for his large medical bills, yet despite his financial worries he could still find the money to indulge himself. Following a very lengthy stay in the Bristol Royal Infirmary in 1975, Montgomery hired a chauffeur-driven limousine to take him the 80 miles or so back to Dartington.

His private life was not going much better. Montgomery had always attracted women who wanted to look after him. As the impetus of his professional life started to decline there seem to have been two women who pursued him in varying degrees of seriousness. Jill Watt, employed at first in concert management before switching to film script work, had known Montgomery and been taken out by him for some years (they had attended a performance of *Salome* by Richard Strauss at The Royal Opera House as long ago as November 1953). She was likely to have been the woman Montgomery invited to dinner from time to time when he was involved in a film score recording session. After the session he would often get badly drunk with Philip Martell and feel disinclined to honour the invitation. Instead, he would give Martell some money and send him up to London to take her out for the evening. 'Of course, Bruce never made any progress,' Douglas Gamley recalled.[17] Martell constantly baited Montgomery for not being married. 'I would love to get married', Montgomery responded, perhaps because he thought it was expected of him, 'but I never meet any fresh girls in Brixham.'[18]

Jill became dissatisfied with being constantly 'stood up': '[This is] to let you know unmitigatedly how cross I am with you, my pet, for so persistently making me feel like giving up reforming you as a bad job, and letting you disappear down the rope. […] If you really find the prospect of having to see me so dismaying that you can't face it, I would much prefer that you say so.'[19] Montgomery replied in similarly firm terms, telling Jill that she should not see him as someone to save from hell, and should she feel so 'do please pause and reflect that you know nothing at

---

11    RBM to Larkin, 1 April 1976
12    Ibid., 11 November 1976
13    Andrew Motion
14    RBM to Lloyds Bank, 1 April 1976
15    RBM to Kelvin (surname unknown), 7 February 1973
16    RBM to Crime Writers' Association, 8 September 1975
17    Douglas Gamley
18    Ibid.
19    Jill Watt to RBM, 21 November 1959

all of my obligations, commitments and problems in connection with my family and my other friends, and only a very little about my professional life [...] no more sermons please'.[20] Jill soon reassured Montgomery that, although she held him in great respect and affection, she had given up on love for him in the romantic sense: 'I think I did reassure you that you've no need to worry any more on that score.'[21] They kept in touch. Jill later fell on hard times and Montgomery did what he could to help, to the extent of lending her money in 1974 that he barely had himself. 'I think that for a little time, back in the dark ages', Montgomery confessed to Brian Aldiss in 1973, 'she [Jill] perhaps carried a torch for me.'[22] Shortly before his death, he offered her the chance to type the manuscripts of his future novels, and she made a start on *What Seems to be the Trouble?*

Jill lived in Windsor, which was very convenient for Montgomery's trips to the film studios, and their meetings took place almost exclusively in London. Another admirer lived in Newton Abbot, close to his home. He had known Audrey Jackman (known as Jackie) since at least 1956 and they met occasionally at the Grand Hotel, Torquay. She was more ardent than Jill and brought out Montgomery's usual defensive tactics. Late in 1959, after he had kept his word not to see her again, Jackie sent Montgomery a stormy letter in which she admits that her previous claim to have destroyed his photos in a fit of pique was not true, and that it was designed, unsuccessfully as it turned out, to bring him flying back to her in a penitent mood: 'I wanted to marry you so much that there was nothing I would not have stooped to in order to bring it about.' She hoped that he would not be offended by this admission. 'I think I would be secretly very pleased', she went on, 'if someone had gone to such lengths to inveigle me into matrimony – even if I didn't want to marry him.' In a phrase suggesting that she knew the end was nigh, Jackie tried to get him to agree that 'some of it was fun, though, wasn't it?'[23] Montgomery did nothing to improve the situation, and she wished that he 'wouldn't be so harsh and bitter' towards her. Eventually he unbent slightly: 'It was comforting to receive a kind word from you instead of that blistering cold silence,' she wrote in May 1960. 'I wish you'd make an effort to see yourself as a kind of marked down prey who got away, rather than as someone who didn't do right by our Nell.'[24]

The problems we have noted that Montgomery had with women are put into vivid context by the relationship, if such it can be called, he had with Audrey Keir Cross. Montgomery had met her husband, John Keir Cross, in a Totnes pub towards the end of the 1950s. Keir Cross (1911–1967) was a freelance writer of, amongst other things, science fiction. Like Montgomery he had written dramatisations of crime stories for the *Connoisseurs of Crime* radio series and towards the end of his life contributed episodes to the BBC radio serial *The Archers*. In an area not known as a haunt of intellectuals, Montgomery and Keir Cross latched on to each other (Montgomery at times complained about the lack of intelligent friends in the area:

20     RBM to Jill Watt, 6 December 1959
21     Jill Watt to RBM, 19 December 1959
22     RBM to Brian Aldiss, 22 July 1973
23     Audrey Jackman to RBM, 28 December 1959
24     Ibid., 31 May 1960

'The loonies up at the Hall[25] can't be regarded as anything but fit for the bin' was one comment).[26] They were both extremely well read in similar fields, and they met when they needed to feed their enthusiasms. These meetings often took place in the convivial atmospheres of licensed premises and a close friendship developed. Keir Cross, like Montgomery, became an alcoholic.

In 1963 Montgomery played the organ at the wedding of the Keir Cross' daughter, Jennifer. He was not originally intending to do so, but the *Bridal Procession* that he had written for the occasion (it was actually a scarcely revised version of one that he had originally composed many years before) had proved too difficult for the village organist at South Brent. John Keir Cross and Montgomery repaired to the local pub before the wedding, with both drinking a good deal. Audrey Keir Cross had to go and fetch her husband so that he could accompany his daughter in the car and escort her up the aisle. Montgomery was very 'well oiled'[27] by this time, and was terribly shy and worried about playing. It was quite difficult to get him on to the organ stool. The bride's mother was a nervous wreck before the service, but Montgomery played well.

Whilst her husband was writing, Audrey ran a farm in the wilds of Devon not far from Totnes. Brian Aldiss recalls driving with Montgomery to visit them at this 'rather miserable farm'.[28] Arriving rather late at night, John Keir Cross asked what they would like to drink. When they both asked for whisky, he went off and came back with three bottles, one each of whisky for them and one of brandy for himself. They sat by the hearth in 'this rather shoddy place',[29] each drinking his own bottle whilst the daughter came in and out rattling milk pails. When the bottles were empty, Aldiss and Montgomery drove away again.

Audrey got to know Montgomery particularly well in the years immediately after she lost her husband, but before that Montgomery and she had become friends. To all appearances it seems that they were more than this. In November 1963 she wrote to Montgomery instructing him to 'tell Anne [Ann Clements, Montgomery's secretary] that I am giving you £2,000 and let the two of us, Anne and I, sort it out from now on […] Accept me for what I am – a genius for knowing what geniuses need and when! I do love you but I don't intend leaving John, so be kind to me.'[30] Montgomery's interest in Audrey was further kindled by a bizarre incident which occurred on the Sunday before Christmas in 1963. Montgomery had invited Audrey and her husband to one of his lavish dinner parties at the Cott Inn. When the time came for them to leave for the party, John Keir Cross had not returned from a visit to his local pub. Audrey drove there to find her husband badly inebriated and refusing either to leave the pub or to go to the party. His natural reluctance to dress up for formal occasions had got the better of him. In an apologetic state, Audrey rang Montgomery and said: 'I feel bad about this. We can't come.' Montgomery, who knew all about such

---

25    Dartington Hall School, an institution renowned for its liberal regime
26    RBM to Peter Oldham, 11 March 1978
27    Audrey Stock
28    Brian Aldiss
29    Ibid.
30    Audrey Keir Cross to RBM, 19 November 1963

drinking binges, told her not to worry and to come on her own if she wanted. Audrey thought about this: after all, she was dressed up and ready to go – so she went.

They had a very pleasant meal; Montgomery behaved well and did not drink to excess despite ordering the customary champagne to start with and an impressive series of wines. Afterwards they went back to Montgomery's dreary flat in Totnes where, as usual, he began to play gramophone records and to drink heavily. At this stage Audrey did not know him very well, but as Montgomery became increasingly drunk he began to confide in her. Before long, though, he became inebriated and retired to bed. Assuming that her husband would not yet be back from his drinking bout, Audrey decided to stay for a while in Montgomery's sitting room playing records. Not long afterwards she heard her husband's sports car screech up outside the flat. Her first reaction was: 'Oh, my God, it's John. He's drunk. He shouldn't be driving that thing!' Her second, realising that Montgomery was likely to answer the door in his pyjamas and dressing gown and that her presence, although she was fully dressed and entirely blameless, was likely to be misinterpreted, was to try and leave the flat without being seen by her husband. As he was already climbing the stairs, there was only one avenue of escape. She opened the sash window of the sitting room and jumped out into Totnes High Street.

Not surprisingly, given that the flat was on the first floor, Audrey smashed her right foot very badly. Still dressed in her evening wear, not even having had time to button her coat, she hobbled into her car and managed somehow to drive home, staying in third gear for the five-mile trip, using her remaining good foot and hoping that no one got in the way. Her son later took her to Plymouth General Hospital where the consultant, having put her foot in plaster, said it was a miracle that she had not wrecked her spine with such an impact.

Whilst Audrey was making her getaway, her husband was demanding to know where his wife was. Montgomery, somewhat confused having been aroused from his drunken slumber, said: 'I don't think she's here.' John Keir Cross, also drunk, did not believe him. The two men went into the sitting room. Seeing the wide-open window and the still-playing gramophone, Montgomery realised what had happened but did not let on to Keir Cross. 'But she isn't here,' he said. Audrey never knew if her husband was too drunk to have noticed her car outside the flat. In the event she told him that she had fallen through a barn roof. In retrospect Audrey realised that she should have brazened the situation out. She had, after all, done nothing improper and should have told her husband that it was all his fault for being too drunk to go to the dinner party.

This was not the end of the matter. Hearing nothing from Montgomery, Audrey was soon writing to him:

> Many, many apologies for the sordid episode of Sunday night [...] Petrified with fear and knowing from past experience that John would not leave without seeing me, I jumped from your sitting room window smashing my foot rather badly. [...] I realise I must leave you. You need a woman who can bring you peace of mind and John will see that we neither of us achieve that. This makes no difference to your money and I will always make sure that you have enough – you are a great man and nothing will stand in your way.[31]

---

31    Ibid., 25 December 1963

Montgomery was worried that word of the incident might leak out, as Audrey had been seen by the doctor she shared with Montgomery and whom they both knew well; she was able to tell him that '[the doctor] will not anything slip, you may sleep soundly on that count'.[32] She went to stay with her mother and hoped Montgomery might go and see her, knowing that her 'mother would accept a visit from you as a normal courtesy. [...] What a bloody awful Christmas [...] Thank you for some glorious moments.'[33]

But Audrey did not leave him alone. A few days later she was on the war path: 'You miserable bastard, what has happened to my "get well" card? I shall soon be "in the pink" and stomping about on both feet so you'd better hurry up and send one.'[34] Waiting to move in to his new house, Montgomery had gone on a short holiday to Cornwall and this had hampered his efforts to restore a modicum of equilibrium. 'I seem to have made a mess of it all round,' he admitted. 'From Cornwall I wrote to you at the wrong Plymouth hospital. Later I sent some flowers to the same wrong Plymouth hospital – and in any case I found out a few days later that by that time you were back at Baron's Hill. Have since tried to telephone, but the noises which come through suggest that my efforts with the telephone people didn't succeed.'[35] He invited her to visit him and see the new house.

The friendship rumbled on. 'Not an easy letter to write,' Audrey told Montgomery in March 1964 after she had been upset again. 'I cannot deny being distressed about yesterday although yesterday was only the inevitable climax to a series of incidents all of which sent me scuttling back behind my rock.' She listed an impressive catalogue of complaints: of visiting him to find that he had arranged for Ann to appear at seven o'clock so that Audrey had to leave at the requested time; of having two telephone calls rejected; of being ditched on a trip to Brixham so that Montgomery could keep a longstanding appointment with his brother-in-law; and, as recompense for this last snub, being asked to lunch and finding Ann's car in Montgomery's drive as 'a hedge against togetherness. I never enjoy threesomes.' Without any reassurance in between, these incidents all added up: 'Less sensitive folk than I could well feel insecure in such a relationship. [...] One doesn't stop loving even when one's common sense tells one to clear out.'[36]

Montgomery claimed that she had been misled by events. He responded in kind to her 'fighting letter', telling her that Ann's presence working on typescripts was part of her job; he had not rejected her telephone calls but merely been busy – as she had been in the past; that he had been prepared to cancel his appointment with his brother-in-law, but had not done so because Audrey had previously cancelled her appointment with Montgomery – and when she changed her mind it was too late (and, after all, they had had four hours together, so he had hardly 'ditched' her); and Ann's car was in the drive because she had taken his to the garage. 'But even if that hadn't been so', he continued, 'the fact that you "never enjoy threesomes" is not,

---

32    Ibid., undated
33    Ibid.
34    Ibid., 2 January 1964
35    RBM to Audrey Keir Cross, 14 February 1964
36    Audrey Keir Cross to RBM, 25 March 1964

I'm afraid going to influence me as a general principle.' He told her that Ann and her husband were 'among the few people who are welcome here at any time they care to come'. He finished in typical vein: 'But I don't like rows, whether by letter or in any other form. You've been very kind and generous to me, and with any luck I shall be able to repay what I owe you in a week or two. [...] I loathe being indebted, and always try to deal with such things at the earliest possible moment.'[37]

His relationship with Audrey Keir Cross begins to explain many darker aspects of Montgomery's character and problems. In particular, he began to tell her of the problems he had in the physical side of his relationships with women, although he never mentioned any of his previous girlfriends by name. Audrey felt at the time that Montgomery's strict nonconformist upbringing was responsible for these problems. 'When I meet and am fond of someone who comes from the same background as myself and has been brought up in a certain way', he told her, 'I stick them right up on a pedestal, and any physical or sexual contact seems to debase them.' Audrey herself experienced this. Montgomery was not a tactile person with anyone, and she cannot recall him once holding her hand or kissing her, although he may have pecked her on the cheek. In the 1950s when Montgomery visited Kingsley Amis in Swansea, people with whom he came into contact found him 'very shy with women but [his] amiability was not clouded by the shyness. [...] Bruce was always very charming.'[38]

One evening after she had been widowed, Audrey was acting as hostess at one of Montgomery's lavish dinner parties at Week where he had his successful friends on show. Both Kingsley Amis and Malcolm Arnold had new wives with them. Plenty of alcohol had been consumed and the badinage had started. Amis and Arnold began to taunt Montgomery: 'You've got an attractive woman there. What are you thinking of, Bruce? Give her a cuddle. This is how you do it', and they proceeded to demonstrate with their own wives. Amis and Arnold were on the sofas, and Montgomery was sitting as always in his armchair to the left of the fireplace. Getting no change out of Montgomery, Amis and Arnold started on Audrey. 'You sit on his knee,' they urged. She did. Montgomery went ramrod stiff, as if Audrey was a porcupine with all her quills out. He hated the physical contact. She did not stay on his knee for long, and because of Montgomery's discomfiture the joke had also been lost on her. Amis and Arnold knew that their friend had a problem with women and it was as if they were trying to get him to do something about it. Apparently Montgomery had not always shrunk from such contact. He had often flirted in an open way with Harry Harrison's wife Joan, and at a science fiction gathering where Amis was also present, she had sat on Montgomery's lap drinking whisky.[39] She confessed on another occasion to having a healthy adolescent crush on him.[40]

Montgomery did not want old friends to see him without a reasonably attractive woman in attendance, but he was not willing or perhaps capable of taking things any further. He had every opportunity to keep attractive and vibrant women but,

37     RBM to Audrey Keir Cross., 26 March 1964
38     Joyce Sims to author, 1 September 1989
39     Joan Harrison to RBM, undated
40     Ibid., undated

as with his laziness in other areas of his life, he could not be bothered to do what they required. He enjoyed the fact that other men might also want the lady he was escorting (Jeni Turnbull, for instance), and he felt he had to make some sort of move. With the help of his charming manner he usually accomplished this fairly easily. The women he was drawn to were not a threat at the start of a relationship. Most were happy to take things slowly, a flirtation with no responsibilities. It was only later that he would find he was in too deep and had to struggle to get out.

Montgomery had this idea that his difficulties might be resolved if he dealt with women of a different class. He used to drive his expensive car to the Narrows in Totnes so that he could sit and watch the women workers come out of Tucker's Toffee Factory. He was fascinated by them. 'I know I won't actually do it, because I don't want to marry one', he told Audrey, 'but I know that I wouldn't be impotent with one of those girls.' He wanted to mix like with like, but there was no way that he could have an ordinary marital relationship with a woman – and yet he seemed to think he could with 'a bit of rough'.[41] It was an experiment he never tried.

Montgomery undoubtedly attracted women. He was gentle, caring, and had a lovely manner. In the Cott Inn women would often glance his way. This was why John Keir Cross began to worry when his wife was with Montgomery. One can only assume that he must have had a string of failures, because eventually Montgomery was afraid of letting women down. He did not want to risk upsetting a woman with his impotence. She might take it as a suggestion that she was not attractive, and Montgomery was such a nice man that he would not want any woman to think this. So in the end he did not take the chance. Geoffrey Bush's suspicion was that Montgomery felt he would be expected to have a strong sexual drive to keep a wife happy, and it was something he knew he did not have. This probably explains why many of his relationships with women ended with him bringing down the curtain when they showed signs of becoming too keen. We have seen this with Nan Feeny and Peggy Bailey in the 1940s, and similar conclusions were reached with Jill Watt and Audrey Jackman at the end of the 1950s. There was also the psychological problem of his deformed foot. Montgomery liked beauty in everything – and his foot was ugly. He could hardly make love to a woman with his shoes on, so if he were to do anything it would have to be displayed. Audrey gained the impression that this added to his worries.

These sexual problems might go someway to explain the mild interest he had in pornography. He was encouraged in this by friends such as Larkin and Robert Conquest. From time to time he exchanged pictures with Larkin, asking him once 'Would you like them back after I've sucked them dry?'[42] There is little to suggest, though, that Montgomery's interest was more than for gentle titillation; even Larkin's much greater enthusiasm was relatively mild in its scope. This interest led to an amusing incident. Conquest, knowing that Larkin was worried about his peccadillo becoming public, wrote to him in the guise of a member of the Vice Squad who had discovered his name on the list of subscribers to a pornographic publication. Larkin, terrified that he would lose his job and reputation, spent most of a day with

---

41    Audrey Stock
42    RBM to Larkin, 24 April 1960 [in *Philip Larkin*, Motion, p. 267]

his solicitor before Conquest admitted the deception. Almost twenty years later, Montgomery was letting Conquest know that his spoof had affected him too: 'I am bound to say that since I first heard that story I've treated all letters and telephone calls with considerable circumspection.'[43]

Although hardly in the same league as the pornography, Montgomery also kept a collection of salacious, at times filthy, limericks which he shared with his friends.[44] He and Larkin occasionally corresponded in adolescently graphic terms. Writing following the publication of Larkin's *The Less Deceived*, Montgomery claimed that

> your next collection – which I imagine will eventuate after the regulation five years' keening, grumbling and general melancholic spleen – will have the ground so well prepared for it that Childe Harold and those old Lyrical Ballads and things just won't be in the picture anywhere. And then think! – there'll be great processions of bosomy girls coming trembling in admiration to you en pèlerinage, and you will be able to take them aside one by one and tell them that not another line will you be able to write, ever, unless you've fucked them first. That'll be the way of it, you'll see, just as it was with Byron, and if Wordsworth hadn't been such an old horse that would have been the way of it with him, too. So perk up! (Much the same result can be obtained more quickly, and also more lucratively, by entering the film business, only there you don't get any admiration with your fucks, so no doubt you're better off, really you are).[45]

Montgomery was showing that he found it difficult to face up to the normal difficulties of life. His drinking was one aspect of this. When John Keir Cross had a drinking binge, he was ready for work the next morning. When Montgomery had experienced a disappointment and went on a drinking spree, he would stay in bed for a week and hide away from everyone. 'Booze is the trouble with me, all right', he told Larkin, 'a happy, daily temporary escape from all my anxieties.'[46] After Audrey Keir Cross had jumped out of his window, he disappeared for a week and would not answer the door. We have already seen that even when he was living with his parents in Brixham he would take to a hotel for a similar length of time. Once Week Meadow was built, it became much easier for him to hide from the world. 'When things get bad for me', he admitted to Larkin, 'I imitate the action of the spider (trap-door), getting into some sort of hole and cowering there.'[47] Harry Harrison heard the same: 'One of my most notable personal characteristics is that I don't take kindly

---

43     RBM to Robert Conquest, 8 September 1975
44     One of the few printable here is:
       There was an old monk named Carruthers,
       Who was given to buggering brothers.
       He would say to each novice,
       'Come up to the office;
       I'll show you an old thing of mother's.'
45     RBM to Larkin, 19 June 1956
46     Ibid., 10 April 1973
47     Ibid., 26 March 1964

to misfortunes.'[48] This was not a new trait; years earlier Amis had noted that 'he [Montgomery] still hates criticism'.[49]

The building of Week Meadow appears to reflect some of Montgomery's main characteristics. One was his love of luxury. It was as if he had to have such an impressive home so that he could copy the lifestyle of the wealthy people in the film world. The quarters for a housekeeper were a sign of this. Audrey Keir Cross though it was a faintly ridiculous idea that someone would be willing to live in two small rooms in a hamlet in the wilds of Devon. Any such person was likely to be a widow with no home of her own, and there was little else in the way of social life in the area. When Montgomery took to his bed for a week, human contact was reduced to even less. He was a very particular man. His bedtime milk had to be exactly the correct temperature, and the housekeeper was expected to check this with a thermometer. When he was drunk in bed, food had to be left on a tray outside his door. It was never likely that Montgomery was going to be flooded with suitable candidates, although the sole person who took up the challenge lasted a reasonable time. Audrey Keir Cross once, and only once, went to dinner during the tenure of this housekeeper. She sat talking with Montgomery in the sitting room until the housekeeper appeared and announced that dinner was ready. They moved through to the adjacent dining room where everything was beautifully laid out. The housekeeper served the meal. It was a very unnatural experience.

Writing to Larkin, Montgomery acted as the expert on housekeepers:

> I didn't answer the bit in your last one about domestic help. <u>Visiting</u> cook-housekeepers who are any good are very difficult to find anywhere; living-in ones are much easier, especially if you're a bachelor, especially if you're an author, especially if you're not decrepit, and especially if you advertise all these facts. Of course, a good deal depends on what sort of house you have and how big it is; no good clamouring for someone 'not as family' if you can't give them quarters to be not as family in. What one looks for is (a) 'Not quite your class, dear'; (b) between fifty and sixty; and (c) a welcoming family not too far away where your treasure can go on weekends off. Readiness to be talked to friendlily – though not, obviously, to talk to you friendlily – is also an advantage. You have to be patient in seeking out all this (plus good cooking), but if you can find it, it's worth having (by the way, try for a non-churchgoer; though admittedly some churchgoers are very tolerant, and beam approvingly no matter what you get up to).
>
> All this is something of a description of my Mrs. Oakman. Perhaps I've been specially lucky – but the principle remains.[50]

Even the excellent Mrs Oakman had her off days: 'Mrs O corpselike first thing', Montgomery observed in his diary, 'but was recovered and back on the job by mid-morning.'[51] The quarters for a housekeeper, and the manner in which she was treated, show that Montgomery expected to be looked after. He had, of course, lived with his parents until the age of 40, and he was accustomed to being cosseted by his mother. He now expected someone else to take over that role. It may well have been a great

---

48    RBM to Harry Harrison, 25 August 1964
49    Amis to Larkin, 6 November 1952 [LKA]
50    RBM to Larkin, 23 April 1964
51    Diary for 1966

shock to him when he finally did move out of Rock Hill House that people no longer ran around to do his bidding in quite the same way. It may in part account for his financial troubles. Although one cannot know the exact financial terms under which Montgomery lodged with his parents, they are unlikely to have been a drain on him. One suspects that his income was mostly pocket money, which made his livelihood less important to him than it is to most people. No wonder he gave the impression of playing at life. Once he had taken the decision to move to the bungalow, his income suddenly became rather more critical. He was no longer playing at life. Unfortunately, he seemed unable to face the realities, and Week provided him with the ideal barrier against the world. Desmond Bagley[52] and his wife, who lived in Totnes, found Montgomery 'semi-reclusive and something of a mystery. [...] We occasionally dropped in at Week – though always by invitation – to be told by Ann that he was "out" or "resting". She would then entertain us and perhaps during the afternoon he would make an appearance. I think he was wide awake on at least one occasion but didn't feel like our company.'[53]

Audrey Keir Cross was indirectly responsible for an episode which is a further indication of Montgomery's *modus vivendi* at the time. He told her once that he was becoming increasingly dissatisfied with his overworked local National Health Service doctor. Audrey had always been very happy with her family doctor, David Shapland, and she asked him whether he could stretch his catchment area to take on Montgomery as a patient. This was not possible but, although he did not normally take private patients, Shapland was eventually persuaded to accept Montgomery on that basis. He was already an admirer of Montgomery's novels and was very pleased to be able to spend time talking to another intelligent and cultured person. They became very close and Shapland, like the others, was soon at Montgomery's beck and call. There was one particular occasion towards the end of his life when Montgomery was suddenly taken very ill indeed. Shapland was at his surgery when the call came through: he dropped everything immediately, sent his waiting patients to a colleague and rushed round to attend to him. He managed to get Montgomery to hospital in the nick of time. When the money began to dry up, Montgomery became peevish and started telling Audrey that Shapland was charging him too much. As with so many other things, Montgomery wanted it all on his own terms. He was very pleased to have, like the film stars, his own private physician. He was happy that Shapland, like Audrey and others, was rushing around doing his bidding. He was very happy with the service he was receiving; his only disenchantment was having to settle the bills.

Everything had to be on his terms. He was a lover of cats, and when he was looking for a new one Audrey Keir Cross would sometimes bring a farm kitten to him for approval. If these kittens did not immediately sit on his lap and behave as he expected a cat to behave, they were rejected: 'I don't want one of these farm cats,' Montgomery would say, and Audrey would be detailed to find a special sort of cat that fitted his bill. Quite a few cats came and went like this. He was simply unable to

52     Desmond Bagley (1923–1983), author
53     Joan Bagley to author, 20 June 1990

take the cats as they were. As with women, he expected them to be what he wanted them to be.

Audrey Keir Cross was a very important figure in Montgomery's life at this time. Given the chaste nature of her friendship with him, she is at a loss to explain the letters she wrote to him. They give the impression that there was some sort of passion underlying their friendship of which she later felt unaware. She certainly did not go into a slough of despond when she stopped seeing him. It could be that stirring up Montgomery was a welcome diversion from her rather humdrum lifestyle of running a farm and attending to an alcoholic husband. She was certainly lively enough to do this. Audrey became more friendly with Montgomery after the death of her husband in 1967, at which time she moved back to London to work for the BBC. She was on 12-hour shifts, with three days on and three days off. For her days off she would often return to Devon to stay with her mother and visit Montgomery. Many people thought that they would marry. Even the way that the waitresses looked at them and served them in the Cott Inn suggested this, but it was never seriously on the cards. David Shapland warned Audrey off: he knew that as a newly widowed woman with considerable problems (she had a 14-year-old son and no pension from her late husband), she might find Montgomery comforting, but he, like her, had been taken into Montgomery's confidence about his difficulties with women.

It was the incautious part of Audrey's nature that particularly interested Montgomery. He was fascinated by the personality of a woman who could jump out of a first-floor window in Totnes High Street. She was so different to the other women he had known. He was also fascinated that her marriage could work so well despite it being between two such different people, one an intellectual and the other rather unconventional. Audrey Keir Cross had to be like that – it was the only way of dealing with the odd life she led at that time. During his time in Abingdon in 1954 Jeni Turnbull had noticed that Montgomery was drawn to unconventional people.

As with other of his women friends, Montgomery managed somehow to persuade Audrey to do things for him. We have seen how she arranged a doctor for him; on another occasion, before electricity had been connected to the building site at Week, she found herself paying to have a generator moved from a farm worker's cottage to Week so that the builders could continue with their work. When Montgomery was having financial problems and not meeting with as much understanding as he expected from the National Provincial Bank in Brixham, she persuaded her own bank manager at Lloyds in Totnes to accept his account. She even borrowed from her mother the £2,000 Montgomery needed to open the account. She did not do these things because she felt he had to be helped. In the case of lending him the money, she was aware that he needed help, knowing from the experiences of her husband that freelance writers rarely have a steady or reliable income. There is no doubt that she felt sorry for this extremely clever man who was useless at coping with the realities of life.[54]

In the end, as with Montgomery's other close friendships with women, this one went nowhere. In 1970 Audrey married her second husband, Peter Stock, and he and Montgomery took an immediate dislike to each other. Montgomery attended the

---

54    Audrey Stock

wedding but was furious to find that David Shapland had been asked to give Audrey away. He had wanted to do it. There is nothing to be surprised about in the way that this latest friendship foundered. With the exceptions of Muriel Pavlow and Jeni Turnbull on whom it seems he was genuinely keen, Montgomery did his best to keep other women at arm's length. We have seen that women found him attractive. His combination of composer and author was some part of the appeal, and involvement with the film world added to his charms. It is undeniable that for some time he moved on the edge of an apparently glamorous world, being on good terms with many distinguished people. When his health began to deteriorate, he brought out the maternal instincts and more in women who admired his talents and thought, rightly in many ways, that he was wasting them. Increasingly Montgomery kept everyone at arm's length. He agreed with the sentiments of Eric Partridge,[55] a near neighbour of his, who claimed that he, Partridge, was not a recluse but someone who liked to be solitary and make 'occasional very <u>short</u> forays to meet people'.[56] Other friends found that in 'his later years he [Montgomery] became more and more reclusive and harder to see, repelling most visits'.[57]

55     Eric Partridge (1894–1979), author
56     Ann Montgomery to Larkin, 16 March 1979
57     Joan Bagley to author, 20 June 1990

# Chapter 17

# 'High time I was under new management': 1957–1976

There was, however, one woman who was not kept at arm's length by Montgomery and who managed to break through his reclusiveness. When Ann Clements started to work for Montgomery in April 1957 as his secretary, she was married to John Clements, a lecturer at Dartington Hall, whom she met when both were at the BBC. Ann was working in the Dartington Hall shop when she heard, through Clements, that Montgomery was looking for a secretary. It was a job she felt fortunate to have secured, being excited by the various milieux in which Montgomery worked.[1]

Ann Clements was in many ways the typical secretary, self-effacing and efficient. She came across as a very ordinary person, both in manner and dress. Despite her appearance of being rather weak and timid, in reality she could be tenacious and determined. It was not long before her role became that of combined secretary and protector. In many ways she was exactly what Montgomery had been looking for and he soon came to rely on her. Here at last was a woman who was prepared to look after him in the manner he expected. He may no longer have had his mother running around after him, or have been able to find a suitable successor to Mrs Oakman as housekeeper, but here was a woman with no children of her own who was ready to treat him as the adolescent he was in so many ways, and to shield him from the world when he wanted to hide. In essence Ann was his housekeeper. She was prepared to go shopping for him, act as cook, and later was even willing to live in the cramped separate quarters originally designed for the housekeeper. She was a most caring woman and a 'vigilant watchdog'[2] rather prone to collecting hypochondriacs, such as her husband. Montgomery fitted her bill as well as she did his.

At the same time Ann's relationship with her husband was going downhill. John Clements had great charisma and enjoyed the attention he received from his female students. One after the other he had two of his admirers stay in the house with Ann and himself. Although she never said so, friends could see that Ann was hurt by having to hear her husband's 'fulsome praises of his young admirers' qualities'.[3] Before long Clements secured a teaching post in Matlock, Derbyshire, for which Montgomery provided him with a glowing reference. This move began the process whereby Ann managed eventually to separate from her husband. Initially she remained in Devon, but by the start of 1967 her husband had become very ill with severe eye and leg problems and she felt that she must go and look after him. Ann

---

1   Molly Townsend to author, 20 October 1990
2   Joan Bagley to author, 20 June 1990
3   Ibid.

remained in Derbyshire for the next three years, broken only by occasional trips with her husband during academic holidays to the house they retained in Devon.

From the very start of her time in Matlock, Ann showed her feelings for Montgomery. 'Do love you EVER SO, poppet,' she finished a letter in January 1967.[4] 'I do miss you so much, and do wish I had been nicer when I was home.'[5] Her letters to Montgomery are very full and detailed, mainly because she did not like telephoning him. The reason for this was that one of her husband's young admirers, a teacher also called Ann, was sometimes in the house and she could not speak freely. By May, during the week of their 25th wedding anniversary, Ann was worried that her husband was going to have his foot amputated. As if this was not bad enough, Ann also had to face increasing demands from Montgomery: from this distance she was still working as his secretary, sorting out his financial affairs and even arranging more mundane matters such as train tickets. She was also having to face emotional pressure from him. 'Darling old chump-headed B.', she wrote, 'of course I'm coming back, you old silly.'[6] Her concern for Montgomery was obvious. At this time he was managing to keep off drink most of the time, but he admitted that his worries about losing her were making him depressed and liable to relapse. 'Keep your pecker up, and your eye off the bottle,' Ann ordered.[7] She checked that he was eating properly. When Montgomery suggested that perhaps they could go for a holiday on the continent, Ann countered with a more modest proposal: 'I remember how you have bursts of enthusiasms for things which cost a lot of money, and sometimes overreach yourself & afterwards regret it.'[8]

The letters between them are a mixture of personal and business matters, and the occasional bursts of rather fruity language from Ann would have surprised the people who knew her as a highly respectable churchgoer and supporter of worthy causes. Montgomery frequently reports on the antics of Tots, his cat, and particularly deplores the carnage wrought on the local livestock. One breakfast was ruined when the cat brought in a bird which lodged behind the fridge before flying around depositing 'blood into my bacon & eggs'.[9] Another letter starts 'CLEMENTS! ATTENTION! YOUR MASTER SPEAKS!' and goes on to tell her that he has switched his whisky from 'Glen Grant to Glenfiddich. Am also working quite hard.' The perils of living in the country are mentioned, particularly for one who had taken sleeping pills for many years: 'Peggy Wales's sodding roosters start heralding the dawn at about 3.30, and go on heralding it, without pause, for the next five or six hours.' More importantly, perhaps, the letter ends 'I love you'.[10] The rooster problem was sorted out a few days later when 'at my earnest entreaty (all quite friendly), Peggy has got rid of her two incessant roosters. Peace at last'.[11] His peace was broken in other ways, though:

---

4       Ann Clements to RBM, 12 January 1967
5       Ibid., 3 January 1967
6       Ibid., 26 April 1967
7       Ibid., 20 February 1968
8       Ibid., 26 February 1968
9       RBM to Ann Clements, 10 May 1967
10      Ibid., 2 May 1967
11      Ibid., 4 May 1967

'Hookes[12] again yesterday. Oh Christ. Sheila[13] again today. Oh Jesus. David[14] again tomorrow. Oh Redeemer.'[15]

By May of 1968 it was clear to Ann that her husband was not going to be well for some time, if ever. This put her in a difficult position and she began to show signs of losing her optimism. She was worried that despite trying to look after both of the men in her life, she had not kept either of them 'at all happy'.[16] It seems that Montgomery made some sort of proposal to Ann which resulted in her being frank with him. 'I think about you all the time, and round you', she wrote, 'about the garden, and cooking, and the house, and how to feel looked after without being smothered, and everything else. Don't worry, love, I'm not changing now; I see how silly I've been, really, to have gone on so long probably making four people miserable in trying to do what I thought was best.'[17] She had no regrets about trying to support her husband, but now there were signs that her husband and his new Ann were getting closer, she was hoping that this would edge her out and smooth the path for her to leave him. The *ménage a trois* was making even the patient Ann restless: 'They both bore me stiff, I'm afraid. Darling, half of the trouble has been that I really couldn't believe that you could really love me, but if you really do after almost three weeks of teetotality, I <u>must</u> be convinced.'[18]

Montgomery himself had not been well, having to stay in hospital with broken bones. By early October he was back at home being looked after by his daily Mrs Worthington, with her husband lifting him in and out of the bath. He was not entirely happy about being teetotal: 'Without booze my mind is hygienic but insipid', he told Ann, 'like distilled water. Ugh.'[19] Montgomery was pressing Ann to marry him. 'I feel a bit old and exhausted', Ann wrote to him, 'and everyone will say you're marrying a mum-figure & hope you won't mind.'[20] A 'mum-figure' was, of course, exactly what Montgomery wanted.

A few days later, in October 1968, Ann plucked up the courage to tell her husband that she wanted to return to Devon and live with Montgomery. He was devastated by this. Typically, one of his first observations was that his new Ann could not stay at weekends without Ann Clements there. What would the neighbours think? The atmosphere became difficult, but even this did not persuade Ann that she could leave him immediately; she was worried he might be left on his own. Montgomery told her not to worry on his account: 'I miss you more than I can say – but at the same time, I <u>can</u> wait, I <u>can</u> manage, I <u>can</u> keep off the bottle and I can get on with my old novel so as to pass the time.'[21]

---

12   RBM's accountant
13   RBM's youngest sister
14   RBM's doctor
15   RBM to Ann Clements, 4 May 1967
16   Ann Clements to RBM, 16 May 1968
17   Ibid., 24 September 1968
18   Ibid.
19   RBM to Ann Clements, 3 December 1968
20   Ann Clements to RBM, 9 October 1968
21   RBM to Ann Clements, 19 November 1968

By the start of 1969 Montgomery was apologising to Ann for being 'petulant and nasty' on the telephone,[22] but it was only because he was afraid of losing her. In February he made a move which showed how much Ann meant to him and how determined he was to marry her. He signed a will of which, with the exception of a small bequest to Mrs Worthington, Ann was the sole beneficiary. She was also the sole executor. Even this had no immediate effect. Ann reported that her husband now had a poor mental state to add to his physical problems. Montgomery was not doing much better. He found Ann's absence difficult, particularly in the evenings ('I miss you banging around in the kitchen')[23] and had taken to drinking again, but had pulled himself together after a phone call from Ann.

Ann was finding her position impossible. She was caught between the Scylla of her husband (depressed, still with mobility and sight difficulties) and the Charybdis of Montgomery (also with mobility problems and facing a constant battle against alcoholism). Friends acknowledged that Ann was faced by a 'terrible dilemma':[24] whether to continue in what for her was an unsatisfactory relationship and let Montgomery, whose health she knew to be unsteady, 'sink into despair',[25] or to leave her husband to his ill-health and support Montgomery. It is hardly surprising that by August she did not know which way to turn. She wrote Montgomery a very gloomy letter in which she claims she cannot leave her husband if he is in danger of going blind and admits that she might have to review her decision to move in with Montgomery; 'My love, I am bound to let you down I think',[26] but this was not to be a final decision unless he agreed with it.

To make Ann's situation more complicated, the last two years had also taken their toll on her. She had not been feeling well, and a lump had been found which might require surgery. The day after she had written the gloomy letter, Ann wrote a more optimistic one. Montgomery received them on the same day and opened the gloomy one first. The combination of news spurred him into unprecedented action. In the past he may have tried to wriggle out of relationships if they threatened to disturb the order of his life, but this time he realised he was in real danger of losing the one woman who matched up to his demands.

For once Montgomery was ready to fight, and the letter he wrote pulled no punches. Telling Ann that if she had to have an operation he would come and see her, he continued:

> And even if hospital isn't necessary, I think I ought to come up in any case. Am most disturbed by the fact that you seem to all intents and purposes to be a prisoner – that, I'm afraid, is what John wants you to be, and for the rest of your life. Sparks,[27] I just can't bear the thought of your wasting the years that remain to you enslaved to a querulous, selfish invalid, permanently tied up in a poky little flat (without hope of a short holiday, even) in company with him and his pea-brained, pig-faced, ever-present popsie. I know

---

22     Ibid., 17 January 1969
23     Ibid., 20 June 1969
24     Molly Townsend to author, 20 October 1990.
25     Ibid.
26     Ann Clements to RBM, 2 August 1969
27     Montgomery's pet name for Ann. She called him 'Bodger'.

the alternative isn't all that marvellous: I'm no prize package. But with me you'd have much more independence – financially, for one thing, and for another, since I'm perfectly capable of looking after myself with Mrs W's assistance, whenever you wanted a day on the Moor or a week with Liz or a month in the Bahamas, you could just <u>have</u> it.

[…] Am shocked and appalled to hear that John has the indecency to create rows when I telephone. Does he think that you're some contemptible little mouse, to have all shreds of independence torn away from you because he is lacking in ordinary civility, self-restraint and, above all, self-respect? Annie, if you stay with him it will be utterly disastrous for you – and, in the end, for him too, because with no hope of anything better to keep you going, and no prospect but unmitigated serfdom, even you are bound to get melancholy and resentful.

He was also blunt about his own position:

Anyway, I refuse to give up hope of having you here; you're all that I truly want from life, and it would be utterly disastrous for me if I had to resign myself to giving you up. There's emotional blackmail for you, if you like! Anyway, after so much waiting I expect I can manage some more. Indeed I must, because it's only the hope that one day you'll come to me here that gives my life any meaning. […] Darling pet, I love you more than I can possibly say.[28]

A few days later Montgomery was clearly confident of claiming Ann when he wrote to Larkin:

Ann Clements — whom I've no doubt you remember — was to have come and settled down here with me this summer, as a permanency, but now her husband has had an eye haemorrhage and she doesn't feel she can ditch him for the time being. So it's a matter of hope deferred. It'll be a very good arrangement for me, though, when it does eventuate. High time I was under new management. I drink too much, for one thing.[29]

Following his forthright letter to Ann, their situation gradually unravelled itself. Ann's lump turned out to be sarcoidosis, a relatively minor inflammatory complaint compared to the leukaemia or Hodgkin's Disease which had been feared. Clements finally sold the house in Devon, and Ann made some progress with encouraging her husband and his younger friend to commit to each other. In October 1969 Ann told Montgomery that she would make a decision on their future early in the New Year; she had no intention of 'stringing' him along any more.[30] The decision was in Montgomery's favour; in March 1970 Ann moved in with him.

Montgomery's constant references to their liaison as an 'arrangement' suggest his approach to the relationship at this stage, and his letters to Larkin, who was also given to unorthodox relationships with women, make frequent allusions to his impending change of status:

Ann will probably be settling in with me early in the New Year. Yes, I know what you mean about needing solitude, and I need plenty of that too, but the fact is that in my life as

---

28    RBM to Ann Clements, 6 August 1969

29    RBM to Larkin, 16 August 1969

30    Ann Clements to RBM, 7 October 1969

organised at present I'm getting too much of it. In that respect, therefore, I think that the new arrangement will be a definite improvement (well, in <u>all</u> respects, damn it). The point is, I can always retire to my study (which psychologically speaking will be surrounded by an impenetrable ring of fire) and pretend to be working. I might even <u>do</u> some work, I suppose.[31]

Charles Monteith recalls Montgomery saying, rather archly: 'My secretary's become my mistress.'[32] A few months later Montgomery explained his domestic situation still further:

Ann and I are now settled down here together, but as to marriage, that will have to wait until she can get a divorce. Meanwhile, we both enjoy plenty of privacy, and sleep and work and have baths in separate parts of the house, so we don't have to live in one another's pockets, and I think it will probably work out extremely well.[33]

Perhaps Ann was happy with these living arrangements, but as always with Montgomery the terms were ones he dictated. A little later their status had not changed. '[Ann] isn't yet exactly my wife (divorce problems)', he told Harry Harrison, 'but has been living with me for three years in, I am very happy to say, sin.'[34] Talk of marriage may have been premature, but Montgomery was clearly confident that this new arrangement was permanent. In early 1971 Ann took over all the domestic accounts, and later the same year Montgomery transferred the bungalow into joint ownership. She was reluctant to follow the matrimonial path again. There was still a reasonable amount in Montgomery's estate, what with the rights of his music and books, and he was keen to marry Ann so that these would pass to her, thus avoiding any squabbles over his will. He had to enlist the help of his old friend Brian Galpin, now a judge, to persuade Ann. When Galpin visited Week with his wife, there was quite a discussion of the matter one evening. Ann did not see any reason for marriage: 'Go on, Brian, give her the law!' Montgomery urged.[35] Whatever was said clearly worked. Ann later told Joan Bagley 'candidly' that she married Montgomery 'in order to safeguard both her financial future and his literary future'.[36]

There are indications that Montgomery played games to try and influence Ann to move in and marry him. In 1969 he went to a dinner of the Detection Club at the Café Royal in London and asked Audrey Keir Cross to go with him. He told her that Ann was not going to be very happy about this. When Audrey suggested that he should have asked Ann rather than her, Montgomery said: 'Why? She's got nothing to worry about.' He was clearly trying to make Ann commit herself. There was another reason for not asking her. Montgomery was in one of what Audrey called his 'Claridges' moods when, despite his precarious financial state, he would insist on doing everything in the grand style by staying at the best hotels and hiring a chauffeur-driven car for the evening. Montgomery knew that Ann could not play

---

31    RBM to Larkin, 24 November 1969
32    Charles Monteith
33    RBM to Larkin, 3 April 1970
34    RBM to Harry Harrison, 10 April 1973
35    Brian and Nancy Galpin
36    Joan Bagley to author, 20 June 1990

the part he wanted on these occasions: she was not comfortable with the grand life and became stiff and buttoned up very quickly. Montgomery did not want the waiters and porters he normally dealt with to see him at a disadvantage, so he did not take her. Audrey, on the other hand, was as happy dealing with this style of life as she was going to the Cott Inn. Others, including Jeni Turnbull, noticed that Montgomery enjoyed playing at life in this way.

On this occasion Montgomery inadvertently caused more trouble for Audrey. He drank heavily during the dinner, after which they went back to her flat in the chauffeur-driven car. Montgomery was sufficiently inebriated to make a beeline for the only bed. Audrey also wanted to sleep as she had to be up for work early, so the pair were forced to share the bed. At about 4am, the chauffeur appeared at the door of the flat in an apologetic state: he had to go off his shift but had not yet been paid. Montgomery's raincoat was still in the car and he wondered whether he should take it back to Claridges. Audrey took the coat and, finding that a rather large sum of money was due, woke Montgomery; despite his condition he knew exactly where his wallet was, and Audrey paid the chauffeur from the large amount she found there. Montgomery was still in bed when she went to work that morning, but he had gone by the time she returned, leaving his bowtie hanging on her dressing table mirror. Rather unwisely Audrey left it there, and when Peter Stock, who was courting her seriously at the time, next paid a visit, he saw it – and there was some explaining to do. It was around this time that Audrey realised there was no future for her with Montgomery. He showed no passion.

In many ways Ann became Montgomery's nurse, but she was an exceptional woman. Molly Townsend, an old friend of Ann's from London days, has noted that 'the support she gave Bruce through his frequent sad periods of alcoholism and his illnesses are beyond praise. From the little we saw of him, I believe he was fully aware of the treasure he had in her.'[37] When Charles Monteith telephoned, he was always pleased when Ann answered, particularly if Montgomery was drinking, as she could always tell him what he needed to know.[38]

Ann had much to endure. In the 1960s Kingsley Amis visited Totnes, and Montgomery worked very hard with no effect at making the occasion a success. He was hampered by the effects of drink, and by the fact that he had clearly forgotten that the invitation had been extended to Amis' brother-in-law. Every few minutes he would say: 'Colin, it is good to see you.' In the 1970s, Amis recalls receiving telephone calls from Ann introducing Montgomery who, when prompted by Amis, would reply with no words, just vague noises. He was probably so drunk that he could not speak. Amis would keep on trying to get a word out of him, with little or no success.[39] Montgomery's sister, Sheila Rossiter, recalled visiting Ann to have coffee one morning and arriving slightly early. Montgomery was still in his dressing gown, drunk and abusive, and demanding to know what she was doing there. Rossiter could not tell whether this was the effect of the previous night's drinking or because he had made an early start. From time to time Ann would pack him off to Moorhaven for

---

37   Molly Townsend to author, 20 October 1990
38   Charles Monteith
39   Sir Kingsley Amis

another course of treatment. Against Ann's wishes Rossiter visited him, and on one occasion found him more or less crawling up the walls. Although he had nothing in his hand, he was flicking the ash off an imaginary cigarette and stubbing it out. It was a disturbing experience; later Rossiter told Montgomery that she did not want to see him like that again, but he did not give the impression of being repentant. In fact, he claimed that he enjoyed it.[40]

In a typically ungenerous comment, Amis found it hard to understand what Montgomery saw in Ann. He thought that someone who had known plenty of attractive film starlets should have had higher standards.[41] 'I say', he wrote to Larkin just before Montgomery was due to visit him, 'why's he going to marry this woman with all those teeth, eh? [...] I can't really ask him, because almost whenever he understands what I'm saying, which doesn't seem to be often, he tends to get slightly cross.'[42] It was true that Ann was slightly gawky and no beauty, but most people who got to know her liked her and realised that she was exactly what Montgomery needed.[43] Amis' judgement might have been coloured by an embarrassing incident which occurred on the last time he saw Montgomery, at a science fiction lunch, on an occasion when he realised that the point of no return had been reached as far as Montgomery's drinking was concerned.[44] After the meal Amis had had enough to drink, but Montgomery wanted more. As Amis had been Montgomery's guest on many previous occasions, he felt that he had to take him and Ann to the Wig and Pen on the Strand, a drinking club to which Amis belonged. They found as secluded an area as they could, albeit in a passage, where Montgomery soon showed that he needed no more alcohol. Amis kept asking if he would like some black coffee, but Montgomery kept on asking for a large scotch and water. He was vomiting where he sat, mopping it up with his handkerchief and promptly starting on another whisky. Amis was furious: he could have been thrown out of the club had the manager seen any of this, responsible as he was for the behaviour of his guest. He was dismayed by Ann's attitude. She sat there, smiling awkwardly, when Amis thought she should have been asking for help in getting Montgomery to a taxi. Had she been good with him, Amis thought, Ann would have sorted the matter out.

This relatively isolated view of Ann, it must be said, is one shared by Audrey Keir Cross. Having herself lived with an alcoholic, she knew that the sober partner had to take charge. Audrey left the guests to take her first husband home during the wedding reception of their daughter because he was becoming socially embarrassing. Ann let Montgomery get away with too much, things that no one else, paid or otherwise, would have tolerated. She did not make him stand on his own feet, and shielded him from having to face up to realities such as completing some work. He needed shaking, otherwise he was liable to slip away like a jelly.[45]

---

40     Sheila Rossiter
41     Sir Kingsley Amis
42     Amis to Larkin, 19 April 1969 [LKA]
43     Charles Monteith
44     Sir Kingsley Amis
45     Audrey Stock

Despite Montgomery's reliance on Ann, he did not always repay her devotion. When she was finding it difficult to leave her husband, Montgomery could become irritable with her and cause an argument. He was not always more amenable after she had committed herself to him. Audrey Keir Cross visited them one day after Ann was living at Week and found her in tears in the garden. It was her birthday, and despite gentle reminders Montgomery had done nothing to celebrate it: he had not wished her a happy birthday or bought her a present or even a card. Audrey was furious. Knowing Ann to be a keen gardener, she drove into Totnes and bought her a tree peony. She then went to see Montgomery and gave him a piece of her mind, reminding him that Ann had left her husband for him and was perhaps still missing some of the normal civilities of a shared life. Rather than showing repentance, Montgomery became insolent: 'I've given her a home,' he said, and went on to list other benefits he considered she had gained. 'What does she want all that nonsense for?' He could be very petulant when sober on such matters as this. Had he been drinking he might have reacted in a very different way, perhaps telephoning the florist for a special delivery. Ann was unlucky to have her birthday on a day when he was teetotal.[46] The truncated diary he kept in 1966 ('I became alcoholically surly, and took it out disgracefully on poor Ann')[47] shows that his reactions were inconsistent, and some excuse for his behaviour might be found in this unsteady health. Despite this, there is no doubt that he was appreciative of Ann. Without her, he once said, he could never have undertaken the complications of negotiating with architect and builders or arranging the furnishings for Week Meadow. When he was still living in Brixham, Ann used to travel there on her motorbike. Montgomery did not like the thought of her making these frequent journeys in the cold, so he gave her a car. She was absolutely delighted with his gift. When they were living together, Ann started an Open University course in art. Montgomery was fully behind this and persuaded her to go on a visit to Italy that had been arranged for the students. The trip gave her great joy, telling friends that it was one of the best experiences of her life.[48] He could undoubtedly be very thoughtful. After he had known Audrey Keir Cross for a time, he would remember that she liked Crescendo, a scent by Lanvin, and buy it for her occasionally. Presumably the musical name stuck in his mind.

Montgomery's precarious health led to a delay in the marriage taking place. The final postponement came at the end of 1975 when Montgomery spent two months in the Bristol Royal Infirmary with hepatitis. 'I'm home again now', he told his sister, Sheila, 'and after the hurly-burly of Ward 15 it's sheer bliss. Ann is putting up with my invalid's tantrums with angelic patience, and of course is looking after me very well. Though convalescence is slow [...] and I still look like something which has spent six months in the grave, still, we're getting on.'[49] Ann and Montgomery were eventually married on 19 February 1976, travelling to and from the registry office in Newton Abbott by taxi. To prepare for it they had taken a few days' holiday at the Old Government House Hotel in Guernsey which, judging from the postcard

---

46    Ibid.
47    Diary for 1966
48    Molly Townsend to author, 20 October 1990
49    RBM to Sheila Rossiter, 10 December 1975 (copy in author's collection)

Montgomery sent to Larkin, was not an unqualified success: 'Very cold, food indifferent, little to do ("We're closed till the Season starts, you see"); not a patch on S. Devon anywise. [...] Hitching day is the 19th. Quel brouhaha!'[50]

The quiet marriage was followed by a nuptial mass at Dartington ('by way of making assurance doubly sure').[51] Writing to thank Larkin for his wedding telegram, Montgomery told him: 'You'll hardly be surprised to hear that my premonitions of disaster started being fulfilled almost before I'd had time to have them.'[52] He promised to enlarge on this in a future letter but failed to do so. Telegrams had arrived from many old friends

> ranging from a Norwegian tweed-maker whom neither of us has seen for years through a collaboration of several of the gigantically tall women who constitute Ann's family [...] and the staff of the local pub (one of whose proprietors dissolved into brandy-laden tears at the thought of such happiness, it was reported to us afterwards). [...] Nothing, needless to say, from KWA [Amis] – not even a scribble on a postcard, despite the fact that I've given him two wedding-presents, not to mention observing faithfully, as godfather, the first sixteen years of birthdays of his obnoxious younger son.'[53]

A few months later he was admitting that 'the old friendship [with Amis] doesn't seem to be what it was'.[54] The following year there was still no word from Amis: 'Possibly he heard me on the radio telling Edward Blishen that despite his manifold talents, I didn't think he was much good at writing detective stories.'[55]

The wedding presents were a mixed bunch. A recording of *Don Giovanni* confirmed Montgomery's opinion 'that absolutely anything from any Mozart opera could be substituted for absolutely anything else from any other Mozart opera without anyone noticing',[56] but he was particularly taken with the miniaturised *Dictionary of National Biography* 'with which Ann, groaning hideously (well, it does weigh about as much as a diesel locomotive) plighted her troth to me'.[57]

---

50    RBM to Larkin, 6 February 1976
51    Ibid., 22 March 1976
52    Ibid.
53    Ibid.
54    Ibid., 11 November 1976
55    Ibid., 27 May 1977
56    Ibid., 22 March 1976.
57    Ibid.

# Chapter 18

# 'The bonelessness of the short-distance funner': 1974–1978

Had it not been for Ann's influence, Montgomery might have gone downhill even more quickly than he did. Despite the reservations that have been expressed about Ann's indulgence of him, without her it is quite possible that Montgomery would never have finished *The Glimpses of the Moon*, and it seems more than a coincidence that he sent the finished typescript to Gollancz within a few months of being married. There had also been a small piece of encouraging news on the musical scene. In December 1975 the BBC Singers broadcast *Venus' Praise*, the cycle of choral songs with string accompaniment he had completed in 1951. Delighted by the performance, Montgomery wrote to thank John Poole, the conductor: 'I hope you and the performers didn't find it too dull. However, although it's dated music, it perhaps makes a change from the aleatory, and from Stockhausen's notation and so forth.'[1] The broadcast spurred Malcolm Arnold into correspondence: 'I though your choral piece on BBC 3 the other day was one of the most beautiful things I had ever heard, and I am more than anxious to hear more of your serious music.'[2] Montgomery was flattered by his old friend's praise, and replied that he hoped music went backwards: 'I have every hope of being an Authentic Minor Composer.'[3] Arnold followed this by writing to the BBC to demand more performances of Montgomery's work, but received only evasive responses.

Despite more than twenty years having passed since his last novel, Montgomery was still held in high esteem in the world of crime fiction. In 1974 the second conference of the Crime Writers' Association was held in Paignton. Montgomery was in a bout of ill health at the time, rather frail and walking with the aid of a stick, and he was not prepared to go the few miles to participate. Desmond and Joan Bagley, however, had invited members to their house in Totnes for a drink before the gala luncheon and they somehow managed to persuade Montgomery to come over. Ann drove him to their house in Totnes.

> By the time he turned up the house was packed. [...] Bruce was quietly ushered into Desmond's study and made comfortable, and we then mentioned to one or two of his oldest friends that he was there (I remember Josephine Bell as one of them, Penny Wallace, Dick Francis, Duncan Kyle among others). Bruce was delighted to see them and was in a particularly outgoing mood, holding court with grace and courtesy. Then the word began to go round that Edmund Crispin in person was present – and there was a steady

---

1     RBM to John Poole, 9 December 1975
2     Malcolm Arnold to RBM, 24 January 1976
3     RBM to Malcolm Arnold, 17 August 1976

swirl of movement as many of the younger or newer writers came into the study to meet the master, obviously awe-struck, fascinated and captivated by him. It was extremely touching – not least for the effect it had on Bruce himself. He stayed much longer than planned and absolutely glowed in the warmth of his welcome.[4]

Dick Francis recalled that Montgomery was 'at the time suffering from sore and inflamed feet, and was consequently wearing bedroom slippers during the height of the day'.[5]

*The Glimpses of the Moon*, Montgomery's final novel, was published on 12 May 1977. Most people were so pleased by its actual appearance that they were willing to overlook some of its defects of plot. Generally it was admired for its humour and high spirits, something not surprising in view of his earlier novels but rather more unexpected given the torments the author had gone through during its very long gestation. 'Satire, wit, farce, the use of language and the movement of dialogue', Jacques Barzun wrote, 'all this added together makes the work a triumph of the baroque that I am the better for having savoured as well as gulped down.'[6] H.R.F. Keating traced its lineage: 'It fulfils every expectation. [...] It is in the line that goes back not only through Innes but through N.F. Simpson, through Beachcomber, through Wodehouse, through a major strain of Dickens, through Sterne, to Urquhart's punch-drunk rendering of Rabelais.'[7] The mention of Wodehouse would have vexed Montgomery: 'Why do I find Wodehouse so unfunny?' he asked an old friend,[8] and it is a very difficult question to answer. One imagines that Wodehouse's use of language and farce would have appealed to him. Michael Innes, with whom Crispin had been compared more than any other writer, was similarly enthusiastic about the new novel: 'it is perhaps true that nobody since Wilkie Collins has successfully achieved the fusing of this type of sensation novel with one or other of the traditional forms of English fiction. Mr Crispin has been having a good try. [...] Indeed, I don't know who has been, at his best, at once so wickedly ingenious and so brilliantly funny.'[9]

The unsigned notice in the *Times Literary Supplement* hit the nail on the head. Having acknowledged that on first reading Crispin's readers might be disappointed by a book that is more comic novel than detective story, it goes on to put matters into perspective:

A second reading, however, alleviates the disappointment and makes it clear that *The Glimpses of the Moon* is in fact a logical successor to the earlier novels, with the difference that an exuberant fancy, which had hitherto been held partially in check by the exigencies of the form, has here been allowed to blossom freely. The result is a gloriously funny book, witty and farcical by turns, with an occasional surprising sidestep into the macabre.[10]

4      Joan Bagley to author, 20 June 1990
5      Dick Francis to author, 11 October 1990
6      *The Bookseller*, 22 January 1977
7      *The Times*, 12 May 1977
8      RBM to John Maxwell, 16 June 1976
9      *Sunday Times*, 15 May 1977
10     *TLS*, 26 August 1977

This is surely true: the tone of the novel is riotously bucolic, with a cast of rustic half-wits and others whose mental equipment appears distinctly sub-standard. Indeed, it has come to something when Gervase Fen seems more or less the sanest person on view. In amongst retarded yokels, incompetent policemen and sadistic farmers there is, for example, the Major, who is obsessed with the jingles from television commercials and takes every opportunity to perform them. He also has an intense dislike of horses ('Horrible treacherous brutes [...] Nip you in the neck as soon as look at you'),[11] a viewpoint doubtless fed by Montgomery's accident in his youth. There is the huge and simian Rector, a worthy successor to another clergyman of doubtful sanity in *Buried for Pleasure*, who dresses up as Madame Sosostris, Famous Clairvoyant, to read palms at the Church Fête, with rolled up rugger socks for his bosom ('I bought myself a forty-two bra, C cups')[12] and who gains enormous enjoyment from chasing burglars ('I'm not', the Rector had once complacently remarked, 'the type of thing you want to meet unexpectedly on a dark night.').[13] There is the Amazonian German woman Ortrud Youings whose violence wrecks the Try-Your-Strength machine at the fête and whose constant infidelities are borne with spaniel-like devotion by her craven husband, the local pig man. There is the landlord of the village pub, The Stanbury Arms, a valetudinarian of colossal proportions who spends all day in bed despite having sufficient energy to exercise on a rowing machine each morning. There is Mrs Clotworthy, a butcher's widow, whose idea of bliss for her 75th birthday is the opportunity 'to cut up a nice pig'[14] and who, by doing so, is inadvertently responsible for a succession of heads, human and porcine, appearing in strange places (atop a raft on the river, for example, or in an armchair in Mrs Leeper-Foxe's dining room). There is Mr Morehen, a quantitative analyst, whose enthusiastic embrace of surliness and socialism is every bit the equal of Primrose in *Frequent Hearses* ('When the Revolution comes', said Mr Morehen, 'you'll be one of the first for the lamp-post').[15] There are the highly respectable Misses Bale, Tatty and Titty, who wheel out for the fête every year what they regard as a Botticelli ('Awful great nineteenth-century daub actually, size of a barn door')[16] so that people can pay to gaze at it in reverence. There is Montgomery's self-portrait, the despondent film composer Broderick Thouless, who has been mentioned previously. And there are countless more.

Inanimate objects also have their eccentricities. When Padmore, a reporter, wonders why Fen and the Major suddenly speed up on a walk, he is introduced to one of them:

> The Major explained that they were speeding up because they were about to pass the Pisser.
>
> Padmore said, 'I see.'
>
> 'Listen,' said the Major. 'It's making its noise again.'

---

11   *The Glimpses of the Moon*, Chapter 2
12   Ibid., Chapter 5
13   Ibid., Chapter 2
14   Ibid., Chapter 3
15   Ibid., Chapter 9
16   Ibid., Chapter 2

There certainly was a noise going on, Padmore realised, and a disquieting one at that. It was being produced by a large, old-fashioned pylon set close against the left-hand side of the lane; and it was owing to the basic character of this noise, the Major explained, that this pylon which issued it was known throughout the neighbourhood as the Pisser (even intensely respectable elderly ladies, the Major truthfully claimed, would ring one another up and say, 'It's such a lovely afternoon, why don't we meet at the gate by the Pisser and go for a walk over Worthington's Steep?').[17]

Fears about the Pisser's eventual detonation are realised, of course, later in the novel.

There is the usual dose of anthropomorphism, but this time the larger array of animals see little significant action. Stripey, a sex-starved tom, and Fred, the Major's pub-hating whippet, lounge around most of the time. Ellis, a tortoise whose jaws are out of alignment and who thus prefers to be fed premasticated pansy petals (much to Fen's inconvenience), seems to exist only so that someone can fall over him. At least the usually somnolent horse Xantippe is spurred into action by the Major at the end.

Montgomery seems to derive particular pleasure from taking swipes at many institutions. British Rail, popular journalism and the modern British novel, about which Fen is writing a survey, all suffer, as does a particular publication:

Fen was not thinking about the murder. Instead, he was smoking a cigarette and reading *The Times Literary Supplement* – nowadays vulgarly retitled T.L.S, without even a full stop after the 'S' – one of three special issues given over to modern Albanian poetry.[18]

Montgomery is particularly savage about Sweb:

'Acronym,' said the Major. 'Stands for South Western Electricity Board. They think that if they call themselves Sweb, don't you know, it'll make people look on them as friends.' He shook his head sadly at the thought of so much innocence exposed in a harsh world, like babies on rocks outside Sparta.[19]

The man from Sweb (a 'terrified little man in grey'[20] ludicrously named, we eventually discover, Humphrey de Brisay) turns out to be a burglar. In this instance Montgomery had special reason to exact his revenge on Sweb. When his bungalow in Week was being built, there had been a number of problems about the electricity supply. At first Sweb had said that it could not connect the house for at least two years, but conceded that if Montgomery paid a supplementary contribution of £150 the installation might be speeded up. He agreed to the contribution, but held it back until Sweb gave him a definite date for connection. This date never came, driving Montgomery to write that Sweb 'prevaricated over so long a period that I can no longer believe anything it says about anything'.[21] In desperation, after a two-year

---

17   Ibid.
18   Ibid., Chapter 10
19   Ibid., Chapter 2
20   Ibid.
21   RBM to A.B. Grayson, 2 March 1964

campaign, he took the matter to the South Western Electricity Consultative Council, but had to install a generator before Sweb finally effected the connection. These experiences are doubtless why Montgomery has the Rector announce about his burglar: 'Could have told you from the first he wasn't from Sweb […] Not nasty enough, for one thing.'[22]

There are further echoes of Evelyn Waugh in the novel. Padmore, the reporter, appears to have had a career of similar misfortune to that of William Boot in *Scoop*:

> In reality he was an expert on African affairs, and had returned from the dark continent three months previously with the cheerless distinction of having been expelled from more emergent black nations, more expeditiously, than any other journalist of any nationality whatever. Even Ould Daddah and Dr Hastings Banda had expelled him, he said – the latter inadvertently, under the impression that he was a Chinese.
>
> 'Underdeveloped countries with overdeveloped susceptibilities,' said Padmore sourly.
>
> There had been no question, he went on, of his trying to knock African aspirations; on the contrary, he sympathized with them. Simply, he had had a run of exceptionally bad luck. He would send off a cable censuring some dissident General at the exact moment when the General's minions were successfully gunning down the palace guards, the Deputy Postmaster and the doorman at the television studios. Or he would praise the enlightened policies of a Minister already on his way to be sequestrated or hanged. Or he would commend the up-to-date safety precautions at an oil refinery which the next day would go up in flames, with fearsome loss of life. As a result of all this, eventually his paper, the *Gazette*, tiring of running indignant news items about their special correspondent's various expulsions, had called him back to London, a call he had answered as soon as he could get out of the Zambian prison where he had been put because of an article drawing the world's attention to how well President Kaunda was always dressed (this had been interpreted as imputing conspicuous waste in high places).[23]

Padmore is not the only character in the novel to have African links:

> The opener of the Fête was a short slim, affable, loquacious Negro, educated at Winchester and New College, who lived twenty miles away, writing lucrative science fiction under the name of Dermot McCartney. (He had begun his writing career with delicate studies of coloured men teetering between two cultures, but these, though gratifying to the *Observer* and the *New Statesman*, had in addition to selling poorly proved to be too much like hard work, since the author had no recollection at all of what Negro culture was like and was obliged to look it all up in books.)[24]

Padmore later learns that McCartney had been brought from the Republic of Upper Volta at the age of three and is much given to sweeping statements about his origins:

---

22   *The Glimpses of the Moon*, Chapter 12
23   Ibid., Chapter 2
24   Ibid., Chapter 5

'My people are mostly dolts, I'm afraid, [...] Dolts or barbarians, or both. They believe things which are either nonsensical or else manifestly untrue, such as that they are collectively capable of managing their own affairs, and that black is beautiful, and that jazz is an art form.'[25]

In many ways, McCartney reminds us of the heads of the rival legations in London from which William Boot has to obtain visas to visit Ishmaelia, neither of whom are natives of the country ('Certainly not! I'm a graduate of the Baptist College of Antigua')[26] and both of whom make similar grand and inaccurate statements about their origins ('we are pure Aryans. [...] In the course of the years the tropical sun has given to some of us a healthy, in some cases almost a swarthy tan').[27] And, at the end of the novel, as if to remove any doubt that Waugh's influence is in the air, Fen quotes Mr Salter of *The Beast* as he disagrees with the Major about how much fun it has been to read all the books for his now-abandoned survey of the post-war novel: 'Up to a point, Lord Copper.'[28]

Despite the comic carnage throughout most of the book, there is a significant difference to most of Montgomery's earlier work, and this is that Fen is an observer for large parts of the novel. He solves the crime, of course, but for longer periods than usual he is either on the sidelines or absent altogether. There are still the little frivolous touches:

Here he [Fen] paused by the mirror, from which, not unexpectedly, his own face looked out at him. In the fifteen years since his last appearance [it was, in fact, rather longer], he seemed to have changed very little. Peering at his image now, he saw the same tall lean body, the same ruddy, scrubbed-looking, clean-shaven face, the same blue eyes, the same brown hair ineffectually plastered down with water, so that it stood up in a spike at the crown of his head. Somewhere or other he still had his extra-ordinary hat. Good. At this rate, he felt, he might even live to see the day when novelists described their characters by some other device than that of manoeuvring them into examining themselves in mirrors.[29]

When Padmore announces his intention to move to Devon and write about murders, including possibly Fen's cases, Fen attempts to dissuade him: 'Crispin writes those up [...] in his own grotesque way. And there's not much money in it, John.' A footnote explains 'I include this fragment of dialogue only at Fen's personal insistence. – E.C.'[30]

But a Crispin novel would not be a Crispin novel if it did not finish with a chase of some sort. The one Montgomery contrives here has little if anything to do with the plot, and it introduces even more people and groups of people on whom he can discharge his spleen. He acknowledged this when confessing that 'It [*The Glimpses of the Moon*] came out a bit longer than I expected, but this, I think, was due to

---

25     Ibid., Chapter 6

26     *Scoop*, Evelyn Waugh, Book I, Chapter 4

27     Ibid.

28     Ibid., Book III, Chapter 3

29     *The Glimpses of the Moon*, Chapter 3

30     Ibid., Chapter 13

multiplicity of characters rather than just to wordiness.'[31] There are cows, horses, men in cars, men on foot, policemen, motor-cyclists, a hippy, and hunt saboteurs whose ineffectiveness is increased by their constant squabbles. The Pisser explodes at a vital moment (' […] as everybody but the experts had always said it one day would')[32], the noise being compared to 'a thousand pitsful of Fu Manchu's death-dealing snakes'[33] – an unsurprising comparison given Montgomery's last film score.

And what about the plot itself? It is clear that Montgomery was having such fun hitting out in all directions that he omitted to concern himself too much with this detail. It is almost as if he knew that there was not much life left in him and was determined to go out with a bang. Having submitted the typescript, he engaged in correspondence with Gollancz about some of the detail of the novel, particularly concerning cutting the length of the chase passage and his elaborate *deus ex machina* of producing a hitherto unknown brother of the murderer. Montgomery himself knew the novel's limitations: 'the whole thing is really a comedy hung on the rather frail and shaky detective framework'.[34] The combination of an unidentified corpse, hacked-off limbs and an amputation were first mooted in Montgomery's notes for *Judgement in Paris*, the abandoned predecessor of *The Glimpses of the Moon*.

One final comment: as this was Montgomery's last literary work, it is highly appropriate that close to the end, as the Rector grapples with reclaiming the criminal soul of the man from Sweb, he should mention the novel that started off 'Edmund Crispin' in Oxford over thirty years previously: 'You could read to me over lunch, then. John Dickson Carr, *The Crooked Hinge*. Good stuff.'[35]

Montgomery was delighted by the book's reception. 'If sales only match reviews, I shall be puffing cigars in a large Roll-Royce' was one reaction.[36] 'Glad you didn't find the new book too unreadable. All very nice reviews to date', he wrote to Larkin, 'particularly, of course, the Innes in the Sunday Times (rather as if Shakespeare had written a favourable notice of Dryden). Glad you remembered some of the old jokes. The high spirits were, I think, precisely due to my narrow escape from the Dread Reaper.'[37] He used a different image when thanking Innes personally: 'It was as though Shakespeare at the height of his powers were to praise some tawdry tragedy by someone like Beaumont. I was flattered and delighted.'[38] The editor of the *Yorkshire Post* visited to write a profile of Montgomery, leaving him to muse that there was no such sign of the London media: 'I suppose everyone thinks I'm long dead.'[39]

---

31   RBM to John Maxwell, 16 July 1976

32   *The Glimpses of the Moon*, Chapter 12

33   Ibid.

34   RBM to Livia Gollancz, 26 July 1976

35   *The Glimpses of the Moon*, Chapter 12

36   RBM to Christopher Francis, 6 June 1977

37   RBM to Larkin, 27 May 1977

38   RBM to Michael Innes, 16 February 1978

39   RBM to Gollancz, 25 April 1977

But despite the book's success and Montgomery's renewed determination to make an immediate start on his first novel for Macmillan, his health and mental state remained precarious:

> Latest medical bulletin. At worst I can hope for another year, which I suppose isn't too bad considering the human body appears to be thrown together like a British Leyland car. If things look good at the end of the year, I can hope for five or six years more – enough, really, in view of the fact that I'm pretty decrepit already, and find life insufferably boring.[40]

This gloomy letter does not tell the whole story. Under Ann's influence Montgomery was showing greater signs of trying to get himself on an even keel and plan for the future than he had for some years. 'I have almost more work than I can cope with', he told a former neighbour, Desmond Bagley,[41] and we have seen that he was making a genuine effort to complete *What Seems to be the Trouble?*; 'my prospects, contractually and so forth, are better than they have been for some time', was the good news for his bank manager.[42] He reassured his accountant: 'I am now virtually completely back to normal, and working very hard to make up for lost time',[43] even though he still only had 'stamina for part time work'[44] and found sitting at a typewriter for more than ten minutes at a time almost impossible.[45] Telling Christianna Brand that he was now writing for Macmillan, he added that 'It would obviously be less laborious for me to sell my body: but unfortunately I'm getting a bit old for that.'[46]

There were times when he managed to stay off the drink. 'As to being on the wagon', he told Brian Aldiss, 'I haven't had a drink for three months now (well, not to put too fine a point on it, it was getting to be a bit much), and am proposing to stay that way for another nine. After that, we'll see.'[47] Larkin learned that 'the craving for booze has now almost entirely vanished, except for times of extreme stress'.[48] This caused minor domestic problems. 'Since I climbed on the wagon, great masses of drink have accumulated in the house.'[49]

Montgomery was exploring the possibility of building a modest guest house in his side garden and had successfully negotiated the purchase of a small amount of adjacent land to grow fruit and vegetables and to keep hens (some years previously he had been financially involved in an enterprise to breed chickens and guinea fowl). He was also proposing to add a room to the house and build a swimming pool: 'you'll have lots of fun eating early strawberries in the new room', he told Larkin,

---

40    RBM to Larkin, 8 August 1977
41    RBM to Desmond Bagley, 27 August 1978
42    RBM to Lloyds Bank, 3 July 1977
43    RBM to Arthur Hooker, 3 July 1975
44    RBM to David Shapland, 20 March 1976
45    RBM to Macmillan, 27 September 1977
46    RBM to Christianna Brand, 6 February 1978
47    RBM to Brian Aldiss, 1 March 1972
48    RBM to Larkin, 1 September 1977
49    Ibid., 4 August 1975

'in the interims sploshing about in my own private waters.'[50] Having heard of a surgeon in Truro who specialised in Dupuytren's Contracture, he considered having a third operation on his hand: 'I miss composing, or just tinkering at the keyboard, very much.'[51] He once flew into a rage at his sister Elspeth when she mentioned some piano music she had recently heard, causing her to flee from the house in tears. It was the next day when Montgomery apologised before Elspeth discovered that this condition made it very difficult for him to play the piano.[52]

He was also trying to get out and about. In 1977 he and Ann planned to visit Oxford for a week in his Daimler (he now had a disabled driver's licence) so that Montgomery could do some research for one of his planned novels. In the same year, on the occasion that Ruth Rendell was admitted to membership, he took Brian Galpin and his wife to a Detection Club dinner at the Café Royal with this warning: 'Many people seek to ingratiate themselves with Club members by announcing that they never read detective stories; but I'm sure that neither you nor Nancy would be guilty of a dreadful solecism like that.'[53] What Montgomery did not know was that Nancy Galpin was an avid reader of detective fiction. After she had talked all evening with many of her favourite writers, it was Montgomery who wrote to Nancy to thank her for the impression she had made. She in turn had noted with satisfaction that many of the writers had sought Montgomery's company.[54] Also in 1977 Montgomery accepted an invitation to be the guest of honour at a Bristol Literary Dinner, taking Ann with him 'because she acts as my chauffeur, and also because I'm slightly crippled at the moment and need a little assistance with changing clothes'.[55] He was impressed with the dinner, having 'at least half a lamb on my plate to start with, with about 95% left congealing in the upshot'.[56]

Unfortunately, he had to pull out of other invitations because of his health, but in all cases he initially accepted them. This in itself marks a change in attitude as for many years he had been very reluctant even to consider public engagements. A typical response was one he gave to the University of Newcastle Literary Society in 1972: 'I'm so sorry [to decline the invitation], but nowadays I never do any lecturing. To be candid, I'm not very good at it; and in addition, I had a spell when it was taking up a great deal too much of my time, so that I was obliged, so to speak, to pull down the shutters.'[57] His variable health was an additional reason. One invitation he accepted initially was to lecture on a course close to his home for the Arvon Foundation with Julian Symons. H.R.F. Keating had been asked to stand by in case Montgomery's health prevented him from attending – which is what happened. When Keating met his students and explained the situation, one lady's face fell like a stone: 'But I only came because of Edmund Crispin,' she blurted out.[58] Writing to Symons when

---

50    Ibid., 25 April 1978
51    Ibid.
52    Elspeth Slaughter
53    RBM to Brian Galpin, 2 September 1977
54    Nancy Galpin
55    RBM to Gollancz, 9 May 1977
56    Ibid., 18 May 1977
57    RBM to University of Newcastle Literary Society, 6 November 1972
58    H.R.F. Keating to author, 28 August 1991

the course was first proposed, Montgomery told him of a new development: 'Great excitement. Have just completed my first book of poems. Of course, they're just doggerel, but there may be some publisher crazed enough to take them, so shall tout them around for a bit.'[59] He sent them to Larkin for comments ('don't hesitate to scribble obscene and insulting remarks in the margins. Larkin holographs are always valuable')[60] and made alterations 'in accordance with your suggestions'.[61]

Two invitations stand out because they show that Montgomery was determined to make the most of what time was left to him. They were both at his places of education. In 1977 he was set to attend a gaudy at St John's College, Oxford, but on being warned by the College Secretary that there was an industrial dispute at the Randolph Hotel, where he had been due to stay, Montgomery decided not to go for that and 'one or two personal reasons'.[62] An invitation that gave him great pleasure was to speak, with the Conservative politician Willie Whitelaw, at a Common Room dinner at Merchant Taylors' School in May 1978. 'My school days were happy ones,' he wrote, accepting with delight. He was particularly pleased at the possibility of renewing acquaintance with one or two of his old teachers who 'somehow managed to teach even a dullard like myself a great deal'. He was keen to look round the school again, 'revisiting the glimpses of the moon', and then 'certainly I'll make a post-prandial speech. I ought to warn you, however, that I am not good at the usual jollish sort, and should probably say a few words, quite seriously, about the status of crime and detective fiction in literature in general. All I can assure you of, here, is that I shall be reasonably brief. Thank you, in any case, for the honour you do me in asking me to make any speech at all.'[63] Not surprisingly, towards the end of April he cancelled for reasons which were not clear but must have been related to his health.

He had visited Peter Oldham in Wales and been open about his state of health: 'I'm only sorry that my "frozen shoulder", Dubytren's Contracture, twice broken left leg, lame feet and, above all, absurd stammer (still, I suppose that if one ingests a couple of bottles of whisky a day for ten years or so, one must expect inconvenient withdrawal symptoms) should have made me a rather cumbersome guest. [...] I only hope that my somewhat tetanic style of utterance didn't make me too much of a bore.'[64] Oldham told Montgomery that he had been 'stimulating company' and apologised for imposing on him a way of life 'so centred in pubs and alcohol as to be potentially rather tedious to an involuntary teetotaller (it would be unendurable to a voluntary one), but I thought you put up with it most nobly'.[65]

Kingsley Amis observed Montgomery's approach to alcohol at this time, and it was not all plain sailing. '[Montgomery] telephoned me recently sounding as pissed as a fart,' he wrote in May 1976. 'I didn't like to ask him if he was, because if, as I strongly suspect, he wasn't, I'd have to say in effect, "Oh, I see, it's just that

59    RBM to Julian Symons, 9 December 1977
60    RBM to Larkin, 8 August 1977
61    Ibid., 1 September 1977
62    RBM to St John's College, 24 June 1977
63    RBM to Merchant Taylors' Common Room: 6 March 1978
64    RBM to Peter Oldham, 24 September 1975
65    Peter Oldham to RBM, 28 September 1975

you still sound it after a year on the wagon," as I've noticed in ex-drunks before. They sometimes go on behaving pissed, too, as you know, which made me have to try pretty hard to sound enthusiastic when he mentioned coming up for a Thurs in the near future.'[66] Later in the year he reported that Montgomery had telephoned him 'sounding sober for the first time since long before his *crise*'.[67] During another conversation a few days later, Montgomery 'maundered on pathetically [...] "I'm tight" he announced unnecessarily after a time. Which means, surely, he hasn't long to go.'[68] A month later and there was more evidence for Amis' fears:

Did I tell you that Bruce was surely back, perhaps intermittently, on the booze? 1) He rings me about something else, I say Have you had a note about Bertorelli's lunch on the 16th? He says No, but I'll come, what was the date again? 2) I write about something else and say at the end Hope to see you on the 16th. 3) He writes and says What's all this about the 16th? Do you mean a Bert. Lunch? I'll assume you do if I don't hear. 4) He fails to show on the 16th, either pissed or thinking he'd asked me to let him know if there was a Bert. lunch. 5) Today in the S Times he reviews a book called Rogue Eagle (I know because I had a proof of it) under the title Rogue Male. Philip [Larkin] says he gets v. articulate letters from him.[69]

When Montgomery hit the drink again the following year, Amis gave Larkin his own explanation: 'Poor old Bruce: he must have been horrified to wake up in the nursing home, find he hadn't knocked himself off after all. I reckon it was realising The G's of the M was no good (I still haven't read it but I trust your judgement) that made him reach for the bottle, or rather vat, don't you?'[70] After one of these periods in hospital Montgomery described his stomach as 'looking as if he'd been strafed by a squadron of MIGs, what with all the plugs and stitches'.[71]

In his final years it seems that Montgomery was a man in torment. Under the influence of Ann – a regular at the Sunday Eucharist at Dartington Parish Church – he took an interest in religion. 'Bruce getting religion?' was Amis' bemused reaction.[72] Montgomery himself seemed barely less surprised: 'I am a Churchman', he told *The Armchair Detective*, 'not a very active one, but the fact that I am one at all in these days is so odd and unexpected that I thought it worth mentioning.'[73] He had never previously displayed any spiritual leanings or attended Church. At Oxford he had often talked a lot about religion whilst not being at all religious; he thought that Christianity was a very hard code to follow and not a soft option at all. Many people who embraced it did not fully understand this.[74] In his state of health it is not difficult to imagine Ann persuading him that religion might bring some comfort. She encouraged him to attend services at the parish church, and he took confirmation

---

66     Amis to Robert Conquest, 18 May 1976 [LKA]
67     Amis to Larkin, 11 October 1976 [LKA]
68     Amis to Robert Conquest, 28 October 1976 [LKA]
69     Ibid., 21 November 1976 [LKA]
70     Amis to Larkin, 28 August 1977 [LKA]
71     Robert Conquest to author, 7 January 1992
72     Amis to Larkin, 28 June 1974 [LKA]
73     *The Armchair Detective*, Spring 1979
74     Colin Strang

classes in his study with the Revd J.G. Bishop, Vicar of Dartington. Like most of Bishop's adult confirmands, Montgomery raised scarcely any questions, but it was clear that he was 'seriously trying to deepen his spiritual life'.[75] After a conditional baptism, held in private on 18 May 1974, Montgomery was confirmed by Bishop Wilfred Westall of Crediton at the main Sunday service. Very occasionally he would attend the midweek evening Eucharist with Ann, having to be helped by her to a seat in the chancel as he shuffled along in his carpet slippers. When he became more ill, the Reserved Sacrament was brought to him at home. At other times he made his confession.

Revd Bishop, who had a particular interest in dreams, noted that in the last months of his life Montgomery

> suffered a few nightmares of hell – and he [Montgomery] associated this without any prompting with Christ in hell suffering 'for three whole days'. He sensed evil as a demiurge attacking Christ: from Gethsemene on Christ too is quite isolated. He had been thinking things through and hoped to make his confession in a fortnight and then receive the Sacrament. Whether he did so is, at this stage, impossible to say [Rev. Bishop was abroad at the time of Montgomery's death].
>
> [...] [This] threw light on B.M's inner turmoil and desolation which I never really reached. My own feeling was that the Christian symbolism of the nightmare augured well for the future. (Once you see your inner conflict in terms of Christ's supreme conflict there is every hope that you too will win through to resurrection). At the time B.M. was a sick man, and I met him in his dressing gown in his study: but there were no intimations, which I registered, that death was near.[76]

It is very difficult to see in this man the author of such ebullient novels as *The Glimpses of the Moon*, so recently completed.

Larkin was due to visit towards the end of September 1978, but early in the month Montgomery was admitted to hospital as an emergency case, this time with another broken femur. Ann suggested Larkin should postpone his visit:

> The idiotic thing is that we haven't any idea how he did it, as he hasn't had a fall and can't recollect bashing it; I suppose his bones are just so brittle that some sort of injudicious heave or bang has done it. The docs say his heart is in good nick, and they are hoping to be able to operate to put a plate in his leg this coming weekend (the 9th), by which time his liver will have settled down as much as possible.[77]

Although Montgomery was keen to be taken to hospital in Plymouth because he knew the staff and it would be easier for Ann to visit, he had been admitted to Torbay at first because the ambulance crew were from there. He was soon transferred. Ann was disappointed at the timing of this latest setback:

> The maddening thing is that Bruce was in the middle of a successful burst of self-improvement when it happened – very little drink, a moderate amount of fresh air and

75    Revd J.G. Bishop to author, 20 September 1989
76    Ibid.
77    Ann Montgomery to Larkin, 7 September 1978

gentle exercise, and a bit or work, regular hair-cuts etc., so he's feeling enormously persecuted.[78]

Montgomery himself had also been quite cheerful. Despite suffering sufficiently to have three weeks of liver-function tests in March 1977, 'my medical consultant says I have remarkable powers of recovery', was his message to Josephine Bell.[79] He told Julian Symons that his health 'still fluctuates a bit […] but I think is showing a steady overall improvement'.[80] But he knew any recovery would not be easy. 'After two years of very uncertain health (including two and a half months in a filthy, Dickensian NHS ward) I seem – touch wood – to be really recovering at long last, though still a bit weak and shaky. But they warned me that convalescence would be a long business.'[81]

Any improvement had come too late, though. From the full-figured young man of some years previously, Montgomery had declined to a spare, stooping figure who needed assistance to walk more than a few paces. In the summer of 1975 Larkin visited Montgomery and wrote to Barbara Pym[82] with his impressions:

> An old friend of mine has been very ill this year: he drank himself into hospital about a year ago; I saw him this summer, and was dismayed at his general frailness, but in the autumn he had some sort of haemorrhage and was an emergency patient for weeks. He's home again now, but too weak still to write.[83]

The following year Montgomery confirmed this: 'The fact is that I'm still a semi-invalid, lacking stamina, and so have to do almost everything in small, fragmented doses, even washing and so forth in the morning. The bonelessness of the short-distance funner.'[84] Invited by Julian Symons to propose the health of the speaker at a Detection Club dinner in 1977, Montgomery was clearly very ill and a much reduced figure. His neck was so thin that it was not touching the collar of his shirt, and his voice was so weak that only those close to him could hear what he said.[85] Josephine Bell found him 'woefully changed' at the same dinner.[86] 'I talked to Bruce on the telephone […] recently', Larkin told Robert Conquest in July 1978, 'he certainly sounds very thick-tongued, but then he always has since the booze got him, and depressed, but no wonder. He's building a swimming pool, of all things, so he can't be entirely without hope.'[87]

The hope did not last. Montgomery did not have the strength to survive the stress of surgery and died in the early morning of 15 September. Ann wrote immediately to Larkin, so that he would receive the news before he saw it in the newspapers:

---

78   Ibid.
79   RBM to Josephine Bell, 23 March 1978
80   RBM to Julian Symons, 3 February 1978
81   Ibid., 27 March 1978
82   Barbara Pym (1913–1980), English novelist
83   Larkin to Barbara Pym, 29 December 1975 [SLPL]
84   RBM to Larkin, 22 March 1976
85   Julian Symons to author, 4 March 1992
86   Josephine Bell to Ann Montgomery, 18 September 1978
87   Larkin to Robert Conquest, 4 July 1978 [SLPL]

It was heart failure, not liver failure, in the end and all very peaceful & easy as far as one could tell. I am trying to say 'it was all for the best' because I really do believe he hadn't much more life in him anyway, and again as 'they' say, he was ready for it because so very tired.[88]

The funeral, conducted by Revd Anthony Cardale of Staverton, took place at the parish church in Dartington, with only a few people in attendance, and Montgomery was buried in the churchyard.

Larkin, writing to Kingsley Amis, gave his immediate view of the death of one of his oldest friends:

I wish I'd seen more of Bruce when he was still on top of things. Whatever one thought of his books, and his sense (sometimes) of what was funny or desirable, he was an original nobody else was the least like, don't you think? And he gave us a lot of laughs, as well as introducing us to things like Dickson Carr and At Swim Two Birds. I feel rather wretched about it, not least because I don't think I've ever seen a Times obit. for a really close friend before and it makes it all sort of realler bumhow comehow.[89]

To Robert Conquest he showed equal regret: 'Funeral today,' he wrote. 'All very sad, and makes the world seem very temporary.'[90] A few months later Larkin visited Ann and she gave him Montgomery's cigarette lighter, which (he told Amis) 'is a bit like inheriting Bix's[91] cornet or St Francis of Assisi's bird table'.[92] Four years later Larkin gave another view: 'I never really made up my mind about him [Montgomery], in the sense that he seemed jolly clever and funny even when giving *written* proofs to the contrary. Bloody fool to kill himself with drink.'[93]

Ann received a lot of letters of condolence after Montgomery's death. Between them they demonstrate the esteem in which her husband was held by his friends, despite the fact that as far as most of them were concerned he had been out of commission for a long time. 'Bruce was one of the best, a real dear', Brian Aldiss wrote, 'and I shall always owe him much for encouragement at the beginning of my career.'[94] Christianna Brand recalled Detection Club meetings where his speeches were always 'witty, able and entirely delightful [...] There has never been a soul to say one unkind word about him.'[95] Charles Cleall remembered 'an intensely private man, deeply reflective and sensitive'[96] whilst Eric Rogers led the tributes from the 'Carry On' brigade: 'Every time we made a new film, Peter [Rogers], Gerald [Thomas] and I always talked about him – let's face it, he was still basically part

---

88    Ann Montgomery to Larkin, 15 September 1978
89    Larkin to Amis, 19 September 1978 [SLPL]
90    Larkin to Robert Conquest, 21 September 1978 [in *Philip Larkin*, Motion, p. 474]
91    Bix Beiderbecke (1903–1931), jazz cornettist and one of Larkin's favourite players
92    Larkin to Amis, 11 April 1979 [in *Philip Larkin*, Motion, p. 474]
93    Larkin to Amis, 23 February 1982 [SLPL]
94    Brian Aldiss to Ann Montgomery, 18 September 1978
95    Christianna Brand to Ann Montgomery, 28 September 1978
96    Charles Cleall to Ann Montgomery, 20 September 1978

of the "team".'[97] Julian Symons emphasised another quality: 'Although we didn't agree about everything (an understatement!) I had the greatest liking and respect for Bruce personally, and for his integrity.'[98] John Whitely, literary editor of the *Sunday Times*, regretted that there would be no more 'of those dry, witty little notices, full of character', and praised Montgomery's 'sheer professionalism' in spending hours of 'valuable time wading through miles of second or third-rate thrillers without ever a groan of complaint'.[99] The author Clive Egleton was appreciative of Montgomery's work at the *Sunday Times*: 'Bruce acknowledged me at a time when most other reviewers didn't want to know.'[100] Philip Larkin was typically generous:

> Bruce was one of the few people – in fact I can't think of anyone else, that really brought new delights into my life, and was always likely to find something fresh and tell me about it. Then again, he was always so very encouraging in the early days, not uncritically, but still very generously. I've always owed him a great deal. […] Monica[101] always said Bruce was the nicest friend I had! Considering what she thinks of some of the others this may not sound a great compliment but I know she warmed to his kindness and good natured courtesy.[102]

Larkin also realised that Ann's 'selfless devotion' was important to Montgomery in his later years. Others picked up on this, too. 'I know something of the care you bestowed upon Bruce', neighbour Eric Partridge wrote, 'and can guess at the strain, the anxiety you've been experiencing all these years, and I profoundly admire you for it.'[103] Audrey Keir Cross, now Audrey Stock, felt the same: 'Your comfort will be the knowledge that you alone were able to sustain him.'[104]

A passage in John Whitely's letter paints a picture of the Bruce Montgomery we have seen at various times, that of the relaxed, unhurried man of music and letters. Whitely regretted that he would not ring again and 'hear his faraway drawl – he always gave the impression of lying in a hammock with bees buzzing faintly in the distance (in fact I really believed it to be so until I once telephoned him in January and got the same impression)'.[105]

---

97    Eric Rogers to Ann Montgomery, 20 September 1978
98    Julian Symons to Ann Montgomery, 16 September 1978
99    John Whitely to Ann Montgomery, 17 September 1978
100   Clive Egleton to Ann Montgomery, 29 September 1978
101   Monica Jones, one of Larkin's girlfriends
102   Larkin to Ann Montgomery, 18 September 1978
103   Eric Partridge to Ann Montgomery, 18 September 1978
104   Audrey Stock to Ann Montgomery, 9 October 1978
105   John Whitely to Ann Montgomery, 17 September 1978

# Postscript

The story of the final years of Bruce Montgomery's life is a sad one, but it must not be allowed to obscure the achievements of his earlier years. By the age of 40 Montgomery had made his mark in four fields: there was a considerable portfolio of his music in the catalogues of major publishers; he was a successful composer of film music; his reputation as an author of detective fiction was very high; and he had done much to raise the status of science fiction literature. Until this point he lived the life of a generous and amusing dilettante socialite. He knew many of the leading figures in his musical and literary worlds, and he enjoyed mixing with them. As a result of his work in films he had the money to lead this lifestyle.

From the early 1960s, though, everything changed. He became an increasingly morose semi-recluse. Illness was one cause. Montgomery may not have been able to do anything about the development of osteoporosis, but he fought little against his alcoholism. There was a history of the abuse of strong drink on his mother's side of the family, but there is no reason to suppose that Montgomery had any particular hereditary disposition towards this trait. Whatever, there is no doubt that a convivial social drinker became an alcoholic. His physical condition, and his attitude towards work, was not improved by the development of Dupuytren's Contracture.

In his *Memoirs*, Kingsley Amis gives his view that Montgomery had 'two genuine and precocious talents which both dried up quite quickly and completely when he was about thirty'.[1] Amis fails to mention the vast amount of film music Montgomery composed by the time he was about 40. But he has a point. It seems that Montgomery had only a limited capacity for any one type of work. In the 1940s he produced a good deal of concert music and novels. In the 1950s it was film scores.

Of much greater significance is a conversation Amis reports having with Montgomery: 'It must have been about then [sometime in the 1950s] that, never one to talk about himself, he said to me almost matter-of-factly, "I can see no point in anything any more and don't get any fun out of anything I do."'[2] Montgomery had always been, in sporting terms, a gentleman and amateur. In 1946 Godfrey Sampson told him that he had an active mind but an indolent nature. His working life had been spent indulging his passions for music and detective fiction. He was fortunate that composing music for films combined many of his interests and was well paid, but unfortunate for a man of his nature that these rewards demanded a thorough professionalism. Montgomery had not previously had to take his work too seriously, but he now found the going had become rather tougher. To support the lifestyle to which he had become accustomed he had to take on more film scores than he was capable of completing. Montgomery was now being judged in the hard professional world, with deadlines to match.

---

1    *Memoirs*, Amis, p. 76
2    Ibid.

There is another point. In both his music and his novels, and particularly in the former, Montgomery's style was nostalgic. This does not mean that there is no stamp of his own personality, but there is always the whiff of a bygone age. He was not an innovator, except perhaps for his contribution to the development of the Movement. This leads to the inescapable conclusion that unless he was willing to experiment, there was nowhere for his work to go. Perhaps his natural talents were incapable of development. In that case we may have to agree with Amis: perhaps he *had* said everything he was capable of. What is more likely, though, is that Montgomery simply was not prepared to make the effort necessary to develop his talents. He did not want responsibility and reacted badly to difficulties in his personal life, and it was the same with his work. During the 1950s he gave Jeni Turnbull the impression that he was a 'marvellous amateur' rather than a professional; life was a game to him. He always wanted to go off to dinner somewhere, to do something to amuse himself. He became a little bored if he had to do anything for too long.[3]

Which brings us back to the letter Montgomery wrote to Philip Larkin:

> What with Kingsley [Amis] becoming a prominent literary figure, and now you, I feel like an ageing hare overtaken by squads of implacable tortoises. There's still time, I suppose, for me to switch to some pursuit more highly esteemed than either film music or detective fiction – but should I be any good at it if I did? And what would become of the big cheques I so much enjoy receiving?[4]

Montgomery wanted to be taken seriously, and he wanted to be taken seriously as a composer of serious music. He saw detective fiction as a diversion and film music as a way of earning a very comfortable living. When the doors to the film world were firmly slammed in his face, Montgomery had to make a choice. He viewed contemporary trends in both music and detective fiction with little enthusiasm. As with his politics he was a firm reactionary. At least he made some attempt to continue with his novels, and the reception of *The Glimpses of the Moon* indicates that there was still an enthusiastic market for such books. But he made no attempt to test the musical water.

Bruce Montgomery was certainly an 'ageing hare'. His career shot explosively out of the traps: 'I like Bruce very much, really,' Kingsley Amis wrote in July 1946. 'I envy him his assurance, but he's much too successful for me.'[5] The lucrative rewards of film music dazzled him, but they also wore him out and were responsible for his increasing reliance on alcohol. His constitution, never robust, was undermined by nicotine and alcohol. His mind was clouded by a lack of sympathy with contemporary trends and doubts about the worth of his life's work. 'I find myself interested in this particular young man's music,' Norman Peterkin at OUP had written to Patrick Hadley in 1944.[6] Given his early achievements and the encouragement he received, the saddest aspect of his final years is that Montgomery felt it had all come to nothing.

---

3    Jeni Turnbull
4    RBM to Larkin, 19 June 1956
5    Amis to Larkin, 1 July 1946 [LKA]
6    Norman Peterkin to Patrick Hadley, 2 November 1944 (OUP Archive)

Robert Conquest, reacting to Kingsley Amis' rather negative chapter on Montgomery in his *Memoirs*, sums up the general view:

I think Kingsley's piece on him in the recent Memoirs was rather deplorable. All that stuff about was he a 'failure' etc, as if life was a competition to 'realize our full potential' etc with KA as referee. Bruce was not ambitious, and certainly had a tendency to procrastination or laziness, but what of that? like many other good men, he wasn't really interested in making his mark or whatever, and none the worse for that. As it was, he wrote what he wanted to and lived his sort of life.[7]

The final word should go to Montgomery himself, from the notes for his speech at a Bristol Literary Dinner in May 1977. It puts into perspective his own relaxed approach to life and the image others had of him.

The late Agatha Christie had one of her houses quite close to mine, and we would visit together whenever she was in my part of the world. Once, kindly invited by her to lunch, I drove up to the entrance to her drive to find that she was seeing other guests off on the local bus and was just setting off homewards on her fairly lengthy walk, when I stopped the car to ask if I could give her a lift. She seemed grateful for this and got into the car, which promptly refused to restart. 'They always do this when I'm in them,' she said, sadly. 'I can't think why it is.' However, the car did start eventually, and when we had gone a little way, Agatha said to me 'Edmund, you don't seem to have written anything for a long time.' I said 'No, Agatha, I haven't.' 'Why not?' I said, 'Well, frankly, I can't think of a plot.' And Agatha, turning to me with a mischievous twinkle in her eye said 'Oh, I shouldn't have thought that would have worried you'.[8]

---

7    Robert Conquest to author, 7 January 1992
8    Notes for talk, GB-Ob. MS. Eng. C. 3919

# Appendix 1

# Montgomery and Detective Fiction

Under the pseudonym 'Edmund Crispin', Montgomery carved for himself an assured and individual reputation in the world of detective fiction as both author and critic. He held very firm views on the form of the detective story and set these out most fully in the introduction to his anthology *Best Detective Stories* (Faber, 1959).

He begins by claiming that, like a rash, people are 'always pronouncing the doom of the detective story'. Mentioning Julian Symons, his future sparring partner, as particularly guilty of this, he rejects this notion, pointing to the continuing success of writers such as Agatha Christie, John Dickson Carr and Ellery Queen. This leads on to a favourite hobby-horse, the invasion of the detective genre by writers of thrillers:

> The drifting, opportunist variety of writer who tinkered with orthodox detective fiction at the time when it was the dominant crime-story form has now abandoned it in favour of the thriller, or the so-called psychological crime tale, or the *soi-disant* 'naturalistic' murder story, all of which are not only intellectually fashionable at the moment, but also (as it happens) very much easier to write. In short, the genre has got rid of its catchpenny hangers-on, and is all the better for that.

Although he does not object to writers presenting crime in a more naturalistic fashion should they wish to do so, he does not see why this should make orthodox detective fiction obsolete, as people such as Symons have suggested it might. These two different types of story are quite capable of existing separately, although Montgomery warns of the dangers of reading too much naturalistic stuff, a surfeit which might lead to people being 'unhealthily obsessed with an eccentric human activity which the majority of people never encounter at first hand during the whole of their lengthy progress from the cradle to the grave'. He showed his colours when writing to H.R.F. Keating, a fellow writer: 'I myself find that more and more of the stuff is gloomy, morbid, sadistic and politically alarmist – a far cry from the days when it was a relaxing entertainment. There are still a few honourable exceptions, of course, but as to much of it, I'd as soon relax with a scorpion or rattlesnake.'[1] He made even more of it when explaining to an American friend why film scores were only partly to blame for his failure to produce another novel: 'I'm also faintly discouraged because the "better" reviewers over here all seem to be highly contemptuous of orthodox detective fiction nowadays. None the less, I'm convinced that there's still a large public for that kind of thing, as opposed to the sub-Chandler thrillers, realistic stodge about police routine, or spineless pseudo-profound guesses at criminal psychology; so I shall push on regardless.'[2] Years later he had not changed

---

1    RBM to H.R.F. Keating, 16 May 1975
2    RBM to Anthony Boucher, 14 March 1960

his view: 'Even nowadays, crime writers are still regarded as inferior inhabitants of a sort of ghetto, while "mainstream" novelists, whom one has never heard of before and never will hear of again, get the awards and the glory.'[3]

Montgomery is firmly of the view that detective fiction is a game between the author and reader. This does not mean that the genre can be accused of 'treating serious matters frivolously': despite 'superficial appearances, it scarcely ever deals with serious matters at all'. The important thing is that it is about mystery, but since the human race finds misdeeds more mysterious than anything else, it is hardly surprising that crime becomes the central focus. Plot is the *raison d'être* of the detective story; attempts to overshadow plot by greater characterisation (something to which he pleads guilty himself) or greater plausibility fail to achieve their object. 'Orthodox detective fiction is in its essence artificial, contrived and fantastic. In trying to make it less artificial, contrived and fantastic you do not improve it: you simply cease to write it.' Montgomery accepts that a plot must be given 'an *appearance* of life', and cites Roy Vickers as an example of an author who manages to include a considerable degree of naturalism whilst never forgetting that 'the proper place for the cart is behind the horse'. Like all good writers of the genre, Vickers is 'predominantly an artificer'. Montgomery thinks it an error to imagine that readers are not capable of enjoying artifice: were that the case, 'we should be obliged to believe that some of the most considerable intellects of our time have been content in their leisure moments to resort repeatedly, for relaxation, to something that is intrinsically quite valueless.' He makes the case that this artifice need not necessarily be devoid of aesthetic pleasure for the reader and compares it to a bridge: we would rather have an unprepossessing but stable bridge than a handsome one that sags in the middle, yet it is possible to have a construction that is both handsome and stable. Detective fiction is '*par excellence* literary engineering'. It is quite possible to mix artifice with aesthetic pleasure, but the author must not neglect structural soundness: embellishments may delight the reader, but 'they will certainly excite derision rather than admiration if the framework which carries them is three-quarters submerged beneath the estuary'.

Montgomery accepts that a successful novel must have more than this rather bare machine, but acknowledges how difficult it is to achieve the right balance of plot and embellishment. Freeman Wills Croft is instanced as an author who adheres in a rather dull manner to the basic formula, whilst Montgomery cites himself as someone who perhaps offers too much over it. 'The ideal method, probably, is to make the non-plot interest of your story a secondary facet of plot, as for example by embodying a clue in a sentence which by way of bonus is an excellent piece of atmospheric or humorous writing in its own right.' The dangers here are that the plot may become absurdly complex whilst the narrative lacks spontaneity.

'What it boils down to is this: that the fully evolved detective story is technically by far the trickiest form of fiction humanity has so far devised. For we have come to demand of it not only a mystery with a plausible solution, but over and above that a mystery with a surprise solution; and over and above that, a mystery with a surprise solution which by rights we ought not to have been surprised at at all.' The

---

3     RBM to John Dickson Carr, 5 November 1976

case for detective fiction relies on people enjoying from time to time an example of 'virtuoso literary *contrivance*'. Montgomery concludes by claiming that the genre has beneficial social and ethical effects. Detective fiction is not morbid; as he has already suggested, crime is not the most important concern ('a fact which regularly gives the impercipients their cue for jibes about characterless corpses on library carpets'), and because the genre is so clearly, almost 'ostentatiously artificial, [...] no one above the level of a moron ever seriously imagines for a single moment that this is what crime in real life is like'. Montgomery had recently read a newspaper article which suggested that the lack of detective fiction in Soviet Russia may be due to its regime's grim reliance on proof of guilt, a reliance which highlights the fact that a convincing surprise ending is better, morally and artistically, than a random one. He knows that if he were to come home one evening to his (at this stage fictional) wife with red stains on his handkerchief, blonde hairs on his jacket and a whiff of another's perfume about him, as well as a perfectly good excuse for it all, he would be much more confident of his wife understanding if she were a reader of detective fiction than if she were not. In life the obvious is often the correct conclusion; detective fiction succeeds because it requires an explanation which, although not the obvious, has to be the true one. It succeeds because it teaches that the evidence has to be trusted above instinct and discrimination, and that jumping to conclusion is not a good way to conduct oneself.

The main characteristics of Montgomery's own writing have been observed in the discussions of his novels, but there are other aspects of his craft that should be considered. The first small problem to solve is that of his pen name. We have seen how he decided on it, but why did he use one? It was not for reasons of secrecy; writing to Livia Gollancz in 1974 he noted that Edmund Crispin 'was never meant to be much of a secret, and certainly isn't meant to be now',[4] and on the back of the green paperback Penguin editions of his novels in the late 1950s his real identity was prominently displayed. Other writers have used pen names for differing reasons, such as John Dickson Carr with his use of the rather transparent Carter Dickson when employing Sir Henry Merrivale rather than Gideon Fell as his detective, or by Ruth Rendell when writing novels of a different kind as Barbara Vine. It seems that the only reason for Montgomery's alias is that he intended keeping his real name for the work as a composer which he had already embarked on before he wrote *The Case of the Gilded Fly*. Perhaps he was influenced in reverse fashion by the composer Peter Warlock who kept his real name, Philip Heseltine, for his work as a critic and musicologist. Montgomery's music shows at times a debt to Warlock, and his persistence in setting texts from the sixteenth and early seventeenth centuries in his vocal music would have gone down well with the arch-Elizabethan Warlock.

We have also seen how Montgomery decided on the name of his detective, but why did he decide on a professor of English Language and Literature? As his views on the genre have made clear, Montgomery was temperamentally in tune with the writers of the so-called Golden Age of Detective Fiction which occurred between the two World Wars. The leading authors of this period often had amateur detectives, following on from the seminal Sherlock Holmes: one has only to think of

---

4    RBM to Livia Gollancz, 28 April 1974

Agatha Christie's Miss Marple, Dorothy L. Sayers' Lord Peter Wimsey or Margery Allingham's Albert Campion to see that it was a logical step for Montgomery to create Fen. The detectives mentioned above seem to be at their leisure to detect whenever they please whereas Fen, at least notionally, has an important job to attend to, not that he ever lets this get in his way. He gives as good an impression of being a dilettante as the rest of them, something he shares with his creator. Fen's status in society is perhaps Montgomery's gesture to the aristocratic blood of detectives such as Wimsey, Campion and Ngaio Marsh's Roderick Alleyn. Whereas some of the Golden Age detectives have regular assistants (Campion's Lugg, for instance, Wimsey's Bunter, Poirot's Captain Hastings or Nero Wolfe's Archie Goodwin), Fen plucks one or more out of the cast Montgomery assembles for each novel. Other amateur detectives have direct links to an officer in the police force, and Fen stays in the tradition by sparring with Sir Richard Freeman, Chief Constable of Oxford (it is no coincidence that he is a knight of the realm). He is likely to have chosen to make his detective a professor because the academic world was about the only one with which he was familiar at the time he wrote his first novel.

Like many of the detectives above, Fen is an idiosyncratic character. His origins in Montgomery's tutor at Oxford have been mentioned, but in time Montgomery began to admit that some of his own characteristics were added to the mix. 'I have only lately realised this in my own case', he told *Harpers Bazaar* in 1953, 'but I have long observed in all the other detective novelists I have ever known that they have some resemblance to their detectives, not necessarily in sex or physique or habits or occupation, but in temperament or aspiration.'[5] Like Montgomery, Fen does not come across as a particularly ambitious person. Like Montgomery, Fen is always happy to treat his audience as intellectual equals. Their main shared traits, however, are mental restlessness and an easy tendency to boredom. There is one notable difference: Montgomery's gentle charm would rarely permit him to be as acerbic and insulting as his detective frequently is.

If setting *The Case of the Gilded Fly* in Oxford was an obvious choice for Montgomery since he was still an undergraduate there when he wrote it, by doing so he was contributing to a noble tradition. Novels such as *An Oxford Tragedy* by J.C. Masterman (1933), *Gaudy Night* by Sayers (1935) and Michael Innes' first detective story *Death at the President's Lodging* (1936) all take place in the city and university. But whereas the college setting is central to these stories, Montgomery's tale makes relatively little use of this enclosed world. He makes even less use of it in the other two novels he set in Oxford, *The Moving Toyshop* and *Swan Song*. Although there is much in Montgomery's later life to suggest that he relished his time in the city and was reluctant to abandon it, at least initially, there is no great justification for attempting to label him an 'Oxford' author, and certainly not in a major way. Later authors such as Colin Dexter, the success of whose novels featuring Inspector Morse has been fuelled by highly successful television adaptations, and Veronica Stallwood use the city as a backdrop to almost all of their work. Instead, Montgomery wrote about milieux of which he had experience, which is why we find ourselves embroiled in the jealousies of repertory and opera companies, schools, colleges, cathedrals and

---

5     *Harpers Bazaar*, December 1953

the film world. There is a sense of a series in Montgomery's novels: previous cases are mentioned, and some characters reappear (such as the decaying don Wilkes, Sir Richard Freeman and Inspector Humbleby).

Montgomery's early novels led some people to compare him with Michael Innes. When Charles Monteith, who became Montgomery's editor at Faber, was introduced to him for the first time at a party at All Souls, Oxford, the first thing he said was 'My God, you're not J.I.M. Stewart!' [Michael Innes' real name] because he had always assumed from their similarity of style that Crispin and Innes were one and the same.[6] In *Bloody Murder*, his important study of crime fiction, Julian Symons puts both Innes and Montgomery in a group of authors which he calls the *farceurs*. Others in the group include Philip MacDonald, A.A. Milne and Ronald Knox. When Innes' first novels were published, critics were quick to hail a new development in the detective story, but, as Symons makes clear, J.C. Masterman had already produced 'very much this kind of "don's delight" book, marked by the same sort of urbanity'.[7] His *An Oxford Tragedy* is certainly urbane: poets such as Pope and Swinburne are quoted, and there are references which make it clear that we are involved in a game with the author. 'Anyone less like the detective of fiction it would be impossible to imagine'[8] is the description of Inspector Cotter. 'You seem to have begun very early to conceal information from the police', Brendel (Masterman's amateur sleuth) tells a suspect at another point, 'that's quite according to the tradition of detective fiction.'[9] Despite these occasional flippancies, though, the tone of Masterman's novel is overwhelmingly sober and a far cry from the work of Innes and Montgomery.

According to Symons, the *farceurs* are writers 'for whom the business of fictional murder was endlessly amusing', and they often demonstrate a carelessness in plotting. Ronald Knox never allowed 'the faintest breath of seriousness to disturb the desperate facetiousness of his style'. Philip MacDonald is cited as one of those authors 'who finds it easy to think of an idea, but hardly ever manage to carry through a fully coherent plot';[10] *Farceurs* also never worry excessively about improbabilities and are not too concerned about hiding the identity of their villain. Montgomery meets all these criteria.

Innes and Montgomery certainly share a characteristic flippancy, even if Appleby (Innes' detective) is a more sober character than Fen. In *Death in the President's Lodging* Innes follows Masterman, and foreshadows Montgomery, in his references to fiction: 'there was a contrivance in a literary tradition deriving from all the progeny of Sherlock Holmes'.[11] And later: 'It was a trick out of fiction rather than out of current burglarious practice.'[12] The urbanity is provided in part in the same novel by the regular allusions to authors including Max Beerbohm, Edgar Allan Poe, Wilkie Collins, Aristotle, Plato and Dickens. Both detectives are happy to trade literary and

---

6    Charles Monteith
7    *Bloody Murder*, Julian Symons, Chapter 9
8    *An Oxford Tragedy*, J.C. Masterman, Chapter 6
9    Ibid., Chapter 8
10   *Bloody Murder*, Julian Symons, Chapter 8
11   *Death in the President's Lodging*, Michael Innes, Chapter 2
12   Ibid., Chapter 5

artistic allusions, with Appleby helped in his knowledge of the art world by being married to a sculptor. In general, Innes draws attention to his learned style in a more ostentatious way than Montgomery. Both authors give characters faintly ridiculous names, or worse; Montgomery often saddles his minor characters with the names of his friends. In *The Daffodil Affair* Inspector Appleby refers to Innes, his creator, by name; in one or two of Montgomery's novels Gervase Fen refers to Crispin, in *The Moving Toyshop* going even further and mentioning his publisher, Gollancz. The erudite tone of both authors is shown in their eagerness to exploit the vocabulary of their readers.

These similarities may be characteristic of their work, but there are also one or two striking differences between the two authors. Innes tends to be rather more expansive than Montgomery, developing his plots and characters on a larger canvas. Because of this, there is a greater complexity to his novels and a more calculating tone. Montgomery often has a more memorable cast of characters and can get sidetracked by them. As with his music, Montgomery knew that it was better for him to keep to smaller structures and control his material.

Montgomery sometimes falls into the carelessness of plotting that marks out the *farceurs*, although his plots are always an adequate peg for his story to hang on. He was aware of this himself: he knew that *Holy Disorders* had 'a rather weak plot',[13] and 'the murder method seems to me far-fetched'[14] in *Swan Song*. Although *Love Lies Bleeding* was one of his favourites, Montgomery still thought that 'the plot might perhaps have been a little better-handled'.[15] Weaned on John Dickson Carr, Montgomery's early novels continue that author's devotion to the locked-room mystery before the tendency gradually becomes less important. A similar fate befalls the Carr-like tinges of the supernatural.

We know Montgomery's view that crime fiction should be treated as a diversion, so it is not entirely surprising that he did not have a particularly high opinion of his work in this field despite the success it achieved and has retained with enthusiasts of the genre. 'Yes, funny the way the old Toyshop lingers on, isn't it?' he wrote to Larkin in 1969. 'I no longer see the attraction, myself, and can only suppose that some of the gusto with which I wrote it has survived the years somehow or other.'[16] Other people think more highly of his civilised and literate novels.

---

13   RBM to Mr Pettersson, June 1975
14   Ibid.
15   Ibid.
16   RBM to Larkin, 16 August 1969

# Appendix 2

# Montgomery and Film Music

Having agreed to compose the score for a film, the first information Montgomery received was usually a copy of the screenplay. It is likely that he made only a cursory study of it, sufficient to gain just an idea of what type of film he was involved with. This gave him time during the period the film was shot to think about the title music. This section of the score was very important; it would, in Gerald Thomas' words, 'bang the drum' for the picture.[1] From the composer's point of view, it might also be the one section of the score in which he could develop a musical idea at any length. It might also provide some musical material that could be used in later sections.

The first time Montgomery went up to the studios was normally after the film had been shot. He saw the rough cut and went away to think about the sort of music he wanted. This was followed by a viewing of the fine cut with the director. At this point a decision would be made about exactly which sections of the film required music. These details were passed to the cutting room which measured and numbered the music sections, thus producing very exact timings. Montgomery took these music measurement sheets away with him, and the next time he was seen at the studios was usually when he arrived for the recording sessions. For the comedy films in which Montgomery mostly specialised, these measurement sheets were very detailed, as we have seen in connection with *Watch Your Stern* (1960). Within each section timings, exact to a third of a second, were given for anything in the action which required pointing and bringing out in the music. Typically, Montgomery would have about three weeks to compose a score. From those of his mature scores which remain in manuscript, it seems that he used a consistent method to compose. The sections were identified by their position within each reel of film. Hence they were numbered 1M1, 1M2, 1M3 and so on within the first reel, and 2M1, 2M2, 2M3 in the same fashion in the second. Each section of the score is written in pencil on a separate collation of 24 stave paper which had previously been ruled out with four bars to a page. The paper is set out for full orchestra. Instruments not used in a particular section are left with blank staves. Full bar rests are omitted. With rare exceptions, Montgomery puts the total timing at the end of each section. Sometimes he puts the culminative timing of the section above each bar, particularly when there are specific actions to point. Occasionally details of the action the music is accompanying are also noted above each bar. As the sections were completed, they were posted to Montgomery's copyist for the orchestral parts to be written out. It was not unknown for his mother to rush to the station towards evening to make sure that the day's work was on the last train to London.[2]

---

1    Gerald Thomas
2    Sheila Rossiter

Starting with *The Duke Wore Jeans* in 1958, Montgomery conducted all his scores. He used the Sinfonia of London, an orchestra formed from top players in London orchestras to specialise in film work. Recording sessions generally took only one or two days. When the film was eventually completed, the editing staff of the production company compiled a music cue sheet. This detailed all the music used for each section of the picture, giving the action the music accompanied, the timings, composer, arranger and publisher. It was approved by the producer of the film and passed to the Performing Right Society (PRS) to write up its own cue sheet so that fees were paid to the correct persons. Generally speaking, the PRS cue sheet is not as detailed as the one produced by the production company.

Thus, to account for Montgomery's film scores there are four possible sources: the music measurement sheets, the autograph scores, the film soundtrack itself, and the music cue sheets, either or both of those produced by the production company and the PRS. It is rare for all four of these sources to survive. Many film production companies have changed ownership or gone out of business since the 1950s, and their archives are often incomplete or lost.

Music measurement sheets for fifteen of Montgomery's films are in the collection of his papers at the Bodleian Library. They are not always complete and are often considerably corrected carbon copies. Montgomery's autograph scores survive either in part or in their entirety for less than half of his films. It was a clause in the standard contract that the score remained the copyright property of, and was retained by, the production company. This was something that in time Montgomery began to question. In 1960, when asked to score *Doctor in Love*, he refused to sign the contract as long as a clause remained which permitted Rank to make further use of the score. His view was that large stocks of such music might deprive him and other composers of future employment: 'In this connection I ought perhaps to add that on several occasions in the past the Rank Organisation has applied to me to re-use, without further payment or obligation, music covered by a clause amended as above; and that I have never hesitated to give such permission – nor am I likely to do so in this particular case.'[3] Despite Rank's threat of not employing him if he persisted, Montgomery asked for the matter to be referred to a higher authority. In the end the clause was removed. Montgomery managed to persuade other companies to amend similar clauses which meant that the scores remained his property and were returned to him after the recording sessions. Those scores which the film companies retained have, it seems, been lost. With the exception of one or two of the short films with which he opened his film career, the scores which remain in the Bodleian collection are all from the later years of the 1950s. In only one instance (*Too Young to Love*, 1959) does a set of orchestral parts survive.

It is not always the case that copies of the actual film are available. Some of the better known pictures, notably those in the *Doctor* and *Carry On* series, are frequently on television. The British Film Institute has viewing copies of three of the remaining films; it has preservation copies, which cannot be viewed at present, of a further eleven; it has no copies of a further seven; it has no record at all of three films. The music cue sheets have fared rather better. The Bodleian collection has the

---

3      RBM to Hugh Parton (Rank), 12 February 1960

detailed film company cue sheets for about half of the films. Fortunately the PRS has its own cue sheets for all but two of Montgomery's films. One of these two films (*Scottish Highlands*, 1952) has an unusual combination of sources. The autograph score survives as do the music measurement sheets, but the British Film Institute has no record of the film and holds no cue sheet.[4]

The existence of these various documents should make it relatively straightforward to identify the music Montgomery composed for each film. Alas, for a variety of reasons this is rarely the case. *The Truth About Women* (1957) is a rare example of a film for which we know he completed all the score. At the recording session Montgomery said to Douglas Gamley, with wide-open eyes: 'You know, Dougie, I finished this one!'[5] The existence of a section on the music measurement sheets for a particular film does not mean that music was actually composed for that section. Subsequent conversations between composer and director occasionally altered a decision made in the original discussion. The existence of a section in Montgomery's autograph score does not mean that the music was actually used in the film. In *Watch Your Stern*, for instance, section 5M1 (at 1 minute 40 seconds a substantial length) remains in manuscript but does not appear on the soundtrack. It is impossible in a case like this to identify the point at which the decision was made to leave this section out of the finished film. It may have been recorded and then abandoned, or the decision not to use it may have been taken before the recording session took place. On reflection, the composer and director may have felt that the action required no background music, or they may have felt that the music composed was not appropriate. Peter Rogers has said that all composed music was recorded for his films. If a section was found to conflict too much with dialogue or action, the volume might be taken down – or it might be left out completely. This happened at the dubbing stage.[6] An instance which appears to confirm this observation occurs in section 10M4A of *Carry On Teacher*. In the autograph this section lasts for 1 minute exactly and builds up to a rousing climax, using material previously heard at the end of the title music to *Carry On Sergeant*. On the soundtrack the section is faded out after 45 seconds.

Even in those rare cases where it appears that the entire autograph score has survived, the lack of a section does not mean that music was not added at the last moment. At the end of the titles in *Watch Your Stern*, a short burst on muted trumpets was taken from a later section of the score. This passage appears on neither the measurement sheets nor the cue sheet. As far as the autograph scores are concerned, the lack of 2M2 where 2M1 and 2M3 survive may mean one of various possibilities: the section was never composed, another composer wrote it, or it has been lost.

It is not always possible to determine from watching those films that can be viewed which music was composed by Montgomery. As indicated earlier, when he got behind with a score he would call in help. The composers who assisted were very skilled at falling in with Montgomery's style. For *Please Turn Over* (1959), Montgomery composed a theme for the titles but asked Eric Rogers to arrange

---

4    A copy has since been located in the archives of British Transport Films
5    Douglas Gamley
6    Peter Rogers

it in a dance style to last for 1 minute 20 seconds. Montgomery had to take the section over for the remaining 12 seconds. The autograph (1M1) shows this clearly. The join between the work of the two composers is seamless. Despite his habit of asking Rogers to arrange such sections, Montgomery could write in a popular style himself (the titles to *Watch Your Stern* show this ability). Without the evidence of the autograph, it would be impossible to tell the compositional history of this particular section. Peter Rogers has suggested that it cannot be assumed Montgomery composed a section merely because it exists in autograph: he could have written out what others had composed for him.[7] This is an unlikely notion. Montgomery asked other composers for help when he was short of time, and under these circumstances it is inconceivable that he would be prepared to copy the scores merely to provide a deception. Any such scores by others would have to be sent to Montgomery, who would need to write them out before posting them to his copyist for the parts to be completed. A pressing schedule would not permit this, and it makes a nonsense of the original reason for the assistance of another composer.

It should be the case that the music cue sheet is the most reliable source for identifying which music in each film Montgomery did or did not compose. It was the last document to be produced after the film was finished. It contained details which had important legal and financial implications for the composer and publisher. Yet, instances of inaccuracies cast doubt upon the veracity of these documents, even in the case of the detailed sheets produced by the film company. Mention has been made above of the added passage at the end of the titles for *Watch Your Stern* which does not appear on the cue sheet. In April 1959, Montgomery asked Eric Rogers to arrange the title music for *Carry On Sergeant* for *Carry On Teacher*.[8] Subsequently this arrangement was used for the titles of both *Carry On Constable* and *Carry On Regardless*. Rogers receives no credit on the cue sheet. On his own copy of the cue sheet for *Checkpoint* (1956), Montgomery has written 'Arr. by Ken Jones 3.23'. This refers to the title music, but is not indicated on the official cue sheet. Sometimes details were left out for contractual reasons. Douglas Gamley assisted Montgomery on the score for *Cartouche* (1955), yet receives no credit at all on the cue sheet. A letter through Montgomery's agents notes that all the rights for the music in the film by Gamley pass to Montgomery.[9] A similar thing happened on Montgomery's last film, *The Brides of Fu Manchu* (1966). Shortly after completing the score Montgomery sent Gamley a note thanking him for his help and enclosing a cheque,[10] yet no mention of Gamley is made on the cue sheet. These difficulties are compounded by the fact that it was general practice to list only the contracted composer on the screen film credits.

*The Brides of Fu Manchu* is an excellent example of the problems encountered in the attempt to account for which music Montgomery actually composed. Film and cue sheet, but no score, survive. Given the knowledge that Gamley assisted Montgomery with the score, and given the cue sheet, it ought to be possible to detail the music

---

7      Ibid.

8      RBM to Eric Rogers, 11 April 1959

9      RBM to AP Watt, 7 November 1955

10     RBM to Douglas Gamley, 28 July 1966

exactly. But given also Gamley's exclusion from the cue sheet and his ability to copy Montgomery's style, it is impossible to draw a satisfactory conclusion. Perhaps Gamley merely arranged some of the score. Music measurement sheets, autograph score, film and cue sheet all survive for *Watch Your Stern*, but even this happy state of affairs leads to some discrepancies, particularly over timings. A comparison of score and cue sheet, for example, shows that section 2M4 in Montgomery's autograph is timed at 42⅓ seconds, whereas on the cue sheet the same section is listed at 38 seconds. There are short sections listed on the cue sheet in Reel 7 which do not survive in manuscript. As the extant autograph sections are numbered consecutively, this suggests that these sections were added at the last moment.

Discrepancies over timing can be explained in various ways. As with the extra passage added on to the titles (1M1) of *Watch Your Stern*, it could be that the decision was taken to continue the composed section with an extract from another section to cover action which had not previously been thought to require music. If it was a section without specific pointing, the music might have been played slightly slower or faster than intended. If, though, as Douglas Gamley recalls about *Carry On Cruising*, Montgomery was capable of both scoring and conducting a section in which handstands are pointed split-seconds apart, this seems a less likely answer. The question of the accuracy of timings must also be raised. With the exception of timings being rounded up or down to the nearest second for the cue sheet, the correlation between surviving autographs and cue sheets seems generally accurate. On this evidence it is fair to assume that sections whose timings have been altered between composition and cue sheet were altered for genuine reasons at the last moment.

Further questions are raised by the sources for *Sins of the Father* (1958). The cue sheet produced by the production company (Emmet Dalton Productions in Ireland) has not survived, and the sheet held by the Performing Right Society lists sections only by time and not by action. However, the music measurement sheets are extant. From these it is possible to make up a more detailed cue sheet, along the lines of the one that would have been produced by the production company. The timings asked for on the music measurement sheets match exactly with the timings given on the PRS sheet. The strange thing here, though, is that the timings on Montgomery's autograph score do not always agree with these documents. It is possible that Montgomery might have needed to change certain timings, but if he did why does the cue sheet show the timings which were originally agreed? Something is wrong here if we believe that the progression was measurement sheets, score, recording, cue sheet. Could it be that the production company did not check the finished film properly and merely assumed the timings were the same as originally measured? This possibility raises doubts about cue sheets for other films for which we do not have so much detail. In the particular instance of *Sins of the Father*, this question cannot be answered conclusively as neither the British nor Irish Film Institutes have a copy of the picture.

There is a further category of work which needs discussing. At least three films for which Montgomery composed either all or some of the music were never completed or released. In 1956 he wrote at least eleven sections for a television film called *The*

*City – Cairo*. The music was recorded on 26 March (a letter in 1975 confirms this),[11] yet it appears that the film was not completed. It was certainly never shown. In 1958 Montgomery wrote to Philip Martell, who had conducted the score, asking ('as the original picture came to grief')[12] if the score could be returned to him so that he could use it for other things. In this case the eleven sections survive in manuscript. As the section numbered M16 is the last, there are five sections missing. In Montgomery's pocket book both Gamley and Ken Jones are listed as being paid 'arrangers' fees'. It may be that they were responsible between them for all the missing sections, yet the possibility remains that some may have been lost.

Montgomery's withdrawal from the score for *Follow That Horse* in early 1960 has already been mentioned – but by then he had already composed an unknown number of sections for the film. After he pulled out, the film company let him know that it was not sure whether it would make use of the music he had written.[13] In the end Stanley Black was engaged to compose the score and Montgomery's music was not used. The autographs have not survived. In 1958 he also composed a very small amount of music for an aborted film called *Anna*, including a pastiche of Bach and Scarlatti. He told the company: 'I'm now going to write the concertina piece for the opening of the picture', but was reluctant to do more because the script 'is still in such a fluid and uncertain condition'.[14] Within three weeks the film had been cancelled.

Given the pressure of time under which these scores were composed and recorded, it would be unrealistic to expect changes not to be made at some stage. This observation does nothing to help as accurate a conclusion as possible to be drawn as to what music Montgomery actually composed for each film. Conclusions can be drawn, but the circumstances vary from film to film. All four main sources, five if one includes correspondence, provide vital information. Although we cannot entirely trust any particular source, the cue sheets are likely to be the most accurate guide to Montgomery's film music.

One last point: although Montgomery often attended the premieres of films for which he had composed the score, it seems that he did not always see the finished version for some years. One evening in the early 1970s Montgomery telephoned Desmond Bagley and his wife to ask, if they were intending to watch a particular thriller on the television,[15] whether he could come and watch it with them. It was one of his scores that he had never heard in its completed version. 'I've never sat through a movie with the composer sitting next to me and it was an odd experience,' wrote Joan Bagley. 'We saw the entire film in its musical context, accompanied by a running commentary. How I wish we'd taped it!'[16]

---

11    RBM to Jack Docherty, 28 December 1975
12    RBM to Philip Martell, 3 October 1958
13    Cavalcade Films to RBM, 4 January 1960
14    RBM to David Deutsch, 23 February 1958
15    Joan Bagley cannot recall the name of the film
16    Joan Bagley to author, 20 June 1990

# Appendix 3

# List of Montgomery's Novels and Other Books

All books were published in London under the pseudonym 'Edmund Crispin'.

As author:

1944    THE CASE OF THE GILDED FLY (Gollancz)

1945    HOLY DISORDERS (Gollancz)

1946    THE MOVING TOYSHOP (Gollancz)

1947    SWAN SONG (Gollancz)

1948    LOVE LIES BLEEDING (Gollancz)

1948    BURIED FOR PLEASURE (Gollancz)

1950    FREQUENT HEARSES (Gollancz)

1951    THE LONG DIVORCE (Gollancz)

1953    BEWARE OF THE TRAINS (Gollancz)
        Beware of the Trains; Humbleby Agonistes; The Drowning of Edgar Foley; Lacrimae Rerum; Within the Gates; Abhorrèd Shears; The Little Room; Express Delivery; A Pot of Paint; The Quick Brown Fox; Black for a Funeral; The Name on the Window; The Golden Mean; Otherwhere; The Evidence for the Crown; Deadlock

1977    THE GLIMPSES OF THE MOON (Gollancz)

1979    FEN COUNTRY (Gollancz)
        Who Killed Baker?; Death and Aunt Fancy; The Hunchback Cat; The Lion's Tooth; Gladstone's Candlestick; The Man Who Lost His Head; The Two Sisters; Outrage in Stepney; A Country to Sell; A Case in Camera; Blood Sport; The Pencil; Windhover Cottage; The House by the River; After Evensong; Death Behind Bars; We Know You're Busy Writing, But We Thought You Wouldn't Mind If We Just Dropped in for a Minute; Cash on Delivery; Shot in the Dark; The Mischief Done; Merry-Go-Round; Occupational Risk; Dog in the Night-Time; Man Overboard; The Undraped Torso; Wolf!

As editor:

| | |
|---|---|
| 1955 | BEST SF (Faber and Faber) |
| 1956 | BEST SF 2 (Faber and Faber) |
| 1958 | BEST SF 3 (Faber and Faber) |
| 1959 | BEST DETECTIVE STORIES (Faber and Faber) |
| 1961 | BEST SF 4 (Faber and Faber) |
| 1962 | BEST TALES OF TERROR (Faber and Faber) |
| 1963 | BEST SF 5 (Faber and Faber) |
| 1964 | BEST DETECTIVE STORIES 2 (Faber and Faber) |
| 1965 | BEST TALES OF TERROR 2 (Faber and Faber) |
| 1966 | BEST SF 6 (Faber and Faber) |
| 1968 | THE STARS & UNDER: A SELECTION OF SF (Faber and Faber) |
| 1968 | BEST SF STORIES OF C.M. KORNBLUTH (Faber and Faber) |
| 1971 | BEST SF 7 (Faber and Faber) |
| 1973 | BEST MURDER STORIES 2 (Faber and Faber) |
| 1974 | OUTWARDS FROM EARTH: A SELECTION OF SF (Faber and Faber) |

# Appendix 4

# List of Montgomery's Compositions

Complete works (with associated incomplete works) are listed here. A further 38 projects which failed to see the light of day for one reason or another are listed in David M.T. Whittle, 'Bruce Montgomery (1921–1978): a biography with a catalogue of the musical works' (unpublished PhD thesis, University of Nottingham, 1998).

Unless otherwise stated, autographs of unpublished concert works can be found in the collection of Montgomery's papers in the Bodleian Library, Oxford.

Where appropriate, the date given for a composition is that of completion.

Opus numbers are Montgomery's own.

For films, cast members are selected, not comprehensive. When the date of release cannot be confirmed, the date of the censors' classification is given.

## Abbreviations

| | | | |
|---|---|---|---|
| A | alto | ob | oboe |
| B | bass | org | organ |
| bd | bass drum | perc | percussion |
| bn | bassoon | pf | pianoforte |
| cel | celesta | pic | piccolo |
| cl | clarinet | S | soprano |
| cnt | cornet | sax | saxophone |
| cym | cymbal | sd | side drum |
| db | double bass | str | strings |
| dbn | double bassoon | T | tenor |
| elec gui | electric guitar | tamb | tambourine |
| eng hn | english horn | timp | timpani |
| euph | euphonium | tpt | trumpet |
| fl | flute | trbn | trombone |
| glock | glockenspiel | tri | triangle |
| gtr | guitar | va | viola |
| hn | horn | vc | violoncello |
| hpd | harpsichord | vn | violin |
| kbd | keyboard | vib | vibraphone |
| mand | mandolin | xyl | xylophone |
| mar | marimba | | |

1     CHESHAM BOIS
Hymn tune for SATB
Date and place of composition: Chesham Bois, Bucks, 1934
Publication: Privately printed in 1934
First performance: Amersham Free Church, date uncertain, but probably 1934

2     THE SANDS OF DEE
Chorus and Orchestra
Date of composition: 1935/6
This work is referred to as 'fortunately lost' in Montgomery's own catalogue

3     MINIATURE SUITE
Piano
Movements: Prelude, Scherzino, Pastorale
Dedication: For Miss E. M. Scandrett
Date of composition: 1937

4     TO HELEN
Violoncello and piano
Date of composition: 31 July 1937

5     NURSE'S DANCE
Piano
Date of composition: 1937

6     RONDO RHAPSODY
Cor anglais, horn, harp and string quartet
Dedication: To H. G. R.
Date and place of composition: April 1938, Paris

7     A SONG FOR CHRISTMAS
Voice and piano
Dedication: For Elspeth and Francis
Date and place of composition: April 1938, Amersham

8     PILGRIMAGE
Part song for SATB and piano or organ
Text: Sir Walter Raleigh (?1554–1618)
Dedication: To My Mother
Date and place of composition: October 1938, Amersham

9     SUMMER NOCTURNE
Two pianos (four hands)
Date and place of composition: March 1939, Amersham

10    UNTO THEE WILL I LIFT UP MINE EYES
Motet for SATB
Text: from Psalm 123
Dedication: To Muriel Pavlow
Date of composition: 1939

11    JESU, THAT DOST IN MARY DWELL
SATB and organ
Text: Gerard Manley Hopkins (1844–1889)
Dedication: To Ann and Dennis Mallett
Date and place of composition: August 1940, Brixham

12    AS THE HART PANTETH
Anthem for SATB and organ
Text: from Psalm 42
Dedication: To Muriel Pavlow
Date and place of composition: September 1940, Brixham

13    DANCE
Piano
Dedication: To Peter Oldham
Date and place of composition: December 1940, Oxford and Brixham

14    STUDY IN F SHARP MINOR (for the right hand)
Piano
Dedication: To Peter Oldham
Date and place of composition: December 1940, Brixham

15    FIVE PIECES FOR STRING QUARTET
String quartet
Movements: Prelude, Reverie, Scherzo, Pastorale, Rondo
Dedication: To Godfrey Sampson
Date and place of composition: April 1941, Brixham

16    SAILOR'S LEAVE
Ballet
Date of composition: 1941
Nothing more of known of this work, and the autograph is lost

17    TWO SKETCHES FOR PIANO, Op. 1 No. 4
Piano
Dedication: To Diana Gollancz
Date and place of composition: July 1941, Brixham
Publication: Oxford University Press, September 1944

18      MAGNIFICAT IN A MAJOR
SATB and organ
Text: from The Book of Common Prayer
Date of composition: 1941–2

19      MY JOY, MY LIFE, MY CROWN!, Op. 1 No. 3
Anthem for SATB and organ
Text: George Herbert (1593–1633)
Dedication: To my parents
Date of composition: By 14 July 1942
Publication: Oxford University Press, October 1944
First performance: 26 August 1945, Yorkshire Summer School, Newburgh, conducted
    by Montgomery
First broadcast performance: 5 August 1949, BBC West Home Service, choir drawn
    from RSCM affiliated choirs conducted by Hubert Crook, with James Levett
    (organ)

20      EVERYMAN: INCIDENTAL MUSIC FOR ORGAN
Organ
Movements: Prelude, Everyman, Beauty, Fellowship, Contrition, Regret, Death,
    Apotheosis
Date and place of composition: November 1942, Oxford
Written for the Student Christian Movement

21      IT IS A SHOW
Voice and piano
Text: John Maxwell [a friend of Montgomery]
Date and place of composition: February 1943, Oxford

22      BLOW, BLOW THOU WINTER WIND
Part song for SATB
Text: William Shakespeare (1564–1616)
Dedication: To Isabel Douglas
Date of composition: 1943

23      FUGUE IN C MINOR
Organ
Date and place of composition: 26 December 1943, Devon

24      SONG
Voice and piano
Text: Philip Larkin (1922–1985)
Date and place of composition: April 1944, Devon

25 CANZONA FOR VIOLIN AND PIANO, Op. 1 No. 1
Violin and piano
Dedication: For Clifford Walker
Date of composition: 1944


26 ROMANCE IN B
Piano
Dedication: P. A. L. [Philip Larkin]
Date of composition: before 14 September 1944


27 SPRING, THE SWEET SPRING, Op. 1 No. 5
Two voices and piano
Text: Thomas Nashe (1567–1601)
Dedication: To Margaret Deneke
Date of composition: 1943
Publication: Oxford University Press, 1945
First performance: 30 March 1946 at Saltburn during Women's Institute competition
    festivals in Yorkshire


28 ON THE RESURRECTION OF CHRIST, Op. 2
Chorus and orchestra [2fl (2nd doubling pic), 2ob, 2cl in A, 2bn; 4hn in F, 3tpt in C,
    3trbn, tuba; 4timp, perc (bd, sd, cym, tri, xyl, bells, gong); harp, str]
Text: William Dunbar (?1456–?1513)
Dedication: In memoriam C. W. [Charles Williams]
Date of composition: By 14 September 1944
Publication: Novello, 15 April 1947


29 OVERTURE TO A FAIRY TALE, Op. 3
Orchestra [2fl (2nd doubling pic), ob, 2cl in A, bn; 2hn in F, tpt in C (*2tr in C),
    (*3trbn); 3timp, perc (bd, sd, cym, tamb, gong); harp or pf; str]
    * not in full score, but in parts
Date and place of composition: 23 February 1946, Devon
Publication: Oxford University Press, October 1944
First performance: 29 February 1948, Torquay Municipal Orchestra, conducted by
    Ernest Goss
First broadcast performance: 29 July 1949, BBC West Home Service, by the West
    Country Studio Orchestra conducted by Reginald Redman


30 SALLY IN OUR ALLEY, Op. 1 No. 6
Part song for SATB
Text: Henry Carey (?1687–1743)
Dedication: To Mr and Mrs Whiting
Date of composition: By 29 October 1945
Publication: Novello, 31 December 1945
First performance: During a summer school in Yorkshire in 1946
First broadcast performance: 6 February 1954, BBC North Region

31     HOMAGE TO DELIUS, Op. 1 No. 2
Piano
Date and place of composition: 16 June 1946, Devon


32     MARY AMBREE, Op. 7
Chorus and orchestra [2fl, ob, 2cl, bn; 2hn, tpt; timp, perc; str] or piano
Text: Anon. (sixteenth century) from *Reliques of Ancient English Poetry* (1765)
     edited by Thomas Percy
Dedication: For Ailsa and Brian [Galpin]
Date of composition: By 19 July 1946
Publication: Oxford University Press, 15 January 1948
First performance: 20 March 1949 during a course under the aegis of Derbyshire
     Education County Music Committee at Eastwood Grange, Ashover
First broadcast performance: 28 July 1949, BBC West Home Service by the West
     Country Singers and West Country Studio Orchestra conducted by Reginald
     Redman


33     AS JOSEPH WAS A-WALKING, Op. 4 No. 2
Carol for treble solo, SATB and organ
Text: Hone's *Ancient Mysteries Described*
Date of composition: By 5 June 1947
Publication: Oxford University Press, 5 June 1947
First performance: During 'A Residential Course for young adult Choralists and
     Pianists' held under the aegis of the Derbyshire Education Committee County
     Music Committee at Eastwood Grange, Ashover, on 22/23 October 1949


34     FAIR HELEN, Op. 4 No. 1
Voice and piano
Text: Anon.
Dedication: To Sydney Northcote
Date of composition: By 20 September 1946
Publication: Novello, 10 October 1947
First performance: 16 October 1949 at Oxford Ladies' Music Club by David Galliver
     accompanied by Montgomery


35     FOUR SHAKESPEARE SONGS, Op. 5
Voice and piano
Movements: Full Fathom Five; Come Away Death; O Mistress Mine; Tell Me Where
     Is Fancy Bred?
Text: William Shakespeare (1564–1616)
Dedication: To Edwina and Godfrey [Sampson]
Date of composition: By 15 March 1947
Publication: Novello, 8 April 1948
First performance: At least two of these songs were performed on 16 October 1949
     at a concert of the Oxford Ladies' Music Club by David Galliver accompanied
     by Montgomery

First broadcast performance: 3 January 1952, BBC West Home Service, by Cecil Cope with an unknown accompanist (not Montgomery) of the second and third songs only

36   CHRIST'S BIRTHDAY, Op. 8
Mixed chorus and string orchestra with piano obbligato
Movements: 1] In the bleak mid-winter; 2] Balulaow; 3] Adam lay ybounden; 4] There came three kings; 5] A maid peerless; 6] Good day, Sir Christèmas
Texts: 1] Christina Rossetti (1830–1894); 2] Wedderburn (1567); 3], 4], 5] and 6] Anon. (fifteenth century)
Date of composition: By 6 August 1947
Publication: Novello, 13 July 1948
First performance: 19 August 1948 at a summer school at Downe House, near Newbury, conducted by Sydney Northcote
First broadcast performance: 20 December 1948, BBC Western Region, of movements 3], 5] and 6] only. Performers unknown

37a   MARCH FOR ORGAN [i]
Organ
Dedication: To Ailsa and Brian [Galpin] for their wedding
Date and place of composition: 19 August 1947, Brixham

37b   BRIDAL PROCESSION [i]
Organ
Dedication: Written for Jennifer Keir Cross for her wedding November 7th 1963
Date of composition: By 7 November 1963
This is the same work as 37a, different only in chord spacings and occasional rhythms

38   FOUR SHAKESPEARE SONGS Second Set, Op. 6
Voice and piano
Movements: Take, O Take Those Lips Away; When Icicles Hang By The Wall; Who Is Silvia?; Under The Greenwood Tree
Text: William Shakespeare (1564–1616)
Dedication: To Pat and Colin Strang
Date of composition: 30 October 1947
Publication: Novello, 21 October 1948
First performance: At least two of these songs were performed on 16 October 1949 at a concert of the Oxford Ladies' Music Club by David Galliver accompanied by Montgomery
First broadcast performance: 3 January 1952, BBC West Home Service, by Cecil Cope with an unknown accompanist (not Montgomery)

39     BARTHOLOMEW FAIR, Op. 9
A comedy overture for orchestra [2fl, 2ob, 2cl in A, 2bn; 4hn in F, 2tpt in C, 2trbn, bass tbn; 3timp, 1perc (sd, bd, tamb, cym, xyl); harp; str]
Date of composition: 27 December 1947

40     CONCERTINO FOR STRING ORCHESTRA, Op. 10
String orchestra
Movements: 1] Moderato quasi allegro; 2] Lento expressivo; 3] Vivace ed energico
Dedication: To Geoffrey Bush
Date and place of composition: 3 March 1948
Publication: Novello, 1 August 1950
First performance: 10 December 1948 at Wigmore Hall, London, by the Riddick String Orchestra conducted by Trevor Harvey
First broadcast performance: 6 January 1954 on BBC West Region (unknown performers)

41     I LOVED A LASS, Op. 11 No. 2
Part song for SATB
Text: George Wither (1588–1667)
Date of composition: By 9 June 1948
Publication: Novello, 15 October 1948

42     GATHER YE ROSEBUDS, Op. 11 No. 1
Part song for SATB
Text: Robert Herrick (1591–1674)
Date of composition: By 17 July 1948
Publication: Novello, 15 December 1948
First (broadcast) performance: 1 June 1951 on BBC North/Northern Ireland Radio (performers unknown)

43     MY TRUE LOVE HATH MY HEART, Op. 14 No. 1
Voice and piano
Text: Sir Philip Sidney (1554–1586)
Date of composition: By 2 September 1948
Publication: Novello, 31 May 1949

44a     WILLY DROWNED IN YARROW, Op. 14 No. 2
Voice and piano
Text: Anon.
Dedication: To Dr Thomas Armstrong
Date and place of composition: 12 October 1948, Brixham
Publication: Novello, 2 May 1952
First performance: 16 October 1949 at a concert of the Oxford Ladies' Music Club by David Galliver accompanied by Montgomery
First broadcast performance: 3 January 1952, BBC West Home Service, by Cecil Cope with an unknown accompanist (not Montgomery)

44b    BONNIE LESLEY
Voice and piano
Text: Robert Burns (1759–1796)
Date of composition: 1948/9
First performance: 16 October 1949 at a concert of the Oxford Ladies' Music Club
    by David Galliver accompanied by Montgomery
Note: This song was originally composed as the first of *Two Scottish Songs* with
    44a


45    WHICH WILL YE HAVE? (or BARABBAS THE ROBBER), Op. 12
Film
Production company: G. H. W. Productions Ltd
Producer: Clifford Jeapes
Director: Donald Taylor
Cast: Frank Adams, Henry Oscar, Michael Callan, Betty-Ann David
Date of composition: 1948
Place of recording: Gate Studios, Elstree
Conductor: John Hollingsworth
Release date: 1949


46a    SUITE IN E MINOR, Op. 13 No. 1
Piano
Movements: 1] Moderato poco inquieto e senza rigore; 2] Poco lento come una
    nannarella; 3] Presto e ritmico; 4] Moderato con morbidezza; 5] Allegro con
    lancia
Date of composition: 1948
First performance: By Ruth Dyson during a tour of Sweden in 1948
Location of autograph: In author's collection


46b    SONATINA FOR PIANO (i)
Piano
Movements: 1] Moderato poco inquieto e senza rigore; 2] Poco lento come una
    nannarella
Date of composition: 1948
1] has similarities with 1] of 46a. 2] is identical with 2] of 46a.


46c    SONATINA FOR VIOLIN AND PIANO
Violin and piano
Movements: 1] Moderato; 2] Suave; 3] Allegro
1] is similar to 25. 3] is an arrangement of 5] from 46a.


46d    CANTILENA FOR PIANO (incomplete)
Piano
Dedication: To Peter Rogers
The single bar of this work is the same as the opening bar of 46a

47     HEROIC MARCH, Op. 15
Military band (exact scoring not known)
Date of composition: 1949
First (broadcast) performance: 11 April 1950 on BBC London Home Service by the
    Band of the Irish Guards conducted by Lt. C.H. Jaeger
The work was commissioned by Lt. Jaeger and scored by him. The complete
    autograph is lost.


48     GO, LOVELY ROSE!, Op. 16 No. 3
Two voices and piano
Text: Edmund Waller (1606–1687)
Date of composition: By 18 November 1949
Publication: Novello, 21 December 1951


49     TO PHYLLIS, Op. 16 No. 1
SATB and piano
Text: Thomas Lodge (1558–1625)
Date of composition: By 1 December 1948
Publication: Novello, 15 March 1950


50     CONCERT WALTZ FOR TWO PIANOS, Op. 13 No. 2
Two pianos
Date of composition: By 16 October 1949
Publication: Novello, 18 March 1952
First performance: 16 October 1949 at a concert of the Oxford Ladies' Music Club
    by David Galliver accompanied by Montgomery and Geoffrey Bush


51a    AN OXFORD REQUIEM, Op. 17
Chorus and orchestra [2fl (2nd doubling pic), 2ob, 2cl, 2bn; 4hn, 3 tpt, 2trbn, bass
    trbn, tuba; timp, perc (bd, cym, sd, trgl, gong); 2harp; str]
Movements: 1] As for man, his days are as grass; 2] But thou, O Lord, art my
    defender; 3] Man that is born of woman; 4] Lord, thou hast been our refuge
Text: 1] from Psalms 103 and 90; 2] from Psalms 3 and 16; 3] from the Burial
    Service; 4] from Psalm 90
Dedication: In memoriam G. S. [Godfrey Sampson]
Date of composition: 7 August 1950
Publication: Novello, 1 December 1950
First performance: 22 May 1951 at the Sheldonian Theatre, Oxford, by the Oxford
    Bach Choir and London Symphony Orchestra conducted by Thomas Armstrong.
The work was commissioned by the Oxford Bach Choir for the Festival of Britain.


51b    MY SOUL, THERE IS A COUNTRY (incomplete)
Ode for Baritone solo, SATB and orchestra
Text: Henry Vaughan (1621–1695)
This incomplete work was probably originally intended as the second movement of
    51a

52      TO MUSIC, Op. 16 No. 2
Part song for AA (or T) TBB
Text: Robert Herrick (1591–1674)
Dedication: For the City Glee Club
Date of composition: By 4 July 1952
Publication: Novello, 30 September 1952
First performance: 19 November 1952 at the Overseas Club, St James, London by
    the City Glee Club (which commissioned the work)


53      VENUS' PRAISE, Op. 18
Chorus and string orchestra
Movements: 1] Ask me no more where Jove bestows; 2] Love for such a cherry lip;
    3] Whenas the rye reach to the chin; 4] More white than whitest lilies far; 5] Love
    is a sickness full of woes; 6] Weep you no more, sad fountains; 7] Come, be my
    valentine!
Texts: 1] Thomas Carew (1595?–1639?); 2] Thomas Middleton (1570?–1627); 3]
    George Peele (1558?–1597); 4] Robert Herrick (1591–1674); 5] Samuel Daniel
    (1562–1619); 6] Anonymous (1603); 7] Francis Andrewes (fl. 1629–1643)
Dedication: To M.B.M. [Montgomery's mother]
Date and place of composition: 11 January 1951
Publication: Novello, 17 August 1951
First performance: 26 April 1951 at the Wigmore Hall, London, by the South London
    Bach Choir and the Strings of the London Classical Orchestra conducted by
    Trevor Harvey
First broadcast performance: 9 December 1975, BBC Radio 3, by the BBC Singers
    and the BBC Concert Orchestra conducted by John Poole


54      THIS IS BRITAIN: LOVE OF BOOKS, Op. 19, No. 1
Film
Production company: Crown Film Unit
Director: Cyril Frankel
Date of composition: 9 March 1951
Date and place of recording: 12 March 1951, Beaconsfield
Release date: 1951


55 TWO HUNDRED MILLION MOUTHS
Film
Production company: Wessex Film Productions
Producer: Ian Dalrymple
Narrators: Leo Glenn, Danilo Colombo
Date of composition: 15 June 1951
Date and place of recording: 18 June 1951, Beaconsfield
Conductor: Muir Mathieson
Release date: 1951

56    AMBERLEY HALL, Op. 20
Ballad opera in one act for three soloists, string quartet and piano
Text: Kingsley Amis
Date of composition: May 1951


57    FLOURISH FOR A CROWNING, Op. 21
Military band [1st fl, ob, solo cl, rep cl, 2nd/3rd cl, E flat cl, E flat alto sax, B flat
    tenor sax, bn; 2hn, solo B flat cnt, 2nd B flat cnt, 2 trbn, bass trbn, euph, divided
    bass; timp; perc (sd, bd, cym)]
Date of composition: 17 July 1952
First (broadcast) performance: 17 March 1953, BBC Light Programme, by the Band of
    the Irish Guards conducted by Lt. C.H. Jaeger (by whom it was commissioned)


58    SCOTTISH HIGHLANDS
Film
Production company: British Transport Films
Producers: Ian Ferguson, Edgar Anstey
Director: Michael Orrom
Date of composition: 5 October 1952
Scoring: 2fl, ob, 2cl, bn; 2hn in F, 2 tpt, 3trbn; timp, perc; harp; str
Date of recording: 8 October 1952
Orchestra and conductor: London Symphony Orchestra, Muir Mathieson


59    THE CENTURY'S CROWN
Chorus and orchestra [2fl, pic, 2ob, 2cl, 2bn; 4hn, 2tpt, 3 tbn, tuba; timp, perc (2
    players); harp; str]
Text: Kingsley Amis
Dedication: To the Glasgow Choral Union [which commissioned the work]
Date of composition: 20 March 1953
First performance: 3 June 1953 in St Andrew's Halls, Glasgow, by the Glasgow
    Choral Union and the Scottish National Orchestra conducted by Charles Cleall


60    VARIATIONS ON A HARROW THEME
Piano and orchestra [2fl, 2ob, 2cl in A, 2bn; 4hn in F, 2tpt in C, 2 tbn, bass trbn;
    timp, str]
Movements: Theme and five variations
Date of composition: 11 May 1953
First performance: 17 June 1953 at the Granada Cinema, Harrow, by the London
    Symphony Orchestra (with unknown soloist) conducted by Muir Mathieson


61    JOHN BARLEYCORN, Op. 22
Ballad opera in three acts
Text: Mary Fairclough
Dedication: R.E.M. [Montgomery's father]
Date of composition: 27 May 1953
Publication: Novello, 15 August 1962

First performance: 7 December 1968 at Wellsway County Secondary School, Keynsham, Bristol

62    A PRINCE FOR CYNTHIA
Film
Production company: BRI: Go Productions
Producer: George K. Arthur
Director: Muriel Box
Cast: Elizabeth Henson, Paul Rogers
Date of composition: 16 July 1953
Date and place of recording: 17 July 1953, Beaconsfield
Conductor: Muir Mathieson
Date of release: 1953
Recording: Excerpts on US LP MGM E-3151

63    THE KIDNAPPERS
Film
Production company: UA Nolbandor-Parkyn Productions
Producer: Sergei Nolbandov
Director: Philip Leacock
Cast: Duncan MacRae, Jean Anderson, Adrienne Corri, Jon Whitely
Date of composition: 26 October 1953
Date and place of recording: 27/28 October 1953, Denham
Orchestra and conductor: Royal Philharmonic Orchestra, Muir Mathieson
Date of release: 22 February 1954

64    DOCTOR IN THE HOUSE
Film
Production company: Group Film Productions
Producer: Betty Box
Director: Ralph Thomas
Cast: Dirk Bogarde, Muriel Pavlow, Kenneth More, Donald Sinden, James Robertson Justice
Date of composition: January 1954
Date of recording: 18/19 January 1954
Date of release: 26 April 1954

65a    CASH ON DELIVERY
Incidental music for revue sketch (scoring unknown)
Date and places of composition: 17 April 1954, Brixham, The Bull at Gerrard's Cross, and the Royal Court Theatre, London
First performance: 26 April 1954 at the Arts Theatre, Cambridge, in 'Joyce Grenfell Requests the Pleasure'.
The surviving autograph suggests that this stage act was a musical representation of a short story of the same name by Montgomery as Edmund Crispin.

65b    PERFIDIA

Incidental music for revue sketch [cl/sax; tpt; drums; pf; vn, va, vc, db]

Dedication: Written for 'Joyce Grenfell Requests the Pleasure'

Authors of text: Paddy Stone and Kenneth Pearson

Date and places of composition: 26 May 1954, Brixham, The Bull at Gerrard's Cross, and the Royal Court Theatre, London

First performance: 2 June 1954 at the Fortune Theatre, London, in 'Joyce Grenfell Requests the Pleasure'

This is a reworking of 65a


66    WHY SHOULD THE SWALLOW RETURN?

Cabaret song for voice and piano

Text: Montgomery

Date of composition: 1954


67    SCOTTISH AUBADE

Orchestra [2fl (2nd doubling pic), ob, 2cl in A, bn; 2hn in F, 2tpt in C, 2trbn, bass trbn; 3timp, perc (cym, bells, glock); harp; str]

Dedication: Muir Mathieson

Date and place of composition: 26 June 1954, Brixham

First (broadcast) performance: 12 August 1954, BBC Overseas Service, by the BBC Concert Orchestra conducted by Muir Mathieson

Based on the score for SCOTTISH HIGHLANDS [58]


68    A SCOTTISH LULLABY

Orchestra [fl, ob, cl in B flat, bn; hn in F; 2timp + tri (1 player); str]

Date of composition: 16 July 1954

First performance: April 1955 at Baron's Hall, Arundel Castle, Sussex, by the Southern String Orchestra conducted by Kathleen Merritt

First broadcast performance: 18 October 1956, BBC West Region, Bournemouth Symphony Orchestra conducted by Charles Groves

Based on the score for THE KIDNAPPERS [63]


69    RAISING A RIOT

Film

Production company: British Lion Film Productions

Producers: Ian Dalrymple and Hugh Perceval

Director: Wendy Toye

Cast: Kenneth More, Shelagh Fraser, Jan Miller, Ronald Squire

Date of composition: October/November 1954

Date of recording: 15 November/1 December 1954

Conductor: Muir Mathieson

Date of release: 1 April 1955

70    BRIDAL PROCESSION (ii)
Organ
Dedication: For Peter [Oldham] and Paul [Pauline Oldham]
Date of composition: 2 February 1955
First performance: 12 February 1955 at Islip

71    DOCTOR AT SEA
Film
Production company: Group Film Productions
Producer: Betty Box
Director: Ralph Thomas
Cast: Dirk Bogarde, Brigitte Bardot, James Robertson Justice, Maurice Denham
Date of composition: 15 May 1955
Date of recording: 16/17 April 1955
Date of release: 25 July 1955

72    MUSIC FOR 'LOOK'
Title and incidental music [various instrumentations] for television natural history
     series
Production company: BBC Television (Bristol), Natural History Unit
Date of composition: Between June 1955 and January 1958

73    ESCAPADE
Film
Production company: Pinnacle Productions
Producer: Daniel M. Angel
Director: Philip Leacock
Cast: John Mills, Yvonne Mitchell, Alastair Sim
Date of composition: 19 June 1955
Date and place of recording: 20 June 1955, Beaconsfield
Conductor: Philip Martell
Date of release: 22 August 1955

74    THE WOODLANDERS
Incidental music for BBC radio serial
Date of composition: 20 July 1955
Scoring: 2fl, ob (doubling eng hn), 2cl in B flat, bn; 2hn in F, 2tpt in B flat, 3 trbn; 3
     timp, perc; harp; str
Date and place of recording: 21 July/1 August 1955, BBC Bristol
Orchestra and conductor: BBC West of England Orchestra, Montgomery

75     CARTOUCHE
Film
Production company: Produzione Venturini
Producer: Johan Nasht
Directors: Gianni Vernuccio (Italy), Steve Sekely (USA)
Cast: Richard Basehart, Patricia Rog, Massimo Serato
Date of composition: 31 August 1955
Date and place of recording: 1/2 September 1955, Elstree
Conductor: Philip Martell

76     KEEP IT CLEAN
Film
Production company: Marksman Films
Producers: Maxwell Setton and James Sloan
Director: David Paltenghi
Cast: Ronald Shiner, James Hayter, Ursula Howells, Joan Sims
Date of composition: 25 November 1955 (part revised 22 February 1956)
Date and place of recording: 24/25 November 1955, Shepperton/24 February, 1956,
     Elstree
Conductor: Philip Martell
Date of release: 1 June 1956

77     GUILTY (or BY WHOSE HAND)
Film
Production company: Gibraltar Film Productions
Producer: Charles Leeds
Director: Edmond Greville
Cast: John Justin, Barbara Laage, Stephen Murray, Donald Wolfit
Date of composition: 12 March 1956
Scoring: fl, ob (doubling eng hn), cl (doubling bass cl); 4hn, 2tpt, 3trbn; timp, perc;
     harp; str
Date and place of recording: 14 March 1956, Beaconsfield
Conductor: Philip Martell
Date of release: 24 June 1956

78     THE CITY – CAIRO
Television film
Date of composition: 25 March 1956
Scoring: fl, ob, 3cl (doubling alto sax and bass cl); 2tpt, 3 trbn; timp, perc; harp, vib,
     str
Date and place of recording: 26 March 1956, Beaconsfield
Conductor: Philip Martell
This film was never completed or released

79     EYEWITNESS (or POINT OF CRISIS)
Film
Production company: Rank Film Productions
Producer: Sydney Box
Director: Muriel Box
Cast: Donald Sinden, Muriel Pavlow, Nigel Stock, Michael Craig
Date of composition: 13 May 1956
Date and place of recording: 14/15 May 1956, Denham
Date of release: 13 August 1956

80     CIRCUS FRIENDS
Film
Production company: Femina Films
Producer: Peter Rogers
Director: Gerald Thomas
Cast: Alan Coleshill, Carol White, Sam Kydd, John Horsley
Date of composition: 15 July 1956
Date and place of recording: 11 and 16 July 1956, Shepperton

81     CHECKPOINT
Film
Production company: Rank Film Productions
Producer: Betty Box
Director: Ralph Thomas
Cast: Anthony Steel, Odice Versois, Stanley Baker
Date of composition: 28 August 1956
Date of recording: 29/30 August 1956
Date of release: 14 January 1957

82     DOCTOR AT LARGE
Film
Production company: Rank Film Productions
Producer: Betty Box
Director: Ralph Thomas
Cast: Dirk Bogarde, Muriel Pavlow, Donald Sinden, James Robertson Justice,
    Shirley Eaton
Date of composition: December 1956
Date of recording: 14/15 January 1957

83     FULL SCREEN AHEAD
Short promotional film
Production company: Rank Film Productions
Cast: Belinda Lee, Betty Box, Ralph Thomas

84     MEET DR SPARROW
Short film for television
Production company: Rank Film Productions

85     SPOTLIGHT ON DIRK BOGARDE
Short promotional film
Production company: Rank Film Productions
83, 84 and 85 all make use of music Montgomery had composed for earlier Rank films

86     THE SURGEON'S KNIFE
Film
Production company: Gibraltar Film Productions
Producer: Charles Leeds
Director: Gordon Parry
Cast: Donald Houston, Adrienne Corri, Sydney Tafler, Mervyn Johns
Date of composition: May/June 1957
Scoring: fl, ob, cl, bn; 2hn, 2trbn, bass trbn; timp, perc; harp; str
Conductor: Philip Martell

87     AT THE ROUND EARTH'S IMAGIN'D CORNERS
SATB
Text: John Donne (1572–1631)
Dedication: For Cecil Cope and the Exeter Elizabethan Singers
Date of composition: June 1957
Publication: Novello, November 1957
First performance: 25 July 1957 in Exeter Cathedral by the Exeter Elizabethan
    Singers conducted by Cecil Cope (who commissioned the work)

88     THE TRUTH ABOUT WOMEN
Film
Production company: Beaconsfield Film Productions
Producer: Sydney Box
Director: Muriel Box
Cast: Lawrence Harvey, Julie Harris, Mai Zetterling, Eva Gabor
Date of composition: June/July 1957
Orchestra and conductor: Sinfonia of London, Muir Mathieson
Date of release: 15 March 1958

89     HEART OF A CHILD
Film
Production company: Beaconsfield Film Productions
Producer: Alfred Shaugnessy
Director: Clive Donner
Cast: Donald Pleasance, Jean Anderson
Date of composition: December 1957/January 1958
Date of release: May 1958

90    THE DUKE WORE JEANS
Film
Production company: Insignia Films
Producer: Peter Rogers
Director: Gerald Thomas
Cast: Tommy Steele, June Laverick, Michael Medwin
Date of composition: January/February 1958
Conductor: Montgomery
Date of release: 31 March 1958
Montgomery wrote the incidental music for this film musical and not the songs

91    CARRY ON SERGEANT
Film
Production company: Insignia Productions
Producer: Peter Rogers
Director: Gerald Thomas
Cast: William Hartnell, Bob Monkhouse, Shirley Eaton, Kenneth Williams
Date of composition: June 1958
Scoring: 2fl (doubling pic), ob, 6cl, bass cl, alto sax, tenor sax, bn; 3hn, 4cnt, bass
    trbn, euph, 2 brass basses, 3perc; gtr
Date and place of recording: 18 June 1958, Denham
Orchestra and conductor: Band of the Coldstream Guards, Montgomery
Date of release: 1 September 1958

92    SINS OF THE FATHER (or HOME IS THE HERO)
Film
Production company: Emmet Dalton Productions
Producers: Robert Baker and Monty Berman
Director: Fielder Cook
Cast: Walter Macken, Eileen Crowe, Arthur Kennedy, Joan O'Hara
Date of composition: September 1958
Scoring: fl (doubling pic), cl; 3hn, tpt; timp/perc, vib; harp; str
Conductor: Philip Martell
Date of release: 1 February 1960

93    CARRY ON NURSE
Film
Production company: Beaconsfield Films
Producer: Peter Rogers
Director: Gerald Thomas
Cast: Shirley Eaton, Kenneth Williams, Hattie Jacques, Leslie Phillips, Joan Sims
Date of composition: January/February 1959
Scoring: 3fl, 2ob, 2cl, 2bn; 4hn, 3tpt, 3trbn, tuba; timp, 3perc; pf, cel, harp; str
Date and place of recording: 3 February 1959, Denham
Orchestra and conductor: Sinfonia of London, Montgomery
Date of release: 1 April 1959

94     CARRY ON TEACHER

Film
Production company: Beaconsfield Productions
Producer: Peter Rogers
Director: Gerald Thomas
Cast: Ted Ray, Leslie Phillips, Kenneth Williams, Hattie Jacques, Kenneth Connor
Date of composition: May 1959
Scoring: 2fl, 2ob, alto sax, 2tenor sax, baritone sax, 2bn; 4hn, 4tpt, 3trbn, tuba; timp, 2perc; harp, pf; str
Date and place of recording: 27/28 May 1959, Denham
Orchestra and conductor: Sinfonia of London, Montgomery
Date of release: 1 October 1959


95     COMING

Voice and Piano
Text: Philip Larkin (1922–1985)
Date of composition: April 1959


96     TOO YOUNG TO LOVE

Film
Production company: Beaconsfield Productions
Producer: Herbert Smith
Director: Muriel Box
Cast: Thomas Mitchell, Pauline Hahn, Joan Miller, Austin Willis
Date of composition: September/October 1959
Scoring: fl, ob, 2alto sax (1st doubling cl1; 2nd doubling fl2), 2tenor sax (1st doubling bass cl; 2nd doubling cl2), baritone sax (doubling cl3); 3hn, 4tpt, 2trbn, bass trbn; 3perc; gtr; pf; harp; str
Date and place of recording: 19 October 1959, Borehamwood
Date of release: 14 March 1960


97     PLEASE TURN OVER

Film
Production company: Beaconsfield Productions
Producer: Peter Rogers
Director: Gerald Thomas
Cast: Julia Lockwood, Jean Kent, Ted Ray, Leslie Phillips, Joan Sims
Date of composition: October 1959
Scoring: 3fl (1 doubling pic), 2ob (1 doubling eng hn), 2alto sax, 2tenor sax, 2cl (1 doubling bass cl), baritone sax, 2bn; 4hn, 3tpt, 3trbn, tuba; timp, perc; harp; gtr, elec gtr; pf; str
Date and place of recording: 19/20 November 1959, Denham
Orchestra and conductor: Sinfonia of London, Montgomery
Date of release: 25 January 1960

98    CARRY ON CONSTABLE
Film
Production company: G.H.W. Productions
Producer: Peter Rogers
Director: Gerald Thomas
Cast: Sid James, Eric Barker, Joan Sims, Hattie Jacques, Kenneth Williams
Date of composition: January/February 1960
Scoring: 3fl (1 doubling pic), 2ob, 2alto sax (1 doubling cl), tenor sax (doubling cl),
    tenor sax (doubling bass cl), baritone sax, bn, dbn; 4hn, 4tpt, 2trbn, tuba, tba (in
    F), euph, ; timp, 3perc; musical saw; str
Date and place of recording: 1/3/4 February 1960, Beaconsfield
Orchestra and conductor: Sinfonia of London, Montgomery
Date of release: 1 April 1960


99    DOCTOR IN LOVE
Film
Production company: Rank Organisation Film Productions
Executive producer: Earl St John
Producer: Betty Box
Director: Ralph Thomas
Cast: Michael Craig, Leslie Phillips, James Robertson Justice, Liz Fraser
Date of composition: April 1960
Scoring: 2fl, ob, 2cl (1 doubling bass cl), alto sax (doubling cl), 2bn; 3hn, 3tpt, 2trbn,
    bass trbn; 2perc (including timp); harp; str
Date and place of recording: 3/4 May 1960, Denham
Orchestra and conductor: Sinfonia of London, Montgomery
Date of release: 1 August 1960


100    FANFARE FOR ANGLO-AMALGAMATED (FILM DISTRIBUTORS)
Film Trademark
Scoring: 4tpt, 3trbn; 2perc
Date and place of recording: 12 May 1960, Denham
Orchestra and conductor: Sinfonia of London, Montgomery


101    WATCH YOUR STERN
Film
Production company: G.H.W. Productions
Producer: Peter Rogers
Director: Gerald Thomas
Cast: Kenneth Connor, Eric Barker, Leslie Phillips, Joan Sims, Hattie Jacques
Scoring: 2fl, 2ob, 2cl (1 doubling bass cl), 2bn; 4hn, 4tpt, 2trbn, bass trbn, tuba; timp,
    3perc; gtr, elec gtr; pf; harp; str
Date and place of recording: 20/21 July 1960, Denham
Orchestra and conductor: Sinfonia of London, Montgomery
Date of release: 1 November 1960

102    NO KIDDING (or BEWARE OF CHILDREN)
Film
Production company: G.H.W. Productions
Producer: Peter Rogers
Director: Gerald Thomas
Cast: Leslie Phillips, Geraldine McEwan, Julia Lockwood
Date of composition: October 1960
Scoring: 2fl, 2ob, 2cl, 2bn; 4hn, 3tpt, 3trbn; timp, 3perc; harp; str
Date and place of recording: 2/3 November 1960, Gate Studio
Orchestra and conductor: Sinfonia of London, Montgomery
Date of release: 1 January 1961

103    CARRY ON REGARDLESS
Film
Production company: G.H.W. Productions
Producer: Peter Rogers
Director: Gerald Thomas
Cast: Sid James, Kenneth Connor, Joan Sims, Liz Fraser, Kenneth Williams
Scoring: 2fl, ob, alto sax (doubling cl), 2cl (1 doubling bass cl), bn; 3hn, 3tpt, 3trbn;
    2 perc; harp; str
Date and place of recording: 2 March 1961, Denham
Orchestra and conductor: Sinfonia of London, Montgomery
Date of release: 1 May 1961

104    TWICE ROUND THE DAFFODILS
Film
Production company: G.H.W. Productions
Producer: Peter Rogers
Director: Gerald Thomas
Cast: Juliet Mills, Donald Sinden, Donald Houston, Kenneth Williams, Ronald
    Lewis, Joan Sims
Scoring: 2fl, 2ob (1 doubling eng hn), 2cl (1 doubling bass cl), 2bn; 4hn, 2tpt, 3trbn;
    timp, 3perc; harp; str
Date and place of recording: 7 February 1962, Denham
Orchestra and conductor: Sinfonia of London, Montgomery

105    RAISING THE WIND
Film
Production company: G.H.W. Productions
Producer: Peter Rogers
Director: Gerald Thomas
Cast: Sid James, James Robertson Justice, Leslie Phillips, Kenneth Williams, Paul
    Massey, Jennifer Jayne, Liz Fraser
Scoring: Pre-recording, 3fl (1 doubling pic), 2ob, eng hn, 3cl (1 doubling bass cl),
    2bn; 4hn, 3tpt, 3trbn, tuba; 4perc, timp; harp; hammond org, pf; str + banjo and
    vocalist

Incidental music, 3fl (1 doubling picc), 2ob (1 doubling eng hn), 3cl (1 doubling bass cl), 2bn; 4hn, 4tpt, 3trbn, tuba; timp, 3perc; harp; str

Date and place of recording: Pre-recording, 14 March 1960, 5/8/18/19 May 1961; Incidental music, 13/14/ July 1961

Orchestra and conductor: Sinfonia of London, Montgomery

Date of release: 18 September 1961

Montgomery also wrote the screenplay for this film


106    CARRY ON CRUISING

Film

Production company: G.H.W. Productions

Producer: Peter Rogers

Director: Gerald Thomas

Cast: Sid James, Kenneth Williams, Liz Fraser, Dilys Laye, Kenneth Connor

Scoring: 2fl, 2ob, 2cl (1 doubling bass cl), alto sax (doubling cl), 2tenor sax (1 doubling cl), baritone sax (doubling bass cl), 2bn; 4hn, 4tpt, 3trbn, tuba; 3perc (including timp); harp; gtr, mand; str

Date and place of recording: 21/22/27 March 1962, Denham

Orchestra and conductor: Sinfonia of London, Montgomery

Date of release: 1 May 1962

Montgomery composed only part of the music for this film


107    MERELY PLAYERS

Radio play with incidental music

Date and place of recording: Script, 8 January 1965; Score, 27 January 1965, BBC Birmingham

Orchestra and conductor: BBC Midland Light Orchestra, Montgomery

Date of broadcast: 31 January 1965, BBC Third Programme

Montgomery wrote both play and incidental music for this BBC commission


108    THE BRIDES OF FU MANCHU

Film

Production company: Fu Manchu Films

Producer: Harry Alan Towers

Director: Don Sharp

Cast: Christopher Lee, Douglas Wilmer, Marie Versini, Heinz Drache

Date of composition: April 1966

Conductor: Philip Martell

Date of release: 1 January 1967

# Appendix 5

# Discography

*The Carry On Suite* (arranged by David Whittle from the scores to *Carry On Sergeant*, *Carry On Teacher* and *Carry On Nurse*)
*Raising the Wind* (title music)
*Fanfare for Anglo-Amalgamated*
The Carry On Album                    ASV                    CD WHL 2119
City of Prague Philharmonic Orchestra/Gavin Sutherland

*Watch Your Stern* (extended titles, arranged by David Whittle)
*Twice Round the Daffodils* (title music)
What a Carry On!                      Dutton                 Vocalion CDSA 6810
Royal Ballet Sinfonia/Gavin Sutherland

*Concertino for String Orchestra*
English String Miniatures, Vol. 3     Naxos                  8.555069
Royal Ballet Sinfonia/David Lloyd-Jones

*Lord, thou hast been our refuge* (from *An Oxford Requiem*)
Let God Arise                         OxRecs DIGITAL         OXCD-81
The Choir of St John's College, Oxford/Matthew Morrison

*Overture to a Fairy Tale*
British Light Overtures               White Line             CD WHL 2140
Royal Ballet Sinfonia/Gavin Sutherland

*Scottish Aubade*
*Scottish Lullaby*
British Film Composers in Concert     White Line             CD WHL 2145
Royal Ballet Sinfonia/Gavin Sutherland

A number of the films for which Montgomery wrote the scores are available on VHS and/or DVD, including those from the *Carry On* and *Doctor* series.

The BBC Sound Archive and the National Sound Archive hold a relatively small amount of further material.

# Bibliography

The vast bulk of Montgomery's personal papers are held in his collection at the Bodleian Library, Oxford. Sources not otherwise identified are from this collection. All letters to and from Montgomery are held in this collection, unless otherwise stated.

When references consist of a name only, these refer to interviews with the author.

## Published Sources

Aldiss, Brian (with David Wingrove), *Trillion Year Spree* (Paladin, London 1988)

Amis, Kingsley, *Memoirs* (Hutchinson, London 1991)

Blake, Lord and Nicholls, C.S. (eds), *The Dictionary of National Biography, 1971–1980* (Oxford University Press, Oxford 1986)

Bush, Geoffrey, *An Unsentimental Education* (Thames, London 1990)

Carr, John Dickson, *The Crooked Hinge* (Xanadu, London 1989)

Critchley, Julian, 'Fen's Creator', *Illustrated London News*, Christmas 1979, p. 47

Drabble, Margaret (ed.), *The Oxford Companion to English Literature* (Oxford University Press, Oxford 1985)

Greene, Douglas, *John Dickson Carr, The Man Who Explained Miracles* (Otto Penzler Books, New York 1995)

Herbert, Rosemary (ed.), *The Oxford Companion to Crime and Mystery Writing* (Oxford University Press, New York 1999)

Jacobs, Eric, *Kingsley Amis, A Biography* (Hodder and Stoughton, London 1995)

Larkin, Philip, Foreword to *Fen Country* by Edmund Crispin (Gollancz, London 1979)

Larkin, Philip, Introduction to *Jill* (Faber and Faber, London 1975)

Larkin, Philip, *Required Writing, Miscellaneous Pieces 1955–1982* (Faber and Faber, London 1983)

Leader, Zachary (ed.), *The Letters of Kingsley Amis* (Harper Collins, London 2000) [LKA]

Meredith, Anthony and Harris, Paul, *Malcolm Arnold: Rogue Genius* (Thames/Elkin, Norwich 2004)

Montgomery, Bruce, 'Edmund Crispin', *The Armchair Detective*, Vol. 12 No. 2, Spring 1979, pp. 183–185

Morrison, Blake, *The Movement* (Oxford University Press, Oxford 1980)

Motion, Andrew, *Philip Larkin* (Faber and Faber, London 1993)

Ross, Alan, *Blindfold Games* (Collins Harvill, London 1986)

Thwaite, Anthony (ed.), *Selected Letters of Philip Larkin* (Faber and Faber, London 1992) [SLPL]

Vaughan Williams, Ursula, *RVW: A Biography of Ralph Vaughan Williams* (Oxford University Press, Oxford 1988)

Wakeman, John, *World Authors, 1950–1970* (The H.W. Wilson Company, New York 1975)

The following periodicals were consulted:

*Cambridge Daily News, The Chesterian, The Choir, Daily Cinema, Daily Film Renter, Daily Telegraph, Derbyshire Advertiser, Evening News* (Glasgow), *Evening Standard* (London), *Exeter Express, Film Daily, Film in Berlin, Film User, The Guardian, Glasgow Herald, Hampshire Chronicle, Hampshire Telegraph and Post, Herald Express, Hollywood Reporter, Intermezzo, John O'London's, Kinematograph Weekly, Librarian, The Listener, London Symphony Observer, Monthly Film Bulletin, Motion Picture Herald, Musical Opinion, The Musical Times, Music in Education, The Oxford Magazine, Oxford Mail, Paignton News, Picture Show, The Radio Times, Record Mirror, Saturday, Scottish Daily Express, Screen International, The Sketch, The Soundtrack, The Spectator, Stage, Symphony, TV Mirror, The Times, Times Literary Supplement, Today's Cinema, Variety, Western Mail, Western Morning News, West Lancashire Evening Gazette, Yorkshire Post*

## Unpublished Sources

*History of Terry's*: privately printed by Northwood Preparatory School, Middlesex
*Taylorian*, magazine of Merchant Taylors' School, Vols 57–59

Whittle, David M.T., 'Bruce Montgomery (1921–1978): a biography with a catalogue of the musical works' (unpublished PhD thesis, University of Nottingham, 1998)

The following archives were consulted:

British Film Institute (BFI): Gerald Thomas Collection (not catalogued)

Faber and Faber: Correspondence with Montgomery concerning anthologies (not catalogued)

Gollancz: Correspondence with Montgomery concerning novels (not catalogued)

Novello: Details of the publication of Montgomery's music

Oxford University Press (OUP): Correspondence with Montgomery concerning music (not catalogued)

Performing Right Society (PRS): Music cue sheets for films

Rank Film Distributors: Music cue sheets for films

Society of Authors: Correspondence with Montgomery (not catalogued)

# Index